If you're wondering why you should buy the new edition of *Public Policy*, here are six good reasons!

1. Case studies have been added at the end of chapters to encourage small group dialog and debate, and energize the next generation of policy-makers to get involved.

2. Immigration, as a policy theme, is now introduced in five of the policy area chapters in Part 3.

3. A section on public finance and taxation helps you understand the budget, its size, and the resources invested in the making of public policy.

4. A discussion of the role of technology looks to the future of public policy and how it is developing in the twenty-first century.

5. With a condensed text and new glossary, this second edition shortens your reading time and makes information easier to find.

6. A chapter on policy termination has been added to Part 2 of the policy process.

PEARSON

SECOND EDITION

PUBLIC POLICY

PREFERENCES AND OUTCOMES

Christopher A. Simon

University of Nevada, Reno

Longman

New York   Boston   San Francisco

London   Toronto   Sydney   Tokyo   Singapore   Madrid

Mexico City   Munich   Paris   Cape Town   Hong Kong   Montreal

Editor-in-Chief: Eric Stano
Marketing Manager: Lindsey Prudhomme
Production Manager: Wanda Rockwell
Text Design and Electronic Page Makeup: Aptara®, Inc.
Creative Director: Jayne Conte
Cover Designer: Bruce Kenselaar
Cover Images: Shutterstock
Cover Printer and Binder: Courier Stoughton
Manager, Rights and Permissions: Zina Arabia
Manager, Visual Research: Beth Brenzel
Manager, Cover Visual Research & Permissions: Karen Sanatar
Image Permission Coordinator: Kathy Gavilanes

For permission to use copyrighted material, grateful acknowledgment is made to the copyright holders on p. 324, which is hereby made part of this copyright page.

Library of Congress Cataloging-in-Publication Data
Simon, Christopher A.
   Public policy : preferences and outcomes / Christopher A. Simon.—2nd ed.
      p. cm.
   Includes index.
   ISBN-13: 978-0-205-74482-4
   ISBN-10: 0-205-74482-6
   1. Policy sciences.   2. Political planning.   3. Political science—Philosophy.   4. Values.
5. Political planning—United States.   6. Public administration—United States.   I. Title.
   H97.S538 2010
   320.6—dc22

                                                                                2009015025

Longman
is an imprint of

www.pearsonhighered.com
ISBN-10:   0-205-74482-6
ISBN-13: 978-0-205-74482-4

Dedication

This book is dedicated to my parents—

Raffi G. and Susan M. Simon.

CONTENTS

ALTERNATE CONTENTS

There is no "one best way" to teach a policy class. There are at least three approaches that I have witnessed or used as an instructor. That is why I have written the chapters in this book to be flexible and independent—to support whatever approach and organization an instructor might prefer. I have also included alternative tables of content—different "menus," if you will—to give instructors a sense of the various ways they might use this book to best support their own course goals.

I have discussed three different approaches to learning and teaching about public policy, described below and on the following pages. Of course, there may be other methods that you find more useful. I am confident that the book will adapt quite easily to fit your preferred method.

MODELS AND PROCESS APPROACH

This is a common approach to learning about public policy. Models and process are learned first and policy substance is reserved for the last portion of the course. Public policy often involves a whole host of complexities, and models are helpful ways of simplifying the articulation of preferences, goals, plans, and outcomes. Understanding the process of public policy may be a useful way to think about policy substance.

FOUNDATIONS

POLICY PROCESS

MAJOR PUBLIC POLICIES

MODELS AND POLICY SUBSTANCE APPROACH

Professors may prefer to juxtapose policy science with social and political values. In this case, the chapter on visions of governance and the chapter on values are assigned initially, followed by three chapters dealing with policy models, analysis, and cost. Setting the stage in this manner allows professors to focus attention on social and political values in relation to democratic governance and policy analysis, prior to discussing applications to major public policies. Policy process becomes a third section of the class or may serve as a reference for students.

FOUNDATIONS

MAJOR PUBLIC POLICIES

POLICY PROCESS

DISCUSSION-DRIVEN NON-ECONOMIC APPROACH

Professors may find that the best way to get students "hooked" on a subject is to initially discuss policy values and theories of governance in relation to tangible policy areas, followed by chapters dealing with policy process. Policy models and analysis may be reserved for graduate student learners. This approach is becoming quite common, as colleges and universities expand degree offerings to include masters or doctoral programs, which may rely on split-level courses.

PREFACE

Public policy is ubiquitous. It impacts our lives every day in countless ways, shaping our choices and the outcomes of those choices. It would be reasonable, therefore, to want to develop an understanding of something so vast and so consequential to our private and public lives, to ask ourselves what public policy ought or ought not be and to discover what it does and does not do. Public policy is affected by two different worlds: the world of the normative—the realm of political philosophy—and the world of the empirical—the realm of science. This book explores both in depth.

The normative aspects of public policy impact policy choices at all stages of the policy process. In order to understand these normative aspects, the book covers briefly two very different notions of liberalism, and introduces students to communitarian thought. It is important to understand that the debate over the nature of government has not ended and can often be a sign of a healthy democracy. Additionally, the early chapters of the book discuss the values of citizens, based on age cohort. Generation Y is the next generation of policy-makers. Many of our students are Generation Y and are curious to know about the values of their peers in relation to older generations of Americans. The discussion of values and philosophy of governance is regularly sprinkled into the subsequent chapters to illustrate and reinforce the book's working definition of public policy.

The empirical aspects of public policy are an equally critical element of the book. In fact, Chapters 2 and 4 are central to understanding much of the empirical aspects of public policy and policy *science*. These early chapters and Part II that follows spend considerable time outlining the policy process model as a basis for understanding how public policy comes to fruition. The chapters are designed to reach students in an introductory course, but the book will also be of value to students in upper-division, policy-specific courses who are reviewing public policy "basics" to arrive at a better understanding of their specific policy area of study. From my own experience years ago as a graduate student, I know that a "unifying" tome (or tomes) in public policy helped to bring concepts and thoughts together and the text should serve well such a purpose, albeit this is not the primary purpose of the book.

The final third of the book deals with policy-specific areas and offers detailed analysis of policy within these areas. Policy history provides an important background to students, helping them to establish some landmarks in the learning process. Once those landmarks have been established—note that Parts 1 and 2 of the book should provide a learning "compass"—many detailed aspects of topical policy areas are discussed with the intent of helping students to understand current policy issues. The end of each policy-area chapter in Part 3 applies policy models discussed in Chapter 2 to the policy area in question. New to the second edition are the inclusion of case studies to encourage small group dialog and debate. Also, I have included several sections tying policy areas to current immigration policy issues. The budget process, Chapter 17, rounds out the discussion of public policy. After reading about policy areas, it should be fairly clear to students that public policy is a substantial investment of resources. It is instructive, therefore, to discuss the budget, its size, and the process by which it comes into being. New to the second edition is a brief discussion of public finance and taxation.

The second edition has provided an opportunity to reflect on the original text and to consider, with reviewer insights, recrafting aspects of the book.

NEW TO THE SECOND EDITION

- *Policy termination chapter added*—A chapter on policy termination was added in Part 2 on the policy process.
- *Real-life current case studies and group projects added*—Although the end-of-chapter questions remain, case studies are group projects used in Part 3 chapters to stimulate group discussion and class-based activities.
- *Glossary of bold-faced key terms*—Each chapter has a section of key terms that have been highlighted in-text. A glossary of more than 250 key terms has been developed, located near the end of the book.
- *Policy additions and updates*—
  - **Immigration** as a current policy theme is introduced in five of the policy area chapters in Part 3.
  - A section on the **State Children's Health Insurance Program (SCHIP)** has been added to the public health policy chapter.
  - **Missile defense** policy is updated in the defense policy chapter.
  - A section on the basics of **public finance** is included in the chapter on the cost of public policy.
  - The environmental and natural resource policy chapter is reframed as **green policy**.
  - . . . and better news still—*Despite all additional material, the book remains efficient. The second edition is significantly shorter than the original text.* That means savings to your students in time and money while having a second edition that keeps them current on national public policy.

There are several people I wish to acknowledge and thank for their support during the writing and editing of this manuscript. My parents, Raffi G. and Susan M. Simon, have played a central role in my life and career—my best friends and constant companions. I cannot imagine getting through this writing project without their strength and support, regular encouragement, sound advice, and excellent dinnertime discussions. Courtney Hepton, the Longman sales representative in Northern Nevada in 2001, got me started on the book project. Executive Editor-in-Chief Eric Stano gave me the go-ahead to write the manuscript as I saw fit and offered sound advice on many occasions. Special thanks also to assistant editor Elizabeth Alimena, project manager Wanda Rockwell, Edex copyeditor Susan Gilbert, and project coordinator Ravi Bhatt of Aptara, Inc.

Also, thanks to Professor Janet Frantz, and the authors, staff, and editors of *The Christian Science Monitor*, *The Navajo Times*, nuclearfiles.org, and *Stars and Stripes*. I would also like to acknowledge the pilot of Marine One depicted in Photo 11.1—a college friend, Major David Heino, USMC. Project Vote Smart (PVS) was very generous, allowing me to access public speeches of prominent political figures—students interested in government and public policy should become more aware of the learning opportunities that PVS offers. My students and colleagues have also offered many helpful suggestions—thanks for your support!

I appreciate the sage advice of the many reviewers who read this manuscript in its many forms:

Stanley P. Berard, *Lock Haven University;* Mittie Olion Chandler, *Cleveland State University;* Michael Coulter, *Grove City College;* Shane Day, *Indiana University;* Andrew Ewoh, *Prairie View A&M;* Kenneth Fernandez, *University of Nevada, Las Vegas;* Celeste Murphy Greene, *San Diego State University;* John A. Hamman, *Southern Illinois University;* Jane Hansberry, *University of Colorado, Denver;* Susan Hoffman, *Western Michigan University;* Michael Licari, *University of Northern Iowa;* Jared J. Llorens, *University of Georgia;* Theo Edwin Maloy, *West Texas A&M University;* Dale Nesbary, *Oakland University;* Michael Nojeim, *Prairie View A&M;* Monica Labelle Oliver, *Georgia State University;* Jim Riley, *Regis University;* Samuel T. Shelton, *Troy State University;* Jon R. Taylor, *University of St. Thomas;* and Leonard Williams, *Manchester College.*

Christopher A. Simon
University of Nevada

1

■ ■ ■

Policy and Visions of Governance

CHAPTER OVERVIEW

The goal of this chapter is to provide you with a *working definition* of public policy. The definition will help you to understand the process by which policy is made and applies to actual policy areas. A good working definition enables you as an individual to consider policy without restricting you to a particular ideological position, a definition that helps you understand your private political and social belief system in relation to the very public process of creating public policy.

The specific goals for the chapter are:

- Provide a working definition for public policy.
- Outline the normative foundations of public policy through a discussion of *classical* and *modern liberal* thought.

A WORKING DEFINITION OF PUBLIC POLICY

Public policy is defined here as what government *ought* or *ought not do*, and *does* or *does not do* (see Box 1.1, *The Definition*). Government, as a group of institutions and processes, is not closed to new policy ideas. Government is constantly changing as our values and priorities adapt, and as a result of cultural diversity, political evolution, and new concerns. How many of us have been involved in a conversation and not had someone—or more usually, several people—discuss the priorities of government and offer specific or general prescriptions of what government *ought* to do?

So, how do we decide what we *ought* or *ought not* do? The answer is: It all depends on what we want out of our **social contract**—the written and unwritten agreement that we continually rewrite stating what we want to do for each other collectively and what we want other members of society to do for us as

BOX 1.1

The Definition

The writings of the late British historian Edward H. Carr inspired my working definition of *public policy*. In *The Twenty Years' Crisis, 1919–1939—An Introduction to the Study of International Relations* (1946, 5), Carr states, "Political science is the science not only of what is, but of what ought to be."

Edward H. Carr

individuals. Our view of the social contract is often a function of our opinions about the **scope of government**—in essence, how big or how small we want government to be and how much we want to pay for the collective and individual benefits government may provide.

In the United States, government can be thought of as something we have agreed to purchase—a little bit like your interest in buying a new pair of jeans or renting an apartment close to campus. As you might know from experience, you usually shop around looking for the pair of jeans you want or for the best apartment. You have two goals: getting what you want for the price that fits into your budget. And, of course, when you go to buy the jeans or sign the lease, you want some assurances that you are not getting ripped off, right? In essence, you want some kind of written or unwritten contractual arrangement with the provider of the jeans or the landlady who is renting the apartment to you. (See Figure 1.1.)

Government has many similarities, except that it involves more than you as an individual—in government, "purchasing" involves millions of people collectively deciding what they want and how much they are willing to pay for it.

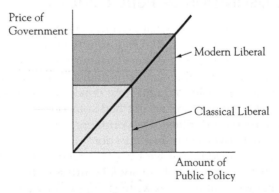

FIGURE 1.1 Price of government versus amount of public policy.

Instead of being based in an economic contract, government is based in a "social contract"—something we have agreed to collectively. Instead of the exchange being called a "purchase" or perhaps a "lease," we call the exchange "public policy."

Sometimes, our collective purchases are not in agreement with our individual preferences. The decision to do something collectively is often made by majority vote; it is more proper to say that government purchases what we think it *ought* rather than saying that government purchases what we *want*. What we think government *ought* to do is a function of our view of the social contract in our liberal democracy.

CLASSICAL LIBERALISM

Classical liberalism was developed during the seventeenth and eighteenth centuries. It emerged in sharp contrast to earlier forms of government, such as monarchies. A series of historical events—for example, the Enlightenment, *Magna Carta* in England, or revolutions against European monarchies—led to changes in a rigid and limited view of human rights and the relationship between government and the individual. This rethinking laid the groundwork for an expanded application of what we call **liberal government**—government *by* the people and *for* their individual and collective benefit.[1] **Classical liberalism** was the earliest approach to **liberal government**.

John Locke's *Second Treatise on Civil Government* served as a logical starting point for the discussion of classical liberalism and its role in shaping public policy. The cornerstone of classical liberalism is a belief in the **ascendancy of individual rights**. Locke argued that individuals have **natural rights**—rights that are an inherent part of each human being in a pregovernment condition known as the **state of nature**. Three important natural rights are: *the right to life, liberty, and personal property*. In the state of nature, individuals must seek to limit the impact of others on their own individual natural rights. If an individual, pursuing her self-interest, were to trespass on the property rights of another individual, then the rightful owner of the violated property would have the right to defend the property through some form of individual justice. The property owner would become the judge in this case and establish a penalty for the offense. In American folk tradition, this form of justice is often referred to as "frontier justice." (See Photo 1.1.)

Because of the tremendous time it takes to continually defend one's property, Locke concluded that individuals will form a civil society and government. Locke's vision of a social contract is conceived to protect natural rights and maximize personal freedom, known in this case as **negative freedom**—in other words, freedom *from* excessive government and other interferences in the lives of individual citizens living within the social contract.

Because we all possess natural rights in an equal quantity to other individuals under the social contract, Locke concludes that all individuals should have an equal opportunity to participate in the limited government and civil society. Every individual should have the right to vote in the elections of leaders. Either

PHOTO 1.1   John Locke (1632–1704)

through direct vote or through elected representation, we can reshape our social contract to better fit our needs.

The social contract also helps us meet our obligation to care for others. Under Locke's classical liberal social contract, our obligation to satisfy the needs of other parties is generally limited to the maintenance of individual freedom or liberty and the protection of individual rights. A guarantee of equal protection under the law would maintain a presumed equality of humanity.

In Locke's view, the role of government is very limited. Society would be civil through maintenance of social order and individual freedom. Civility is viewed as a function of human rationality and self-interest. Order and freedom, in turn, would allow individuals maximum opportunities to engage in economic and social relationships for individual and/or collective benefit. Public policies limiting the positive use of personal freedom could serve to limit human spirit and ability, impinging on individual rights and possibly diminishing civil society.

Lockean liberalism continues to shape public policy debates, choices, and outcomes. The Republican Party tends toward classical liberalism, often opposed to the growth of government programs viewed as performing a social welfare function. Republicans often oppose the growth of government regulations viewed as limiting the personal freedom of individuals and businesses.

Classical liberals believe that as government increases its scope of power, the freedom and liberty of the individual declines. As larger and more powerful governments arise, a greater number of decisions are developed publicly and individuals pursuing their individual self-interest make fewer decisions. Reliance on individual rationality and civility in solving problems or meeting defined needs is replaced by public policy. American conservatives are concerned that the growth of public policy increases the likelihood of passive powerless citizens.

Many political scientists use **economic theory** and classical liberalism as the basis of their analyses of public policy; in essence they study what public policy *does* (using economics) in relation to what classical liberalism would indicate it *ought to do* (using classical liberal philosophy). In *An Inquiry into the Nature and Causes of the Wealth of Nations* (1776), Adam Smith proposed that:

- Individuals are rational economic self-maximizers, pursuing their individual good in the private realm of the marketplace and in the public sphere of government and civil society.
- Government is almost exclusively established to protect the individual and his or her property rights and other natural rights . . . to replace the state of nature in which members of a social contract no longer find a workable existence.

Smith (see Photo 1.2) wrote centuries ago, but his thoughts still shape the American conservative view of **classical liberalism**. Authors such as Ludwig von Mises, Friedrich von Hayek, and Milton Friedman—strong believers in capitalism and proponents of a limited social contract—have played a significant role in shaping the choices of policy-makers such as President Ronald Reagan, who believed government should not provide as many benefits to citizens and should cost less.

Although often leery of big government, most American classical liberals (American conservatives) are willing to consider a role for the national government in maintaining some degree of equity in society. In part, their policy preferences can be attributed to the ideas of John Stuart Mill. **Mill extended liberalism to include a role for government in promoting social justice.** (See Photo 1.3.)

Mill argued that inequality is a function of the development of societies that in some way limit the freedom of the individual and potentially limit opportunities for that individual. Mill illustrates the conflicting values that classical

PHOTO 1.2 Adam Smith (1723–1790)

PHOTO 1.3 John Stuart Mill (1806–1873)

liberalism represents: Does one recognize the human condition or does one blindly follow Locke's principles? By identifying social justice as a legitimate concern, Mill's work had the potential to expand the role of government.

Mill's work inspires many Americans to recognize the existence of social inequalities and to support means to rectify those inequalities. Affordable health care, for instance, shapes contemporary politics. Access to health care is shaped by an individual's ability to pay. Does economic condition, therefore, dictate one's ability to live a healthy life? If so, then social inequality is bound to occur. Or, is health care an assumed basic right that government must promote? If the latter is true, then affordable health care must be promoted as part of the social contract.

MODERN LIBERALISM AND PUBLIC POLICY

Modern liberalism is based solely in human reason in establishing a notion of rights and liberties, referencing historical evidence to support an *evolving* vision of "good" public policy and "good" government. The foundations of modern liberalism can be traced through the work of many modern philosophers, but for purposes of simplicity I will focus on three major philosophers and their influence on modern liberalism—Jean Jacques Rousseau, Immanuel Kant, and John Rawls.

Jean Jacques Rousseau

From the perspective of Jean Jacques Rousseau, individuals are part of a society, a community, identifying themselves through mutual association. **Positive freedom**—freedom to act within societal boundaries—is an important basis of equality within a society or community. Rousseau envisioned a government that would promote equality and freedom because, in his view, neither were absolute principles—both were relative and variable. Good government, therefore, would promote a general set of principles important to all citizens known as the **general will**. Government should promote *positive freedom* as well as equality and social order—individual freedom *to* achieve, *to* succeed, and *to* gain individual happiness. (See Photo 1.4.)

For Rousseau, the general will of the citizens was best determined through community involvement in government. He encouraged active involvement of citizens in town hall meetings. Political leaders were to act as agents of the people rather than elected independent decision-makers. According to the well-regarded twentieth-century professor of philosophy George Sabine, the Rousseau general will is often vague and difficult to apply.

- First, it assumes that the general will as a majority view is always right, when in fact it may be highly inaccurate.
- Second, it assumes that individuals' personal preferences are a function of their membership in the society or community, when in fact preferences may be shaped by individual self-interest.

PHOTO 1.4   Jean Jacques Rousseau
(1712–1778)

- Third, it is unclear in Rousseau's thought whether the general will directly emerges from the mass society or community, or whether it emerges from enlightened individual thought of an educated elite within society.

Despite these stated challenges, can we apply Rousseau's ideas to a discussion of modern liberalism and public policy in the United States? The answer is an emphatic yes.

- First, **the establishment of national public policy goals in the United States is consistent with Rousseau's notion of societal goals and principles**. Examples of this can be seen in many twentieth-century policies such as the War on Poverty and the War Against Cancer, efforts intended to promote social equity through economic and health care policies.
- Second, **Rousseau's general will as applied through mass society involvement in establishment of societal goals is consistent with a growing role of citizen-policy-makers in the United States**. In the 1960s, public policy in the United States increasingly turned to citizens to shape public policy rather than relying solely on policy experts. Prominent political scientists such as Robert Dahl and Carole Pateman illustrated the importance of citizen involvement in policy-making in a democracy.
- Third, **Rousseau's views of freedom and equality are consistent with many modern liberal public policy goals in the United States.** Rousseau's thoughts influenced the prominent early-twentieth-century American social philosopher John Dewey. Dewey's writings on social and political theory in a modernizing American society link our eighteenth-century democratic principles to pragmatic public policy goals in the areas of social welfare, education, and political participation intended to

promote core societal values. Dewey's writings have and continue to serve as a roadmap for many of the domestic public policies that promote equality and fairness.

Immanuel Kant

The work of Immanuel Kant helps us to understand what a social contract means in a foundational sense. **Kant questioned the metaphysical (or religious-based) foundations of political philosophy.** In *Critique of Pure Reason,* Kant dissects the notion that through reason we can arrive at the proposition that there is a Creator. Without going fully into Kant's argument, it is important to realize that without the concept of a Creator, the notion of the preexistence of equality in the state of nature as espoused by Locke comes into question.

Kant argued that human understanding is not uniform because individual approaches to understanding are not uniform. When we study society and the inequities within society, individuals' power of reason might lead to different conclusions about what society could or should do to limit inequalities, or even result in one not seeing or comprehending inequality. Development of a standard approach to understanding becomes central to explaining phenomena, their causes and effects, and the ability to predict or change the direction of phenomena. If we form agreement on *how* to "see," and determine, via scientific theory, what we "see" might mean, then the idea of uniform knowledge and understanding is made possible. (See Photo 1.5.)

Kant's ideas led to the questioning of Locke's assumptions about the state of nature and the capacity and role of government. Kantian thought draws our attention to the condition of individuals. We discover the variations in the condition and state of individuals, variations not yet fully explicated

PHOTO 1.5 Immanuel Kant
(1724–1804)

through scientific analysis. Absent Locke's notion of individual natural rights and natural law (and given that scientific research has shown that inequalities exist between individuals), it would appear that we do not enter the social contract as equals and our existence under the social contract may remain unequal in significant ways. Kant proves to be critical to modern liberal thought because his ideas lead to important questions about the nature of classical and modern liberalism:

- His questioning of the basis of rights serves to confirm some elements of Rousseau—namely, the notion that rights emerge from human society rather than from an otherworldly "Creator."
- His argument in favor of uniform science for observation, inquiry, and analysis of phenomena nods to the uniqueness of individual human observation and therefore the unique role each individual may play in the establishment of social norms and principles.
- The role of science in identifying inequities and causes of inequities in society affirms the evolving nature of the general will and the role of enlightened policy-makers in shaping the general will. Science and social norms and principles must be brought together, shaping our understanding of what government ought or ought not do, and does or does not do.

John Rawls

Possibly the most prominent modern liberal philosopher is John Rawls, who outlined his principles in *A Theory of Justice* (1971). Building on the ideas of Kant, Rawls's primary assumption is that individuals are capable of reason. Rawls argues that individuals desire the maximum freedom possible in order to achieve their maximum benefit. This necessarily produces inequities resulting from individuals pursuing their individual, selfish benefit, their personal notion of good. Rawls concludes that this dilemma necessarily relates to a central tenet of modern liberal social contract theory: the idea of "justice as fairness"—a reasonable social position where individuals pursue their private interests while preserving the rights of other members of society to preserve their freedom to maximize their benefits, too. (See Photo 1.6.)

Two general principles emerge from Rawls's modern liberal social contract. The first principle would include the concept of ***equal representation*** (Rawls's First Principle) of individuals and therefore interests via the vote process, a position consistent with Lockean classical liberal views. The presence of a social contract and the processes of governance would likely be to the advantage of all parties to the contract. Because all individuals are assumed to be rational and reasonable, it is likely that all individuals gain something from the social contract and have equal opportunities to gain and use political power (Rawls 1971, 61).

According to Rawls' Second Principle (***difference principle***), wealth and income distribution do not have to be equal for all members of society, but the end result of distribution must always benefit all parties to the social

PHOTO 1.6   John Rawls (1921–2002)

contract. In short, the justness of individual outcomes is judged in relation to the outcomes of other members of society. The difference principle justifies policies for the redistribution of individual property or wealth to promote social and economic justice.

Although Rawls goes beyond the two major principles discussed, it has been made sufficiently clear that his vision of modern liberalism outlines a much broader social contract compared to Locke's. Rawls draws his argument almost entirely from what is known or generally understood to be the essence of human motivations, desires, and general characteristics, as known through objective scientific inquiry—systematic thought based solely on human reason. Natural rights and natural law are absent from Rawls' theory.

Constitution

THE NATURE OF LIBERALISM IN THE UNITED STATES

Our social contract and policy process first emerged from constitutional powers and principles, guided by a belief in a Creator or divine being who had granted to us certain natural rights and liberties. Over time, we have come to recognize the incompleteness of our social contract, which in the past excluded women and minorities from full membership in society and may continue to do so (see Schneider and Ingram 1993). Also, we do not fully agree on the existence of a Creator or divine being; therefore, Locke's assumptions are derogated, and the modern liberal assumptions, based instead on rational social contract construction, are elevated.

The political process today is driven to a large degree by a discussion of political rights and equality-related issues. Perhaps a subject of perennial debate, equality has moved toward the center of political and social discussions. Today, many individuals accept that policies promoting equality of condition and outcome are necessary. With an enlarged definition of what equality means and with a connection drawn between equality and freedom—a connection not drawn in Locke's vision of liberalism—the scope of government has necessarily grown and continues to grow, as we continue to define the meaning of equality and freedom. In terms of political parties, proponents of modern liberalism are more likely to be Democrats than Republicans, although both major political parties tend to espouse elements of both classical and modern liberalism.

COMMUNITARIANISM: ANOTHER WAY OF VIEWING SOCIETY AND POLICY

Although liberals—classical and modern—continue to debate the meaning of liberalism, communitarians often reject the social contract as the sole basis of our society—of a "good" society. Communitarians generally do not see the strength of American society in the promotion of narrowly defined individual rights. Rather, they tend to see individuals as members of groups or communities within larger groups and communities—society is a filigree, the complexity and strength of which is an important dimension in a self-governing liberal democracy. As such, individuals are not truly independent of one another and do not blindly pursue their self-interest.

Rather than relying on a system of laws to protect individuals from one another, communitarians believe that the nature of the community shapes the conditions of civil society. Political liberals are drawn to public policy and law, but communitarians place greater emphasis on informal voluntary human cooperation to solve problems. In the United States, communitarians often point to Alexis de Tocqueville's description of American communities in his early-nineteenth-century analysis, *Democracy in America.* Writing in what has become the foundational work in the communitarian tradition, the French social observer addressed two critical themes within American political and social ethos: individualism and community affiliation.

Communitarians often find Lockean liberalism and its emphasis on the individual to be unrealistic. Individuals are by nature social beings and as such develop informal relationships with one another for mutual economic, political, and social benefit. Within "community," individuals establish and/or maintain shared traditions and social norms—important elements in establishing community values and in defining "virtuous" behavior (Etzioni 2001). Community members often recognize a collective benefit from mutual support that cannot easily be translated into individual benefit.

Communitarians are interested in the development of social trust. In their view, trust is the foundation upon which all other social, political, and economic relationships and institutions are based, thrive, and endure. Absent interpersonal trust, social and political institutions will experience member conflict and failure. Scholars such as Francis Fuyukama and Robert Heilbroner have concluded that the nature of interpersonal trust, as well as the structure of society and government, shapes the strength of nations within the world economic community; economic position will influence what we ask of government and what we get in return.

Considering both classical and modern liberalism in light of what we are now learning about communitarian thought, it seems that some level of trust is necessary to either enter into or maintain the social contract. John Rawls recognized this need in *A Theory of Justice,* particularly when he alluded to the development of "social union." Rawls went further in *Political Liberalism,* in which he grappled with the coexistence of modern liberal principles in relation to the existence of community and/or civic society. Therefore, much of the work of communitarian scholars is not an outright rejection of liberalism and its principles; rather, it is an attempt to either strengthen or maintain core elements of liberalism. Communitarian ideas have a great deal to do with the strength of civil society and how that strength influences the efficacy of public institutions and the value of what institutions produce: namely, public policy.

In addition to trust, communitarian scholars are interested in intergenerational connectedness, in other words, the establishment and maintenance of traditions and "good" social, political, and economic values. Of course, the definition of "good" traditions and values often depends on a scholar's political predispositions. Nevertheless, there is some agreement regarding the notion that democratic values (i.e., freedom, social order, and equality) are important concepts that must be transmitted intergenerationally. Additionally, individuals must learn from others the value of political and social participation.

In *Making Democracy Work: Civic Traditions in Modern Italy* (1993) and *Bowling Alone* (2000), Robert Putnam offers credible evidence to support the communitarian views. His analysis of the relative strength of civic community in relation to the strength of liberal democracy demonstrates that weak communities are generally associated with weak or crumbling government institutions and failed public policies. Putnam's study of Italian regional government demonstrated the stark differences that exist between Italian regions, due in large part to differences in the strength of social capital (e.g., social trust; civic participation; a belief in the value of social, political, and economic institutions), which serves as the basis of strong communities. In *Bowling Alone,* Putnam analyzed the strength of social capital in the United States and found a significant decline in traditional forms of civic engagement. Although new forms of engagement are emerging and require further study, the foundation of American liberal democracy—namely community—has not fared well in recent decades. Communitarian scholars find that strong civic communities are the basis of strong classical or modern liberal democracies; liberalism is the "ideal," but communitarian principles are the realization and preservation of that ideal. Government alone, through public policy, can neither create nor maintain a classical or modern liberal reality. Rather, it is people and working cooperatively that creates the society that we collectively desire.

Why would it be important to understand the nature of community in relation to a discussion of public policy? Consider my definition of public policy: What government *ought or ought not do, does or does not do.* Looking at the principles of classical and modern liberalism, many of the issues surrounding the definition are addressed by classical and modern liberal scholars. For instance, the confiscation of private property by government would probably be something that ought not to happen in a society governed by classical liberal principles, but it might happen in a modern liberal society in order to meet the requirements of the "difference principle."

How do we reach agreement on what government ought or ought not do on a case-by-case basis? We have not locked (no pun intended) ourselves into one or another form of liberalism . . . our social contract is continually evolving. How, then, do we discuss change? Fortunately, many issues that are discussed do not rise to the level of social contract revision; they are simply things related to the stresses and strains of living in proximity to one another. In some cases, issues can be considered in light of government responsibility as well as community responsibility. Productive discussion would require trust and an accepted forum for discussion of ideas; hence, one reason why communitarian perspectives and principles might be important to us.

Second, the issue of freedom arises when discussing the social contract and more importantly public policy. The freedom promised by liberalism is grounded in the notion of human rationality or at least reasonability. Through the power of reason and rationality, individuals and groups of individuals could solve many problems without relying on government, which sounds similar to Locke's classical liberal perspective. More accepting of government, even Rawls would likely not support the notion that all issues can or should be dealt with via government policy or litigation. The strength of liberal democracy is arguably found in the wisdom of government leaders and the judgment of the citizenry. For Tocqueville, the loss of community and civic traditions would mean increasing reliance on government to solve problems via public policy; acting alone and without the active support of citizens, government policy may not meet "needs."

Third, social, political, and economic values are the foundation of public policy. We do not have a unified vision of "good" social, political, and economic values. Beyond general values related to liberal democracy, American values are very diverse. Given our pluralist tradition, perhaps it makes sense that we disparage those individuals or groups who demand or desire to institute one set of "good" values.

Values and the discussion of values are important in the policy process. Certain issues such as abortion are often witness to intense policy debates about what political "rights" ought to be protected by government. The abortion policy issue, of course, is also tied to a discussion of morality. Other issues, such as gun control and smoking, are often connected to a discussion of personal freedom and rights. In essence, the discussion of public policy is also a discussion about values.

So, if public policy is about values—as well as rights—where can this discussion occur? Again, this brings us back to the need for an accepted forum for discussion, a place where we can trust each other to react to each other's views in a rational and/or reasonable manner. Where can we reach agreement on what values we collectively wish to promote through public policy? Absent civic traditions and social capital, the discussion of values would look more like a war than the reasoned discussion desirable in liberal democracies. **Communitarianism** can cherish and nurture the civic forums for healthy and constructive public debate, affirming the values we share, identifying our differences, and offering the possibility of peaceful resolution to political and social conflict. Nevertheless, in the pursuit of the "good" we can overlook the voices of the less powerful in our community—liberalism and communitarian thought is a balancing between individual rights and community, as well as between our vision of how society "ought" (philosophy) to function and how it "does" (science and social science) function.

Lessons Learned from Chapter 1

SPECIFICS

- Public policy is what government ought or ought not do, does or does not do.
- The judgments we make about what government ought or ought not do are related to generally accepted principles of government and society.
- The U.S. government was initially established on the basis of classical liberal thought, which envisions limited government and the protection of citizens' "natural rights."
- Modern liberal thought does not support the idea of natural rights, but argues that rights are based in human reasonableness and rationality, evolve over time, and are agreed upon collectively. Modern liberalism concludes that government should protect citizens from the inequalities that are created by society.
- Whereas classical and modern liberals focus on the issue of rights and government protection of rights, communitarians focus on citizen–government interaction and the never-ending dialogue about basic values. Values, it is argued, are the basis of society and effective government.
- The principles of classical and modern liberalism and communitarianism are effective in illustrating some of the ways we think about what government ought or ought not do.

THE BIG PICTURE

Public policy is a function of disparate visions of governance. It is unlikely that the debate over what government does or does not do will be based solely in objective applied social science policy analysis. Such analyses are often thought to be a universally accepted approach to studying the impact of government policies and the efficiency of government policy (i.e., do benefits outweigh the costs?). In many respects, this scientific approach is the basis of Kantian critiques of the power of human reason and the modern liberal view of social justice. The former argues for the use of scientific, mathematically based approaches to understanding, whereas the latter requires government identification and

BOX 1.2

"Liberalism" versus "liberalism"

When speaking of "liberalism" (with a lower case "l"), one must be cognizant of certain distinctions. Someone who is a *liberal* may or may not be "left-leaning." The "liberalism" discussed here is largely related to the philosophical foundations of government. This discussion is essential because of the proposed revised definition of public policy; one's philosophical vision of government will likely shape what is expected from government. In the United States, someone who is politically and socially conservative is more than likely a *liberal*. Being a "liberal" means that one identifies with a particular philosophical foundation of government. An American "conservative" is often identified with the rejection of, or deep-seated skepticism about, the need for political and social change. American conservatives prefer the status quo, possibly because it benefits them to have things remain the same. American conservatives generally support the principles of classical liberalism. Conversely, someone who is an American "Liberal" (with an upper case "L") identifies with a particular political ideology that often supports political and social change—as opposed to simply maintaining the status quo—as the preferred method of establishing a desirable government and society. American Liberals generally support the principles of "modern liberalism."

monitoring of socioeconomic disparity in order to meet the needs of social justice. Objectivity is often claimed, but in every policy there is a normative foundation to be found.

The lack of appreciation for deeply held philosophical differences between classical and modern liberalism, and the role of value debate as addressed by communitarians, means that a cacophony of numbers generated by different ideological camps are not understood for what they likely represent; namely, normative differences hiding behind numbers. As Ted Lowi concluded in *The End of Liberalism* (1969), the ideological debate is being replaced by a power struggle. This power struggle plays itself out in part through competing claims to knowledge regarding the state of society and the capacity of government to positively impact societal conditions. Under such conditions, cogent public policy-making becomes supremely challenging. (See Box 1.2, *"Liberalism" versus "liberalism."*)

Key Terms

classical liberalism
communitarianism
economic theory
general will
modern liberalism
negative freedom

liberalism
positive freedom
public policy
scope of government
social contract

Questions for Study

1. How does philosophy of government impact public policy?
2. What is the difference between a philosophical liberal and a communitarian?
3. What is the working definition of public policy used in this chapter? Discuss how our normative views of government impact what government does or does not do. Provide an example.

Bibliography

Barber, B. 1988. *Strong democracy: Participatory politics for a new age.* Berkeley, CA: University of California Press.

Barker, E., ed. 1947. *Social contract: Locke, Hume, Rousseau.* London: Oxford University Press.

Bellah, R., R. Madsen, W. Sullivan, A. Swidler, and S. Tipton. 1985. *Habits of the heart: Individualism and commitment in American life.* New York: Perennial Library.

———. 1992. *The good society.* New York: Knopf.

Carr, E. H. 1946. *The Twenty Years' Crisis, 1919–1939: An introduction to the study of international relations.* London: Macmillan & Company.

Corwin, E. 1928. Reprint, 1971. *The 'higher law' background of American constitutional law.* Ithaca, NY: Cornell University Press.

Dahl, R. 1971. *Polyarchy: Participation and opposition.* New Haven, CT: Yale University Press.

Dewey, J. 1888. *The ethics of democracy.* Ann Arbor, MI: Andrews.

Etzoni, A. 2001. *The monochrome society.* Princeton, NJ: Princeton University Press.

Fuyukama, F. 1995. *Trust: The social virtues and the creation of prosperity.* New York: Free Press.

Gardiner, P., ed. 1969. *Nineteenth century philosophy.* New York: Free Press.

Goodin, R. 1982. *Political theory and public policy.* Chicago: University of Chicago Press.

Gray, J. 1986. *Liberalism.* Minneapolis: University of Minnesota Press.

Hartz, L. 1955. *The liberal tradition in America: An interpretation of American political thought since the Revolution.* New York: Harcourt Brace.

Heilbroner, R. 1993. *21st Century capitalism.* New York: Norton.

Hero, R. 1998. *Faces of inequality: Social diversity in American politics.* New York: Oxford University Press.

Hobbes, T. 1950. *Leviathan.* New York: Dutton.

Kantorowicz, E. 1957. *The king's two bodies: A study in medieval political theology.* Princeton, NJ: Princeton University Press.

Kraynak, R. 1987. Tocqueville's constitutionalism. *American Political Science Review.* 81(4): 175–95.

Lazlo, E., and J. Wilbur. 1968. *Value theory in philosophy and social science.* New York: Gordon and Breach Science Publishers.

Lipset, S. 1990. *Continental divide: The values and institutions of the United States and Canada.* New York: Routledge.

Locke, J. 1947. *Two Treatises of Government.* Edited by T. Cook. New York: Hafner Publishing Company.

Lowi, T. 1969. *The end of liberalism: Ideology, policy, and the crisis of public authority.* New York: Norton.

Pateman, C. 1970. *Participation and democratic theory.* Cambridge: Cambridge University Press.

Putnam, R. 1993. *Making democracy work: Civic traditions in modern Italy.* Princeton, NJ: Princeton University Press.

———. 2000. *Bowling Alone.* New York: Simon & Schuster.

Rawls, J. 1971. *A theory of justice.* Cambridge, MA: Harvard University Press.

———. 1993. *Political liberalism.* New York: Columbia University Press.

Sabine, G. 1989. *A history of political theory,* 4th ed. Fort Worth: Harcourt Brace College Publishers.

Sandel, M. 1982. *Liberalism and the limits of justice.* London: Oxford University Press.

Schneider, A., and H. Ingram. 1993. Social construction of target populations: Implications for politics and policy. *American Political Science Review.* 87(2): 334–47.

Smith, A. 1776. *An inquiry into the nature and causes of the wealth of nations.* London: W. Strahan and T. Cadell.

Tocqueville, A. 1958. *Democracy in America.* New York: Mentor Books.

Toffler, A. 1971. *Future shock.* New York: Bantam Books.

Von Hayek, F. 1944. *Road to serfdom: The dangers inherent in social planning.* Chicago: University of Chicago Press.

———. 1960. *The constitution of liberty.* Chicago: University of Chicago Press.

Von Mises, L. 1981. *Socialism.* Indianapolis: Liberty Fund.

Walzer, M. 1983. *Spheres of justice: A defense of pluralism and equality.* New York: Basic Books.

Endnote

1. Eastern Europe witnessed an expansion of liberalism in the late twentieth century, with the collapse of the Soviet Union.

2

■ ■ ■

Theories of Public Policy: How Choices Are Made

CHAPTER OVERVIEW

In this chapter, the empirical aspects of public policy or policy "science" will be discussed. **Policy science** pursues reliable, valid, and universally understood techniques for developing public policy. The empirical aspect of public policy helps us to develop a more detailed understanding of *why* policies come to fruition.

The specific goals for the chapter are:

- What is science and how does it relate to public policy studies?
- Discuss policy models that will be used to study specific policy areas.

THE IMPORTANCE OF SCIENCE IN STUDYING PUBLIC POLICY

To advance, science requires cumulative knowledge. Newly acquired knowledge must build on past knowledge. The accumulation and sharing of knowledge leads to greater complexity in understanding, making possible the prediction of future phenomena. Also, *methods* of understanding must be identified and accepted by scientists if science is to progress. A generally accepted method of understanding forms the basis of *rational* scientific discourse. A **scientific theory** is a tentative basis of understanding. Theories provide scientists with a unified way of thinking about phenomena. Objective science produces uniformly accepted methods of describing a policy problem, leading to a normatively uniform outcome—a critical yet often overlooked assumption in discussions of policy models. A good theory is able to describe, explain, and predict the phenomena surrounding public policy. (See Box 2.1, *A Good Theory.*)

BOX 2.1

A Good Theory

A good theory is able to:

- Describe
- Explain
- Predict

THE RATIONAL–COMPREHENSIVE MODEL

Charles Lindblom outlined the rational–comprehensive approach in his classic article, "The Science of Muddling Through" (1959). The first step in the rational–comprehensive approach involves careful identification of a problem. All aspects of the problem must be empirically studied, thoroughly defined, and understood. Agreement on problem definition ("is") should produce agreement on problem solution ("ought").

Once agreement is reached on problem description, in both a general and specific sense, the rational–comprehensive model requires that policy-makers identify an exhaustive list of potential solutions. Science plays a significant role at this point, requiring policy-makers to fully understand methods of limiting or eliminating the undesirable impacts associated with policy problems. Problem identification shapes problem solutions. Problems inaccurately described or understood produce faulty solutions.

A third step in the rational–comprehensive approach involves the selection and application of a solution. Government deals with a multitude of problems and limited resources for addressing those problems, so important choices have to be made. Choices attempt to maximize the benefit of a policy while simultaneously limiting costs.

In the fourth step, using empirical analysis, policy outcomes are compared with policy goals to determine whether: (1) the problem has been properly addressed; if not, then policy adjustments will be made, more clearly identifying a problem, policy solutions, and expected outcomes. Policy goals are juxtaposed with outcomes to determine whether the policy requires adjustment[1] so as to produce desired outcomes; or, (2) policy is inherently flawed and should be terminated. (See Box 2.2, *Rational–Comprehensive Model*.)

There are potential drawbacks to the rational–comprehensive model. First, it is often difficult for policy-makers to agree about what government ought or ought not do; yet, agreement on values is assumed. Second, it is frequently impossible to agree on the description of a particular problem. Third, high costs are associated with the employment of the rational–comprehensive approach. Finally, the rational–comprehensive approach requires in-depth problem and policy solution analyses, requiring significant time commitment and fiscal resources.

BOX 2.2
Rational–Comprehensive Model

- Identify problem
- Identify all solutions
- Implement the best solution
- Measure the impact on the problem

With limited time available, problem identification and policy solutions must be designed in a relatively expedient manner and be understandable to policy decision-makers. Highly detailed analyses may confuse policy-makers who lack the time to read detailed analyses. Also, details and proposed alternative solutions to policy problems may produce rancor among policy-makers and slow down the policy-making process. Finally, it is often difficult to determine whether a particular policy has had the intended impact, producing the expected benefit at a given cost. Policy outcomes are not immediate; it may take years to determine whether there has been the intended impact, during which time policy-making institutions often change priorities. Policy-makers come and go throughout the policy process, often due to election outcomes. The public has a hand in encouraging elected representatives to refocus the goals of a particular policy or perhaps terminate specific policies. Due to shifts in policy goals, what may have been considered a success at one point in time could be seen as failure at a later time.

INCREMENTALISM[2]

Charles Lindblom (1959) proposed an alternative to the rational–comprehensive model, which he believed better described public policy decision-making, known as **incrementalism**. The model's premise is that most decision-making is neither complete nor final; rather, a series of small decisions—successive limited comparisons—are made on a regular basis over time. Unlike the rational–comprehensive model, policy-makers do not agree on detailed policy goals or a process of achieving such goals; in fact, most policy debate does not end with the creation of policy. Policy continues to evolve over time for both empirical and normative reasons.

Continued debate inspires conflict and growing policy complexity as normative issues are addressed and empirical evidence is collected. Conflict and complexity often lead to rancor in political institutions. One way of reducing conflict is to reach agreement on very general policy goals and values. For example, classical and modern liberals would likely agree that a civil society is one that does not allow its citizens to starve; therefore, it is likely that some agreement could be reached on the role of social welfare policy. Basic agreement streamlines the policy process, limits policy alternatives, and expedites the formulation and implementation of public policies.

In the process of reducing conflict and complexity, incrementalism often leaves policy-makers and policy scientists without a clear understanding of policy solutions. The problem is not identified in a narrow sense, so specific solutions are often left to other decision-makers in the policy process (public administrators and clientele groups) who often have great personal and biased interest in particular policy processes and outcomes.

Incrementalism assumes that problem definition and policy goals and alternatives are regularly revisited and revised over time. Small decisions about policy objectives, goals, and outcomes are made during each decision-making cycle, but discussion and debate over the core goals of policy are often avoided. Policy adjustments are usually made in reaction to changing conditions.

Despite its ease of application, incrementalism poses a serious challenge to democratic policy making. The approach frequently avoids making the tough and comprehensive decisions about what government ought or ought not do, does or does not do. In this sense, incrementalism has the potential to be quite dangerous. At the foundation of liberal democracy lies the assumption that governance involves a regular and open discussion of values and goals but incrementalism is process-driven rather than goal-driven.

In his work on policy analysis, Yehezkel Dror was somewhat skeptical of incrementalism, fearing its value-neutral goals, amoral stance, and potentially negative impact on citizens. Dror found that incrementalism could produce public policies that have a life of their own, slowly growing and evolving without full consideration of their need, desirability, or effectiveness.

PUBLIC CHOICE

Public choice is primarily grounded in classical liberal philosophy. Advocates of public choice envision limited or **minimalist** government, one that meets only the basic needs of citizens associated with the protection of citizens' natural rights. Public choice theorists conclude that government solutions, particularly utopian policy solutions designed to create a "good" society, are flawed and should be eliminated, particularly if a net social gain cannot be demonstrated (see Tullock 1969, 196). Expansive public policy is seen by public choice theorists as an unjust limitation of personal freedom. Public choice is generally concerned with the preservation of the civil order necessary to maintain individual preference and marketplace solutions.

Public choice theorists concede that the pure pursuit of individual gain through the marketplace potentially leads to the destruction or loss of *public goods*—basic necessities often held in common and needed by all citizens in order to survive (e.g., air or water). Public goods are often limited in supply—individuals pursuing their personal gain might stockpile public goods or misuse goods in pursuit of individual benefit, thus reducing the access to public goods for use by others—a condition often termed the "tragedy of the commons." Theorists conclude that government must regulate public goods so as to prevent misuse or destruction.[3]

Public choice theory is a valuable tool for understanding the policy process; the motivations of individual citizens in the political process are often shaped by self-interest. According to Anthony Downs in *An Economic Theory of Democracy* (1957), political parties attempt to capture vote majorities by pledging support for a particular set of issues—the "benefit." Individuals choose to vote for a particular candidate based on the perceived benefit of choosing that candidate and his or her political party's agenda as well as the perceived "costs" associated with the vote choice. In order to capture the majority of votes cast, political parties and their candidates adjust their policy positions so as to attract needed votes. The election process functions as a political marketplace, where voters and candidates bargain over policy benefits and tax costs associated with benefits; candidates and voters pursue their individual self-interest, but simultaneously meet the interests of a majority of citizens.

Through the election process voters affect the size and scope of government and amount and types of public policy. Voters also influence tax costs. Tax cost equates to a loss of personal economic freedom, surrendered to or taken by government, used to pay for *public goods and services*. Voters are assumed to be rational—consuming accurate information on costs and benefits of a particular vote choice. In reality, not all voters collect uniform quantities and quality of information, in part due to the costs (resources and time) associated with compiling information. Because political parties generally represent a large number of issues over long periods of time, voters can, at times, simply vote for a political party, remaining ignorant of many of the details of a particular candidate's issue stance, relying instead on a general or vague understanding of a political party's philosophy of governance. Often, the act of voting is a cost without a perceived individual benefit; for example, an election where one candidate is expected to win by an overwhelming majority. Under such conditions, an individual might consider that the act of voting is futile . . . there may be no direct benefit from the act of voting beyond the emotive benefit of participating in the democratic process.

Public choice theory offers an explanation of interest group politics. Many goods and services provided by government offer a general benefit for all citizens (e.g., defense, police protection, and basic education), but the cost and benefit per citizen is usually relatively small. Other goods and services offer **selective benefits** (e.g., farming subsidies and Social Security)—all members of society usually share the costs associated with these policies, but the direct benefits are offered to a fraction of the population. Interest groups pursue both types of benefits but are often interested in selective benefits.

Through collective action, interest groups reduce the costs of information for their membership as well as for elected officials (through information campaigns and lobbying), offering a select benefit in return for group affiliation or support. With lower costs and recognizable benefits, interest groups take an active role in elections, pooling resources to support campaigns, in an effort to affect the election of candidates supportive of their cause.

Public choice, therefore, offers us a normatively grounded model for what public policy *ought* to look like in a minimalistic Lockean classical liberal democracy. Public choice theorists have attempted to outline the public policy environment that would maximize personal freedom—to paraphrase the title of James Buchanan's well-known and classic account, somewhere between anarchy and Hobbes's absolutist government, *Leviathan*. Public choice theory is also highly empirical, attempting to explain why government and public policy develop as they do. *Public choice* touches on both normative and empirical elements in the definition of public policy.

GROUP THEORY

James Madison, one of the distinguished authors of the U.S. Constitution and later the fourth U.S. president, spent considerable time in *Federalist Papers #10* and *#51* discussing the nature of political pressure groups. In Madison's view, individuals coalesced into groups based on shared opinions, beliefs, and political and social values—political and social preferences that shape public policy. If allowed to become a dominant force in society, such groups could use their political, social, and economic power to constrain the public and private behaviors of citizens who hold different political and social preferences. Madison termed the result of such group control factional "tyranny." Madison and his fellow constitutional Founders designed the American political system so as to limit the impact of any one faction or interest group on other members and groups in society and to prevent group domination of the political process.

A variety of groups shape the prioritization and selection of policy issues and solutions. The most visible groups are political parties. Political parties are unique groups because they represent more than one interest or priority: Political parties represent a coalition of various interests. Unlike "special" interest groups, the primary goal of political parties is to win elections. The ability of a political party to shape public policy is determined by the election of its candidates. Once in office, an elected official generally pursues a policy agenda that is consistent with the party he or she represents, as well as the interests of those individuals in his or her state or district—*constituents*. As groups, political parties are unique because they incorporate a myriad of issues into their political messages. Parties shift policy preferences in order to gain votes, usually from moderate voters who represent the middle ground of American public opinion.

Political parties often pursue policies that provide both general and specific benefits. In order to win elections, parties attempt to demonstrate that their more general policy goals will benefit all citizens in some way; this is critical to gaining the support of voters in the political "middle ground." Concurrently, political parties often provide select benefits to their more staunch ideological and financial supporters. Groups pursuing narrowly defined policy goals—special interest groups—often help finance the campaigns of a party's candidates and seek specific policy benefits in return, should the party's candidate(s) win the election or gain control of a branch of government. Therefore, parties are pulled in several policy directions simultaneously.

The **group theory** perspective helps explain political party policy preferences and the actions taken by elected officials.

Group theory is more commonly associated with interest group politics,
often referred to as "special interest" or simply "interest groups." Unlike political parties, interest groups represent a very narrow band of policy preferences.
Interest groups do not choose candidates for political office; instead they support the campaigns of political party candidates who pledge support for particular policy preferences. A group's primary goal is to achieve a policy outcome
that is consistent with the preferences of their leaders and members. (See
Photo 2.1.)

Interest groups may pursue *select* or *generalized* benefits from government. A select benefit produces positive outcomes for individuals who are
members of the interest group, but would likely not benefit nonmembers. Corporations and trade associations operating in various industries seek to shape
policy that will improve the economic conditions for members of their industries. Selective benefits shape individual choices to join interest groups.

Interest groups may also pursue *generalized benefits*, which benefit
group members and nonmembers. As an example, consumer advocacy
groups often pursue regulatory policies designed to make products and services safer for all consumers. One dilemma that emerges for interest groups
pursuing generalized benefits is known as the *free-rider problem*. Free-riders
are individuals who benefit from the actions of interest groups without having

PHOTO 2.1 Groups making themselves heard.

to incur any direct costs (such as membership dues). When generalized benefits are offered, there may be limited incentive for many individuals to join an interest group's pursuit of a particular policy goal; with a more limited membership, an interest group may face difficulty in achieving its desired policy goals.

In *The Logic of Collective Action: Public Goods and the Theory of Groups,* Mancur Olson (1965) analyzed interest group formation and proliferation from a political economy perspective. He concluded that groups providing *selective* benefits to their members were more likely to survive and grow than groups pursuing *nonselective* or *generalized* benefits. The free-rider problem, he argued, would offer little economic incentive for individuals to join the latter groups, thus reducing potential economic resources available to so-called "public" interest groups. Hence, economic groups—business groups such as trade and commodity associations—would be more likely to exert effective influence in the policy process than would nonselective benefit groups. As it turned out, Olson's prediction was inaccurate. Partially a result of changing societal values, many individuals join public interest groups for value-related reasons rather than economic self-interest. Public interest groups have grown in both number and influence.

In *Policy Design for Democracy* (1997), Anne Schneider and Helen Ingram concluded that general political and social values frequently shape the direction of public policy and quite possibly the likelihood of interest group formation. According to Schneider and Ingram, general political and social values dictate which groups and individuals are seen as "deserving" or "undeserving." Individuals and groups considered undeserving often have lower socioeconomic status in society, and are predominately comprised of individuals from historically disenfranchised social and economic groups.

The growth and proliferation of interest groups have led to a cacophony of demands upon government. With so many different groups pursuing a variety of different policy goals—and some interests not represented at all—the ability of government leaders to accurately prioritize the preferences of citizens is difficult. In his book, *The End of Liberalism,* Ted Lowi argued that one of the central tenets of a liberal society—political equality—is either severely distorted or thwarted by the socioeconomic bias of interest group formation and their ability to influence government policy-making. The result is a society in which individuals—via group membership—pursue their own gain through public policy, largely ignoring the need to pursue majoritarian policies beneficial to society as a whole. Group theory is a valuable theoretical tool when trying to understand the policy-making process and its outcomes.

SYSTEMS THEORY

Systems theory is largely an adaptation of ideas developed in the biological sciences. Political scientist David Easton (1965) first proposed the use of systems theory to better organize the study of politics and policy. Easton argued that although much research had been conducted in the areas of political

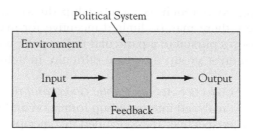

FIGURE 2.1   Model of political system.

parties and elections, interest group theory, institutional power and processes, and public opinion, there was a need to unify these analyses through a model of politics. Easton identified a number of general elements in the policy system: *political environment, input, political system, decisions or policy outputs, and feedback.*

The **political environment** is the source of various demands on government. Individuals and groups operating in the political environment regularly attempt to shape government policy choices by placing demands upon government leaders and institutions through, for example, voting in elections or interest group influence. General societal conditions that exist in the policy environment often shape policy—for example, economic decline, increasing crime rates, or international terrorism. In Easton's model, the political environment shapes the **inputs** (demands or information) into the policy process. (See Figure 2.1).

The **political system** element of the model is often termed the "black box." In Easton's model, the *type* of political system is not critical to a general study of politics and policy. Politics is simply the "authoritative allocation of values," and the black box is a generic way of thinking about government institutions. This approach is helpful because it allows each student of policy to think of government institutions in their own way.

The policy **decisions** made by government institutions are the **outputs** of government. Outputs are a reflection of what leaders within government institutions and dominant individuals or groups feel government *ought* or *ought not* do, *does* or *does not* do. Outputs may achieve the goals intended or they may not. Our view of outputs may be that they either succeeded or failed and need fine-tuning. Ruminations on policy outputs are a form of **feedback** that serves as an input into the black box in future policy-making decisions.

INSTITUTIONALISM

Institutionalism is a classic approach to the study of politics and policy-making. Aristotle's *Politics* focused much attention on types of government and institutional arrangements, identifying the good and bad qualities. Institutionalism is a highly descriptive method of the study of politics and policy. The goal of the institutional approach is to discover the nature of institutional powers, the methods by which institutions make policy choices, and how institutions and institutional actors interact with one another. The powers, structure, and governing rules of institutions are considered the basis for understanding policy decisions and outcomes. Institutionalism focuses on aggregate institution-level powers in relation to outcomes, rather than placing specific emphasis on the decisions and behavior of individual members in any particular branch of government.

Many of the powers associated with particular political institutions are not clearly enumerated in the U.S. Constitution and evolve over time. Also, many institutional powers are informal and are frequently not clearly visible, making the analysis of institutional power a challenging method of understanding institutional outcomes. The most complete set of enumerated powers are found in Article I of the Constitution—the powers of the Legislative Branch of the national government. Despite a detailed enumeration, the powers of the Legislative Branch have evolved and grown over time to include the use of the commerce clause and the "necessary and proper" clause (Article I, Section 8) to enlarge the scope of legislative power to shape and "nationalize" American politics and public policy (Lunch 1987).

Many of the powers of the executive and judicial branches can be attributed to the growth of implied and assumed institutional powers. Presidential power and influence fluctuate but remain a central part of policy-making, offering the legitimacy of a nationally elected figure and his or her administration to the policy-making process (See Photo 2.2.). Presidential power is shaped by an

PHOTO 2.2 "The goal, before this decade is out, is landing a man on the moon and returning him safely to the earth." —President Kennedy

incumbent's image, character, and popularity. In *Presidential Power: The Politics of Leadership,* Richard Neustadt concluded that presidential power is shaped by the leader's ability to persuade others to follow a policy course. Fluctuations in popularity can alter presidential power and influence. In many cases, the president's popularity is shaped by conditions largely out of his or her control, such as economic cycles and the impact of international crises on American politics and society. In domestic policy, the president's power may be weakened by poor economic or social conditions, yet his or her power is most needed in those circumstances. Conversely, international crises may bolster a president's authority in foreign affairs. The most notable recent example of this is the terrorist attack against the United States on September 11, 2001. Although a tragic event occurred domestically, public opinion polling indicates that the president's foreign policy powers were bolstered. The 9/11 attack was a unique circumstance impacting presidential powers in the short term.

The judicial branch of government has the fewest clearly enumerated powers. Only the chief justice of the Supreme Court is mentioned as a judicial officer, but the size and specific powers of the Supreme Court were not discussed. The Judiciary Act of 1789 established the basis of the national system of courts. Beyond certain narrowly defined jurisdictional powers outlined in the Constitution, the judiciary's role in the policy process has largely been a function of the courts' power of judicial review—established in the case *Marbury v. Madison* (1803). The judiciary now plays a major role in shaping the policy process, with the courts taking an active role in shaping public policy and determining its consistency with Constitutional principles.

Institutions have slightly different constituencies. The legislative branch often focuses attention on the needs of members' states or congressional districts, although national policy goals also receive attention. The president is the only nationally elected leader (note: the vice president is also elected nationally) representing the demands of a very large and diverse constituency. Courts are generally concerned with the maintenance of rights and liberties and the rule of law. Institutionalism focuses attention on the division of powers among branches of government and offers legitimacy to the policy process. The checks and balances of institutional powers often means that public policy is scrutinized from many different angles. The model provides a greater understanding of how policy goals can be tailored to various needs.

ELITE THEORY

Elite theory concludes that society is stratified, with a powerful minority at the top tier—the *elites*. The majority of citizens—the *mass public*—are at the bottom tier and do not play any significant role in the governing process. The mass public is largely passive, uninformed, and disinterested in politics and public policy, except when policies directly affect them as the consumers of public goods. The mass public has very little power to influence demand. Elite actors

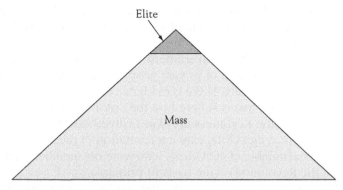

FIGURE 2.2   Model of elite theory.

shape policy preferences and the mass public generally accepts the outcomes, so long as their appetites or passions are satisfied. (See Figure 2.2).

Elites may hold different views about government and society, but are generally thought to agree on one issue: Power must be concentrated among elite actors, and the political goals and values that legitimize the elites and guarantee elite social, economic, and political gain must be preserved. According to C. Wright Mills in *Power Elite* (1956), the mass public can impact political and social elites (e.g., through elections), effectively changing elite control of government. Elite theorists might point to the 2006 congressional election as an example of a shift in the governing elite, moving from Republican to Democratic control of the U.S. Congress. The elite Republican political actors maintain a prominent role, but do not have the same level of power they once possessed. Over time, so the theory goes, the power will continue to shift between the established political elites (major political parties).

The elite members of a society usually possess a significant socioeconomic advantage over members of the mass public. Individuals within the mass public often rise to prominence, but those elevated individuals enter elite circles through elite acceptance. Elites control the reins of power and use their authority to design public policy so as to fulfill their personal interests; however, they do not actively execute policy. Rather, a barrier exists between elites and the mass public, composed of public administrative agencies and personnel loyal to the values and policies promulgated by political elites.

There has been much discussion of how elite theory can be applied to American democracy and policy-making. According to Charles Beard, an early and prominent voice in the political science literature, many of the values undergirding American democracy are actually a function of elite politics. Many of the Founders were highly influential, well-educated, wealthy landowners with a substantial interest in either maintaining or elevating their social, political, and economic status in postrevolutionary America. From an elite theory perspective, the colonial grievances against the British were trivial and directly impacted a very small portion of the population. The individuals most hampered by British rule were the colonial elites who inspired revolution for personal gain, delegitimizing the British ruling elite and replacing it with the principles of liberal democracy: a belief in the rule of law, universal suffrage (albeit limited to wealthy White landowners), the protection of private property rights, and representative (though limited) government. The principles of liberal democracy, particularly the protection of private property, were especially beneficial to the wealthier colonial rebels. There is evidence to deny the elitist claim; particularly, the tremendous losses suffered by the colonial rebel elites—many either lost their lives in the Revolutionary War or lived out their days in relative poverty. Additionally, critics of the elite interpretation of the American rebellion say that a substantial number of individuals who were not members of the colonial elite fought in the Revolution on the basis of principle.

A contrary point of view claims that the modern liberal elites began their rise to prominence in the late nineteenth century, with the emergence of Progressivism. American conservatives argue that Progressives who have served as members of the governing elite effectively redrafted the social contract in a way that diminishes critical elements of its eighteenth- and nineteenth-century foundations. Government bureaucracy grew tremendously over the course of the twentieth century and government programs intended to establish more than just economic, social, and political conditions have emerged and flourished. From an elite theory perspective, it could be argued that much of what Progressivism accomplished had the effect of manipulating the *mass* public—client-citizens or denizens—thus increasing the powerbase of those elites who use government to magnify their own political, social, and economic well-being.

In either case, elite theory is a tool for understanding the policy process that surrounds a particular political or policy-making scenario. Elite theory is often grounded in certain assumptions about obscure groups whose activities are best described on a grand scale and applied to individual cases of politics and policy. Elite theory is not always guided by the principles of scientific empiricism. Often, elite theory literature is deductive, theory-sustaining work.

GAME THEORY

Game theory recognizes that we do not always agree about the prioritization of public policy preferences, nor do we always agree on policy specifics. Where disagreement is present, conflict of some type is likely to occur; however, conflict does not always have to result in cataclysmic events. In the case of policy-making in our democratic institutions, conflict is often constrained by institutional rules and by constitutional guarantees of individual liberty, rights, and property. Conflict is generally limited to public debate, often followed by some form of compromise in the decision-making process.

There are different types of decisions in the policy process. At times, conflict can be described as *zero-sum*—a situation in which an individual or group gains a benefit as a result of the conflict and outcome, while the opposing individual or group loses some form of benefit. Zero-sum outcomes are generally not desirable, particularly in the case of most domestic public policy. Public policy is intended to be beneficial to members of society as a whole. Furthermore, public policy should not result in a loss of rights or property for any individual or group of individuals. An outcome that strips an individual of rights or property would violate the ultimate goal of our social contract: namely, the protection of the individual.

A second type of outcome in public policy is called *non-zero-sum,* also referred to as *Pareto-optimal.* In non-zero-sum, conflict and compromise result in a gain for some individuals, but no losses for individuals who do not receive a benefit from a particular policy. The principles of modern liberalism pursue *Pareto-optimality*—the creation of a just society in which individuals receive some benefit from being a member of the society, and net losses are avoided.

According to the theory, games can be either competitive or cooperative. In competitive games, each party is trying to achieve an individual "win" rather than focusing on a generalized benefit. Game theorists often use the prisoner's dilemma to illustrate competitive games, a fictional situation in which two individuals, partners in crime, are arrested and placed in different cells or different interrogation rooms. Both individuals have the opportunity to admit guilt or implicate their partner and receive a reduced prison sentence. If both remain silent, the prison sentence may be longer for both (assuming they are found guilty). If both admit guilt and agree to implicate their partner, the prison sentence may be shorter for both. Ultimately, the shortest prison sentence will occur for one individual if he or she admits guilt, while the other criminal remains silent. (See Figure 2.3).

The prisoner's dilemma model illustrates that although a particular decision made by an individual may appear to be in his or her rational self-interest (in this instance, "squealing" to the police so as to maximize personal benefit and minimize personal cost), the outcome may also be impacted by decisions made by others. Without knowing the decisions and goals of others, yet having

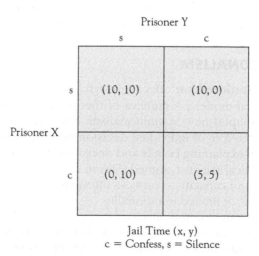

Jail Time (x, y)
c = Confess, s = Silence

FIGURE 2.3 Model of the prisoner's dilemma.

some idea of possible outcomes, decision-making involves maximizing personal gain within the context of a competitive environment requiring strategy and maneuvering—what may appear to be a good decision at one point in time may prove costly when the decisions of other individuals or groups are revealed. In the policy process, some decisions and strategizing remain hidden, making it difficult to decide a beneficial course of action. For example, in defense policy, the goals of other nation-states or nonstate actors (e.g., terrorists) may be unclear until an emergency occurs.

In cooperative games, the policy preferences of other individuals or groups are made public. Many domestic policy decisions are a function of cooperative games. Major political parties, for instance, publish policy preferences through party platform documents, official reports, and political speeches. A cooperative game is an event in which both parties are attempting to maximize their self-interest and reduce their costs, arriving at an outcome that is acceptable to both parties. Outcomes are generally Pareto-optimal.

Different actors in the policy-making process favor different forms of "games." Political compromise is a hallmark of legislative and legislative–executive politics. Senators, representatives, and the president pursue their individual and collective policy priorities, realizing that outcomes may not be entirely satisfactory or optimal. At best, they hope to achieve an outcome that offers the maximum benefit possible, given the political compromises that often must be made. Conversely, interest group politics are often driven by a desire to achieve a win without compromise. Interest group politics can move the policy process into the realm of a zero-sum game, in which some groups and individuals win while others lose. Zero-sum games are often associated with policy-making through court decisions. Judicial processes are highly adversarial, generally producing decisions that proclaim winners and losers. The cost of litigation, however, encourages compromise, for example, "out-of-court settlements." In recent years, the courts have also pursued nonadversarial procedures, encouraging parties involved in many legal disputes to engage in constructive dialogue leading to non-zero-sum outcomes before choosing to litigate.

NEO-INSTITUTIONALISM

Neo- or **new institutionalism** effectively synthesizes many of the previously discussed theoretical models. A number of theoretical perspectives on politics and policy have shaped new institutionalism. First, the rise of behavioralism drew attention to the role of individual decision making and the characteristics of the individual in explaining beliefs and decisions. Herbert A. Simon, a Nobel Prize–winning political scientist, argued (Simon 1976) that individuals lack complete information and capacity to process information fully; thus, human decisions are "bounded" or limited in rationality.

A second influence on the development of new institutionalism is public choice theory. Public choice posits that individuals will pursue their self-interest in maximizing personal benefit. Complete information is not required—just the ability to recognize one's interest and to pursue that interest as one sees fit.

A third major influence on new institutionalism is game theory. Game theory can be applied to marketplace bargaining, where individuals purchase goods and services viewed as personally beneficial. Public policy formulation involves bargaining on the part of various actors operating in what could be considered a very complex marketplace. Game theory helps us understand how actors arrive at a compromise acceptable to the majority.

New institutionalism recognizes that institutions change over time, influencing the subject, type, and quality of decisions made. Institutional rules, processes, and structure are not static. Individuals operating within institutions bring with them different values and priorities and consequently shape the organization—as membership changes, so too does the organization. Informal social norms and behaviors develop within organizations, creating important venues in which decisions are made and goals accomplished. The overwhelming emphasis on formal structure and function found in old institutionalism is now seen as a narrow and largely insufficient treatment of decision making in politics and public policy.

Lessons Learned from Chapter 2

SPECIFICS

- Science plays an important role in guiding public policy.
- Policy scientists think about policy in complex ways, focusing on goals and methods of achieving goals.
- In order to simplify complex ways of thinking about public policy, policy scientists have developed and used a variety of policy models.
- All the models are valuable in their own way, and each provides us with a unique and important understanding of politics and policy.

CHARACTERISTICS OF A GOOD MODEL

- A good model helps you to *describe* policy-making.
- A good model will help you to *explain* public policy or policy-making.
- A good model has *predictive* power. Predictive power requires that a theory be able to explain that which has yet to occur based on what is known prior to the prediction.

THE BIG PICTURE

Public policy is both normative and empirical. In Chapter 1, we discussed the normative aspects of public policy—the "big ideas" that shape our individual and collective decisions about what government *ought* or *ought not* do. In Chapter 2, we discussed the basis of the empirical element of public policy—the issue of what government *does* or *does not* do. As you probably figured out, policy science shapes our view of government and what it can and cannot do, thus shaping the realities of public policy. Only by understanding phenomena will we be able to shape those phenomena in a way that pleases us individually or collectively.

Key Terms

elite theory
game theory
group theory
incrementalism
institutionalism

new institutionalism
policy science
public choice
scientific theory
systems theory

Questions for Study

1. Discuss the importance of science in public policy. How are theories developed?
2. Compare the rational–comprehensive model to the incremental model of public policy. Which theory do you find more applicable? Why?
3. Choose one theory of public policy, and use it to explain a public policy with which you are familiar.

Bibliography

Aristotle. 1943. *Politics*. Translated by B. Jowett. New York: Modern Library.

Baumgartner, F., and B. Leech. 1998. *Basic interests: The importance of groups in politics and political science*. Princeton, NJ: Princeton University Press.

Beard, C. A. 1941. *An economic interpretation of the Constitution of the United States*. New York: Macmillan.

Benfield, D. 1974. The A Priori-A Posteriori Distinction. *Philosophy and Phenomenological Research*. 35(2): 151–66.

Berry, W. 1990. The confusing case of budgetary incrementalism: Too many meanings for a single concept. *Journal of Politics*. 52(1): 167–96.

Browne, W. 1998. *Groups, interests, and U.S. public policy*. Washington, DC: Georgetown University Press.

Buchanan, J. 1975. *The limits of liberty: Between anarchy and leviathan*. Chicago: University of Chicago Press.

Cleaveland, F. 1966. Congress and urban problems: Legislating for urban areas. *Journal of Politics*. 28(2): 289–307.

Dales, J. 1975. Beyond the marketplace. *The Canadian Journal of Economics*. 8(4): 483–503.

Downs, A. 1957. *An economic theory of democracy*. New York: Haspes.

Dror, Y. 1971. *Design for policy sciences*. New York: Elsevier.

Dunning, W. 1913. The political theories of the German idealists. *Political Science Quarterly*. 28(2): 193–206.

Dye, T., and H. Zeigler. 1972. *Irony of democracy: An uncommon introduction to American politics,* 2nd ed. Belmont, CA: Wadsworth.

Easton, D. 1957. An approach to the analysis of political systems. *World Politics*. 9(3): 383–400.

Easton, D. 1965. *A systems analysis of political life*. New York: John Wiley & Sons.

Hardin, G. 1968. The tragedy of the commons. *Science*. 162: 1,243–48.

Howell, R. 1973. Intuition, synthesis, and individualism in the *Critique of Pure Reason*. *Nous*. 7(3): 207–32.

Hrebenar, R., and R. Scott. 1982. *Interest group politics in America*. Englewood Cliffs, NJ: Prentice Hall.

Kant, I. 1900. *Critique of Pure Reason*. Translated by J. Meikeljohn. New York: Wiley.

Kitchner, P. 1980. A priori knowledge. *The Philosophical Review*. 89(1): 3–23.

Lasswell, H. 1950. *Politics: Who gets what, when, and how*. New York: Peter Smith Publishers.

Lindblom, C. 1959. The science of "muddling through." *Public Administration Review*. 19(2): 79–88.

Lowi, T. *The end of liberalism: Ideology, policy, and the crisis of public authority*. New York: Norton.

Lunch, W. 1987. *The Nationalization of American Politics*. Berkeley, CA: University of California Press.

McLean, I. 1986. Some recent work in public choice. *British Journal of Political Science*. 16(3): 377–94.

Mills, C. 1956. *The power elite*. New York: Oxford University Press.

Neustadt, R. 1960. *Presidential power: The politics of leadership*. New York: Wiley.

Olson, M. 1965. *The logic of collective action: Public goods and the theory of groups*. Cambridge, MA: Harvard University Press.

Ostrom, E. 1990. *Governing the commons: The evolution of institutions for collective action*. New York: Cambridge University Press.

Parenti, M. 1988. *Democracy for the few*, 5th ed. New York: St. Martin's Press.

Premfers, R. 1981. Charles Lindblom and Aaron Wildavsky. *British Journal of Political Science*. 11(2): 201–25.

Rycroft, R., and J. Szyliowicz. 1980. The technological dimension of decision-making: The case of Aswan High Dam. *World Politics*. 33(1): 36–61.

Schneider, A., and H. Ingram. 1997. *Policy design for democracy*. Lawrence: University of Kansas Press.

Simon, H. 1976. *Administrative behavior: A study of decision-making processes in administrative organizations*. New York: Free Press.

Summerfield, D. 1991. Modest a priori knowledge. *Philosophy and Phenomenological Research*. 51(2): 39–66.

Truman, D. 1951. *Governmental process: Political interests and public opinion*. New York: Alfred A. Knopf.

Tullock, G. 1969. Social cost and government action. *American Economic Review*. 59(2): 189–97.

Wilson, J. 1973. *Political organizations*. New York: Basic Books.

Court Case

Marbury v. Madison 5 U.S. 137

Endnotes

1. In their analysis of rational–comprehensive policy-making, Rycroft and Szyliowicz conclude that it is most useful to make adjustments to technical aspects of policy. Additionally, their study focuses on the use of rational–comprehensive policy-making and planning in capital projects— policies involving the construction of physical structures such as dams, roads, and bridges. In these instances, policy is usually a long-term and expensive process involving the need to carefully coordinate particular portions of a project. Rational–comprehensive approaches are particularly valuable in urban planning (Cleaveland, 1966). As the author points out, however, the ability of key policy-makers in high-level positions (e.g., Congress) to manage the microlevel elements of urban planning is particularly challenging, resulting at times in disappointing policy outcomes.

2. As a model for understanding the policy process and as an alternative to the rational–comprehensive model, incrementalism may suffer from overuse. Incrementalism is a fairly simple idea that seemingly covers many aspects of the policy process; yet its greatest weakness may be that it has been expanded in definitional form to the point where elements of the model tend to contradict other elements of the model. In his 1990 article, William Berry addresses some of the limitations imposed on incrementalism by an ever-evolving definition of its basic tenets.

3. For a thoughtful discussion of the role of government in relation to the private marketplace, see Dales (1975).

3

■■■

Values and Public Policy

CHAPTER OVERVIEW

Our working definition for public policy is: what government ought or ought not do and does or does not do. The first half of the definition—namely: *ought or ought not*—reflects the role of political and social values in policy-making. In "The Influence of Social Values on Public Policy Determination," Shuchman (1962, 175) defines **values** as "a normative standard of the desirable, functioning as an operational force in human behavior." Values possess the following characteristics: "(1) oughtness, (2) associated reactions of guilt, anxiety, condemnation, or approval; and (3) a sense of self-appraisal or appraisal of others" (Shuchman 1962, 175–176). Values are part of our emotive selves, shaping our preferences and influencing our policy choices.

The specific goals for the chapter are:

- Discuss political values, their relationship to civic engagement, and impact on policy preferences.
- Discuss how values have changed in the post–World War II period.
- Using survey data, illustrate important value differences that exist between age cohorts.

REGIME VALUES

Regime values, generally accepted by a large portion of the population of a nation, are those values that have been encoded into, and establish the basis of, some form of social contract. At times, government uses forms of coercion to encourage citizens to adopt regime values as their own—for example, through education (low-level coercion) or the threat of punishment (high-level coercion). In a free democratic state, regime values are often limited in number and may evolve over time.

Democratic theorists believe that shared core values are critical to the maintenance of American democracy. American core values are related to a belief in individual freedom, political and social equality, and the maintenance of social order; nevertheless, the meaning of these values has changed due to: (1) changing social and political engagement on the part of Americans, and (2) cultural shifts that have occurred across generations. Developing awareness of regime values represents one element of **political socialization** experience, but it is not the sole basis of the individual's value structure.

CIVIC ENGAGEMENT, SOCIAL CAPITAL, AND VALUES

Many democratic theorists see political and social engagement as the critical intergenerational link that preserves fragile democratic values and social traditions. In his work on Italian social and political engagement (*Making Democracy Work: Civic Traditions in Modern Italy,* 1993) and more recently on the status of American public life (*Bowling Alone: The Collapse and Revival of American Community,* 2000), Robert Putnam demonstrates a strong connection between good governance and the level of citizens' engagement in social and political institutions. He finds that citizens in a healthy democracy are actively engaged in their communities. Liberal democracy operates best when citizens live as members of a community rather than isolated individuals.

The status of social and political engagement in society is termed **social capital** by Putnam (1993, 2000), which incorporates civic engagement, political and social trust, intergenerational connectedness, and community networks. Scholars studying social capital frequently base their work on the observations and conclusions of Alexis de Tocqueville, the early-nineteenth-century French observer who spent considerable time studying the nature of social and political life in American communities. Tocqueville found that the strength of American democracy lay in the nature of civil existence, which although not fully inclusive of ethnic and racial minorities at the time of his writings, nevertheless did place tremendous emphasis on the establishment of cooperative networks and associations.

Civic involvement often occurs through involvement in various voluntary organizations. Some are closed organizations, which limit the type of individuals allowed to join. Civic clubs that allowed only men or women to join are examples of closed civic organizations (e.g., Rotary[1] or Soroptimists). Conversely, other civic organizations are open to all community members. Most churches, for instance, encourage people of all races and ethnicities to attend their services. Neighborhood groups maintain neighborhoods for the benefit of all residents. Individuals choose to participate in civic organizations; their decision to participate may be due to socialization experiences that are related to a predisposition to join a particular group, economic self-interest, or a need to engage in social interaction with others of like mind.

Remaining engaged in a community often means that an individual has established a basis of trust with other individuals. Individuals often have an emotional or economic link to other community members. Shared experiences build interpersonal trust and shared value structures. Civic networks have the capacity to create greater awareness and tolerance of heterogeneity of thought. Civic involvement often leads to dialogue about values and priorities, which Tocqueville considered essential for the continued success of American democracy.

Tocqueville saw American community life as one explanation for the nation's need for only limited government. What public policy existed at the time was offered legitimacy through dialogue-rich community policy-making processes. Tocqueville concluded that a decline of what is now termed *social capital* would likely result in the growth of government bureaucracies and a more limited role for citizens in policy-making.

Although a decline in social capital may or may not produce the growth of government bureaucracies, our relative happiness or unhappiness with government bureaucracy and public policy is probably related to declining levels of social trust and citizen civic engagement (Putnam 1993, 2000). Citizens who are detached from civic life are often more cynical, distrustful, and more likely to be frustrated with government institutions and public policy. Conversely, civically engaged citizens are frequently more optimistic and efficacious.

In "American Ideals versus American Institutions," Samuel Huntington (1982) envisions American democracy as an ongoing rather than finished product: "The United States has no meaning, no identity, no political culture or even history apart from its ideals of liberty and democracy and the continuing efforts of Americans to realize those ideals" (Huntington 1982, 36). The core social and political values or ideals comprise what Huntington terms the ". . . American Creed. Support for liberal, democratic, individualistic and egalitarian values." (Huntington 1982, 1). Vibrant dialogue-rich civic engagement in public institutions and effective public policy are essential preconditions for the realization of American ideals.

BASES OF INDIVIDUAL VALUES

A discussion of regime or core values offers some legitimacy to the issue of what government ought or ought not do, but our policy priorities are also a function of our individual social and political values. Individual values are shaped by many things, including family social capital and value structure, parental/legal guardian social and economic status, race, ethnicity, education level, gender, and geographic region. **Family social capital** relates to the nature of family intergenerational value exchange and continuity. An individual who comes from a conservative family, for instance, might be exposed to traditional values and mores that are passed on from generation to generation.

Race and ethnicity shape individuals' political and social values. In part due to historic discrimination and political disenfranchisement, racial and ethnic minorities in America have until only relatively recently become more actively included in reestablishing and legitimizing core values.[2]

Familial traditions and ethnic subculture variations also shape the nature and scope of participation. In a study of the civic and political involvement of Italian and Jewish youth, Greeley (1976) found that: ". . . ethnic heritage seems to have an independent influence outside of family socialization experiences" (Greeley 1976, 204). Ethnic heritage tended to influence tolerance and trust of other individuals, likely explaining predilections to participate in the broader community.

Socioeconomic status also shapes value structure. Wealthier and more educated individuals frequently place greater priority on prosocial values. Tocqueville once commented on the lack of widely disparate economic and social status among Americans, perhaps contributing to greater unity in terms of general political and social values, but times have changed. An expanding income gap may contribute to great social divisions.

Finally, geographic location can shape individual—and community—value structures. In *American Federalism: A View from the States* (1966), Daniel Elazar identified three major types of political cultures within American states: individualistic, moralistic, and traditionalistic. Individualistic political subcultures are characterized by fairly limited civic engagement and place significant emphasis on private choice rather than public policy solutions. Moralistic political subcultures have fairly expansive civic activity and greater acceptance of public or communal solutions to individual and collective problems. Government is often viewed as a partner, working with civic groups to create better communities. Traditionalistic subcultures emphasize citizen deference to political and social elites, who set policy priorities.

ECONOMICS AND SOCIETAL VALUE CHANGES

Core and individual values shape public policy priorities and choices. Citizens' values tend to evolve over time, but crisis can lead to rapid value shifts. A dramatic value shift occurred when the Baby Boom generation came of age. Ronald Inglehart documented this significant change in public values in his book, *Culture Shift in Advanced Industrial Society* (1990). Inglehart's thesis is that advanced economies become less **materialistic** and more **postmaterialistic**. **Materialists** are interested in their own individual economic benefit, whereas **postmaterialists** are interested in societal issues such as the general quality of life and social and economic fairness. Baby Boomers were the first generation raised in the advanced post–World War II U.S. economy and are more postmaterialistic.

How does economic prosperity lead to value changes? As societies become more affluent, basic goods—for example, food, clothing, and shelter—become more readily available. As basic *material* needs are more readily met, people are able to turn their attention to other goals. Individuals become more outward-looking and less self-interested. They become more postmaterialistic, focusing on societal-level needs and conditions and quality of life issues.

Individuals witness these changing economic conditions during the adult phase of their lives, a point where their basic values have already formed. Adults have already been socialized by parents, friends, and teachers to adopt certain values and to engage in certain types of acceptable social behavior. These *political socialization* experiences have a profound effect on the value structure of individuals. Therefore, *economic change* and the potential for value evolution are moderated by *socialization experiences* and the *values adopted by an individual earlier in life*—a phenomenon known as a **cohort effect**.

The political socialization and public opinion literature carefully documented the shift in values, beliefs, and opinions that emerged among post–World War II birth cohorts. The studies generally found that children and young adults were less likely to be deferential to parental values and beliefs; rather, members of the Baby Boom cohort were more likely to adopt widely divergent sets of values, beliefs, and opinions (see Jennings and Niemi 1968, 1974; Niemi, et al. 1978).

Unlike more socially and politically conservative materialists, postmaterialists tend to define freedom in a broad sense. Rather than seeing the citizen–government relationship as one of freedom *from* (negative freedom) government influence, postmaterialists tend to see freedom in terms of government actively protecting political and social behavior—that is, government actively promoting an individual's freedom *to* (positive freedom).

Positive freedom is consistent with the postmaterialists' conception of political and social equality. Postmaterialists tend to define equality in very broad terms, or at least are more willing to engage in dialogue about the definition of equality. For earlier generational cohorts, equality meant "equality before the law," albeit frequently applicable to only a narrowly defined social strata in society, generally, White males. Postmaterialists were more likely than were materialists to see equality as "equality of condition" or "equality of opportunity" or perhaps "equality of outcome." For example, in terms of discrimination issues, postmaterialists are more likely to advocate greater political and social tolerance of individual lifestyle choices and behaviors. Equality is at times broadly defined by postmaterialists to include the "rights" of animals and plants to exist in a pristine natural habitat.

Postmaterialists often place significant emphasis on the issue of political rights and liberties for individuals and groups. Although individual rights are central to both classical and modern liberal ideals, group-based approaches to the discussion of political rights is germane only to modern liberal thought and redirects public policy toward a renewed evaluation of government, its scope, and its roles. Postmaterialists are more likely to adopt a Rawlsian or modern liberal perspective on political rights. The postmaterialist tends to invite greater regulation of individual or group behaviors seen as harmful to the greater good.

The postmaterialist approach to public policy is also shaped by their discontent with large government. The welfare state, while serving an important role in meeting the basic needs of disadvantaged individuals and groups, is considered a carryover from a more materialist past. Meeting a citizen's basic needs is important, but does little more than maintain a status quo—it does not help individuals grow and improve themselves. Postmaterialists often find a place for public assistance to meld with private sector opportunities—a **Third Way**.

The **Third Way** approach to governance is often seen in efforts to "streamline" government—protecting basic rights, yet encouraging citizen involvement. Public policy priorities that are more efficiently and effectively developed and executed in the private sector may be privatized or contracted out to private industry or to nonprofit civic organizations. Government may develop partnerships with the private and nonprofit sectors to accomplish shared goals. Third Way approaches have gained some strength in public policy-making both domestically and internationally. In nearly all the postindustrial "developed" societies in the world, Third Way politicians have been elected to positions of governing authority and have significantly reshaped public policy goals.

Postmaterialists tend to support direct citizen influence in the policy process. One dilemma facing postmaterialists in their attempt to engage in the policy process is related to the **technical information quandary** (see Pierce and Lovrich 1986)—in essence, the increasingly detailed and technical language of policy-making in a highly technological policy atmosphere. For postmaterialists, the rise of **technocracy**—government by experts—challenges democratic policy-making and the active inclusion of citizen "voice." Postmaterialists value the role of individual citizens pursuing their interests in the context of the community "good."

Postmaterialists are less deferential to political elites than were earlier generational cohorts and more likely to engage in protests against policies of government and private industry that are not conducive to their value structure. The rise of **corporatism**—big government and corporations working in tandem to orchestrate public policy and the private marketplace—is often viewed by postmaterialists as detrimental to democratic society. Postmaterialists have sought to adopt the best aspects of traditional communities and societies and overlaid it with a new, more inclusive value structure to create sound public policy for the twenty-first century.

HOW VALUES HAVE CHANGED AND CONTINUE TO CHANGE

Society's values substantially impact public policy. Values consciously and subconsciously guide the choices of citizens and policy-makers. They serve as lenses through which we "see" phenomena and help us to determine whether a particular social condition ought to be addressed in a public or private setting. The value frameworks of individuals frequently relate to competing theories of democracy and the social contract, different perspectives on what ought or ought not be done by government.

Tracking public opinion indicators representing either classical or modern liberal values is one method of understanding the policy direction of the past, present, and future. Values change over time, reflecting changing public policy priorities. Since 1948, the American National Election Study (ANES) has biannually tracked the political and social values, beliefs, and opinions of individuals. The study is one way of demonstrating the changes that have occurred in social and political values over several decades. By studying the values, opinions, and beliefs of these age cohorts, we will develop a better understanding of the continuity of public policy issues. We might also cautiously speculate about future public policy priorities.

This section will describe social and political values of five age cohorts:

- Generation Y—individuals born after 1978
- Generation X—individuals born between 1965 and 1978
- Baby Boomers—individuals born between 1946 and 1964

PHOTO 3.1   Mother and daughter with grandmother.

- Silent Generation—individuals born between 1928 and 1945, a smaller generational cohort whose adolescence occurred during World War II
- World War II Generation—individuals born between approximately 1919 and 1927, who were young adults during the Depression and war years

Younger generational cohorts come from multiethnic backgrounds. Many individuals openly identify themselves in terms of their heritage and identify with values that are unique to their ethnic backgrounds. Due to educational and occupational activities, however, it is apparent that some overarching cohort linkage ties different subcultures together. Generation X and Y cohorts are more likely to attend college than their parents and grandparents, and are more likely to have pursued postgraduate education. (See Photo 3.1.)

Generations X and Y are fairly confident that they will achieve their social and economic goals. Having grown up during periods of unprecedented economic growth, they tend to be highly optimistic about their ability to obtain the job of their choice. They tend to feel that government has a role in the economy, maintaining economic stability and ensuring fairness in the labor market.

Generations X and Y do not have the same level of interest in politics or social institutions as earlier age cohorts. In a 2008 ANES[3] time series study of Americans, more than 10 percent of Generation X and nearly one-fifth of Generation Y respondents indicated that they have almost no interest in public affairs. About 17 percent of Generation Y respondents indicated that they were interested in public affairs "most of the time"; approximately 23 percent of Generation X respondents were interested in public affairs "most of the time." (See Table 3.1).

Younger generational cohorts attend religious services at a much lower rate than their parents' or grandparents' generations. Approximately 60 percent

TABLE 3.1   Interest in Public Affairs (2008)

		Hardly at All	Only Now and Then	Some of the Time	Most of the Time
Age	World War II	13.3%	13.3%	50.0%	23.3%
Cohort	Silent Generation	6.4%	16.4%	43.3%	33.9%
	Baby Boomers	7.3%	22.0%	40.9%	29.8%
	Generation X	12.8%	27.9%	36.0%	23.3%
	Generation Y	18.6%	31.7%	32.8%	16.9%
Total		10.7%	24.1%	38.9%	26.3%

Source: National Election Studies, Time Series Data File. Survey Research Center, University of Michigan, 2009, www.umich.edu/~nes/ (accessed March 19, 2009).

of Generation Y respondents indicate religious service attendance. Of those who attend religious services, Generation Y individuals are the least likely to attend weekly (or almost weekly). Involvement in community institutions, such as churches, synagogues, mosques, and temples, tends to influence individuals' political and social values. (See Table 3.2).

TABLE 3.2   Religious Attendance (2008)

		Does Respondent Attend Religious Services?	
		Yes	No
Age	World War II	74.2%	25.8%
Cohort	Silent Generation	73.1%	26.9%
	Baby Boomers	68.1%	31.9%
	Generation X	63.2%	36.8%
	Generation Y	60.7%	39.3%
Total		66.5%	33.5%

		Religious Attendance			
		Every Week	Almost Every Week	Once or Twice a Month	A Few Times Per Year
Age	World War II	63.3%	14.3%	12.2%	10.2%
Cohort	Silent Generation	55.8%	11.5%	18.7%	14.0%
	Baby Boomers	37.6%	16.7%	23.4%	22.3%
	Generation X	26.8%	18.0%	30.3%	24.9%
	Generation Y	23.6%	16.7%	32.5%	27.2%
Total		36.8%	16.0%	25.4%	21.8%

Source: National Election Studies, Time Series Data File. Survey Research Center, University of Michigan, 2009, www.umich.edu/~nes/ (accessed March 19, 2009).

TABLE 3.3   Can People Be Trusted? (2008)

		Can't Be Too Careful	Most People Can Be Trusted
Age	World War II	72.5%	27.5%
Cohort	Silent Generation	65.9%	34.1%
	Baby Boomers	64.6%	35.4%
	Generation X	71.5%	28.5%
	Generation Y	80.8%	19.2%
Total		69.9%	30.1%

Source: National Election Studies, Time Series Data File. Survey Research Center, University of Michigan, 2009, www.umich.edu/~nes/ (accessed March 19, 2009).

Generations X and Y—particularly Generation Y—have markedly lower levels of social trust when compared to most of the other older age cohorts studied. Survey respondents from Generation Y are the least likely cohort to believe that most people are trustworthy. Generation Y overwhelming believes that people have the capacity to take advantage of them. (See Table 3.3).

Generations X and Y tend to be skeptical of government and often exhibit a low level of confidence in political institutions. Members of these age cohorts possess very low levels of confidence in government officials. Combined, they are marginally more likely to believe that elected officials are "crooked" when compared to earlier age cohorts.

More than 45 percent of Generation Y respondents feel they have no say in government. There has been speculation in media and academic treatments that Generations X and Y are composed of "disaffected" individuals who do not feel that older generations listen to them or respond to their needs. The evidence here does not offer support for that contention. (See Table 3.4 and Table 3.5)

TABLE 3.4   Are Government Officials Crooked? (2008)

		Hardly Any Are Crooked	Not Very Many Are Crooked	Quite a Few Are Crooked
Age	World War II	11.3%	45.3%	43.4%
Cohort	Silent Generation	9.1%	40.9%	50.0%
	Baby Boomers	5.4%	40.0%	54.6%
	Generation X	6.7%	36.9%	56.3%
	Generation Y	7.1%	39.0%	54.0%
Total		6.8%	39.3%	53.8%

Source: National Election Studies, Time Series Data File. Survey Research Center, University of Michigan, 2009, www.umich.edu/~nes/ (accessed March 19, 2009).

TABLE 3.5   People Like Me Have No Say in Government (2008)

| | | No Say in Government? | | |
		Agree	Disagree	Neither Agree Nor Disagree
Age	World War II	35.5%	51.6%	12.9%
Cohort	Silent Generation	55.3%	35.2%	9.5%
	Baby Boomers	51.4%	41.8%	6.8%
	Generation X	48.7%	41.2%	10.1%
	Generation Y	45.8%	32.8%	21.5%
Total		49.9%	39.2%	10.9%

Source: National Election Studies, Time Series Data File. Survey Research Center, University of Michigan, 2009, www.umich.edu/~nes/ (accessed March 19, 2009).

The generational cohorts differ in terms of their ranking of eleven major policy areas. The rankings are a rough measure of policy priority differences. The World War II generation ranks funding for the War on Terrorism as their number one priority, whereas Baby Boomers rank science/technology as their top issue. The Silent Generation and Generations X and Y place high priority on social and environmental policy funding. Border security issues rank as more important for the World War II generation and Baby Boomers when compared with the Silent Generation and Generations X and Y. A generation that fears not seeing the benefits of Social Security, Generation X places this policy as the second most important issue in its policy priorities. (See Table 3.6).

TABLE 3.6   Policy Priority Rankings By Generation (2008)

World War II	Silent Generation	Baby Boomers	Generation X	Generation Y
War on Terror	Welfare	Science/Tech.	Environment	Public Schools
Science/Tech.	Environment	Environment	Social Security	Welfare
Child Care	Foreign Aid	Child Care	Welfare	Child Care
Social Security	Science/Tech.	Foreign Aid	Public Schools	Environment
Environment	Crime	Public Schools	Child Care	Crime
Border Security	Child Care	Border Security	Science/Tech.	War on Terror
Foreign Aid	Aid to Poor	Aid to Poor	Border Security	Foreign Aid
Public Schools	Public Schools	War on Terrorism	Foreign Aid	Border Security
Crime	Social Security	Crime	Aid to Poor	Science/Tech.
Aid to Poor	Border Security	Social Security	War on Terror	Aid to Poor
Welfare	War on Terror	Welfare	Crime	Social Security

Source: National Election Studies, Time Series Data File. Survey Research Center, University of Michigan, 2009, www.umich.edu/~nes/ (accessed March 19, 2009).

TABLE 3.7 Government-Provided Health Insurance? (2008)

		Favor	Oppose	Neither Favor Nor Oppose
Age	World War II	56.7%	40.0%	3.3%
Cohort	Silent Generation	43.5%	41.3%	15.2%
	Baby Boomers	53.9%	33.3%	12.8%
	Generation X	58.2%	26.6%	15.1%
	Generation Y	63.2%	24.0%	12.7%
Total		55.1%	31.3%	13.6%

Source: National Election Studies, Time Series Data File. Survey Research Center, University of Michigan, 2009, www.umich.edu/~nes/ (accessed March 19, 2009).

Government is seen to have a narrow role in the choices of individuals, but an expansive role in solving what are viewed as collective or group-related problems. Nevertheless, Generation Y survey respondents tend to see government as an important mechanism in reducing the impact of personal and group decisions. In other words, government should play a role in reducing the level of risk associated with living and alleviate the consequences associated with that risk. By way of illustration, Generation Y is particularly supportive of government-provided health insurance. (See Table 3.7).

Because their political and social values tend to be less grounded and stable (as discussed in Yankelovich 1991), Generations X and Y tend to experience more dramatic shifts in terms of their value priorities and policy preferences. Generally, members of these age cohorts are driven by pragmatism; policies are important so long as it can be demonstrated that policies serve a valuable purpose for disadvantaged groups, individuals, or themselves.

In the 2008 ANES study, Generation Y tended to be liberal-minded. Generation Y leans, on average, further to the left than any generation in this study.[4] Although strongly centrist, Generation X has a higher percentage of left-leaning members than either the Baby Boomers or the Silent Generation. The World War II cohort respondents tended to be right-leaning centrists.

In terms of social and political groups, Generation Y remains among the most enthusiastic of all age cohorts studied. The level of support for a variety of different groups representing a variety of different values may contribute to significant changes in the nature of public policy in the future. Looking at the highest and lowest levels of support, varying levels of support should not be construed as "likes" or "dislikes" but simply generational priorities.

In the 2008 ANES time series study, Generation X respondents exhibited high levels of support for Feminists. Other groups receiving high levels of support from Generation X were: Christians, Rich People, Muslims, and Gays and Lesbians. Generation X respondents exhibited, within-cohort, lowest levels of support for Atheists, Illegal Immigrants, Catholics, and Christian Fundamentalists.

The groups garnering the highest level of support from Generation Y respondents were Asians and Feminists. Other highly favored groups for Generation Y were: Christian Fundamentalists, Catholics, Muslims, and Jews. The groups for which Generation Y, on average, exhibited the least support were: Atheists, People on Welfare, Christians, and Labor Unions. It is important to note that the differences between group support is often very small—the purpose here is to look at a ranking of levels of support.

Although the least likely to watch TV news, Generation Y respondents report reading the newspaper about two days a week. Generation Y is also moderately more likely to pay attention to local news when compared to all other cohorts studied. Generation Y's average viewing of Internet news is not significantly higher than Baby Boomers or Generation X respondents.

Until the September 11 attacks, Generation Y had very limited exposure to the potential for political violence to impact their lives. In their childhood and early teenage years, they were exposed to Operation Desert Storm, a conventional military campaign for the United States and allied nations of short duration and with limited U.S. casualties. A short economic slowdown in the early 1990s was followed by one of the most noteworthy periods of economic growth in U.S. history. Domestically, the struggle for equal rights continues, but was by no means as pronounced during Generation Y's early years of political awareness. Baby Boomers and Gen-Xers are much more likely to remember the struggle against racial segregation and severe inequality for women in the workplace. Gay rights remains a major political issue, but the more pronounced aspects of the struggle for equal protection occurred in the 1980s when gays were more likely stigmatized and blamed for the rising HIV-AIDS epidemic. Their values are not inconsistent with their socialization experiences. The post–September 11 War on Terrorism will likely continue to shape the political and social values of Generation Y, as well as the three other generational cohorts—witness the high average levels of support for major religious groups, religious differences often playing central roles in political and social violence. Also, Generation Y has a high level of interest in social and education policy issues, as previously mentioned, policy areas that often are seen as ameliorative in relation to our appreciation and understanding of each other and differences in need. Changes in values, beliefs, and opinions will, in turn, impact the prioritization of public policy. The dramatic economic slowdown in 2008–2009, the social turmoil created by job losses and home foreclosures, and corporate scandals will likely have a significant impact on the values, opinions, beliefs, and policy priorities of Generation Y.

The generation shift could, in part, be a function of the normalization and acceptance of a modern liberal social contract, a Rawlsian form of social contract; yet, important elements of classical liberalism remain in evidence. In many respects, Generation Y may represent a synthesis of perspectives on the ongoing debate about what government *ought* or *ought not* do. Generation Y tends to believe that government's primary function is to maintain equality by focusing on the primacy of the individual. Individuals are responsible for their lives and their status within society, unless their status is a function of socially

TABLE 3.8 Government Should Do More or Less (2008)

		Less Government	About the Same	More Government
Age	World War II	25.8%	54.8%	19.4%
Cohort	Silent Generation	44.0%	34.6%	21.4%
	Baby Boomers	47.9%	32.5%	19.6%
	Generation X	45.0%	36.0%	19.0%
	Generation Y	45.3%	39.4%	15.3%
Total		45.4%	35.7%	19.0%

Source: National Election Studies, Time Series Data File. Survey Research Center, University of Michigan, 2009, www.umich.edu/~nes/ (accessed March 19, 2009).

constructed inequalities. Generation Y tends to support equality of opportunity through their support for women and minorities; yet, they tend to reject illegal immigration and may be less inclined to support a broader view of equality.

Generation Y demonstrates a low level of interest in public affairs and yet strong support for government solutions. Their focus is primarily on groups, valued in different ways. Public policy may, therefore, become a function of the times, rather than built on long-lasting principle, but is nevertheless demanded of government rather than made available through the marketplace. A new definition of public policy then is likely to emerge, namely, *public policy is what government must do, does, or does not do.* (See Tables 3.8–3.10).

There is some possibility, therefore, that public policy may become less grounded in a stable set of social values, sporadically changing as the will of the citizens, government leaders, and institutions change. With less reliance on stable core values, public policy of the future might produce less consistency in policy choices. Changing definitions of the public and private good could result in the blurring of the lines between public necessity and private property and

TABLE 3.9 Strong Government or Free Market? (2008)

		Stronger Government	Free Market Approach
Age	World War II	62.3%	37.7%
Cohort	Silent Generation	65.4%	34.6%
	Baby Boomers	74.0%	26.0%
	Generation X	76.2%	23.8%
	Generation Y	78.4%	21.6%
Total		71.2%	28.7%

Source: National Election Studies, Time Series Data File. Survey Research Center, University of Michigan, 2009, www.umich.edu/~nes/ (accessed March 19, 2009).

TABLE 3.10   Cooperation or Self-Reliance? (2000 Election Survey)

		Cooperative	Self-Reliant	Depends
Age	World War II	58.3%	38.6%	3.0%
Cohort	Silent Generation	52.2%	46.4%	1.4%
	Baby Boomers	54.5%	43.1%	2.4%
	Generation X	58.8%	38.9%	2.3%
	Generation Y	59.7%	40.3%	
Total		55.5%	42.4%	2.1%

Source: National Election Studies. Survey Research Center, University of Michigan, 2005, www.umich.edu/~nes/ (accessed February 1, 2005).

individual rights. Conversely, public policy may become more clear and consistent due to the social consensus of Generation Y, producing policies that most citizens and leaders can support.

Lessons Learned from Chapter 3

SPECIFICS

- Values play a significant role in shaping policy choices. Chapter 3 shows how the regime in which an individual lives, his or her socialization experiences, and the nature of the times impact values and policy choices.
- Public policy preferences will likely change over time as Generations X and Y attain important policy-making positions in government. Individuals in the two generations have had different socialization experiences and were raised under different familial and societal conditions, leading them to be less civically and politically engaged and more pragmatic about certain aspects of public policy. Alternatively, Generation X and Y have a high regard for individuals and groups who have high ideals.

THE BIG PICTURE

For Generations X and Y, the lesson to be drawn from this chapter is: The public policy that you will soon be making is a function of the choices made in the past, but is to a great extent a function of your preferences. In learning about how values shape public policy, you notice that the political regime in which you live invites a discussion of policy preferences. In the recent past, the Baby Boom generation changed the course of public policy as their postmaterialist value base became the foundation of public policy. Survey research indicates that Generations X and Y have their own value sets and policy preferences; in time, public policy will likely reflect the new generations' preferences.

Key Terms

cohort effects
corporatism
family social capital
materialist
political socialization
postmaterialist

regime values
social capital
technical information quandary
technocracy
Third Way politics
values

Questions for Study

1. Discuss three different social and economic influences that may shape an individual's values, opinions, and beliefs.
2. What is postmaterialism? What role did it play in American public policy in the twentieth century? Are you a postmaterialist? Explain.
3. Choose four examples from your reading to illustrate generational differences in relation to public policy priorities. What is your generational cohort? With which generational cohort do you most closely identify? Your own cohort? Another cohort? Several cohorts? Explain.

Bibliography

Aaron, H., T. Mann, and T. Taylor, eds. 1994. *Values and public policy.* Washington, DC: The Brookings Institution.

Annenberg Foundation 2007. *A republic divided.* New York: Oxford University Press.

Bellah, R., R. Madsen, W. Sullivan, A. Swidler, and S. Tipton. 1985. *Habits of the heart: Individualism and commitment in American life.* New York: Perennial Library.

———— 1992. *The good society.* New York: Knopf.

Bender, D., ed. 1989. *American values: Opposing viewpoints.* San Diego, CA: Greenhaven Press.

Carrow, M., P. Churchill, and J. Cordes, eds. 1998. *Democracy, social values, and public policy.* Westport, CT: Praeger.

Craig, S. C., and M. D. Martinez, eds. 2005. *Ambivalence and the structure of political opinion.* New York: Palgrave.

Dawson, R., K. Prewitt, and K. Dawson. 1977. *Political socialization,* 2nd ed. Boston: Little, Brown, and Company.

Douglas, M., and A. Wildavsky. 1983. *Risk and culture: An essay on the selection of technological and environmental dangers.* Berkeley, CA: University of California Press.

Elazar, D. 1966. *American federalism: A view from the states.* New York: Crowell.

Fried, C. 1970. *An anatomy of values: Problems of personal and social choice.* Cambridge, MA: Harvard University Press.

Greeley, A. 1976. *Ethnicity, denomination and equality.* Beverly Hills, CA: Sage.

Hero, R. 1992. *Latinos and the U.S. political system: Two-tiered pluralism.* Philadelphia, PA: Temple University Press.

————— 1998. *Faces of inequality: Social diversity in American politics.* New York: Oxford University Press.

————— 2007. *Racial diversity and social capital: Equality and community in America.* New York: Cambridge University Press.

Huntington, S. 1982. American ideals versus American institutions. *Political Science Quarterly.* 97(1): 204–38.

Inglehart, R. 1990. *Culture shift in advanced industrial society.* Princeton, NJ: Princeton University Press.

Jaros, D. 1973. *Socialization to politics.* New York: Praeger.

Jennings, M. K., and R. Niemi. 1968. The transmission of political values from parent to child. *American Political Science Review.* 62(1): 169–84.

————— 1974. *The political character of adolescence: The influence of families and schools.* Princeton, NJ: Princeton University Press.

Kohn, M. 1977. *Class and conformity.* Chicago: University of Chicago Press.

Lea, J. 1982. *Political consciousness and American democracy.* Jackson: University Press of Mississippi.

Lunch, W. 1987. *The nationalization of American politics.* Berkeley: University of California Press.

Narcos, B. 2007. *Fueling our Fears: Stereotyping, Media Coverage, and Public Opinion of Muslim Americans.* Lanham, MD: Rowman & Littlefield.

Niemi, R., D. Ross, and J. Alexander. 1978. The similarity of political values of parents and college-age youths. *Public Opinion Quarterly.* 42(4): 503–20.

Pierce, J. C., and N. P. Lovrich. 1986. *Water resources, democracy, and the technical information quandary.* Millwood, NY: Associated Faculty Press.

Putnam, R. 1993. *Making democracy work: Civic traditions in modern Italy.* Princeton, NJ: Princeton University Press.

————— 2000. *Bowling alone: The collapse and revival of American community.* New York: Simon & Schuster.

Richman, S. 1995. *Separating school and state: How to liberate America's families.* Fairfax, VA: Future of Freedom Foundation.

Shils, E. 1997. *The virtue of civility: Selected essays on liberalism, tradition, and civil society.* Indianapolis: Liberty Fund Press.

Shuchman, H. 1962. The influence of social values on public policy determination. *The Journal of Conflict Resolution.* 6(2): 175–82.

Smith, T. A., and R. Tatalovich. 2003. *Cultures at war: Moral conflicts in Western democracies.* Orchard Park, NY: Broadview Press.

Tocqueville, A. 1958. *Democracy in America.* New York: Mentor Books.

Von Mises, L. 1981. *Socialism: An economic and sociological analysis.* Indianapolis: Liberty Fund Press.

Wanta, W. 1997. *The public and the national agenda: How people learn about important issues.* Mahwah, NJ: Lawrence Erlbaum Associates.

Welch, S. 1993. *The concept of political culture.* New York: St. Martin's Press.

West, E. 1994. *Education and the state: A study in political economy.* Indianapolis: Liberty Fund Press.

Western, J. W. 2005. *Selling intervention and war: The presidency, the media, and the American public.* Baltimore, MD: Johns Hopkins University Press.

White, J. 2003. *The values divide: American politics and culture in transition.* New York: Chatham House/Seven Bridges Press.

Yankelovich, D. 1991. *Coming to public judgment: Making democracy work in a complex world.* Syracuse, NY: Syracuse University Press.

Court Case

Brown v. Board of Education 347 U.S. 483 (1954)

Endnotes

1. Until the late twentieth century, Rotary was a male-only organization. It has recently opened its membership to women.
2. For an excellent account of racial minorities and political enfranchisement, see Lawrence Bobo and Frank Gilliam Jr. 1990. "Race, Sociopolitical Participation, and Black Empowerment," *American Political Science Review.* 84(2): 377–393. Also, see Rodney Hero's broader analyses of public policy and racial and ethnic minorities: *Latinos and the U.S. Political System: Two-Tiered Pluralism* (1992), *Faces of Inequality* (1998), and *Racial Diversity and Social Capital: Equality and Community in America* (2007).
3. I reviewed recent ANES election studies conducted by Survey Research Center, University of Michigan.
4. ANES 2008 Time Series, V083069 7 pt. Liberal–Conservative scale, ANOVA V083069*Cohort, Chi-Square: 70.52 (p<0.01)

4

■ ■ ■

Policy Analysis

CHAPTER OVERVIEW

Policy analysis is a critical part of policy-making. Before a policy is put into place, analysts try to determine the most effective and efficient method of achieving policy goals. Budget constraints and citizen demands mean that government must choose policy options wisely.

As mentioned earlier, Immanuel Kant challenges us to consider methods of analysis. Kant saw a need for uniformity in methods of analysis, so as to arrive at compatible and comparable conclusions. Uniformity in policy analytic techniques is just as critical as in other scientific endeavors.

Although many tools are used by policy analysts, economic analysis is a major focus. Economics is used to describe choices made by individuals, private-sector corporations, and government. In theory, economics describes options, allows for comparison, and provides rational choices.

Economics may also aid in the understanding of policy impacts. Monetary impact is a valuable method of measuring costs and benefits emergent from public policy. Economics gives us the ability to compare costs with benefits, illustrating the magnitude of a policy option.

The specific goals for the chapter are:

- Discuss the role of economics in policy analysis.
- Discuss the rise of policy "sciences" and the growth of public policy.
- Describe the tools of policy "science."
- Discuss the limitations of policy "science."

ECONOMICS

At its very core, economics is the study of exchanges of wealth. In a state of nature, human beings focus their attention on the acquisition and use of goods used to satisfy their needs. Goods often have value. Possession of goods is a form of wealth. At times, individuals no longer want more goods. They might have a surplus or it may not suit their tastes. Exchange behaviors follow, in which one form of wealth is exchanged for another form of wealth. In the exchange, it is expected that individuals will desire to either gain wealth or at a minimum not lose wealth. This optimal or "efficient" situation is known as a *Pareto optimal* outcome.

In modern society, certain individuals or groups of individuals—a corporate body—intentionally create surplus material items to be sold to other individuals or groups using a financial exchange process—that is, monetary wealth exchanged for material wealth. (See Box 4.1, *Supply and Demand*.) If an individual or corporate body produces a good for which consumer demand exists, it can set prices such that net gain or **net profit** can be maximized in relation to the supply available. If the demand for an item is high and supply is low, then prices may be higher than if demand was low and supply was high. Rational individuals try to obtain more goods at a lower cost. Producers maximize profit by keeping average costs of production low in relation to the marginal cost of producing more items for sale at a given price. When demand is high and supply is low—when, at a given price, the marginal costs of production exceed the average cost of production—it is likely that either a given producer or competing producers will try to increase sales of a good, until that point where supply meets demand and prices decline to a point where marginal costs equal average costs. Under those circumstances, the marketplace has reached equilibrium.

As outlined previously, the model of **free market economics** guides many of the choices made in public policy and in the private sector. The model makes certain assumptions about the nature of goods and the usage of those goods. First, the model assumes that goods are **rivalrous** (see Weimer and Vining 1992, 41) in their use. In other words, the owner of a particular property is the individual who paid a price agreed to by a seller. A good example of this might be a pair of glasses. When I purchase my glasses, no one else can own them. Second, the model assumes that property is **excludable** (Weimer and Vining 1992, 41)—the owner of a property is the only person who has control over the use of the property. A good example of excludability is home ownership—the person or persons who own a home can exclude others from entering the home and enjoying the benefits that emerge from the property.

Some goods are nonrivalrous, but are excludable. In other words, it is possible that multiple parties could enjoy the good or service simultaneously, but under certain conditions it is possible to limit the use of a good or service. Canals can be viewed as an example of such a good. Frequently, canals are produced privately and then made available for public use. Once built, a canal could be seen as having some minimal costs for maintenance and repair; for that reason, it might be sensible for the canal's owner to charge a usage fee for the maintenance and continued operation of the canal. In strictly economic theory terms, it would be inefficient for the owner of the canal to charge an amount that would result in a profit for him or her; in reality, of course, profit or rent is one motivation for the construction of the canal. Again in theory, the only other circumstance under which the canal owner would raise user fees would be under conditions of traffic congestion, for example, when the canal became too crowded with users. Higher fees would effectively exclude some users from canal usage. Reduced canal congestion might lower the costs to users in terms of travel time.

BOX 4.1

Supply and Demand

I like going to Greece, but it costs money. So, I have to plan my visit so that I can get the best price possible.

Sunset at Temple of Poseidon at Sounion

This chart provides a simple way to think about it.

P = Price; Q = Quantity

b = Lower quantity of rooms available at a higher price

c = Higher quantity of rooms available at a lower price

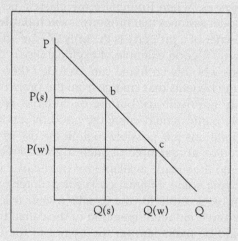

Model of supply and demand

Not all property is held privately. For example, **public goods** or **communal goods** are commonly found in both tribal and modern societies. Some public goods are referred to as pure public goods, which are nonexcludable and nonrivalrous. Air is an example of a pure public good. We all breathe air and it is

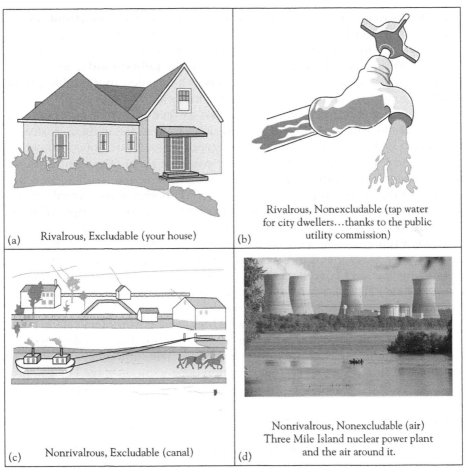

(a)   Rivalrous, Excludable (your house)

(b)   Rivalrous, Nonexcludable (tap water for city dwellers…thanks to the public utility commission)

(c)   Nonrivalrous, Excludable (canal)

(d)   Nonrivalrous, Nonexcludable (air) Three Mile Island nuclear power plant and the air around it.

FIGURE 4.1   Rivalry and excludability

impossible to limit the use of air by other individuals. Additionally, air is also used by factories, automobiles, and airplanes as a convenient place in which to expel smoke and exhaust fumes. Because public goods have a low per person cost and a variable per person benefit, public goods are easily overused, resulting in depletion, damage, or destruction. Protection of quality and availability is important. Because public goods are nonexclusive, people might *not* contribute to the repair or replenishment of public goods. Known as **free riders**, these individuals selfishly benefit from the efforts of others. (See Figure 4.1.)

Sometimes, public goods are leased or sold by government to individuals who desire excludable usage of the good. The use of public lands for grazing can be considered a **marketable public good**—the forage and water were sold or leased for use, but the land itself remains under government ownership. In the nineteenth century, grazing on public lands was seen by ranchers as posing minimal or no cost to the environment and society. Environmental interest groups argue that environmental and social costs of grazing are very high (e.g., damage to public lands due to overgrazing, native species endangerment, or the **opportunity costs**[1] associated with grazing compared to other uses). Given the new perspective on costs, grazing rights would either be terminated or the price imposed should be very high. Environmentalists see public lands as a pure **public good** requiring careful management. Ranchers view public lands as a modified **marketable public good**—a good that could be subject to market forces and bought or sold.

A final category of goods are known as **free goods**. Free goods are nonexcludable, which means that all individuals have access to them. However, individuals seek the excludable use of the goods. If goods are not consumed by an individual, then other individuals will consume them. The rain forests in South America are an example of a free good. One of the inefficiencies that emerges in the case of free goods is the overconsumption and eventual exhaustion of the goods. Demand may not fluctuate on the basis of supply or price.

The potential economic circumstances discussed offer some role for government. Even if society were composed of solely private goods, it would be necessary for government to protect the welfare and private property of citizens, enforcing laws governing the contractual legal use or to prevent misuse by other individuals. Government would play a role in economic relationships to prevent large-scale economic inefficiencies.

In agrarian-based societies, the need for a large government role in maximizing social welfare is not as great as it is in industrialized modern society. Agrarian societies offer many opportunities for self-sufficiency, whereas in modern industrial societies, citizens are often dependent on wage labor to provide the monetary resources necessary to purchase needed goods and services.

RISE OF POLICY SCIENCES

In the United States, social movements in the mid-1800s paralleled the rise of industrialization, and culminated in the Progressive movement in the early twentieth century—a movement whose goals and vision impacted contemporary politics and society. A consideration for social welfare has become a growing part of U.S. government responsibility over the last century. Policy response to the Great Depression in the 1930s established a new vision of the social contract in modern society. Government was no longer simply involved in promoting social and political order or in the expansion of individuals' freedom from government (a response to millennia of aristocratic rule). A new vision emerged that promoted individual equality and freedom to exercise individual social, economic, and political rights.

The massive changes in society impacted both the scope and objective of public policy. Public policy's new role moved from regulatory to distributive and redistributive, steering us toward a more perfect society . . . a "good" society. At the very heart of the movement was a belief that policy can produce predictable changes. The rise of *behavioral science* made this vision a new reality.

Behavioral science argued that individual behavior was in part a function of various stimuli. With a greater understanding of the individual's conditions (social–psychological), it was possible to predict the response to a given stimulus. It was believed that stimuli via public policy incentives could produce a desired response. Educational opportunity, for example, was found to produce the desired policy outcome: economic and social improvement. Welfare benefits and job training have been shown to produce the desired policy outcome of successful employment. Behavioral science provides great hope to society. If human behavior and condition could be described and predicted, then it would be possible to shape human behavior and conditions toward a desired outcome.

Policy science guides policy choices and designs with the intent of producing a desired outcome. The complexities of policy analysis have contributed to the development and growth of policy science, harnessing the knowledge and tools of the hard sciences (e.g., biology and chemistry), social sciences (e.g., sociology, psychology, and anthropology) and humanities (e.g., history and philosophy). Policy science helps leaders better understand all aspects of human society, its problems, and the solutions to those problems.

Policy analysis is primarily concerned with the consideration of several policy alternatives, each expected to produce different policy outcomes. Policy analysis requires careful systematic and empirical study (Lasswell 1971, 1). Policy analysis involves all aspects of the policy process, from the early stages of policy adoption and formulation to the implementation and evaluation of public policies. Policy analysis is important in modern complex society because public policy is so vast, public problems are sophisticated and often interconnected, and public policies have tremendous social, economic, and political implications. Public policy is a dynamic process, operating under changing social, political, and economic conditions. Policy analysis helps us to understand how social, economic, and political conditions change and how public policies must evolve so as to meet the changing needs of an evolving society.

GROWTH OF PUBLIC POLICY

Government spending patterns illustrate the scope of public policy. Public policy is often a function of direct government expenditure, although a variety of indirect costs of regulation cannot be easily and consistently quantified. According to the *Statistical Abstract of the United States*, the direct costs of state and national government totaled an estimated $5,186.2 billion in 2008.[2] This figure represents roughly 36.3 percent of the estimated 2008 gross domestic product of $14,264.6 billion. In other words, government expended over one-third of the gross domestic product to provide services and direct payments to individuals and groups for the purpose of fulfilling public policy goals.

Where is public policy growing the fastest? Based on estimates, it appears that state-level policy, measured by expenditure patterns, is growing the fastest. Between 1990 and 2008, state-level budget outlays increased by nearly 70 percent in real 2008 dollar terms. By comparison, the national government policy financing has increased by approximately 55 percent. In terms of size and cost, public policy is a "growth industry."

Government expenditure illustrates the size of public policy; it tells us little, however, about the scope of public policy. The expansion of public policy occurred for several reasons, but *one common theme found behind all public policy is a perceived need for a public solution to particular social, economic, or political dilemmas, furthered by a belief that such policy is consistent with what government ought to do under the terms of the social contract.*

Public policy analysis is an integral part of the policy-making process, from the initial stages of decision-making to the evaluation of public policies as implemented. Policy analysis requires an interdisciplinary approach—a solid understanding of the theoretical developments within a variety of science and social scientific disciplines and the practical applications of the information available. In that sense, public policy analysis helps us to bridge the gap between developing an understanding of what government ought or ought not do and what government does or does not do.

As government grows and policy challenges become more numerous, complex, and interrelated, policy analysis plays a larger role in making certain that decisions in one policy area are consistent or at least compatible with decisions made in other policy areas. Government development and growth tends to parallel population growth and the heterogeneity of needs associated with a diverse population. Therefore, policy analysis must also seek to overcome the complexities of consumer needs, yet advance equal policy outcomes.

CENTRAL QUESTIONS FOR PUBLIC POLICY ANALYSIS

Robert Brewer and Peter de Leon outlined five questions that must be considered by policy analysts at all stages of the policy process:

1. What goal values are sought, and by whom?
2. What trends affect the realization of these values? Or, where did the problem originate?
3. What factors are responsible for the trends? Or, what are the driving or influencing factors?
4. What is the probable cause of future events and development—especially if interventions are not made?
5. What can be done to change that course to realize or achieve more of the desired goals, and for whom? (Brewer and de Leon 1983, 12–13).

The first question can be viewed as having some normative characteristics. It asks policy analysts to consider what government ought or ought not do. The tools used to answer this question can be found in the realm of philosophy. It requires policy analysts to consider how citizens wish to live as individuals and as members of a society. It may also require the prioritization of values and desires because often it is not possible to meet all desires simultaneously. Philosophy also helps policy analysts and citizens understand values in terms of human-centered or nature-centered ethics—what is acceptable and what is not acceptable in terms of policy preferences. For example, if an individual or a society values something that would systematically harm other individuals, ethical guidelines might dissuade policy analysts from pursuing particular public policies.

All five of these questions can be addressed empirically; that is, various elements of the questions can be studied systematically, using a form of measurement. Beyond the five central questions, policy analysis—the empirical study of public policy choices—is conducted for a number of more specific reasons. For example, a public policy may not be effective or efficient. Policy analysis is conducted to determine what is causing the policy to not meet its goals and offer ways of improving policy process and outcomes. Policy analysis is also used to plan for contingencies—for example, emergencies brought on by a random act of nature or that are human-caused. Policy analysis is also used to make resource allocation decisions. There may be several policy alternatives, but money is in limited supply. Policy analysis is a way of making choices about relative costs and benefits.

In *Analysis for Public Decisions* (1989, 49), E. S. Quade identifies five critical points where policy analysis is particularly important:

- ***Issue framing stage***
  When a proposed policy is first considered by elected officials, it is often very difficult to frame the policy issue in a way that is tangible and understandable. Policy analysts help to define the proposed policy and outline its goals.
- ***Policy choice stage***
  In the policy process, elected officials often consider a number of different policies; again, it proves difficult to compare these alternatives without a thorough analysis of their similarities and differences. Policy analysts makes the comparisons possible, calculating expected outcomes and estimated costs.
- ***Current and future relevance analysis***
  Many public policies are designed to solve both current and future problems. Although policy is often designed to deal with contemporary issues, it must be able to adapt to future needs. In this third part of the process, policy analysts attempt to forecast future needs based on past and present conditions.
- ***Output/Impact analysis***
  Policy outcomes can be found in a variety of different forms—tangible outputs and not-so-tangible impacts. It is often difficult to determine whether the policy itself resulted in desired change or if other exogenous or external factors were the most direct cause. Nevertheless, it is important to determine whether policy is responsible for the desired change—if it is not responsible, then there would be no need for the policy.
- ***Futuristic projections***
  Policy analysis studies trends and makes educated guesses about the future directions of public policy and develops general plans to meet projected policy needs. Futuristic projections analysis often serves as the basis for entirely new policy areas. For instance, supply shortfalls in strategic metals has led current policy analysts to explore the feasibility of interplanetary or lunar mineral extraction and recovery policies possibly implemented decades or centuries from now.

TOOLS FOR POLICY ANALYSIS

There are two types of empirical analysis: **qualitative studies** and **quantitative studies**. Qualitative studies involve a variety of different tools, but only two major types will be discussed here: archival analysis and personal interviews. Quantitative studies discussed will include: benefit/cost analysis, **demography**, and survey research. Types of data and data analysis will be discussed briefly.

Archival analysis is particularly important in public policy analysis. Policy history—what was done in the past, why it was done, and how much it cost—helps policy analysts learn important lessons that can be applied to current or future problems and goals. Historical analysis may illuminate hidden costs and pitfalls that might lead to policy failure, thus improving policy success rates.

Personal interviews are also an important tool for improving current public policy and informing future policy design. Interviews of former elected and appointed officials may reveal the decision process by which policy was adopted, and which choices were avoided. Through personal interviews, it is possible to document past experience for future use.

Interviews with clientele groups or individuals are also valuable. Clientele are often eager to talk about the positive and negative aspects of public policy, frequently offering an "insider's view." For instance, individuals who have lived in government-owned and operated tenements in major urban areas understand the day-to-day challenges to the quality of life as well as, if not better than, government agents tasked with managing housing. Directly impacted by public policy, the clientele have a sense of how public policy benefits or injures them and how public policy could be recrafted to better serve their needs.

Quantitative studies involve the use of numbers to describe phenomena. The analysis of numbers can simplify the study of public policy, because numbers have assigned values that may have a more universal meaning. In the strictest sense, monetary values are often understood by individuals. Other numerical values have meanings that are frequently ephemeral and often socially constructed.

In quantitative analysis, information is numerical in form, referred to as "quantitative data." The data are collected and processed in several different forms. Some data are **aggregate-level data** or grouped data. For instance, data that describes a group—a city, county, state, gender, ethnic group or particular race—are aggregated to reflect that group as a whole. In aggregated form, data analysis allows policy analysts to describe social or economic conditions in very general terms, making it difficult to pinpoint policy problems and to craft and direct policy more efficiently and effectively to those individuals or groups being served. **Individual-level data** often describe a person. For example, the Internal Revenue Service (IRS) collects individual-level data via tax documentation on an annual basis.

Benefit/Cost Analysis

Benefit/cost analysis compares the amount of expected or known benefits produced by a particular policy choice with the expected or known costs associated with that choice. Of the two elements in the generic equation, costs are often more easily computed. Costs are usually measured in monetary terms. Known costs of labor and supplies are easily computed. Although **hidden costs** are always associated with any policy decision, such costs can be estimated given previous experiences in prior public policy endeavors. **Opportunity costs**—the costs associated with choosing a particular policy over an alternative policy—can also be estimated.

Benefit is difficult to calculate because aspects of public policy benefit are not easily measured in dollar terms. For example, it may be impossible to quantify the benefit one gains from climbing to the top of El Capitan in Yosemite National Park, but the benefit exists. Individual clientele and policymakers have a tremendous influence on the quality of a policy outcome or output, but the calculation of a "benefit" is often aggregated, overlooking nuances.

The determination of benefit/cost (B/C) ratios is not a one-time event. Public policy is dynamic and requires that policy-makers adjust policy to changing conditions and needs. When change of policy direction or emphasis occurs, it usually requires increased resource expenditures. For example, if a public school administrator determines that students' reading disabilities are impeding their progress in school, it might be necessary to increase resources devoted to reading programs. The goal would be to increase policy benefit as a result of increased expenditure. The increased benefit is called a **marginal benefit**, whereas the increased cost is a **marginal cost**. In B/C analysis, if benefit does not increase at a rate greater than cost increases, then a policy change is not efficient.

Demography and Policy Analysis

In policy analysis, the changing nature of society's needs must be continually monitored. People move, social and economic conditions change, and public policy must evolve to meet new challenges. Demographers have special skills to monitor these changes. Compiling data collected from local and state officials and private entities, demographers track patterns of change and make general predictions about future trends. The analysis helps policy-makers determine the feasibility, need, and likely success of a policy.

Demographic data helps policy-makers determine whether social and economic change is occurring in an equitable manner. For instance, the growth of suburban areas in the United States during the 1950s, 1960s, and 1970s resulted in a noticeable demographic change in urban areas. Often characterized by the expression "White flight," American suburbs were populated by middle-class Whites who no longer wished to live in multicultural urban communities. As a result, many businesses shifted their attention to the burgeoning White suburban middle class, effectively reversing or limiting economic growth in urban areas. Individuals who remained in urban areas, primarily persons of color, were witness to significant economic decline. Demographic analysis played an important part in documenting the rise of economic and social inequality that arose in the post–World War II era. Although the analyses were interpreted by political conservatives and liberals in different ways, the findings themselves played an important role in developing

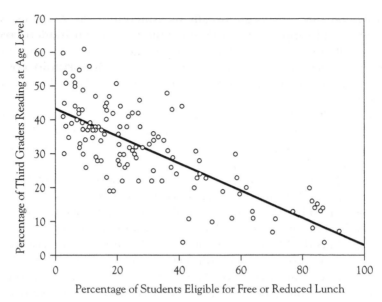

FIGURE 4.2   Correlation between test scores and economic disparity measure.

public policies intended to remedy the inequities, the impacts of which could be studied in future demographic analysis. (See Figure 4.2.)

The Use of Public Opinion Surveys

Generally, public policy analysis is concerned with formulating public policy, choosing alternatives, and studying outcomes. Public opinion can shape policy alternatives chosen. If the public is not supportive of a policy choice, a negative or noncommittal public response could effectively delegitimize it. Policy analysts may then consider changing the policy approach or goals. The use of mass survey techniques, such as mail or telephone surveys, allows policy analysts to efficiently collect information on the opinions, beliefs, and values of individuals.

Decision Theory

In many respects, decision theory is an extension of statistical analysis and economic theory. **Decision theory** explores contingencies associated with a policy. The approach is especially useful *after* a particular policy has been adopted by government. Following policy adoption, the details of policy practice are often reviewed, and policy goals and methods formally adjusted.

Government agencies in charge of meeting the new goals seek methods of standardizing the process of decision making, linking process to predictable outcomes. Decision theory involves determining the probability that various events will occur and factoring that probability into decision analysis. It is important for policy analysts to consider the probability of particular events arising, and the cost and outcomes associated with dealing with these events for reasons of policy efficiency and effectiveness, as well as equity. For efficiency reasons, the cheapest and most effective alternatives are usually adopted. For reasons of equity, uniform decisions protect clientele.

Experimentation

Experiments are often effective methods of determining a causal connection between the presence of a public policy and particular outcomes. True experimental design requires the random assignment of individuals to two groups: an **experimental group** and a **control group**. The experimental group is comprised of those individuals who receive a **treatment**, which is a proposed policy or policy variation that is believed will yield more effective or efficient policy outcomes. A control group, similar to the experimental group, is not given the treatment and then compared to the experimental group to see whether the groups are different after the treatment is administered. In a true experiment, all external influences that shape outcomes are prevented, a concept known as **experimental control**. In reality, public policy experiments are frequently not truly randomly assigned. Experimentation with new policies or policy strategies is often conducted in particular states or localities that may not reflect the general population. Additionally, it is difficult to control other influences on policy outcomes.

In social welfare policy, welfare reform plans were first tested via policy experimentation at the state level. In Wisconsin, former Governor Tommy Thompson launched a series of welfare reforms that led to the reduction of individuals on the state's welfare rolls. The policy innovation seemed to yield positive outcomes and inspired national welfare reform in 1996. In Figure 4.3,

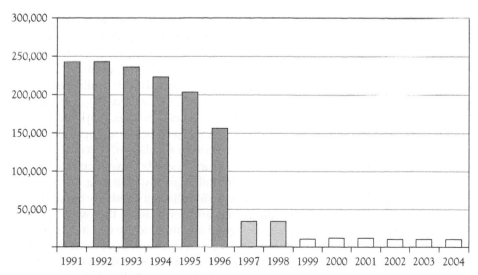

FIGURE 4.3 Welfare caseloads in Wisconsin 1991–2004. (AFDC/TANF)

Note: 1999–2004 data was reported by the Wisconsin Department of Workforce Development as annual average caseload data.

Source: Data from Wisconsin Department of Workforce Development.

welfare caseloads in Wisconsin began to decline from 1993–1996. After the new policy was established in 1997–1998, welfare case loads dropped dramatically; however, policy experts are divided on whether reform was the causal factor.

OUTCOMES OF PUBLIC POLICY ANALYSIS

The outcomes of public policy analysis are highly varied. Through policy analyses, policymakers develop a greater understanding of a policy problem and possible solutions. Policy analysis projects costs and possible benefits that will emerge from adoption of a particular policy alternative. Decision-makers are usually interested in efficient alternatives—greatest benefit for the least cost.

Nevertheless, policy analysis should not be thought of as the solution to government waste and mismanagement. At best, policy analysis offers us some guidance in our choices between alternatives; it does not guarantee that our choices will be morally or ethically wise, nor does it ensure that outcomes will occur as anticipated. Unanticipated events may reshape policy priorities and goals. Policy analysis cannot predict the future with absolute certainty.

ETHICS AND POLICY ANALYSIS

At its best, policy is about improving the condition of individuals' lives within the context of a generally accepted set of political, social, and economic values that serve as the foundation of a social contract. In a classical liberal society, the primary role of government is reflected in public policy: namely, the establishment of legal protections to limit violations of an individual's property rights, life, and personal freedom. In classical liberal society, military and criminal justice functions of government would play prominent policy roles.

Conversely, modern liberal societies have a more expansive role for government in protecting individual rights and promoting social, political, and economic equality. Government is proactive, actively involved in building a better future for all individuals under the social contract. In that sense, government is seen to have some role in the management of goods (private, marketable, free, and public). **Externalities** occur with all types of goods; through public policy, government tries to limit negative impacts through regulation. Government also uses incentives to encourage specific uses for goods. For instance, the federal government has entered the realm of marketable goods, charging low rates for public land grazing, encouraging ranchers on adjacent lands to expand their livestock operations. In the late nineteenth and for most of the twentieth century, public land grazing policy was designed to stimulate growth in agricultural production, particularly in the American West. In this way, government spurred economic growth with cheap marketable goods, while simultaneously improving the lives of rural citizens. (See Box 4.2, *Is Public Policy Spiraling out of Control? Nonmainstream Viewpoints.*)

What seems to be a simple difference of opinion regarding the meaning of liberalism (classical or modern) is, however, much deeper. At its core, policy

BOX 4.2

Is Public Policy Spiraling Out of Control? Nonmainstream Viewpoints

As public policy has moved beyond the relatively limited government functions of a more classical liberal society, it has had to face a series of hard questions related to ethics and to the role of liberal democracy in public policy. It seems odd that such a question would be asked: What is the role of liberal democracy in public policy-making? Yet, it is a question that has arisen on a number of occasions, largely because public policy is moving so rapidly to solve complex and ever-expanding problems. Increasingly, elected officials and citizens struggle to understand the general direction of public policy. Policy analysts are highly specialized and highly trained individuals often speaking in the very technical language of their particular policy area. Under such conditions, it becomes difficult for public policy to meet both standards of the general definition—that is, ought versus ought not, does versus does not. Elected officials and citizens find themselves unable to clearly see the normative criteria of policy being met and at times find it difficult to understand what it is that government is doing. As Max Weber said in *Structures of Power*, "The political master finds himself in the position of 'dilettante' who stands opposite the 'expert,' facing the trained official who stands within the management of administration" (Jenkins-Smith 1990, 45). In other words, there is the potential threat that democracy will be replaced by technocracy in the policy-making process.

The late Friedrich Hayek, an important figure in the so-called Austrian School of Economics, wrote about the concerns surrounding the rise of technocratic policy-making in his books, *The Road to Serfdom* and *Constitution of Liberty*. Hayek predicted the decline of representative policy-making. Hayek saw the rise of technocracy as potentially reducing individual power, centralizing it, and placing it in the hands of government policy analysts, who would become primary decision-makers.

Other critics of policy analysis see the outcomes of the growth of government policy as not producing the utopian visions that were intended. **Dystopians** often see the decline of personal privacy of individuals. In a complex policy environment, policy analysts require tremendous amounts of data to form their decisions and policy strategies. In many instances, these data are about individuals in society. Dystopians see the data collection process and use of the data collected as a limitation on the privacy rights of individuals. Additionally, the data aggregation process has the potential to treat a person as a "number," thus dehumanizing individuals.

analysis makes assumptions about the proper role of government in manipulating individual preferences. A classical liberal policy often manipulates the individual using disincentives—for example, crime is punished, often mercilessly. Modern liberal policy is more likely to manipulate the individual through incentives—for example, purchase an alternative energy vehicle and government offers a tax rebate. Either way, **ethics** (an individual's core beliefs regarding right and wrong) begs us to consider the degree and manner in which government ought to manipulate our preferences. Determining what government ought or ought not do can be traced to ethical belief systems and social contract theories.

Lessons Learned from Chapter 4

SPECIFICS

- Economic theory plays a substantial role in guiding policy analysis and policy choices. Money, and what we get or expect to get for the money we spend, is a very important part of how we invest our public funds.
- Policy "science" really began to develop in the post–World War II period, when policy analysts were able to study policy choices in a more sophisticated way. It was also a period of time when public policy grew quite substantially, and citizens and government leaders and administrators became more aware of the need for well-grounded policy investments that would benefit society.
- Qualitative and quantitative tools are used in policy "science." These tools come from a variety of different fields, such as economics, anthropology, history, political science, psychology, and sociology.
- Policy "science" looks for public solutions to problems. Critics of policy science argue that it is ultimately grounded in normative values that favor public solutions to social or individual problems. Although several of these critics are political conservatives who favor limited government, there are also political Liberal critics who fear that public solutions have not produced the outcomes promised by policy analysts.

THE BIG PICTURE

Public policy analysis is a highly complex process. Policy analysis has been a part of government since the foundation of civilized society. For the most part, it has been an effort on the part of government to manage the social, political, and economic relationships between individuals. In the earliest examples, public policy analysis centered around economic issues, standardizing the contract process and creating uniform methods of tax collection. Additionally, government policy analysts dealt with (and continue to deal with) the regulation and use of goods in society, particularly public and free goods. Over time, government has played a larger role in the use of private and marketable goods, too.

Public policy analysis is built on a foundation of values. Ideally, policy analysis is designed to help government meet goals that are firmly grounded in commonly shared values. Critics often see public policy analysis as highly technocratic, at times setting aside the issue of values and replacing them with a discussion of problem identification and methods to best achieve a particular policy goal. The role of democracy in policy-making has been the subject of much debate in both academic and practitioner circles, as well as in the political arena. Increasingly, the role of democracy in policy analysis and policy-making has been highlighted as critically important.

With that in mind, we have become more aware of the difficulty in identifying policy analysis as a "science." In an applied sense, policy analysis is more often seen as a useful tool for achieving particular ends. Policy analysis will likely never be a "pure" science, one that holds up completely disinterested objectivity as a goal to be achieved. The strength of democratic policy-making is that it tends to involve a very broad discussion, or at least affirmation, of that which everyday citizens, elected officials, and policy analysts believe government *ought* or *ought not* do.

Key Terms

aggregate-level data
behavioral science
benefit/cost analysis
control group
decision theory
demography
dystopians
ethics
excludable
experiment
experimental control
experimental group
externalities
free good
free market economics

free riders
hidden costs
individual-level data
marginal benefit
marginal cost
marketable public good
net profit
opportunity costs
policy analysis
public goods
qualitative studies
quantitative studies
rivalrous
treatment

Questions for Study

1. Discuss three central questions in public policy analysis.
2. What is policy "science"? What is its role in public policy? What are the tools used by policy "science"?
3. Discuss dystopian thought regarding policy analysis.

Bibliography

Bardach, E. 2000. *A practical guide of policy analysis: The eight-fold path to more effective problem solving*. New York: Chatham House.

Bobrow, D., and J. Dryzek. 1987. *Policy analysis by design*. Pittsburgh, PA: University of Pittsburgh Press.

Brewer, G., and P. DeLeon. 1983. *The foundations of policy analysis*. Pacific Grove, CA: Brooks/Cole Publishers.

Goehlert, R., and F. Martin. 1985. *Policy analysis and management: A bibliography*. Santa Barbara, CA: ABC-Clio Information Services.

Haas, P., and J. F. Springer. 1998. *Applied policy research: Concepts and cases*. New York: Garland Publishing.

Hawkesworth, M. 1988. *Theoretical issues in policy analysis*. Albany: State University of New York Press.

von Hayek, F. 1944. *Road to serfdom*. Chicago: University of Chicago Press.

———. 1960. *The Constitution of Liberty*. Chicago: University of Chicago Press.

House, P., and R. Shull. 1991. *The practice of policy analysis: Forty years of art and technology*. Washington, DC: The Compass Press.

Jenkins-Smith, H. 1990. *Democratic politics and policy analysis*. New York: Thomson Learning.

Kane, J. "Econometrics: An applied approach—data." www.oswego.edu/~kane/econometrics/schools.html (accessed September 4, 2004).

Lasswell, H. 1971. *Politics: Who gets what, when, and how*. New York: Peter Smith Publishers.

Nagel, S. 1984. *Contemporary public policy analysis*. Tuscaloosa: University of Alabama Press.

———. *Policy Analysis Methods*. Commack, NY: Nova Science Publishers.

——— ed. 1994. *Encyclopedia of policy studies*. 2nd ed. New York: Marcel Dekker.

——— ed. 1999. *The substance of public policy*. Hauppauge, NY: Nova Science Publishers.

Quade, E. 1989. *Analysis for public decisions,* 3rd ed. Englewood Cliffs, NJ: Prentice Hall.

Sunshine, R. A. 2009. "Congressional Budget Office Director's Blog, Troubled Asset Relief Program, January 16, 2009." http://cboblog.cbo.gov/?p=197 (accessed April 26, 2009).

Walker, W. 1994. *The policy analysis approach to public decision-making.* Santa Monica, CA: RAND.

Weimer, D., and A. Vining. 1992. *Policy analysis: Concepts and practice*. Upper Saddle River, NJ: Pearson Prentice Hall.

Endnotes

1. Opportunity costs are the costs incurred when one chooses a particular course of action and thus loses potential benefits from taking an alternate course of action. For example, if I have $2 and I choose to buy ice cream with the money as opposed to buying a gallon of gasoline, then I have incurred an opportunity cost by depriving myself the benefit of traveling 20 miles in my truck on the gallon of gasoline I could have purchased.

2. The total includes $247 billion in Troubled Asset Relief Program disbursements. See Sunshine, Robert A. "Congressional Budget Office Director's Blog, Troubled Asset Relief Program, January 16, 2009." http:// cboblog .cbo.gov/?p=197 (accessed April 26, 2009).

5

■ ■ ■

Agenda Setting

CHAPTER OVERVIEW

The agenda-setting process is the first step in understanding public policy. Although we may or may not agree with specific methods, government has a role in meeting our needs. Providing for the common defense is one function of government that is rarely questioned in terms of its legitimacy, but exactly what government does or does not do in this policy area is subject to continual debate.

Philosophical differences illustrate societal divisions about policy choices and priorities. Proponents of classical liberalism argue that many issues on the policy agenda should be left to the private sector. Proponents of modern liberalism, however, argue that many agenda items promote social justice. For example, government-sponsored health care is generally disliked by classical liberals but often supported by modern liberals.

The specific goals for the chapter are:

- Discuss how agenda setting works and how issues are framed.
- Discuss the major policy actors and their roles in setting the policy agenda.
- Use policy theories to explain agenda setting.

HOW DOES AGENDA SETTING WORK?

In his book, *Agendas, Alternatives, and Public Policy,* John Kingdon outlines the agenda-setting process. According to Kingdon, the policy agenda can be thought of as a series of streams, circumstances, or activities within public policy institutions and processes. The **problem stream** contains potential policy problems, some more well-known than others, some more likely to be acted upon than others. The **policy stream** contains a series of potential solutions to policy problems. Finally, there is the **politics stream**—those policy issues and solutions that emerge as policy outcomes. The politics stream is a function of the status and philosophy of agenda-setters.

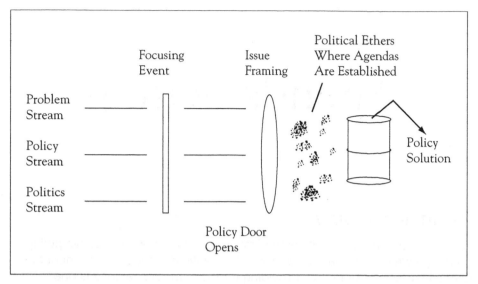

FIGURE 5.1   One way to think about agenda setting.

These streams can operate separately from one another. Individuals and groups are continually identifying problems to be solved by government. Solutions to "problems" abound, but many are never tried. Politics and political institutions are constantly changing, so the political stream is in flux.

When a **focusing event** occurs, the circumstances or behaviors of actors within the policy streams often converge: A **policy window** has opened—the problem stream has become evident to the political stream actors and institutions, and particular solutions within the policy stream may become part of the policy agenda. According to Kingdon, however, the agenda-setting process is often haphazardly chosen from the policy garbage can (Kingdon 2002). (See Figure 5.1.).

In 2007, a major freeway bridge collapsed in Minnesota, killing several individuals and raising serious concern about the safety of bridges in the United States. This terrible disaster led to a number of efforts to inspect bridges nationwide to prevent similar disasters from producing enormous fatalities. Bridge safety issues are not new, but when catastrophic events occur, our concerns are heightened. (See Box 5.1, *Minnesota Bridge Collapses.*)

Issues are more likely to reach the policy agenda if they can be shown to play a role in maintaining the regime's legitimacy and place on the world stage. In his joint session speech to Congress only days after the collapse of the World Trade Center, President George Bush clearly delineated the reasoning behind a war on terrorism. One of the reasons for the "war" was based in basic regime values. As a political system, the United States was considered legitimate and important to world events, an ally of all freedom-loving people. Through his speech, President Bush sought to tie the need for a particular

BOX 5.1

Minnesota Bridge Collapses

BRIDGE COLLAPSE SPOTLIGHTS AMERICA'S DEFERRED MAINTENANCE

The tragic rush-hour collapse in Minneapolis of the I-35W Bridge over the Mississippi River is again forcing a re-examination of the nation's approach to maintaining and inspecting critical infrastructure.

According to engineers, the nation is spending only about two-thirds as much as it should be to keep dams, levees, highways, and bridges safe. The situation is more urgent now because many such structures were designed 40 or 50 years ago, before Americans were driving weighty SUVs and truckers were lugging tandem loads.

It all adds up to a poor grade: The American Society of Civil Engineers gave the nation a D in 2005, the latest report available, after assessing 12 categories of infrastructure ranging from rails and roads to wastewater treatment and dams.

"One of America's great assets is its infrastructure, but if you don't invest it deteriorates," says Patrick Natale, executive director of ASCE.

Among scores of recent examples:

- Last month, a 100-year-old steam pipe erupted in midtown Manhattan, killing one man and causing millions of dollars in lost business.
- The inadequacies of levees in New Orleans became horrifyingly clear in the aftermath of hurricane Katrina. The city is still recovering.
- In 2003, the Silver Lake Dam in Michigan failed, causing $100 million in damage.

America's 577,000 bridges are of particular concern because they are subject to corrosion. According to the Web site of Nondestructive Testing (NDT), which advocates not damaging structures during testing, the average lifespan of a bridge is about 70 years. Bridges are inspected visually every two years. However, NDT notes, "It is not uncommon for a fisherman, canoeist, and other passerby to alert officials to major damage that may have occurred between inspections."

In the federal government's rating system, any bridge that scores less than 80—on a scale of 1 to 100—is in need of rehabilitation. A bridge scoring below 50 should undergo reconstruction under federal guidelines. In 2004, 26.7 percent of U.S. bridges, urban and rural, were rated deficient, down from 27.5 percent in 2002, according to the U.S. Department of Transportation.

Source: Scherer, Ron, "Bridge Collapse Spotlights America's Deferred Maintenance," *The Christian Science Monitor,* August 3, 2007, 1.

---

issue on the policy agenda through an association with regime values, goals, strength, and legitimacy.

Within a year of giving the speech, however, President Bush's popularity sagged substantially because many Americans questioned the way in which problems were being framed and saw policy solutions as being unworkable and too costly. Even in the case of a major event such as September 11, the agenda-setting process and the opening of policy windows is fraught with difficulties for actors in Kingdon's three streams. (See Box 5.2, *A Policy Window Opens. An Agenda is Established.*)

BOX 5.2

A Policy Window Opens. An Agenda Is Established

Framing
Event—
Policy
Window
Open

Tonight we are a country awakened to danger and called to defend freedom. Our grief has turned to anger, and anger to resolution. Whether we bring our enemies to justice, or bring justice to our enemies, justice will be done.

I thank the Congress for its leadership at such an important time. All of America was touched on the evening of the tragedy to see Republicans and Democrats joined together on the steps of this Capitol, singing "God Bless America." And you did more than sing; you acted, by delivering $40 billion to rebuild our communities and meet the needs of our military. . . .

Appeal to
Political
Stream

Framing

Americans are asking, why do they hate us? They hate what we see right here in this chamber—a democratically elected government. Their leaders are self-appointed. They hate our freedoms—our freedom of religion, our freedom of speech, our freedom to vote and assemble and disagree with each other. . . .

Policy
Stream

Our response involves far more than instant retaliation and isolated strikes. Americans should not expect one battle, but a lengthy campaign, unlike any other we have ever seen. It may include dramatic strikes, visible on TV, and covert operations, secret even in success. We will starve terrorists of funding, turn them one against another, drive them from place to place, until there is no refuge or no rest. And we will pursue nations that provide aid or safe haven to terrorism. Every nation, in every region, now has a decision to make. Either you are with us, or you are with the terrorists. From this day forward, any nation that continues to harbor or support terrorism will be regarded by the United States as a hostile regime.

Problem
Stream

Policy
Stream

Our nation has been put on notice: We are not immune from attack. We will take defensive measures against terrorism to protect Americans. Today, dozens of federal departments and agencies, as well as state and local governments, have responsibilities affecting homeland security. These efforts must be coordinated at the highest level. So tonight I announce the creation of a Cabinet-level position reporting directly to me—the Office of Homeland Security.

Solution

And tonight I also announce a distinguished American to lead this effort, to strengthen American security: a military veteran, an effective governor, a true patriot, a trusted friend—Pennsylvania's Tom Ridge. He will lead, oversee and coordinate a comprehensive national strategy to safeguard our country against terrorism, and respond to any attacks that may come.

Interpretation:
Keep the
Policy
Window
Open!

These measures are essential. But the only way to defeat terrorism as a threat to our way of life is to stop it. . . .

Source: President George W. Bush, September 20, 2001, Address to a Joint Session of Congress and the American People, www.whitehouse.gov, accessed August 16, 2007

THE PRESIDENT AS AGENDA SETTER

The presidency has witnessed an ever-expanding role in shaping the policy agenda. In the nineteenth century, presidents tended to be literalists, who generally exercised the powers enumerated in the Constitution and had limited implied powers. Congress and state government leaders were more likely policy leaders than was the president.

Presidential powers expanded in the twentieth century. A protector of the people, Theodore Roosevelt's "bully pulpit" exemplifies presidential **stewardship**. President Woodrow Wilson renewed the tradition of presidents delivering a State of the Union Address to Congress. FDR used "fireside chats" to speak directly to the people about his policy agenda. President Kennedy used media exposure and the backdrop of Cape Canaveral, Florida, to deliver a speech placing lunar exploration on the policy agenda. He indicated that America would reach the moon before the end of the 1960s. Through this speech, Kennedy was able to shape the policy agenda beyond his own presidency. Similarly, President Obama has used the power of political speech in his quest to establish a long-term policy agenda for economic stimulus and free market regulation.

Eroding public support generally limits a president's ability to shape agendas. Despite his speaking ability, Ronald Reagan could not convince the public that limiting social welfare was a legitimate agenda item. Reagan succeeded in reducing the growth of welfare expenditures, but he was unable to enact many of his ambitious free market ideas.

In foreign policy, the president is frequently offered greater deference due to his role as commander in chief. Political scientist Aaron Wildavsky discussed this phenomenon in his **two presidencies thesis**: The presidency was really both a foreign policy presidency and a domestic policy presidency. In foreign policy, the president would likely have greater power in setting the agenda and in formulating policy. At times, the president can choose particular foreign policy agenda items with a high likelihood of success, but choosing wisely is important. President Lyndon B. Johnson's Vietnam policy drew public ire.

CONGRESS AND THE POLICY AGENDA

Congress is composed of 535 elected legislators, serving different constituencies and possessing different policy priorities. Through political compromise, a network of committees, and legislative gamesmanship, legislators establish some form of policy agenda. Unlike the presidency, Congress lacks strong leadership providing clear guidance on policy priorities and agenda items. Congressional committees and membership impact the agenda-setting process. Due to the process by which Congress formulates policy, many agenda items never become public policy. As the presidential powers in establishing the policy agenda have grown, Congress's powers in this area have tended to wane a bit. Congress has tried to reassert its power in establishing the policy agenda.

In 1995, for the first time in decades, the Republican Party gained control of both the U.S. Senate and U.S. House of Representatives. They used this opportunity to promote their Contract with America—an attempt to frame the policy agenda in a way that was significantly different from that of then-President Bill Clinton. In 2007, the Democratic Party regained control of both houses of Congress. The Democrats have attempted to use their new power to reframe the domestic and international policy agenda.

CONGRESSIONAL–EXECUTIVE RELATIONS AND AGENDA SETTING

Congressional–Executive relations play a role in agenda setting, as well as in other elements of the policy-making process. In the agenda-setting process, presidents are particularly interested in advancing agenda items that will have a reasonable chance of becoming policy. In order to accomplish this goal, the president often lards his agenda with items that will be appealing to legislators seeking to bring benefits back to their constituents.

The president's task is complicated: First, the president's agenda is often national in scope, whereas legislators are interested in local benefit. Second, different terms of office impact the time horizons of legislators. Third, although the president faces term limits, members of Congress and the Senate do not. Assuming they are reelected, members of Congress may serve for decades. Finally, the president's agenda-setting ability is complicated by **divided government**. When the president and the majority of Congress represent different political parties, the agenda-setting process becomes complicated.

COURTS AND THE POLICY AGENDA

Traditionally, the courts used narrowly defined legal reasoning known as **constitutionalism**, steering the court away from many policy entanglements. Nowadays, the courts are more inclined to operate on principles of **judicial positivism**, using legal reasoning to determine the substantive meaning and expected outcomes of policy.

The transition to positivism gained momentum in *Lochner v. New York* (1905). In *Schecter Poultry v. United States* (1935), the Court made a critical decision regarding the constitutionality of President Franklin D. Roosevelt's (FDR's) New Deal legislation. In this case, FDR essentially asked the Court to support his policy agenda—creating a national government role in economic management and social welfare provision. Although the Court effectively denied the policy, it *de facto* created a judicial agenda-setting role. In *West Coast Hotel v. Parrish* (1937), the Court effectively reversed its position on New Deal legislation and supported FDR's policy agenda.

The courts deal with policy areas emergent in legal cases brought before them. In this sense, the courts remain *reactive* rather than *proactive* in their agenda-setting activities. Courts move slower in shaping the policy agenda, largely because their decisions are based on **legal precedence**. Although rare, the courts may reinterpret, nullify, or confirm decisions made in the past in relation to new cases brought before them.

At times, the court establishes the agenda *prior to* legislative or executive action. Civil rights provides a good example of the courts shaping the policy agenda. *Brown v. Board of Education, Topeka, Kansas* (1954) served as a catalyst for policy change by deciding that "separate is inherently unequal." By reversing court precedent, the Supreme Court put desegregation on the policy agenda. More than that, the Court opened the agenda to a new dialogue on the meaning of equality—a dialogue that continues to this day. The courts have increasingly become major actors in establishing and advancing the policy agenda, particularly in areas where the elected branches have proven reticent to become involved.

PRESSURE GROUPS AND AGENDA SETTING

Pressure groups use group cohesiveness and structure to influence the policy agenda:

- Pressure groups often have well-developed organizations designed to aggressively recruit new members. Members are often attracted to the select benefits of membership, such as information and solidarity.
- Pressure groups often have a tremendous capacity to raise money from their membership and other interested parties. Monetary resources are used to maintain the group organization, and to support political campaigns of candidates sharing their views. The contributions buy access to political elites and the chance to explain group views about the policy agenda.
- Pressure groups collect and organize information, simplifying the decisionmaking process for policy leaders. Congress, state legislatures, and local government representatives have staff researchers and personal advisers, but the capacity of these personnel is often insufficient in meeting the growing demands on elected decision-makers. **Think tanks**— pressure group organizations devoted almost solely to policy research— often tap the intellectual resources of leading scholars, producing highly detailed information and position papers disseminated to elected officials. Elected officials may use the bite-sized information provided by pressure groups to carry forward a policy agenda.

Large economic groups, such as General Electric, have tremendous resources for gaining access to elected officials and shaping policy agendas. Multiple points of contact in the policy process—contact with elected officials, public administrators, and policy clientele groups—increases the likelihood of successful issue framing and agenda setting.

Some interest groups have more limited resources, but given the nature of the times, changes in cultural values, and public opinion, they might succeed in shaping the policy agenda. A notable example is Ralph Nader's Common Cause. Automotive safety was a growing concern in the 1960s due to horrific traffic fatalities. The circumstances contributed to Common Cause's success in shaping the auto safety policy agenda despite the lack of a large resource base and highly sophisticated group organization. Common Cause was one of the first noteworthy **public interest groups**.

BUREAUCRACY AND AGENDA SETTING

Bureaucracy plays a major role in shaping the policy agenda. Existing government agencies and policies are rarely completely successful. A policy that might have worked last year may require fine-tuning in succeeding years, prompting public sector bureaucrats to pursue new ways of delivering goods and services desired by elected leaders, pressure groups, and clientele.

Bureaucratic agenda setting is highly dependent on the *type* of agency and the *age* of the agency. In *Inside Bureaucracy* (1967), Anthony Downs observed that older agencies are often populated by bureaucratic **conservers**, who focus on agency survival rather than agency change or growth. New agencies are more likely to have younger and more enthusiastic public sector bureaucrats, eager to produce a positive change in society and willing to refocus the policy agenda in order to achieve their goals.

MEDIA AND AGENDA SETTING

The media spends significant time focusing on government successes, but perhaps even greater attention on policy failures. It often also focuses attention on problems for which there is no proposed solution. In each instance, the information presented to the attentive public shapes public opinion, if only for a very short time. The media can shape the policy agenda by heightening awareness of problems that could be solved through government policy.

A recent example of media involvement in agenda setting relates to child abductions. Abductions are a serious problem in the United States; sadly, often associated with child molestation and murder. In the summer of 2002, a young Southern California girl was abducted while playing in front of her family home. The girl was discovered within 48 hours, sexually molested and murdered. Due to several abduction cases that summer, the media focused attention on a serious problem that was not being sufficiently addressed by public policy. The media effectively framed the issue and established the policy agenda for new strategies such as the "Amber Alert" system, which was designed to notify citizens, police, and media as soon as an abduction was reported. The immediate results of the Amber Alert system included the successful recovery of abducted children and the capture of several suspected child kidnappers.

ELECTIONS AND THE POLICY AGENDA

Major electoral shifts related to political, social, or economic turbulence can also play a significant role in shaping the policy agenda. Termed **realignment** by political scientist V. O. Key, electoral shifts produce overwhelming and long-lasting majorities for a particular political party and have a tremendous impact on agenda setting. In realigning elections, it is more likely that the president and congressional majorities will share similar policy agendas. Political scientists argue that realignment has been replaced by **dealignment**, characterized by divided government, weaker presidencies, and smaller and less stable congressional majorities. Post election, a majority party often hails their new electoral mandate, but dealignment indicates that electoral outcomes will probably not result in lasting impacts on the policy agenda.

CULTURAL CHANGE AND AGENDA SETTING

In *Culture Shift in Advanced Industrial Society* (1990), Ronald Inglehart documented the rise of the Baby Boom generation, which brought with it a new set of values and policy preferences. The Baby Boom generation and subsequent age cohorts tend to be less materialistically driven and more concerned about quality of life issues and political and social equality. With a different view of what government *ought* to do, generational differences have shaped what government *does* or *does not* do.

Arguably, agenda setting is related to perceived individual or collective risk. All aspects of life carry some level of risk, but its meaning and acceptability is politically and culturally defined. Political and cultural values play a tremendous role in defining unacceptable risks. Political processes and participants shape the policy agenda to manage these risks. As politics and culture change, so too do perceptions of risk, frequently altering perspectives of what government *ought* or *ought not* do.

BIASES IN POLITICAL PARTICIPATION AND AGENDA SETTING

Anne Schneider and Helen Ingram have written extensively about the role of **target populations** in agenda setting. Political and social values play a tremendous role in the labeling of different groups in society. Drug-addicted individuals and criminals are often labeled "undeserving" members of society. Individuals or groups labeled "undeserving" recipients of public policy benefits often have lower levels of education and income. With limited political and social capital, the "undeserving" are often systematically excluded from equal participation in agenda setting.

Reflect back on group perceptions reported in Chapter 3—it is clear that individuals often view groups differently. The issues represented by certain groups have variable chances of success in becoming part of the policy agenda when compared with others. In large part, the ability of the clientele groups to legitimize their need is shaped by deeply ingrained cultural norms and by socioeconomic biases. There is a strong cultural and economic bias in agenda setting. Systematic bias in public policy making creates barriers to equal participation and may pose a very serious challenge to the long-term legitimacy of a democracy.

EXPLAINING AGENDA SETTING

Rational–Comprehensive Model

Agenda setting often involves the use of rational–comprehensive principles. This approach aids in the understanding of phenomena. Through the use of scientific principles, policy analysts manipulate phenomena so as to produce desired

outcomes. The model tends to ignore the questions of *ought*, leaving those issues for elected officials and the citizenry to debate. In its purest form, the rational–comprehensive approach is often used by public administrators in the
agenda-setting process; less so by elected officials, political parties, pressure
groups, or individual citizens. Unfortunately, the model is subject to misuse by
individuals and groups falsely claiming objectivity in analysis.

Individuals and groups who are left-of-center politically generally do not
find fault with the use of the scientific aspects of the rational–comprehensive
approach. The issue of an expanded role for government is less of a concern if
the rational–comprehensive model is used to limit the inequalities found in society and to advance the principles of modern liberalism. Modern liberalism
generally requires the use of rational–comprehensive agenda setting in identifying and solving economic, political, and social inequality.

For individuals and groups who are right-of-center politically, the rational–
comprehensive model is generally disliked, seen as a tool used to justify the
growth of government. Government involvement is viewed as a constraint on
individual freedom, particularly economic freedom. By relying on the rational–comprehensive model to set policy agendas, the normative questions
surrounding the proper role of government are assumed away, replaced by assumed objective scientific findings. For the classical liberal, the limits of government policy and hence the policy agenda should be determined a priori
rather than a posteriori.

Despite their criticisms of the model, right-of-center individuals and
groups use the rational–comprehensive approach when it fits their purpose. A
good example of this is the invasion of Iraq in 2003. A tremendous amount of
evidential material regarding Iraqi violations of United Nations weapons-related
resolutions was used to establish a "rational" defense policy agenda and to then
prosecute a war. Later, the empirical evidence was found to be questionable as
to its validity and reliability.

Concerns regarding the use of the rational–comprehensive approach to
set the agenda are often moot. The best laid plans, the best evidence discovered
and presented, often has less to do with what becomes part of the policy
agenda than do the political and cultural constraints. Although elements of the
rational–comprehensive approach can help advance an agenda item, it appears
unlikely that the rational–comprehensive approach will ever be the definitive
element in the agenda-setting process. Emotive reasons often play a larger role
in shaping the policy agenda than do hard "facts."

Institutionalism

The structure of government plays a tremendous role in explaining how certain
items become part of the political agenda, whereas other issues never become
a topic of serious discussion for elected and appointed government decision-
makers. The general institutional powers of the branches of government were
initially established by the U.S. Constitution. For the most part, the U.S. Constitution was designed to limit the ability of the federal government to get many

things accomplished. The checks and balances that shape the relationships of the branches, the staggered terms of office, and multiple, often overlapping, constituencies make it very difficult for a unified policy agenda to be established. Institutionalism can tell us a great deal about why so many issues never make it through a policy window and onto the policy agenda.

In order to become part of the policy agenda, most issues are subject to debate within and between the branches of government. Debate frequently produces political compromise—a position agreed upon by a majority of decision-makers regarding the meaning and role of proposed agenda items. If a compromise cannot be reached, or if the item is not seen as a pressing part of the policy agenda, then it will likely fail to gain traction.

A good example is the issue of sex education in public elementary and secondary schools. In the 1980s, members of the Religious Right framed the issue in terms of a particular form of Judeo–Christian morality, arguing that public school sex education ought to teach abstinence because it was morally wrong to have premarital sex. Conversely, political Liberals argued that teaching abstinence for the aforementioned reasons violated the First Amendment— abstinence for moral reasons was a religious choice and should not be a part of the public school curriculum. Instead, public school sex education should focus on methods of avoiding unwanted pregnancies and preventing the spread of sexually transmitted diseases. The debate became so contentious between individuals on the political right and those on the left that the issue as it was framed did not become a part of the policy agenda.

In the twenty-first century, abstinence education has resurfaced as both an agenda item and as public policy. How did it achieve this status? In large part because it was framed in a way in which there could be some basic agreement within and between government institutions. Abstinence education was framed in terms of women's public health. Evidence suggests that adolescent sexual involvement can lead to increased risk for cervical cancer in women, partially due to the transmission of the Human Papilio Virus (HPV). Additionally, the use of prophylactics has been shown to be ineffective in managing the transmission of many sexually transmitted diseases. In other words, the risks associated with sexual behavior among young people may now be seen as unacceptable by a significant portion of society—at least, significant enough to open an agenda policy window for this issue, albeit through alternative policy channels. In a new twist, science has created a vaccine for HPV, which if effective, would weaken the pro-abstinence education position by changing how the issue is framed as an agenda item.

Garbage Can Theory

In his book, *Agendas, Alternatives, and Public Policy,* John Kingdon delineates the value of the garbage can model in explaining the agenda-setting process. There are any number of good ideas for public policy, continually proposed by pressure groups, think tanks, political staffers, public administrators, and interested citizens. Why is it that some policy issues are adopted as part of the policy agenda and other ideas remain in the shadows? Kingdon argues that issues and policy solutions arrive on the policy agenda almost by chance. Emergencies, unanticipated events, and the ever-changing tide of politics cause policymakers to *react* to conditions and needs. When the need arises and when circumstances thrust items onto the policy agenda, there is a frantic search for practical and reasonable-sounding solutions.

The garbage can theory argues that, desirable or not, the agenda-setting process is reactive. In some ways, the garbage can theory demonstrates the benefits of a policy agenda-setting structure that is flexible enough to address unanticipated needs. In another sense, it may explain why some issues are considered at a particular point in time, whereas other issues, which may be of long-term importance, lack the political and social momentum to become part of the policy agenda.

Group Theory

Pluralism, or group theory, claims that the agenda-setting process is a highly competitive arena where pressure groups jockey for position. Pressure groups are primarily concerned with obtaining either selective benefits for their membership or more generalized benefits they believe to be in the public's best interest. In either case, pressure groups seek to shape the agenda in a way that is most beneficial to their goals. The policy agenda is largely a function of which pressure groups—regional, national, or international—are most successful in advancing their interests.

In *End of Liberalism* (1969), political scientist Theodore Lowi, a famous critic of the potentially destructive nature of pressure group domination, described a condition known as **hyperpluralism** in which an ever-expanding number of pressure groups lobby political and administrative decision-makers to shape policy in a manner that best suits their groups' needs. Agenda setting under the condition of hyperpluralism would be driven by the most well-organized, financed, and articulate pressure groups. Democratic policy-making within the structure of a representative government would be distorted, producing biased policy outcomes. Group theory helps us to understand why certain issues dominate the policy agenda, whereas other issues are less frequently discussed or largely ignored.

In the mid-1980s, Mothers Against Drunk Driving (MADD) became a well-recognized pressure group intent on limiting adolescent alcohol-related deaths on the highways and roads. Over time, the group became a powerful pressure group in Washington, actively lobbying Congress to address MADD issues. The pressure group was very successful in shaping the policy agenda. Federal, state, and local authorities responded with education programs to discourage teenage drunk driving.

During the same period, other groups that were less organized, less powerful, and who were not part of dominant target populations were often unable to shape the agenda. For example, in the 1980s Native American tribes fought to open tribal lands to gambling casinos. The money raised would be used to improve the social and economic conditions of tribal members. Increased resources would result in improved health care services and educational opportunities. Nevertheless, the tribes had limited resources in their effort to set one aspect of the agenda. It took several years of lobbying Congress and several court battles—generally, coming up against powerful business pressure groups who viewed Native American casinos as a direct threat to their interests—before Native American gambling became a more prominent part of the policy agenda.

Lessons Learned from Chapter 5

SPECIFICS

- Issue framing and "open" policy windows contribute to the successful adoption of an issue onto the policy agenda.
- Public (e.g., Congress) and private institutions (e.g., the media) play important but varying roles in shaping the policy agenda.
- Cultural change impacts the policy choices of citizens and impacts agenda-setting. Agenda-setting is a function of what citizens think government *ought* or *ought not* do, which will impact what government *does* or *does not* do.
- The *rational–comprehensive, institutional, garbage can* and *group* theories of public policy offer four very different, but convincing, explanations of policy agenda-setting.

THE BIG PICTURE

Agenda-setting is the first step in the policy process. Before an issue can be acted upon, it must become a recognized part of the policy agenda. Additionally, the issue must be prioritized. Although part of the policy agenda, some issues are given relatively low priority, whereas other policy areas are given much greater priority. How an issue becomes part of the policy agenda may play a role in shaping its prioritization. Issues that are related to perceived emergencies or high risks are often given much higher policy priority. Additionally, issues that are placed on the policy agenda by popular presidents are often seen as important national goals that must be met. Conversely, issues viewed as of parochial or local concern, assuming they become part of the policy agenda, may not be considered extremely high priorities.

A variety of individuals and groups shape the policy agenda. Most notably, the constitutional branches of the national government play extremely important roles in agenda-setting. It is important, however, to realize that each branch of government has different powers, different constituencies, and different limitations in terms of tenure of office. Institutional checks and balances complicate matters further.

In addition to the constitutionally established branches of government, there are other important factors to consider when thinking about the agenda-setting process. Political parties establish competing policy agendas that will presumably be enacted upon following the party's victory in elections. Pressure groups lobby Congress, the president, and public administrative agencies with the intent of shaping the policy agendas of elected officials. Additionally, pressure groups may be party to legal suit or may submit *amicus curiae* briefs with the intent of shaping judicial interpretations and decision-making.

Finally, it is important to consider the potential for inherent inequalities in the agenda-setting process. In theory, all citizens and their policy concerns should receive equal hearing and consideration. In fact, political, social, and economic limitations result in inequality within the agenda-setting process. Some individuals and groups have greater influence in shaping the policy agenda than do others. This is due, in part, to deeply ingrained cultural perspectives about various types of individuals and groups within society. In essence, some individuals and groups may be consciously or subconsciously viewed as less deserving of the benefits of public policy than are others. The result is that some policy agenda items are ignored because they are not seen as fully worthy of government attention. It is a serious concern for democratic theorists pondering the possibility of a fully fair and equal agenda-setting process.

Key Terms

conservers	policy window
constitutionalism	politics stream
dealignment	problem stream
divided government	public interest groups
focusing event	realignment
hyperpluralism	stewardship
judicial positivism	target population
legal precedence	think tanks
policy stream	two presidencies thesis

Questions for Study

1. What is issue framing? How does framing impact agenda-setting? Provide an example.
2. Identify and discuss three institutional or individual actors who, according to the text, often play prominent roles in agenda setting.
3. Using three policy models, explain the agenda-setting process using a policy example.

Bibliography

Aristotle. 1985. *Nichomachean ethics.* Translated by Terence Irwin. Indianapolis: Hackett.
Dearing, J., and E. Rogers. 1996. *Agenda setting.* Thousand Oaks, CA: Sage.
Downs, A. 1967. *Inside bureaucracy.* Boston: Little, Brown.

Inglehart, R. 1990. *Culture shift in advanced industrial society.* Princeton, NJ: Princeton University Press.

Key, V. O. 1966. *The responsible electorate: Rationality in presidential voting (1936–1960).* Cambridge, MA: Harvard University Press.

Kingdon, J. 2001. A model of agenda setting with applications. *Michigan State University Law Review.* 2001(2): 331–37.

_____. 2002. *Agendas, alternatives, and public policy.* New York: Longman.

Larocca, R. 2006. *The presidential agenda: sources of executive influence in Congress.* Columbus: Ohio State University Press.

Lowi, T. 1969. *The end of liberalism: Ideology, policy, and the crisis of public authority.* New York: Norton.

Nash, R. 1960. *Wilderness and the American mind.* New Haven, CT: Yale University Press.

Renaud, J. P. "Governor says bay area residents should pay overruns of bridge project." *NewBayBridge.Org* (reported from *Los Angeles Times,* www. newbaybridge.org/medianews/2004_08_17%201atimes_bridge_overruns.html (accessed September 15, 2005).

Riker, W., ed. 1993. *Agenda formation.* Ann Arbor: University of Michigan Press.

Schneider, A., and H. Ingram. 1993. Social construction of target populations: Implications for politics and policy. *American Political Science Review.* 87(2): 334–47.

_____. 1997. *Policy design for democracy.* Lawrence: University of Kansas Press.

Shilts, R., and S. Sward. 1989. "Hundreds dead in huge quake Oakland freeway collapses—bay bridge fails," *The San Francisco Chronicle,* October 18, 1.

Sigelman, L. 1979. A reassessment of the two presidencies thesis. *Journal of Politics.* 41: 1,195–205.

Wildavsky, A. 1966. The two presidencies. *Trans-Action.* 4: 7–14.

Court Cases

Brown v. Board of Education 347 U.S. 483 (1954)

Dred Scott v. Sanford 60 U.S. 393 (1857)

Lochner v. New York 198 U.S. 45 (1905)

Plessy v. Ferguson 163 U.S. 537 (1896)

Schechter Poultry Corporation v. United States, 295 U.S. 495 (1935)

West Coast Hotel Company v. Parrish, 300 U.S. 379 (1937)

6

■ ■ ■

Policy Formulation

CHAPTER OVERVIEW

Demands on government are legitimized through the agenda-setting process. In the policy formulation process attention is focused on outlining alternative methods of meeting demands. Policy formulation is one of the most challenging processes government faces. When an issue is adopted as an agenda item, there is often a sense of urgency. Policy formulation is our attention at work as we identify what government *ought* or *ought not do*, *does* or *does not do*.

   The specific goals for the chapter are:

- Discuss *how* policy is formulated.
- Identify the major participants in policy formulation.
- Use policy theories to explain policy formulation.

HOW IS POLICY FORMULATED?

Policy formulation is the detailed process of using normative and empirical methods to define a policy goal, explore alternatives to achieve the goal, and then choose a preferred policy solution. Defining, exploring, choosing, and planning are the basic elements of policy formulation. The issue of defining a policy goal is often highly normative. For example, classical liberals might say that health care ought not be provided by government; a modern liberal would likely say just the opposite. Given these divergent views, it comes as no surprise that policy goal definition is challenging for policy-makers. Through political compromise, Congress and the president create generally defined policy goals. Other participants in policy formulation, such as bureaucrats and pressure groups, often focus on specific policy goals.

   Once a policy goal has been defined, the process of exploring policy alternatives begins. Policy analysts play a major role in identifying alternatives to achieve particular policy goals. Whether quantitative or qualitative methods are used to explore and identify policy alternatives, the primary concern of policy analysis is to explore various ranges of potential policy benefit (i.e., to what degree and in what manner will the policy goal be achieved?) in relation to various levels of financial commitment.

Economic analysis aids in the uniform comparison of alternatives because money-based comparisons of benefits and costs is understandable. For example, if I have to choose between a gyro served at a restaurant on one side of campus and a sandwich served at another restaurant on the other side of campus, I can make the choice on the basis of a couple of factors. What are the goals I am trying to achieve? I am trying to relieve hunger and I want to enjoy the meal. In my mind, a gyro is (at least) twice as good as a sandwich. Additionally, the sandwich costs twice as much. So, two strikes against the sandwich idea. I'm heading for the gyro—my plan in action. The whole process was quantified in terms of costs and benefits, and there was a goal and there were at least two alternatives, the third being that I would choose not to eat. (See Photo 6.1.)

Policy analysis is a bit more complicated than my lunch choice. The goals are often vaguely defined; a myriad of choices exist; and, multiple actors make collective choices, which complicates decision-making. For example, let us say that a city wants to clean up its air pollution problem—its goal. As you might guess, there are several causes of air pollution, not all of which could be solved quickly. So, the city decides to narrow its goal to just limiting air pollution produced by city buses. There are a series of choices to address the problem, two of which might be: (1) get rid of all city buses permanently, (2) replace old buses with new buses that do not produce air pollution. First, the policy analyst would have to determine the costs and benefits of each alternative. Second, assuming that alternative (2) was chosen, the policy analyst would then study and price out a series of bus configurations and compare the bus price with expected

PHOTO 6.1 Much more than an economic choice—for me, at least!

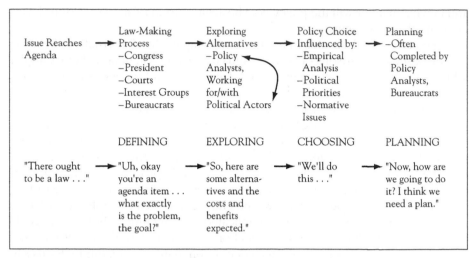

FIGURE 6.1   Policy formulation process

pollution reductions. The costs and benefits of each alternative would be compared and a choice would be made. (See Figure 6.1.)

Policy planning, the final stage in the policy formulation process, is extremely time-consuming. Policy plans are shaped by empirical analysis leading to the adoption of a particular policy alternative, built around certain assumptions about policy methods, costs, and benefits. Frequently, policy is not funded at the level assumed in analysis, forcing formulators to produce the level of expected benefit with fewer resources.

Policy planning requires that goals and methods are strictly adhered to in order to meet policy requirements. The creation of rules and procedures is, therefore, a critical part of policy planning. Planning also requires that a clear sense of future needs be determined for successful policy continuation. With long-term vision, policy planning considers the issue of **goal enlargement** or **goal drift/shift**, which occur when goals are more broadly defined over time or when policy goals evolve as policy problems change.

In the previous examples, the policy formulation was fairly simple. Imagine, however, a situation where a multitude of individuals and groups identify the goal differently, pursue different alternatives, try to then choose one of the myriad of alternatives, and then struggle to establish a policy plan. In essence, this is an uncomplicated description of the complicated process by which policy formulation occurs at the national level.[1] As a brief reminder, Chapter 4 provides a general sense of the tools used throughout the policy process.

MAJOR ACTORS IN POLICY FORMULATION

A variety of institutional and extrainstitutional actors are involved in policy formulation. The national-level institutional actors were discussed in earlier chapters: Congress, president, and federal judiciary. Within the institutions of government, there are also public bureaucracy and personal staffers, who play a significant role in illuminating policy alternatives for institutional actors.

Pressure groups, particularly groups that have advanced a particular policy agenda, often seek to play a role in the policy formulation process if their goals are adopted as agenda items. Interested individuals (e.g., clientele) may also contribute to policy formulation.

Congressional Policy Formulation

With its committee system, Congress is a highly specialized branch of government. In its initial stages, congressional policy formulation occurs within the confines of a committee or committees to which the policy concern has been assigned. Congressional committees then assign policy formulation responsibility to a subcommittee. Subcommittees define and explore the policy issue by requesting policy analysis or more detailed policy exploration by associated administrative agencies. The **Congressional Budget Office** (CBO), **Congressional Research Service** (CRS), and **General Accounting Office** (GAO) conduct a significant portion of the technical work for congressional policy formulators.

Created in 1974 to help Congress establish greater control over the budgeting process, the CBO studies the costs-related factors associated with policy formulation and may, if requested, discuss the financial feasibility of policies proposed in legislative bills. The CBO also analyzes policy proposals within the president's budget as reported to Congress. Using its own economic and budgetary assumptions, the CBO studies the president's budget to determine the feasibility of proposed policies in terms of costs and benefits compared with other policy goals. Ultimately, public policies cost money; therefore, policy formulation is tempered by budgetary constraints and the fiscal demands of other policy priorities. Given budget limitation, CBO evidence regarding new policy feasibility is particularly critical.

Initially created in 1914 as the Legislative Reference Service, the **Congressional Research Service** (renamed following the 1970 Legislative Reorganization Act) conducts the bulk of policy research for members of Congress and congressional committees. The CRS deals with policy areas in both domestic and foreign policy and is committed to conducting timely and impartial analyses of existing policy areas as well as providing information and assistance for elected representatives seeking to build effective policy in new policy areas.

> CRS is organized into five interdisciplinary research divisions: American Law; Domestic Social Policy; Foreign Affairs, Defense and Trade; Government and Finance; and Resources, Science and Industry. Within each division, CRS staff are organized into smaller sections, which focus on specific areas of public policy.[2]

The CRS plays a critical role in congressional policy formulation. CRS personnel help legislators craft policy, provide assistance in the drafting of legislation, and aid in the development of committee hearing questions and topics.

Created in 1921, the GAO focuses attention on policy evaluation and auditing, which is closer to the end of the policy process rather than the early stages of policy formulation. Nevertheless, GAO analyses of past policy events and outcomes can have a tremendous impact on future policy formulation. The GAO's recommendations can help policy formulators avoid potential pitfalls that could lead to policy failure. Additionally, the GAO's auditing process provides guidance to policy formulators as they consider ways of defining measurable policy goals.

The personal staff of congresspersons also play a role in policy formulation. As elected representatives, members of Congress often contemplate policy formulation in light of the parochial demands of constituents as well as the national interests. Congressional staffers tend to be more attuned to constituency and contribute to the policy formulation process by crafting legislation to meet local needs. Staffers make recommendations regarding committee hearing proceedings and develop questions their boss (i.e., the elected representative) might consider asking during congressional committee hearings. Staffers identify expert witnesses whose testimony will help the elected representative promote particular policy alternatives.

Staffers often act as liaisons between elected officials and government agencies—both the aforementioned congressional agencies and Executive Branch agencies—requesting information and reports that will advance a representative's policy preferences. With a multitude of time commitments, congresspersons rely heavily on their staff in the policy formulation process.

Congressional policy formulation is often highly detailed, often conducted within committees and subcommittees. In the end, however, choices must be made based on the exploratory studies conducted and analyzed, and legislative bills must be reported to the parent chamber for a floor vote. In the floor vote process, representatives who were not a part of the detailed committee policy formulation discussions and debates are able to consider the proposed policy and must decide to support it as is, amend it, or reject it. Amendments may be made for normative reasons—for example, a philosophical disagreement regarding a policy—or perhaps just pure self-interest. The Senate has very limited rules of debate and proposed policies are much more likely to be assailed by a stream of germane and nongermane amendments, undoing months of committee research intended to define, explore, and choose a good policy plan. Congressional policy formulation allows for a great deal of normatively driven debate and reformulation of policy proposals. Although an important part of policy-making, these "last minute" reconfigurations of public policy formulation may actually increase the likelihood of policy failure or, at the very least, reduce its effectiveness.

Presidential Policy Formulation

In the nineteenth century, the president did not have the powers nor the bureaucratic structures needed to help him in the area of domestic policy formulation. In the twentieth century, however, the powers of the presidency in the domestic policy formulation arena grew tremendously, and public bureaucracies sprouted up to help the president accomplish his new policy tasks.

In 1920, Congress established the Bureau of the Budget (BOB), giving the president the power to submit a proposed national budget annually. A larger role in budgeting meant that the president also had greater say in the policy formulation process. Budget allocation proposals often translate as policy choices.

In the mid-1930s, the **Brownlow Commission on Economy and Efficiency** was tasked with determining the administrative support needs of a modern presidency. The commission recommended the establishment of a major bureaucratic support structure now known as the **Executive Office of the President (EOP)**. Currently, EOP contains more than 16 different suboffices and departments.[3] In establishing EOP, Congress and the president recognized the chief executive's growing responsibility in policy formulation. EOP policy analysts develop public policies for the president's policy agenda, eventually proposed in draft form for congressional review, revisions, and approval or disapproval. The structure of EOP facilitates effective policy formulation.

Courts and Policy Formulation

The Court studies public policy formulation in terms of its impact on individual rights and its breadth and potential impact on intergovernmental relationships. In the 1950s and 1960s, the Court began to more actively constrain policy formulation that limited individual rights or negatively impacted citizen privacy. The Court saw a role for itself in examining the differential impact of public policy on minority groups and through its decision process let policy-makers in the elected branches and public bureaucracy focus greater attention on the need for greater equity in public policy.

Policy could be nondiscriminatory in a legal sense, but could unintentionally produce greater inequality. For modern liberals, the Court's role in shaping equitable outcomes, effectively demanding an emphasis on social justice, is viewed as a positive development. By focusing on policy formulation that produces *fair outcomes,* the judiciary demonstrates concern for *all* members of society, particularly those individuals and groups not effectively represented through the political process (Fredericksen 1971).

Reviewing public policies and the policy formulation process, the courts seek to confirm or negate the constitutionality of policies, essentially guiding policy-makers' future plans. At times, elected policy-makers have resisted the judiciary's role in policy formulation, leading judges to establish court-mandated policy goals, supervise policy implementation, and scrutinize policy outcomes.

The scope of national public policy formulation is impacted by the courts' vision of the proper scope of powers of the national government in relation to state governments—in other words, the federal relationship. In the nineteenth century, the national courts generally adopted a *dual federalism* model. National public policy was limited to the powers of the national government as enumerated in the Constitution. Over time, the national courts envisioned a broader role for the national government. Commerce Clause decisions in the 1930s effectively expanded the role of national public policy in shaping the economic and social conditions of individuals within states. The courts legitimized cooperative federalism (see Chapter 10), with overlapping state and national policy responsibilities.

In the last twenty years, however, the Supreme Court has sought to limit the scope of national public policy through the application of the Tenth and Eleventh Amendments to the U.S. Constitution. The changing judicial philosophy of the Court, a function of Reagan and George H. W. and George Bush judicial appointments, might result in the national government sidestepping policy areas out of deference to "state's rights."

A good policy-maker will understand the role of the courts and legal precedents, hoping to avoid potential pitfalls. Policy formulation is a proper place to design public policy that will succeed rather than be found unconstitutional in application.

Interest Groups and Policy Formulation

Established interest groups frequently employ policy analysts who formulate policy alternatives. Policy analysts are able to access and comprehend government data that serve as the basis of policy recommendations. If an interest group is able to get an issue on the policy agenda, then they are likely to gain access to the formulation process, offering testimony, presenting pre-drafted legislative bills, and detailing prospective costs and benefits of attractive policy alternatives.

Interest groups use similar strategies to shape presidential policy formulation, although direct access to the president is often more limited. Interest group leaders may serve as members of a presidential commission or task force, developing policy solutions for pet agenda items. The political preferences of a sitting president determines the membership of executive commissions and task forces—not all interest groups have equal access to Executive Branch policy formulation.

Interest groups may influence policy formulation through the courts. As a party to a court case, interest groups try to shape policy formulation via litigation. If not a party to a case, interest groups may choose to file *amicus curiae* briefs, detailing reasons why the case should be decided in a particular manner. The *amicus* brief might include policy alternatives consistent with the group's preferences.

Many of the details associated with policy formulation are written by bureaucrats and codified into a system of rules and regulations known as administrative law. The process of rule-making is subject to oversight by the three branches of government and is designed to respond to public concerns, often expressed during administrative rule-making hearings or meetings. Interest groups have the motivation and expertise needed to attend and actively participate in the rule-making process.

Public Bureaucracies and Policy Formulation

Departments and agencies within public bureaucracy are often staffed by individuals with particular policy interests. It is not surprising to find that they are often advocates for a particular policy direction. Bureaucrats may intentionally or inadvertently imprint policy with their personal values. Although bureaucrats are often careerists, there are changing patterns of employment. Individuals serving in key roles in bureaucratic policy formulation retire, replaced by individuals with different values, beliefs, and opinions. Personnel changes may lead to differences in policy formulation.

The U.S. Forest Service (USFS) and U.S. Bureau of Land Management (BLM) are two examples of how personnel changes impacted agency rules and procedures. In the early twentieth century, both agencies were driven largely by the traditional interests of logging, livestock grazing, and mining. Public bureaucrats who operated these agencies created a system of rules that made the public lands accessible to their clientele. By the late twentieth century, the USFS and BLM were beginning to change. A new generation of organizational leaders, often more postmaterialist in their value orientation, were less friendly to traditional interests, preferring instead to see the public forests and lands preserved for the use of *all* citizens. The new bureaucratic elites tended to be more sensitive to the issue of environmental protection. Building on statutory changes such as the Wilderness Act of 1964, bureaucrats crafted administrative rules and regulations, guided by new values and scientific evidence, advancing efforts at environmental protection.

International Influences on Policy Formulation

We live in a world that is being transformed by globalism. Domestic policy formulation is heavily influenced by international bodies, such as the United Nations, and treaty agreements made with other nations. The influence of internationalism on domestic public policy became more evident following the collapse of the Soviet Union and other Eastern Bloc nations. The United States, identified as the last remaining superpower, found itself operating in a multilateral world rather than the bilateral context of the Cold War.

The Cold War ended during the George H. W. Bush administration and the new multilateralism quickly became apparent. In 1992, President Bush attended the Rio Summit, an international conference dealing with world environmental conditions and the need to reduce greenhouse emissions. Representing the most economically powerful nation, President Bush faced a highly contentious situation. Although evidence regarding the volume of U.S. greenhouse gas emissions was not seriously contended, proposals for improving environmental conditions would have seriously impacted U.S. domestic policy in areas ranging from agriculture to energy use. Farmers would be forced to reduce or eliminate their use of high-nitrogen fertilizers, which damage aquatic life in streams, rivers, and estuaries. The use of fossil energy would be severely limited.

In another bow to globalism President Clinton signed the North American Free Trade Alliance (NAFTA) in 1993, an agreement initially developed during the George H. W. Bush administration. The agreement has impacted the domestic economy in a number of ways, lowering trade barriers to Canadian and Mexican goods flowing into the United States and vice versa. The treaty will likely impact the ability of domestic industries to shape economic policies. A new system built on the ideas of "free market" capitalism will force domestic economies to be less reliant on government social and economic policy, widening exposure to international competition. The emergence of globalism means that policy formulation must consider goals and impacts beyond national boundaries: Does the policy as formulated advance an international policy agenda or work against the forces of globalism? Policy formulation will have to balance national interests with the general principles of ratified treaties promoting cooperative economic, social, and political alliances with other nations.

Globalism makes policy formulation very challenging. Elected representatives serve at the behest of American voters, yet they must also consider other responsibilities that extend beyond the nation's borders. At times, that means putting aside domestic interests in order to receive the benefits associated with being part of the global community.

Globalism and its impact on policy formulation are applauded by both classical and modern liberals, but for very different reasons. Classical liberalism is based on a belief that government should primarily work to preserve our basic individual freedoms—our right to life, liberty, and property. Beyond that, government should not take an active role in economic planning or social engineering. Many free market capitalists argue that classical liberal principles are consistent with their intentions. The use of economic barriers to free trade are seen as examples of government efforts to restrict the economic freedom of individuals and corporations to pursue their economic self-interest and expand their property in ways they find desirable. Therefore, the new globalism—particularly efforts to open markets and eliminate barriers to free trade—is welcomed by many classical liberals/free market advocates. Conversely, global policies that restrict free trade (e.g., international environmental agreements) are rejected by classical liberals.

Modern liberals tend to see globalism as one solution to international economic disparity. Economic and social disparity is viewed as a significant source of global tension, which manifests itself in the form of international and civil wars, terrorism, starvation, malnutrition, disease proliferation, and various other social, economic, and political maladies. International aid organizations and the redistribution of income are seen as possible solutions to grave inequalities. A world without borders—a world focused on the principles of global justice—is seen by modern liberal thinkers as one solution to the many tensions that exist in the world today. Given the complexities of working with multiple national governments, there is movement toward a more powerful role for global governance bodies to formulate overarching policies. The zero-sum game of nation-focused policies may work against modern liberal policy goals favoring equality, fairness, human rights, and environmental justice.

Citizen Stakeholders and Policy Formulation

Citizens can shape policy through interest group membership and elections, but they may also choose *direct* participation in the policy formulation process. Significant citizen or interest group impacts on policy formulation at the grassroots level are sometimes referred to as **bottom-up policy-making**. By way of distinction, **top down policy-making** is policy created by one level of government (frequently national and state government) and imposed on lower levels of government and citizens.

Open meeting law requirements require administrative policy-makers to seek public input and demonstrate administrative action in response to public concerns or demands. If they cannot act on the citizen input, administrators must explain why the public suggestions are not feasible. A citizen **stakeholder**—an individual who has a stake in policy formulation and outcomes (i.e., all of us, whether we take an interest or not)—may or may not be a direct beneficiary of a particular policy. Some stakeholders believe that their involvement is critical to prevent problems from arising that might influence them in a negative manner—or, ensuring that policy has some type of secondary positive benefit for them individually or the community in which they reside. Citizen stakeholders do not always attend open meeting sessions to offer hostile criticisms of public policy. For the most part, citizens are genuinely interested in policy success, but are often interested in balancing individual and collective interests.

Open meetings do not attract regular citizen participation in the policy formulation process. For the most part, open meetings are a venue for one-way communication between policy formulators and citizen stakeholders. Policy-makers listen and take notes on the public input, but are generally not able to provide immediate feedback. The communication pattern often leaves citizen stakeholders frustrated.

Citizen advisory boards and collaborative policy-making are two other venues for citizen participation. The approaches offer unique opportunities for citizens to play a more active role in setting the policy agenda and formulating public policy. Professional policy-makers provide some level of policy education to citizen participants so they can understand the complexities and limitations faced by policy-makers in the policy formulation process. Professional policy-makers may also provide general guidelines regarding the limitations placed on citizen advisory board participants—they may not be allowed by law to participate in formulating all aspects of a particular policy. Advisory board member input often illuminates problems unique to a community being served.

DEMOGRAPHIC CHANGES AND POLICY FORMULATION

In times past, policy analysts looked for a "one size fits all" solution and policy formulation took on a generic approach to meeting citizen needs. As public policy has become more sophisticated, policy analysts and elected officials see the need to properly link policy goals and methods with clientele being served.

Policy decision-makers must balance current and future needs. Immigration patterns have been of particular interest. An improved understanding of Hispanic immigration in the southwestern United States, for instance, has had a tremendous influence on social welfare, health, housing, labor, and education policy formulation. Many individuals emigrating from Mexico and other Latin American nations acquire low-salaried employment in service industries, agriculture, and production plants. Individuals employed in these economic sectors may find it difficult to obtain affordable housing and health care. Labor conditions are regulated to protect workers. Additionally, educational opportunities for the children of the Hispanic population require greater awareness of bilingualism.

Social trends within society shape policy formulation. Two-parent families are no longer the norm in American society. Divorce rates have risen to approximately 50 percent. Family courts may award joint custody to parents, impacting children's socialization and education experiences. The percentage of children born to unwed parents or to nontraditional families (e.g., gay parents) has become a recognized part of the American social fabric. Policy formulation related to children and to families, such as education, welfare, physical and mental health care, drug, crime, and housing policy must consider the condition and changing needs of the American family in order to develop policies that work.

Another demographic change is the "graying" of the United States. A larger segment of Americans is retired and increasingly in need of assistance in their daily lives—for example, dealing with traditional household activities, and transportation to and from medical appointments. The trend is a growing issue due to the retirement and aging of the Baby Boom population. Public policy formulation increasingly responds to this long-term demographic phenomenon.

EXPLAINING POLICY FORMULATION

Incrementalism and Policy Formulation

Incrementalism is a good way to consider the policy formulation process. The theory implies that policy is formed over time. Each Congress and each budget cycle may reshape or reprioritize certain elements of a public policy. Policy formulation is not a one-time process; existing policy areas are forever being reshaped and reinterpreted. According to incrementalism, decisions of the past are a foundation upon which new decisions or choices are made. Incrementalism simplifies decision-making; thus, policy-makers deal with only small portions of policy formulation in any given time period.

Policy-makers generally lack the time or resources necessary to construct the "perfect" policy. Efforts to define a policy problem are generally limited by the ability of policy-makers to collect and interpret information regarding the impact of social, economic, or political phenomena on individuals. Continual change means that problems are regularly explored by social scientists, attempting to better understand the nature of society. How we explain phenomena partially determines the choice of policy solutions. As understanding evolves, solutions evolve.

In the formation process, the incremental model offers policy-makers the chance to make a successive number of limited comparisons regarding policy formulation and direction. Additionally, incrementalism means that policy-makers avoid large and potentially contentious discussions regarding policy "oughts." Normative discussions are replaced with a series of limited discussions regarding what government will or will not do in a particular policy area as a result of how policy is formed over time.

Incrementalism means that no single group of elected or appointed officials has the final word on policy formulation. A policy initiated years ago by a Democratic president and Congress may very well continue in existence only to be marginally changed in terms of policy formulation by a Republican president and Congress. Incrementalism offers continuity in public policy formulation and may ensure some level of political, economic, and social stability. It may also mean, however, that the momentum of public policy formulation changes so slowly that problems intended to be solved are never completely remedied. Incrementalism offers us a balance between a rapidly moving policy formulation process that may be incomplete and thus fail to achieve its intended outcome, and a policy formulation process that moves slowly but responsively toward alleviating problems that may be chronic rather than immediately solved.

Group Theory and Policy Formulation

Public policy formulation is often driven by the goals of various interest groups who pressure government to meet particular goals or solve particular problems. Interest groups spend considerable time and money trying to increase public and policymaker awareness of particular issues and solutions, in their quest to influence policy formulation.

Elected officials and civil servant personnel are often interested in the analyses conducted by interest groups. Interest groups might represent a significant portion of the clientele served by a particular public policy. Attention to the needs and desires of clientele is an important part of policy formulation.

After policy has been statutorily adopted, interest groups still have many opportunities to shape policy formulation. Laws often provide general guidance to public agencies, which operationalize laws. Agencies often create specific definitions of policy goals and administrative rules needed to operate policy on a day-to-day basis. Interest groups and individuals—as noted previously—have an opportunity to participate in administrative rule-making; and thus, shape policy formulation at the bureaucratic level.

Interest groups seeking selective benefits may have the added advantage of minimal inter-group competition in the policy formulation process. At one time, agricultural and industrial groups lacked any real competition from environmental groups in shaping economic policies that related to their production goals. Access to policy decision-makers was fairly unilateral and policy formulation produced outcomes nearly tailor-made to meet these groups' needs. Despite the rise of environmental groups, agriculture groups remain quite powerful in shaping the Farm Bill and related policies.

One concern that emerges from interest group influence in policy formulation relates to equity and the promotion of the general welfare of all citizens. Regardless of whether they receive direct benefits, public policy is paid for with citizens' tax dollars.

Neoinstitutionalism and Policy Formulation

Neoinstitutionalism demonstrates that policy formulators operate under a series of constraints. Institutions, such as the presidency, Congress, and the courts, are very old. Over the years, the institutions have adopted a number of formal and informal processes and rules restricting decision-making in some manner. Prior to the twentieth century, the presidency as an institution was limited by simple reliance on a limited number of formal powers and an equally limited number of offices and staff personnel tasked to formulate public policy. With the rise of progressive politics in the twentieth century and the ever-enlarging role for the chief executive in formulating public policy, there was a subsequent growth in presidential personal and civil servant staff. The Executive Office of the President, which emerged in the late 1930s, has grown tremendously and includes a multitude of political appointees and career bureaucrats who formulate public policy. Nevertheless, these presidential "helpers" have also served to constrain presidential decision-making in relation to policy formulation. Due to the overwhelming amount of information available for policy formulation, the president often faces time constraints and data overload, possibly impairing successful policy formulation. The great irony that emerges is that in the attempt to formulate policy in an expeditious manner, the president often systematically limits information that may prove valuable to policy success or failure.

Additionally, the institution of the presidency has formal and informal culture, subcultures, and processes that guide policy formulation decision-making. There are many information processing points within the Executive Branch, where policy analysts digest and summarize information before it reaches the president. Information processing and reforming means that the president is offered limited choices with information that is no longer "raw" or unprocessed. With predigested information, the president usually shapes policy formulation in very small ways—at the margins—and within the limited scope of choices offered him.

Congress faces similar limitations related to institutional processes and rules. Congressional leadership may constrain the policy formulation process and therefore limit available alternatives. Committee leaders and members seek to achieve floor vote victories for purposes of committee and individual prestige; so formulation is shaped by the need for political success. Additionally, the Congress has established a strong and well-organized institutional and personal staff system composed of a number of individuals and offices—each shaped by individual values and professional norms—that digest and interpret information and constrain choices available to legislators.

Lessons Learned from Chapter 6

SPECIFICS

- The policy formulation process involves four major steps: defining, exploring, choosing, and planning. Each step involves normative and empirical issues, what we *ought* or *ought not* do, and what government *does* or *does not* do.
- Policy formulation is conducted in different ways by different political institutions. Congress and the Executive Branch have different constituencies and different methods and goals in policy formulation. The courts are primarily concerned with policy formulation that meets standards of political and social justice, but are cognizant of the public's values and opinions.
- Incrementalism, Group Theory, and Neoinstitutionalism are three policy models that help illustrate the policy formulation process.

THE BIG PICTURE

Policy formulation is a very challenging part of the policy process. Unlike the policy agenda-setting or adoption stage, which is at its foundation a normatively driven process related to the question of "ought" or "ought not," policy formulation generally relates to issues of what government does or does not do. Formulation requires that policy-makers develop some level of understanding of problems and realistic solutions.

A central issue in policy formulation is the ability of a particular solution to affect change. In many instances, the policy formulation process is not deterministic, meaning that policy-makers cannot be entirely confident that a particular solution will produce a desired outcome. Policy phenomena are often organic, not mechanistic.

Although in one sense policy formulation is really about determining the best and most efficient method of solving an identified policy problem, it is, ultimately, a matter of preference. Due to the limited capacity of information to provide decision-makers with a clear empirically based set of alternatives, choice is often clouded by personal and group values. Policy formulation is often shaped by interest groups, citizen stakeholders, and political parties who find a particular policy alternative to be most desirable given their values and preferences. These individuals and groups frequently play a role in policy formulation, providing decision-makers with information and policy alternatives they believe will match their personal or group values and priorities. Policy formulation is a cyclical process. As policy goals evolve, so too must policy solutions.

Decision-makers continually adjust public policies already in operation as new information and new demands shape or reshape policy goals. Political institutions respond differently in the policy formulation process. Each institution has its own particular powers and methods of operation and each institution has different resources available to it.

Key Terms

bottom-up policy-making
Brownlow Commission on Economy
   and Efficiency
Congressional Budget Office
Congressional Research Service
Executive Office of the President
   (EOP)

General Accounting Office
goal drift/shift
goal enlargement
policy formulation
stakeholder
top-down policy-making

Questions for Study

1. What are the major steps in policy formulation? Discuss and provide examples.
2. Identify and discuss three major influences/actors that shape the policy formulation process.
3. Use three policy models to describe and explain the policy formulation process.

Bibliography

Congressional Budget Office. 2007. "CBO Fact Sheet," www.cbo.gov/ (accessed August 17, 2007).
Congressional Research Service. 2005. "CRS: History and mission," www.lcweb.loc.gov/crsinfo/whatscrs.html#hismiss (accessed August 17, 2007).
Dye, T. 2001. *Top down policy-making.* New York: Chatham House.
Easton, D. 1965. *A framework for political analysis.* Englewood Cliffs, NJ.: Prentice Hall.
Edwards, G., S. Shull, and N. Thomas, eds. 1985. *The presidency and public policy-making.* Pittsburgh: University of Pittsburgh Press.
Eyestone, R., ed. 1984. *Public policy formation.* Greenwich, CT: JAI Press.
Fredericksen, H. G. 1971. *New public administration.* Tuscaloosa: University of Alabama Press.
Jones, C. 1970. *An introduction to the study of public policy.* Belmont, CA: Wadsworth.
Ripley, R., and G. Franklin. 1975. *Policy-making in the federal executive branch.* New York: Free Press.
Sabatier, P., ed. 1999. *Theories of the policy process.* Boulder, CO: Westview Press.
Sharkansky, I. 2002. *Politics and policy-making: In search of simplicity.* Boulder, CO: Lynne Rienner.
Shull, S. 1999. *Presidential policy-making: An end-of-century assessment.* Armonk, NY: M. E. Sharpe.
Van Beuren, E., E. H. Klijn, and J. Koppenjan. 2003. Dealing with wicked problems in networks: Analyzing an environmental debate from a network perspective. *Journal of Public Administration Research and Theory.* 13(2): 193–212.

Endnotes

1. Interestingly, government tells us what it will do, but with rare exception, it does not tell us in absolute terms what it will not do—one noted example is constitutional prohibition on voting discrimination related to race and gender for those individuals 18 years of age or older.

2. http://www.lcweb.loc.gov/crsinfo/whatscrs.html#hismiss (accessed March 22, 2009).

3. The Executive Office of the President (EOP) contains the following units: Council of Economic Advisers, Council on Environmental Quality, Domestic Policy Council, National Economic Council, National Security Council, Office of Administration, Office of Management and Budget, Office of National AIDS Policy, Office of National Drug Control Policy, Office of Science & Technology Policy, Office of the US Trade Representative, President's Intelligence Advisory Board and Intelligence Oversight Board, White House Military Office, and White House Office.

   Source: http://www.whitehouse.gov/government/eop.html (accessed March 22, 2009).

7

■■■

Policy
Implementation

CHAPTER OVERVIEW

Public policy implementation is where the rubber meets the road—where public policy becomes a reality. Policy studies regularly document the successes and failures associated with implementation. Inability to choose an optimum policy solution is a common challenge facing implementation. Although implementation successes or failures are often case specific, it is possible to draw general conclusions about the process.

The specific goals for the chapter are:

- Discuss four major types of policy implementation.
- Discuss issues surrounding implementation.
- Discuss the major participants in implementation.
- Use policy theories to explain policy implementation.

A THEORETICAL MODEL OF POLICY IMPLEMENTATION

Richard Matland (1995) developed a synthesized model of policy implementation, identifying six factors shaping implementation success:

- *Statutory compliance*
  Statutes often encapsulate policy goals and implementation should be oriented toward goal accomplishment. Statutory compliance alone may overlook issues of efficiency or effectiveness of policy implementation. Also, it does not mean that the statute or compliance with the statute is consistent with constitutional principles, generally accepted ethical standards, or democratic governance. Narrowly defined, compliance is a managerial function; regardless, it is one important dimension of implementation.
- *Bureaucratic accountability*
  Public policies are implemented by bureaucrats working in agencies. In theory, bureaucrats are hired on the basis of knowledge, skills, and abilities,

and implement public policy in a politically neutral manner. As Matland and many others have noted, bureaucrats are not politically neutral. Elected officials use oversight to check bureaucracy and guide it toward compliance with political intent. Implementation might indicate that bureaucrats are doing what they are told to do, rather than what they would prefer to do or perhaps what they know would work.

- *Statutory goals accomplished*
  Statutory goal accomplishment means that a desired output was produced. For example, a statute might state that police officers cannot racially profile and might get into trouble if they disproportionally arrest persons of color. What if officers then began to have unofficial quotas on the number of people of color they could stop or arrest? Would that lead to "statutory compliance?" Of course not. Racial profiling laws were never intended to stop law enforcement officers from preventing crime. The goal of racial profiling law was to prevent intentionally discriminatory law enforcement practices.

- *"Local goals" accomplished*
  Policy made at the national level tends to focus on very generic policy goals. However, policy is implemented in states and local communities. It is important that public policy fit local need as well as meet national policy goals. Implementation of a policy at the local level is often judged in terms of its ability to meet local needs because local governments and citizens are primarily interested in how policy helps them. Elected officials, particularly legislators seeking reelection, view implementation in terms of how constituents are benefited by policy.

- *Political climate improvement*
  Matland views politics in terms of values allocation. Values often explain the level of joy or displeasure in the policy environment and within implementing agencies. Successful implementation means that something has improved as a result of public policy. Improvement might entail better support for the political process; in essence, successful implementation might give individuals renewed hope that demands can be made of government, policy enacted, and positive outcomes produced.

- *Learning*
  Matland contends that one of the most important things to emerge from successful implementation is learning. Although statutory compliance and the meeting of goals are obviously of great interest, learning is central to making things even better. Learning means that policy improves over time, and more complicated goals can be pursued and likely achieved.

According to Matland, policy implementation studies can be divided into two general categories: top-down approaches and bottom-up approaches. Top-down approaches assume:

1. Statutory language is complete, concise, and applicable.
2. Implementation is an administrative function.

Anything that impedes compliance is viewed as a **barrier**. The statute is not seen as a barrier; so, environmental factors are often identified as problematic. The goal is to remove barriers to compliance, essentially clearing the ground in front of policy implementation rather than working with existing conditions. Historical considerations are ignored; top-down implementation is about setting conditions and creating compliance. The second assumption (above) means that top-down implementation is not viewed as a political process—simply the enforcement of agreed-upon standards, rules, and processes. Local-level complaints about policy implementation are seen as barriers that must be overcome rather than recognized and considered.

In the bottom-up approach, policy is implemented by local-level administrators and elected officials; people working closest to policy clientele. Bottom-up implementation generally assumes that statutes are not complete and concise. Through policy networks known as **advocacy coalitions**—comprised of interested citizens and pressure groups, and administrators—policy is formulated and implemented. Specific goals for policy are defined in the implementation phase and strategies to accomplish those goals are agreed upon. For the bottom-up approach, the recognition of current and historic context is central to good implementation. Accountability is a function of the democratic process that includes elected officials as well as sovereign citizens. The rules defining bottom-up policy are created and legitimized through a wide array of advocacy coalition participants.

Matland brings the two aforementioned disparate approaches together in his **ambiguity–conflict model**. He identifies cross-cutting dimensions in policy implementation: policy ambiguity and policy conflict. According to Matland, policy ambiguity emerges in two major forms:

- ***Ambiguity of goals***
  Statutory conciseness and clarity are important ways of clarifying goals. Top-down implementation is particularly concerned with reducing ambiguity in goal formation, whereas bottom-up implementation finds that ambiguity provides greater opportunity to reduce conflict through compromise at the local level.
- ***Ambiguity of means***
  There are two important dimensions to consider: (1) technological wherewithal for effective implementation and (2) financial resources needed to pay for implementation efforts. For example, fire control on public lands is a public policy, but implementation would be difficult if there were neither fire fighting equipment (technology) nor funds to pay for firefighters (resources). As Matland succinctly states, "The degree of ambiguity inherent in a policy directly affects the implementation process in significant ways. It influences the ability of superiors to monitor activities, the likelihood that the policy is uniformly understood across the many implementation sites, the probability that local contextual factors play a significant role, and the degree to which relevant factors vary sharply across implementation sites" (Matland 1995, 159).

Policy conflict comes into play when individual decision-makers do not agree on the basic premise for policy, let alone implementation of it. Policy conflict is best seen in inter- and intra-institutional bargaining activities. Policy conflict usually means that policy is a product of significant compromise, likely reducing statutory conciseness and clarity. Typically, "bargaining mechanisms such as side payments, log rolling, and oversight . . . [and] coercive [methods of compliance]" are visible in cases of policy conflict (Matland 1995, 156). Also, jurisdictional friction and methods of implementation may serve as sources of policy conflict. Conflict is a clash of values (Matland 1995, 157).

Matland identifies and discusses four conditional relationships associated with the ambiguity–conflict model.

Administrative Implementation (Low Policy Ambiguity, Low Policy Conflict)

Policies with low levels of ambiguity and conflict are generally very concise and clear policies. Low levels of ambiguity mean that a policy is clearly defined in terms of process and goals. Low levels of conflict decrease the likelihood that policies are vaguely written as the basis of compromise.

Concise statutes mean that implementation is built around rational "programmed" administrative decisions. "The central principle in administrative implementation is outcomes are determined by *resource*. The desired outcome is virtually assured, given that sufficient resources are appropriated for the program" (Matland 1995, 160). In "Administrative Implementation," resources are fairly stable. Technology is clear and exists prior to the establishment of policy. Administrative personnel are stable. "Implementation failure occurs because of technical problems: the machine sputters" (Matland 1995, 161). Compliance in implementation is further assured through normative mechanisms (e.g., mutual agreement), coercive mechanisms (e.g., statutes and rules), and remunerative mechanisms (e.g., salary and benefits).

Political Implementation (Low Policy Ambiguity, High Policy Conflict)

Policy goals are clear, but policy complexity produces goals conflict. Administrative solutions are less feasible due to a lack of agreement, and normative considerations shape policy implementation choices. Politics becomes the basis by which choices are articulated and *power* becomes the definitive factor in shaping prioritization and choice adoption. Purpose becomes less relevant in political implementation and agreement on process (or "actions") "is sufficient" (Matland 1995, 164). Policy ambiguity is low, but resources are controlled by policy actors outside of the implementing organization; resource allocations cannot be assumed. Allocation decisions are based on power relationships rather than administrative rationality or the compliance mechanisms of administrative implementation.

Experimental Implementation (High Policy Ambiguity, Low Policy Conflict)

Matland used the early years of Head Start as an example of experimental implementation. The goal of Head Start was generally agreed upon; however, the policy implementation was unclear largely because it was something that had not really been tried before. As Matland states, ". . . outcomes will depend largely on which actors are active and most involved" (Matland 1995, 165). Early Head Start implementation techniques were largely innovations tried in program offices across the nation. Circumstances of clientele and the general environment—i.e., *contextual factors*—will shape the degree of policy ambiguity and implementation choices. Policy technologies may not exist prior to implementation; therefore, technologies will be developed on a needs-oriented basis. Statutory compliance will be unclear because statutes will likely be vague due to limited understanding of policy problems and solutions. Statutory goals might or might not be met; local goals were more likely to be met because the policy implementation was shaped by environmental conditions. At times, heavy influence from environmental factors can result in "**capture**," meaning that the implementation process is significantly shaped by individual and group interests at the local level. Administrative accountability may be limited, but policy-learning opportunities will likely be substantial.

Symbolic Implementation (High Policy Ambiguity, High Policy Conflict)

Symbolic policies are strongly rooted in normative positions regarding government and society. Symbolic policies are intended to reaffirm values and associated policy goals. Values tend to vary based on locality, and local goal fulfillment is of particular importance. Conflict is high and groups compete to symbolically enshrine their value set. According to Matland (1995, 169), "Competition ensues over correct 'vision.' Actors see their interests tied to a specific policy definition and therefore similar competing coalitions are likely to form at differing rates." Microlevel interests shape symbolic policy and policy implementation. Resource control is centered in the policy environment, used to influence policy implementation choices, goals, and application.

Accountability is not assured. Statutory compliance is less relevant in this model. Local policy goals and *coalition strength* are paramount and shape value impacts on outcomes. Symbolic implementation tends to work well in top-down as well as bottom-up policy. (See Figure 7.1.)

FIGURE 7.1 Typology of implementation

Source: Matland, R. E. 1995. Synthesizing the implementation literature: the ambiguity-conflict model of policy implementation, *Journal of Public Administration and Theory: J-PART.* 5(2): 145–174.

	CONFLICT	
AMBIGUITY	**Low**	**High**
Low	*Administrative Implementation* **Resources** Example: Smallpox erradication	*Political Implementation* **Power** Example: Busing
High	*Experimental Implementation* **Contextual Conditions** Example: Headstart	*Symbolic Implementation* **Coalition Strength** Example: Community action agencies

ISSUES SURROUNDING IMPLEMENTATION

Policy-makers wish to *control* and *steer* public policy. Control by elected officials and by senior bureaucrats helps maintain statutory objectives and promotes agency accountability. Control increases the ability to link statutory goals with outcomes.

Steerage

Steerage keeps policy focused on intended goals. Policy implementation may not reflect policy goals and adjustments must be made. Steerage exists on two levels: the political and the administrative. Political steerage is often referred to as "oversight." Administrative steerage is shaped by rational–comprehensive and incremental choices, but is often influenced by pressure and clientele groups.

Tractability

Successful policy implementation requires **tractability** (Mazmanian and Sabatier 1981, 1), the ability of public policy to control, influence, or reshape phenomenon in order to achieve a policy goal. Tractability requires policy-makers to describe, explain, and predict phenomena associated with a policy problem. Predictive power allows us to understand how policy will impact problems. Tractability is important in establishing accountability for implementing agencies, highlighting significant accomplishments.

In many cases, it is difficult to provide solid evidence that a problem is tractable and that policy will lead to particular outcomes. If there is no single explanation for why a problem exists, then it is very difficult for policy-makers and policy implementers to identify solutions. (See Box 7.1, *Litter: An Intractable Problem with Many Potential Causes* and Box 7.2, *Speeding through Crosswalks: A Much More Tractable Problem.*)

Target Group Identification

Target groups are the individuals or organizations whose behavior is directly impacted by public policy. Target groups are often described in terms of: (1) size and (2) behavioral aspects associated with policy implementation.

Mazmanian and Sabatier (1981, 8–9) conclude that the size of the target group must be manageable, otherwise implementers will face many difficulties: "In general, the smaller and more definable the target group whose behavior needs to be changed . . . the more probable that the statutory objectives can be achieved." Smaller target groups are usually less diverse, and narrowly tailored policies can be formulated and effectively implemented. Unfortunately, target populations are often ill-defined and misunderstood, leading to unintended policy outcomes.

Federalism

Many nationally formulated public policies are implemented at the local and state level. Some policies are **unfunded mandates**, requiring local and state

BOX 7.1

Litter: An Intractable Problem with Many Potential Causes

Policy-makers can identify public litter as a problem with wide-ranging impacts. First, litter is a health hazard. Second, litter gives the impression of public apathy and can be the first step in elevated crime levels in a neighborhood. Once it has been decided that public litter is a problem that must be solved, policy formulators must identify reasons why people litter and how to best control this behavior. One reason might be a lack of trash receptacles. Individuals get tired of carrying garbage and simply drop it on the ground. A second reason might be that "litterbugs" do not expect to be punished for their behavior. Getting rid of the trash appears to be a pure "benefit" to them. A third reason might be a lack of pride in one's surroundings or perhaps a lack of awareness of the needs of others. Although getting rid of the trash is a benefit to the person littering, it ends up becoming a "cost" to other individuals who have to pay to have it picked up or who have to wade through it. Litter becomes a cost for reasons related to health and crime, as addressed previously. A final reason for litter might be related to socioeconomic deprivation in a community. Perhaps the city does not provide adequate trash collection. Additionally, litter may not be the cause of public apathy, but it may be a symptom of apathy related to socioeconomic and even racial disparity issues that are not being addressed by policy-makers.

After identifying the nature of a problem and the potential causes for it, policy-makers must identify solutions. Clearly, the problem of litter is related to any one of a number of causes. Simply regulating behavior and sending police officers out into the streets to issue citations will not solve the other problems identified with the issue of litter. In fact, it is doubtful that approaching this problem with any single policy solution would prove to be fruitful and might exacerbate other policy problems.

---

governments to implement national policies using their own financial resources and personnel. Conversely, **funded mandates** are implemented with financial support—**grants-in-aid**—from the national government. Grants-in-aid often imply a long-term commitment to the implementation of a particular public policy. In times of budgetary crisis, resource streams may disappear, constraining the implementation process.

Veto Points

Veto points are places within the policy process where policy can be changed or eliminated. Policy implementation is fraught with veto points, particularly within implementing agencies.

Agency structure impacts implementation. Most agency structures mimic the **bureaucratic model**, which reduces the number of veto points. In bureau-

BOX 7.2

Speeding Through Crosswalks: A Much More Tractable Problem

An advertisement for pedestrian safety.

Policy problems that are related to a narrow spectrum of potential causes are much more tractable and easily solved; therefore, implementation proves to be much more straightforward. Speeding through school crosswalks is one example of a fairly narrow policy area and one that can be much more easily solved. Speeding through a crosswalk poses a serious hazard to children on their way to and from school. There are at least two reasons individuals might speed through a crosswalk: (1) they are in a hurry and see the "benefit" of speeding to be greater than the "cost" of getting a traffic fine and (2) they are unaware of the existence of the crosswalk. The policy solutions are fairly obvious. First, the public could be made more aware of the costs of speeding through public information campaigns and through the presence of police officers issuing tickets. Second, the use of crosswalk monitors, lights, and signage would make motorists more aware of the presence of the crosswalk.

"The City of Bellevue's School Crosswalk Enhancement Project provides an example of how engineering improvements can change driver behaviors. In a two-year project, the city worked with schools to identify traffic concerns. The first year of the project focused on changing driver behaviors through education programs, enforcement activity, signing, and pavement marking. In the second year, physical engineering improvements were installed if the problem behaviors had not improved. At Somerset Elementary and Bennett Elementary the city installed raised crosswalks, curb extensions, and bollards. At both schools there was a history of drivers speeding through the school zone and parking on or near the crosswalks. The raised crosswalk acts like a gentle, smooth speed bump to reduce vehicle speeds and to make students more visible as they cross. Curb extensions, or curb bulbs, bring a semicircle of sidewalk out into the crosswalk. This shortens the pedestrians' crossing distance and eliminates parking on or near the crosswalk providing an unobstructed view for the pedestrians. The bollards (three foot posts) are positioned back from the edge of the curb extensions to keep pedestrians a safe distance back from the road. Plaques were installed on the bollards with tips on how to safely cross the street. These physical engineering improvements reduced average speed through the school zone and eliminated parking near the crosswalks." (www.wtsc.wa.gov/school_safety_programs.html, accessed January 30, 2005.)

cracies, decision-making authority is controlled by a small group of senior agency administrators. Administrative implementation works well in the hands of bureaucracy.

Vague statutory directives require agencies to have **active managers**, delegating decision-making authority but cognizant of the need for accountability. Active mangers must also deal with policy input from pressure groups, concerned citizens, clientele, and other policy stakeholders. When decision-making authority is delegated, the number of veto points increases substantially, as more policy actors shape implementation choices.

The **organizational culture**, or implementing agency's organizational norms, shared values, and informal processes, may act as a veto point. Agency personnel are usually career civil servants who have seen any number of statutes implemented. Often, they can sense the potential for a statute to bolster or detract from existing agency goals, priorities, and culture. When a statute detracts from the agency's culture, personnel will likely resist change.

The **legal standing** of pressure groups and clientele is another veto point. Legal standing means that those individuals or groups who are directly impacted by a statute have the right to take legal action regarding the decisions of the implementing agency. Policies that deny an individual their constitutional rights are particularly contentious.

Well-heeled interests often use their legal standing to shape implementation for their personal benefit. Powerful corporations impacted by regulatory implementation have the financial and legal resources necessary to fight implementation decisions. Heavily regulated, corporations have little difficulty demonstrating direct interest and legal standing. However, many individuals lack the resources necessary to turn their legal standing to their advantage. Bias creeps into implementation when agency choices are motivated by attempts to reduce the potential for serious legal challenges from the powerful corporate interest, while ignoring the unexercised legal standing of less powerful individuals and groups (Mazmanian and Sabatier 1981, 13).

A Changing Policy Environment

Policy implementation is a long-term and dynamic process. A few environmental factors that must be considered:

- Target group change—The ever-changing nature of target groups and resources available to meet their needs must be a continual consideration for policy implementers.
- Technology—Advances in technology may reduce the cost of policy implementation. Technologically backward agencies are often inefficient and ineffective.
- Public attention—Public attention is often directly related to media coverage. The media play a role in all aspects of the policy process. Initially, the media is interested in the "hot topic," but if media awareness wanes, then all too often, public attention declines. Policy implementation may suffer from a lack of public attention, lower prioritization, reduced

funding, and diminished effectiveness (Mazmanian and Sabatier 1981, 16–17).

- Public opinion—as registered through elections—results in changes in the policy-making and oversight process. Elected officials lose reelection bids or retire from office. New officials often have different priorities, which may negatively impact the implementation of existing policy.

When You Can't Steer, You Slip

Policy implementation faces "a unique kind of politics" (Bacharach 1977, 37). Once formulated, policy faces continued scrutiny and constraint by a dynamic and changing cohort of elected policy-makers operating at the national, state, and local level. Individually or collectively, these factors have the potential to cause **slippage** in the policy implementation process—a reduced ability to produce outputs consistent with policy goals. Mazmanian and Sabatier discuss a series of factors related to slippage, as noted in the picture (Mazmanian and Sabatier 1981, 21–22). (See Box 7.3, *Issues in Policy Implementation: Out to Sea.*)

MAJOR PARTICIPANTS IN POLICY IMPLEMENTATION

Bureaucracy

Bureaucracy establishes administrative rules guiding the implementation process. The rules made by bureaucrats, **administrative law**, require public hearings and, in many instances, legislative and/or executive oversight. Once established, federal administrative rules are published in the Federal Register. At the state level, administrative law is usually published in the individual state's administrative code manuals. Administrative judges and magistrates are the first line of judicial enforcement in administrative law cases. Administrative laws also guide the day-to-day implementation of statutes.

When statutory implementation leads to the creation of new agencies and new personnel positions, new personnel-related rules may be needed. Personnel structures must be reorganized to fulfill statutory requirements. Position descriptions for personnel must be rewritten and offices and administrative staff must establish new goals, priorities, and standard operating procedures.

Pressure Groups

Public hearings for administrative rule making are an excellent venue for pressure group influence on the implementation process, an opportunity to shape interpretations of statutory intent, which guides bureaucratic decision-making. Pressure groups able to establish legal standing may challenge administrative rules through the court system.

Pressure groups can also act as an important source of support for bureaucrats in the implementation process through information campaigns, legislative lobbying activities, and testimony at oversight hearings. Pressure group **information campaigns** may maintain public awareness of a policy issue. Legislative **lobbying** is another important method by which pressure groups

BOX 7.3

Issues in Policy Implementation: Out to Sea

The easiest way for me to think about all of this is to consider sailing. As a kid, I used to crew on sailboats like the one in the picture. Most of what happens to a sailboat is similar to what happens in policy implementation; in fact, sailing is a form of implementation, to include sea-sickness. I'm sure that policy implementers can testify to occasional nausea.

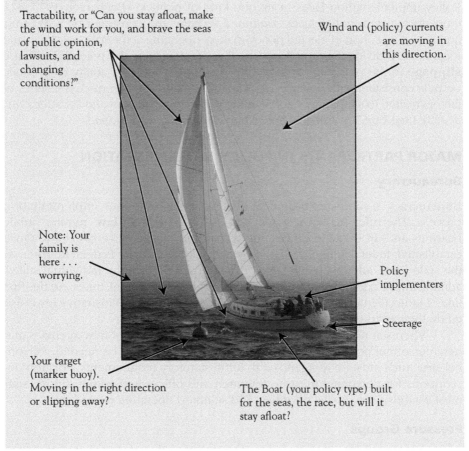

Tractability, or "Can you stay afloat, make the wind work for you, and brave the seas of public opinion, lawsuits, and changing conditions?"

Wind and (policy) currents are moving in this direction.

Note: Your family is here . . . worrying.

Policy implementers

Steerage

Your target (marker buoy). Moving in the right direction or slipping away?

The Boat (your policy type) built for the seas, the race, but will it stay afloat?

might help bureaucrats during the implementation process, using contributions as a tool for gaining access to legislators and shaping choices. Finally, pressure groups may provide **expert testimony** during oversight hearings, an opportunity to hail the success of implementation or influence policy changes.

In the policy process, relationships can develop between pressure groups, administrative agencies, and legislative committees, referred to as the **iron triangle** or **subgovernment model**. The pressure groups, agencies, and committees develop a symbiotic relationship that advances policy agendas. Although this relationship was discussed previously in terms of the agenda-setting process, it continues on throughout the policy process. In the implementation process, the exclusivity of iron triangles can have a tremendous impact on policy priorities and outcomes.

Clientele

Policy clientele have varying degrees of influence on policy implementation. Societal values play a significant role in who is listened to in the implementation process. Anne Schneider and Helen Ingram found that some clientele groups are seen as being more "deserving" than others. Convicted criminals, users of illegal drugs, and the chronically indigent—are often viewed by policy-makers and agency implementers as being undeserving recipients of public policy. Their voices and concerns are frequently overlooked in the implementation process. Racial-, gender-, and age-based discrimination systematically excludes large segments of the population from voicing their interests and concerns in *all* stages of the policy process. Age-based discrimination frequently impacts both *younger* and *older* individuals.

The Clinton administration paid significant attention to policy issues concerning young adults. Clinton placed special emphasis on listening to the concerns of young women and racial and ethnic minorities. The increased emphasis in this area of public policy may turn out to have been symbolic— only time will fully inform us of its lasting impact in equalizing clientele input in the policy process. (See Photo 7.1.)

PHOTO 7.1 Sometimes, meetings can keep you in stitches

Judicial System

The court system becomes particularly involved with policy implementation when individuals or groups claim that their constitutional rights are violated either by a statute or administrative rules governing the implementation process. These groups or individuals must demonstrate legal standing. Not all public policies offer pressure groups or clientele equal access to legal recourse. Litigation costs also limit access to the judiciary. Litigation is not always the best solution to problems in policy implementation. **Alternative dispute resolution (ADR)** is an attempt to solve conflicts prior to a full legal hearing before a judge.

EXPLAINING POLICY IMPLEMENTATION

Rational–Comprehensive Model

Rational–comprehensive approaches assume there is a clear theory related to the problem to be solved and a readily identifiable solution. If theory is clear and widely accepted, the rational–comprehensive approach will likely guide the creation of strict policy guidelines, rules, and regulations for policy implementation. At times, apparently reasonable policy solutions are based on inchoate theories and prematurely generated data, ultimately resulting in policy failures. If policy theory is faulty, then clear and concise implementation processes will be for naught.

Elite Theory Explanation

The elite theory explanation of implementation can be highly convincing. Policy implementation is often a function of decisions made by a relatively small group of powerful policy-makers. Policy will vary, depending upon the controlling elite. A policy area that is important to the controlling elite may be infused with particular normative and empirical theories regarding the cause and nature of a policy problem. The chosen theory will impact the solutions to the problem and the methods by which these solutions are put into place.

As different elites gain control over the policy formulation and implementation process, policy problems will be viewed differently. Implementation of new and existing policy will likely evolve. Administrative Implementation provides the least amount of flexibility in terms of the evolution of policy; in this case, changes in implementation will frequently require significant statutory changes, which necessitate the revisiting of statutory provisions by legislatures and political executives. The range and depth of elite control will have to be much greater in policy areas subject to Administrative Implementation. Elites can use the oversight function as a method of reshaping policy implementation, particularly in marginal ways.

Elite theory also applies to policy implementation and the role of mass and social elites. The mass media play a significant role in framing, prioritizing, and maintaining issues on the policy agenda. Policy implementation often loses public support when the policy issue becomes less visible in the media.

Issue agenda and issue framing is controlled by private business executives, editors, and the journalists who finance, choose, and develop news stories (Edelman 1988); their story choices impact public awareness, which in turn impacts the policy process.

Incrementalism

Public policy implementation is by no means a perfect science. Statutes do not provide complete policy guidelines, so implementing agencies and policy formulators must try different approaches to solving policy problems. With enough tinkering, agency administrators hope that policy goals will be achieved.

Incrementalism helps us recognize that policy formulation and implementation is a continual process. Through many iterations of a policy, decision-makers can arrive at better approaches to identifying and describing a problem and implement plausible solutions. Policy problems evolve and circumstances change, requiring adjustments for effective policy implementation.

Group Theory

Implementation often involves a substantial amount of administrative rule making. Pressure groups that have a significant interest in the implementation of a particular public policy will likely attend and actively participate in agency rule-making hearings. Well-organized groups often have legal counsel and policy experts who can argue in favor of particular implementation rules and methods. Agency administrators often take seriously the arguments made by pressure group attorneys and policy analysts, possibly to the detriment of individuals with only a rudimentary understanding of policy specifics (Pierce and Lovrich 1986).

Group theory also does an adequate job of explaining and describing other pressure group tactics in shaping implementation. Groups send lobbyists to meet with elected and appointed decision-makers. Lobbyists try to use their influence to shape statutory guidelines and administrative rules. Pressure group leaders seek to provide testimony to legislative committees during oversight hearings, another important method of shaping the implementation process. Additionally, group theory is a useful way of understanding pressure group interaction with the judiciary. Groups can influence implementation through lawsuits or *amicus curiae* briefs filed in Supreme Court cases.

Lessons Learned from Chapter 7

SPECIFICS

- Implementation involves a great deal more than simply putting policy into effect—in many cases, policy has to be created because original formulations produced in the statute-making process are too vague or are incomplete.

- Policy implementation is categorized on the basis of the level of policy ambiguity and conflict.
- There are four types of policy implementation: administrative, political, experimental, and symbolic.
- Implementing agencies, pressure groups, and political and social elites can exercise tremendous power over policy implementation, impacting implementation by helping to decide what government *ought* or *ought not* do, and what government *does* or *does not* do.

THE BIG PICTURE

This chapter offers a general model of policy implementation, discussing implementation types as a function of statutory completeness, level of policy conflict, and organization theory. The implementation literature offers a general understanding of how policy moves from formulation to outcomes. Knowledge of implementation is imperfect, but the academic literature does confirm a few principles related to policy implementation success: (1) clear understanding of a policy problem, (2) demonstrable solutions to the problem, (3) well-defined target groups, and (4) strong and sustainable support for the public policy being implemented.

Key Terms

active managers
administrative law
advocacy coalitions
alternative dispute resolution
   (ADR)
ambiguity-conflict model
barrier
bureaucratic model
capture
expert testimony
funded mandates
grants-in-aid

information campaigns
iron triangle
legal standing
lobbying
organizational culture
slippage
steerage
subgovernment model
target groups
tractability
unfunded mandates
veto points

Questions for Study

1. Discuss three major institutional/individual actors in the policy implementation process.
2. According to Richard Matland, what are four major types of policy implementation? Identify and discuss.
3. Identify three policy models and demonstrate how the models could be used to explain policy implementation. Provide examples.

Bibliography

Bacharach, S. 1977. Introduction to *Reward systems and power distribution in organizations: Searching for solutions*. Edited by T. Hammer and S. Bacharach. Ithaca: New York State School of Industrial and Labor Relations.

Bardach, E. 1977. *The implementation game: What happens after a bill becomes a law*. Cambridge, MA: MIT Press.

Downs, A. 1967 *Inside bureaucracy*. Boston: Little, Brown.

Edelman, M. 1988. *Constructing the political spectacle*. Chicago: University of Chicago Press.

Hanf, K., and T. Toonen. 1985. *Policy implementation in federal and unitary systems*. Boston: Martinus Nijhoff Publishers.

Hill, M. 2002. *Implementing public policy: Governance in theory and practice*. London: Sage.

Honig, M. 2006. *New directions in education policy implementation*. Albany, NY: SUNY.

Iyengar, S., and D. Kinder. 1987. *News that matters: Television and American opinion*. Chicago: University of Chicago Press.

Lowi, T. 1969. *End of liberalism*. New York: Norton.

Matland, R. E. 1995. Synthesizing the Implementation Literature: The Ambiguity-Conflict Model of Policy Implementation, *Journal of Public Administration Research and Theory: J-PART*. 5(2): 145–174.

Mazmanian, D., and P. Sabatier. 1981. *Effective policy implementation*. Lexington, MA: Lexington Books.

Nakamura, R., and F. Smallwood. 1980. *The politics of policy implementation*. New York: St. Martin's Press.

Palumbo, D., and D. Calista, eds. 1990. *Implementation and the policy process: Opening up the black box*. New York: Greenwood.

Pierce, J., and N. Lovrich. 1986. *Water resources, democracy, and the technical information quandary*. New York: Associated Faculty Press.

Schneider, A., and H. Ingram. 1997. *Policy design for democracy*. Lawrence: University of Kansas Press.

Taylor, D., and S. Balloch. 2005. *The politics of evaluation: participation and policy implementation*. Bristol, UK: Policy Press, University of Bristol.

Washington Traffic Safety Commission. 2005. "Programs: The city of Bellevue's school crosswalk enhancement project." www.wtsc.wa.gov/school_safety_programs.html (accessed January 30, 2005).

Whitford, A. 2007. Decentralized policy implementation, *Political Research Quarterly*. 60(1): 17–30.

8

■ ■ ■

Policy Evaluation

CHAPTER OVERVIEW

Evaluation provides important feedback to policy-makers and administrators for improvement to public policy and the achievement of desired policy outcomes. Policy evaluators concentrate on the *does* or *does not do* elements of public policy. Good policy evaluation is based on purely objective analysis. When the empirical world collides with the normative world, things often become a bit messy. The effective policy evaluator is able to dance through the minefield of politics bearing important messages for policy-makers to consider.

The specific goals for the chapter are:

- Discuss the purpose of policy evaluation and the skills needed to conduct a good evaluation.
- Discuss the *types* and *methods* of evaluation.

SKILLS OF A GOOD POLICY EVALUATOR

The late Stuart Nagel (2002) considered the required skills of a good policy evaluator:

- ***Policy expertise***
  Evaluators should have a solid understanding of the policy area being evaluated. Graduate school studies in public policy and/or public affairs help to develop an understanding of policy history, contemporary public policy, and future trends. A good policy evaluator understands multiple policy areas; often, public policies are interrelated.
- ***Public administration and management***
  Policy evaluators must understand how and why public administration works in the manner it does, variations in administrative style and operation, and the types of constraints under which administrators operate. Conceptualizing public administration requires an understanding of the philosophy of government and the dynamic nature of the social contract— the foundation of our liberal democracy. Social contracts evolve and values

change. A product of Progressivism, public administration values equity, efficiency, accountability, fiscal integrity, effectiveness, and responsiveness (Wilson 1989).

- *Organizational theory*
  Evaluators must be sensitive to organizational differences and circumstances. Every organization has different standard operating procedures, operates under different leadership, and has different employees. Additionally, organizational culture is a critical element that will shape organizational outcomes. In some instances, organizations compete with other organizations for resources. Alternatively, organizations may develop cooperative relationships with other organizations to meet organizational goals. Public–public and public–private organizational partnerships have become more common in the policy implementation process. An evaluator who understands how organizations work internally and how they relate to their "environment" will have a greater understanding of how policy implementation works, where pitfalls arise, and where policy success is realized.
- *Research methods*
  Policy evaluation relies on both qualitative and quantitative **analysis**. Quantitative analysis will likely always play a dominant role in policy evaluation. Effective policy evaluators must develop strong skills in statistical analysis.

(See Box 8.1, *A Policy Evaluator's Toolbox;* Box 8.2, *Policy Sciences and Evaluation;* and Box 8.3, *Policy Analysis Versus Policy Evaluation.*)

BOX 8.1

A Policy Evaluator's Toolbox

Knowledge/Skill/Ability	Source
Policy Area Expertise	Experience; policy sciences, political science courses.
Public Administration or Management	Experience; public administration/political science courses.
Organizational Theory	Experience; public administration, organizational psychology, cultural anthropology courses.
Research Methods/Statistics	Experience; economics, statistics, political science, policy studies, sociology, psychology courses.
Ethics and Philosophy	Experience; philosophy, comparative religion, cultural diversity, history, political science courses.

BOX 8.2

Policy Sciences and Evaluation

The policy sciences are grounded in normatively driven Progressive politics. As the late Charles Merriam argued, there is a need for a more reasoned approach to politics. As Merriam saw it, politics is frequently a highly wasteful process. Ignorant and self-interested individuals and groups pursue their objectives without any due consideration for the "higher" purposes of government—namely, efficient, effective, and equitable outcomes. The politics of the past, according to Merriam and others, were driven by power and brute force. Issues of justice were grounded in the notion that "might makes right." Merriam rejected this notion of government, concluding that the modern era would place its faith in grounded principles of general social, economic, and political advancement, rather than the interests of a narrow group of very powerful individuals.

For the Progressive-minded, policy sciences should focus on the development of reasoned approaches to the study of social, political, and economic phenomena; identify problems that can be solved through social action; and develop acceptable solutions to these problems. Policy science was seen as a liberating force in public policy, removing the influences of political "mumbo-jumbo" and encouraging "the constructive possibilities of human nature." Policy evaluation—an important part of the policy sciences—was born of this vision and continues to be guided by related principles.

BOX 8.3

Policy Analysis Versus Policy Evaluation

As discussed in Chapter 4, policy analysis often focuses on the questions of what government *ought* or *ought not* do and how normative priorities can become empirical realities. Policy analysis is conducted early on in the policy cycle, particularly during the policy formulation process, and helps guide policy choices and plans. Policy evaluation, however, is very carefully focused on existing public policy—policy that is being implemented or has been implemented.

Pointing out this distinction may seem rather pedantic, but it is a very real concern. At the time at which it is conducted, policy evaluation should attempt to measure only the impact, output, efficiency, and effectiveness of public policy. The information generated may, at a later time, serve as the foundation of future policy analysis and policy adjustments, but superior policy evaluations cannot be conducted in a fair and impartial manner if normative issues cloud the evaluation process. Without objective evaluation, it is impossible for policy-makers and administrators to have a clear sense of what policy *is* and *is not* doing. Important empirical findings must be juxtaposed with the goals of public policy and considered in future policy cycles if public policy is to advance and improve.

Given the importance of evaluation, is the distinction between *policy analysis* and *policy evaluation* understood and observed in the policy process? Frequently, the answer is: no. Policy evaluation and analysis are often confused, assumed to be one and the same. The result of this confusion is an inability by many policy-makers, administrators, and policy evaluators to separate objective conclusions about a public policy from normatively based advocacy for or rejection of public policy. In other words, the results of evaluation study are frequently viewed as either a sign of loyalty to the proponents of particular policy goals or as a serious affront.

Policy evaluators face the same constraints as did the legendary Cassandra, daughter of Priam, the King of Troy in the *Iliad*. Like Cassandra, evaluators speak truths to those who hold positions of power, but are often ignored; their "truths"—particularly painful truths—negated. At times, the evaluators involved are castigated for their efforts. Policy analysis is often driven by advocacy and the analysts are often praised by individuals and groups whose ideas they support. The policy evaluator does not have the luxury of working within such an inviting setting. Whether the evaluator's evidence demonstrates policy success or failure, the evidence will likely draw the attention of policy critics and apologists who either reject or embrace the findings.

GENERAL PURPOSES OF EVALUATION

Evaluation occurs for several reasons. According to Carol Weiss (1998), these purposes can be divided into two general categories: *overt* and *covert* purposes.

The overt purposes of **policy evaluation** are to determine: (1) the process by which a policy is being implemented and to develop a better understanding of the progression and pitfalls associated with implementation and (2) policy impacts and outcomes. Overt evaluation is done "above board," so the policy evaluator has fewer ethical dilemmas. Evaluation results are usually objective, intended to help policy-makers and implementers to develop efficient, fair, and effective policy outcomes.

Covert evaluation is often used to protect agencies from destructive "political storms." Covert evaluation is conducted for at least three reasons: (1) *postponement*, (2) *ducking responsibility*, and (3) *window dressing* (Weiss 1998, 22).

Postponement means that agencies are trying to fend off external pressures. Elected officials, clientele groups, and policy advocates or critics may be searching for information regarding agency implementation or may be pressuring the agency. An implementing agency or administrator may use evaluation to delay the distribution of information or slow the decision-making process.

Ducking responsibility is a classic example of covert evaluation. Evaluation is conducted to shed responsibility for failures and shift blame. Agencies document that they have "just" followed the rules and have not been involved with the policy failure. Ducking responsibility is unconstructive; it does not help policymakers seeking to improve outcomes.

Window dressing is a third reason for covert evaluation. The approach "offer[s] legitimacy" (Weiss 1998, 22) to agencies as they go about the implementation process. It is a method of reducing constraints imposed by elected officials via oversight and grassroots efforts to influence agency decision-making in the implementation process. Agencies claim that evaluation was conducted using objective empirical techniques for the purpose of justifying implementation decisions. Window dressing evaluations may also be done for public relations purposes to build support for a policy.

INTERNAL VERSUS EXTERNAL EVALUATIONS

Internal policy evaluators are individuals or teams drawn from an agency's own personnel. External evaluators are individuals or teams drawn from professional evaluation organizations, either for-profit private firms or not-for-profit organizations, such as a research department in a public university.

Internal Evaluation

Internal evaluations have one immediate advantage, namely, the evaluators are often well-known and trusted members of the organization being evaluated, who understand an implementing agency's organization, culture, processes, and goals. Familiarity reduces the time and effort necessary for an evaluator to learn "how" a policy is implemented. Evaluators must develop a policy narrative, drawing conclusions about (1) how a policy is being implemented, (2) the success of the implementation, and (3) constructive advice on how to improve policy implementation processes and outcomes.

Internal evaluations face several challenges. First, there is the potential for subjectivity to cloud the evaluation process and outcomes. Internal evaluators often feel a real or perceived pressure to produce positive evaluation results, aware of possibly uncomfortable relations with colleagues and supervisors if the evaluation is critical. Second, internal evaluators may ignore data damaging to the implementing agency image. Third, policy formulators, pressure groups, and clientele may disregard internal evaluation **findings**, if they do not trust the implementing agency. Finally, internal evaluators may suffer from groupthink— as members of the agency being evaluated, the evaluators might find it difficult to think outside the agency paradigm or may be constrained in their ability to consider the outcomes and impacts of policy implementation. Internal evaluators may consciously or subconsciously introduce bias into evaluation studies and findings.

External Evaluation

External evaluations are viewed as more accurate and objective. External policy evaluations may be conducted by private firms or by public organizations (e.g., universities' policy workshops) specializing in evaluation studies. Agencies prefer external evaluators who are objective, but who couch findings in an understanding of policy goals, horizons, and complexity; implementing agency processes and culture, and the nature of the target groups being served.

TYPES OF EVALUATIONS

Informal Evaluations

Sometimes implementing agencies wish to conduct small, unscientific informal studies of policy implementation processes and outcomes. Through **informal evaluation**, adjustments can be made at various stages in the implementation process. In the case of new policies, particularly policies that are not well defined through statutory guidelines, implementing agencies may find it necessary to build policy processes incrementally, and through trial and error determine an optimum process to achieve a satisfactory policy outcome. Public administrators, however, tend to be conservative and do not like to take big risks. Administrators realize that their decisions can impact the provision of resources and could damage their ability to demonstrate fiscal integrity and accountability. Therefore, informal evaluations may be conducted to determine whether policy-related decisions are producing desirable outcomes.

Informal evaluation often relies on the experience of policy administrators rather than solely on scientific objectivity. Through their collective experiences in a particular policy area, administrators often have a good idea about what is feasible and what will result in policy failure. Administrative personnel who have worked for a long period of time with a specific target group develop a sense of policy impacts. Informal evaluations are usually conducted by internal evaluators. In fact, many informal evaluations are conducted by individual personnel who collect and study readily accessible information. The nature of the evaluation usually does not demand the expense of inordinate amounts of resources to collect and analyze data. (See Box 8.4, *Data and Developing Confidence in Numerical Measurement.*)

One problem that emerges from an overreliance on informal evaluations is it often tells only a tiny portion of the story about policy implementation. Placing great faith on the experience of administrators, the approach may wrongly assume that data collected are valid and contain reliable measures of implementation processes and outcomes.

Formal Evaluations

Formal evaluations usually require a significant time commitment by evaluators and a substantial financial commitment on the part of a policy implementing agency. Implementing agencies operating under severe budget constraints may wince when faced with the cost of conducting a formal policy evaluation. Nevertheless, formal evaluation is likely to confirm or disconfirm the success of implementation efforts.

Postpolicy evaluations are one way of reducing the costs of evaluation, although postpolicy evaluations usually occur because evaluation is thought to be something that occurs "at the end." At other times, postpolicy evaluation is a function of timing—agency administrators do not establish evaluation teams or contract out for evaluation services until policy implementation has commenced. Postpolicy evaluations are typically used in the case of policies that are supported by grants-in-aid from other levels of government or from private granting institutions. Granting agencies usually require evaluation studies for purposes of accountability. Postpolicy evaluations are incapable of demonstrating the *impact* of a public policy on a target group. Because nobody really knows the condition of the target group *prior to* the implementation of a public

BOX 8.4

Data and Developing Confidence in Numerical Measurement

Collecting data involves more than simply determining its *type*. Policy evaluators must be aware of the quality of the data. First, data must be shown to have high levels of *validity*. In other words, the policy evaluator must be able to demonstrate that the measures developed through operationalization accurately represent theoretical concepts. *Face validity* is a nonstatistical approach to justifying an empirical measure for a concept. This approach appeals to intuitive sense that a measure reflects a theoretical concept. For example, *net income* is likely to be one way of measuring the concept of *socioeconomic status*. Other approaches to determining validity involve statistical analysis. *Concurrent validity* determines whether multiple measures of a concept are positively correlated (or vary in the same or very similar way) with one another. For example, if *net income, number of years of formal education completed,* and *occupational prestige* were used as measures of *socioeconomic status,* concurrent validation of the measures would be expected to yield very high positive correlations between the measures. *Discriminant validity* analysis assumes that measures that do not describe the same concept should not be correlated. For example, in a policy evaluation study of antiterrorism policies related to airport security, it would not be expected that a measure of the concept *socioeconomic status* (e.g., income) would be correlated with a measure of the concept *clientele satisfaction* (e.g., feelings toward airport security personnel).

The *reliability* of measures is also very important in policy evaluation. Measurement must be demonstrated to be consistent, otherwise the results of policy evaluation may not reflect that which is occurring. Reliability analysis requires the use of statistics to determine the consistency of a measure. *Test-retest* analysis measures the same phenomena repeatedly. If the results of measurement are the same from measure to measure, then the reliability of the measurement can be assumed.

Validity and reliability are very sophisticated topics that can be simplified through an analogy. Pretend for a moment that you are shooting a crossbow at a paper target. You have a scope with crosshairs on the crossbow to guide your arrows to the center of the target. If you find all your arrows stuck in the bull's-eye, then your scope measure of the center of the target is valid and reliable. If you find that your arrows are clustered together elsewhere on the target, then the scope's measure of the center of the target is not valid but it is reliable. Finally, if you find that your arrows are randomly distributed on the target, then the scope's measure of the center of the target is neither valid nor reliable.

policy, it is impossible to use a postpolicy evaluation approach to empirically demonstrate a change in the target group's condition.

Pre-/postpolicy evaluations are much better at demonstrating the changes brought about by the implementation of a public policy. A target group's condition prior to the implementation of a public policy is duly noted through prepolicy study. Following the policy influence on the members of the target group, an identical study is conducted to record their postpolicy condition. It is very important that identical measures are used in both the pre- and postpolicy evaluation. If the measures are not identical, then it is impossible to conduct an accurate comparison.

Whereas the pre-/postpolicy approach provides greater understanding of the condition of a target group prior to and following interaction with a public policy, it is uncertain as to whether the impact was a function of public policy or the result of changing societal conditions, unrelated to policy. For example, a welfare-to-work program may find that there was a significant increase in employment among their unemployed clientele, but was that increase in employment a function of a welfare-to-work program or was it a function of changing economic conditions?

It would be helpful if a pre-/postpolicy evaluation had at least two groups to study—one group that was served by a public policy (an **experimental group**) and another group that was similar to the target population but was not served by the public policy (a **control group**). If there was no change in the latter group while there was a significant positive change in the former group (or if the change in the latter group was not as positive as that of the former group), then the policy evaluator could conclude that the public policy, as implemented, is achieving a positive outcome and having an impact on the target population.

One problem with the policy experiment approach relates to ethics. In order to develop a control group it is necessary to deny government services to individuals who are very similar to the target population being served by public policy. An individual's constitutional rights are likely to be impinged, particularly if it is shown that the status of the experimental group is improving in an expected manner. In other words, the control group would be denied the benefits of public policy for purposes of experimentation.

In addition to demonstrating the presence or absence of positive policy outcomes, evaluators may also focus on different types or amounts of influence a public policy seeks to exert on a target population. This is very similar to medical studies scrutinizing the differential impact of medications or dosages on patients. In regulatory policy, for instance, it is often not necessary to use maximum penalties to dissuade an individual or organization from doing things deemed illegal or deleterious to the public welfare. This approach to evaluation is especially valuable to policy analysts trying to produce efficient and effective public policy. If it can be shown through policy evaluation that a simpler and more cost-effective approach to policy implementation produces the same effect as more expensive and sophisticated approaches, then it is likely that the cheaper, yet equally effective, approach should be adopted.

As with the control group scenario, offering different types and levels of service delivery may face scrutiny by target groups and other policy stakeholders. Few people are pleased to discover they were treated like test animals. If individuals or groups have been given lower quality services that do not produce the desirable effect, then they might feel discriminated against by their government. (See Box 8.5, *Qualitative Approaches to Evaluation*.)

BOX 8.5

Qualitative Approaches to Evaluation

In some instances, a public policy is not conducive to quantitative analysis. The policy may seek to produce qualitative outcomes and must, therefore, be evaluated on those terms. Although a pre-, post-, and interim evaluation design is possible, the analyses cannot be shown to have a *significant* impact on target populations without a concerted effort on the part of the policy evaluator to weave a narrative demonstrating desired policy impacts. Internal evaluations that are based in qualitative methods are usually highly suspect and are less likely to be accepted by individuals and groups who are skeptical or critical of the public policy. External evaluations using qualitative methods are often seen as potentially misleading, but the fact that these studies are being conducted by individuals and groups from outside the implementing organization tends to lend a higher degree of credibility. The evaluator's or evaluation team's track record in conducting objective policy evaluations is also of considerable importance when conducting external policy evaluations based in qualitative analysis.

Qualitative analysis requires a high level of creativity on the part of the evaluator or evaluation team. Rather than focus on formal organizational structure, qualitative process analyses focus on the informal relationship between policy actors within and outside the implementing agency. The evaluator uses personal interviews and archival data as the basis of qualitative **process evaluations,** which study the systematic organizational methods by which policy goals are accomplished. Interviews are difficult to obtain and take a considerable amount of skill on the part of the interviewer. Additionally, interviews require a time commitment on the part of the interviewer and interviewee. It takes time to answer questions and it takes time to develop the level of trust necessary to obtain accurate and complete responses. Finally, the evaluator using the interview technique must sift through hours of transcripts and written notes, trying to develop a narrative or series of narratives that describe the informal processes of policy implementation and then juxtapose that informal process with the formal processes associated with the achievement of policy goals.

Personal interviews are frequently used by evaluators conducting outcome evaluations. The evaluator might wish to conduct interim interviews with policy implementers and clientele groups. Following policy implementation, evaluators may wish to meet again with agency personnel and clientele to discuss the outcomes of the policy, outline things that went well and things that could be improved about the process of implementation, and discuss the policy impacts, quality of service, and areas of improvement associated with policy implementation.

In some cases interviews are conducted on an individual or one-on-one basis. As noted previously, interviews are expensive and time consuming. In order to maximize the use of the qualitative policy evaluation technique, focus groups are frequently used. A group of individuals from the implementing agency or clientele is invited to participate in focus groups. Although more cost effective, there is the possibility that individuals will be apprehensive in expressing views that are not consistent with the opinion of the majority of individuals present. Additionally, a form of group-think may develop—individuals will construct a group narrative rather than offer individual views; the result is that variation is diminished and evaluation results may seem stilted.

Lessons Learned from Chapter 8

SPECIFICS

- Evaluation is a highly technical process of determining whether a policy is meeting the goals it was intended to meet.
- Evaluations can be either *formal* or *informal.*
- Evaluations study the *impacts* of policy as well as the *processes* by which policy goals are accomplished.
- Evaluations can be conducted either *internally* or by *external* evaluation teams.
- Two major methods of evaluation were discussed: *quantitative* and *qualitative.*

THE BIG PICTURE

The effectiveness of policy evaluation is dependent on the type of evaluation conducted, the skill level of the evaluator or evaluation team, and the level of trust present between the evaluator or evaluation team and the individuals or agencies under study. I have outlined two major types of policy evaluation here: internal and external evaluation. Both approaches have certain strengths and certain weaknesses. Clearly, internal evaluators are faced with certain constraints associated with being a member of the implementing agency. Evaluator bias may consciously or subconsciously affect evaluation processes and outcomes. Nevertheless, internal evaluation may be capable of greater consonance between evaluation process and policy intent as defined by statute and informal policy implementation processes and subgoals. Internal evaluators may be able to gather information with greater ease due to their knowledge of the organization.

External evaluators are often viewed as being more objective in their analysis. As nonagency personnel, external evaluators may be better able to see policy and agency implementation in a holistic manner; able to compare their analyses with evaluation studies conducted under similar circumstances and of related policy. In that sense, the external evaluator or evaluation team's experience and collective knowledge covering a wide variety of evaluation studies is highly valuable to implementing agencies. Not being members of the implementing agency, however, makes the collection of relevant information more difficult and requires building trusting relationships with key actors within the implementing agency being evaluated.

Additionally, the skill level of the evaluators or evaluation teams is critical to the evaluation process. Internal and external evaluators must be chosen on the basis of their skills in—among other things—objectivity, ethical standards, statistics, quantitative and qualitative methodology, organization theory, personnel administration, and policy expertise. In the case of internal evaluation teams, the implementing agency must be committed to the provision of continual training for the evaluator or evaluation team. External policy evaluators must also be committed to continual training and retraining, but it is difficult for the implementing agency to know that skill levels are continually being improved—one way of measuring the knowledge, skills, and abilities of an external policy evaluator or evaluation team is through careful study of their past work.

An evaluation cannot be conducted in an ad hoc manner. For evaluation to be accurate and complete, it is necessary for evaluators to be active observers of public policy as it is being implemented. Evaluation must parallel the goals and processes of implementation. Goals must be operationalized for implementation *and* evaluation. Processes must be clearly identified and standards established in a manner that can be measured for purposes of evaluation. Benchmarks must be built into the policy evaluation and implementation process, which will serve as instruments of comparison between the implementing agency's goals and outcomes. Most public policies are highly complex and require months or years to achieve desired outcomes. In this case, implementing agencies and evaluators must work together to identify distinct policy phases. Each of these phases should have identifiable subgoals that must be met. Evaluators can then conduct studies with a greater understanding of what should be accomplished by a certain point. If the policy phase goals are not being met, then evaluation can be used to correct or adjust policy implementation processes and outcomes.

An important thing to remember about policy evaluation is that it is as much an art as a science. Many of the principles of policy evaluation discussed emphasize the use of a scientific method of evaluation, but a good policy evaluator is also aware that evaluation must fit policy and agency type. Just as one would not build a skyscraper out of bricks or mud, a policy evaluator must choose his or her media and tools carefully, constructing an accurate story about a policy and how it is being implemented.

Key Terms

analysis
control group
ducking responsibility
experimental group
findings
formal evaluations

informal evaluation
policy evaluation
postponement
process evaluations
window dressing

Questions for Study

1. What are three major purposes of evaluation? Identify and discuss.
2. What is the difference between formal and informal evaluation?
3. What are three major challenges to policy evaluation? Identify and discuss.

Bibliography

Berk, R., and P. Rossi. 1998. *Thinking about program evaluation,* 2nd ed. Newbury Park, CA: Sage.

Davidson, E. 2005. *Evaluation methodology basics: The nuts and bolts of sound evaluation.* Thousand Oaks, CA: Sage.

Merriam, C. 1972. *New aspects of politics.* Chicago: University of Chicago Press.

Mohr, L. 1995. *Impact analysis for program evaluation,* 2nd ed. Newbury Park, CA: Sage.

Nagel, S. 2002. *Contemporary policy evaluation.* New York: Nova Science Publishers.

_____, ed. 2002. *Handbook of public policy evaluation.* Thousand Oaks, CA: Sage.

Rogers, P., Hacsi, T., Petrosino, A., and T. Huebner, eds. 2000. *Program theory in evaluation challenges and opportunities: New directions for evaluation.* San Francisco, CA: Jossey Bass.

Stufflebeam, D. 2001. *Evaluation models.* San Francisco, CA: Jossey Bass.

Sylvia, R., Sylvia, K., and E. Gunn. 1997. *Program planning and evaluation for the public manager,* 2nd ed. Long Grove, IL: Waveland Press.

Weiss, C. 1998. *Policy evaluation.* Upper Saddle River, NJ: Prentice Hall.

Wildavsky, A. 1979. *Speaking truth to power: The art and craft of policy analysis.* Boston: Little, Brown.

Wilson, J. 1989. *Bureaucracy: What government agencies do and why they do it.* New York: Basic Books.

9

■ ■ ■

Policy Termination

CHAPTER OVERVIEW

Termination occurs for many reasons. Sometimes, philosophical differences guide termination decisions. A new political majority may deem a policy or program something in which government *ought not* engage. In other cases, termination is a function of government efficiencies. Government *does* many things; however, not all of them are done very well.

The specific goals for the chapter are:

- Define termination.
- Discuss reasons and roadblocks in termination.
- Detail a theoretical model of termination.
- Present a case study of termination.

DEFINITION OF TERMINATION

Termination is defined by Brewer and deLeon (1983) as: ". . . the deliberate conclusion or cessation of specific government functions, programs, policies, or organizations." The definition is complex. First, is the word "deliberate." In considering the nature of politics and political institutions, "deliberate" might not be the first word that comes to mind. Policy is a function of political compromise. Compromise often involves dilution of policy goals, resulting in vagueness.

Cessation means that things come to a stop. In public policy, it does not mean a gradual slowdown or a reconsideration or an adjustment or even a new direction . . . it means STOP. It is not always very easy to figure out exactly what is being done and what exactly should be stopped.

Finally, "specific" is difficult to determine. In reading about specific policy areas, one very quickly realizes that policies, programs, organizations, and government functions are interconnected. Dissembling one area will result in unintended consequences in another area.

KEY ACTORS IN TERMINATION

President

In an earlier time, presidents had a great deal of power in terminating policies or programs. Congress may have authorized a policy or program or agency, perhaps even funded it, but presidents had the power of rescission. **Rescission** means that the president could simply decide not to use the funds for their intended purpose, effectively removing the lifeblood (i.e., money) of a policy, program, or agency. Rescission effectively terminated a policy, program, or agency. Presidents could also use the power of **deferral**, which means that they would decide not to spend certain resources approved by Congress during a certain period of time, preferring to spend the monies at a later time.

Presidents often used the powers of rescission and deferral in a reasonable manner. Over time, however, presidents began to use rescission as a method of destroying programs that they didn't like. President Nixon used rescission quite heavily. In the 1970s, Congress effectively limited the president's power of rescission, requiring the president to seek Congressional approval prior to using either rescission or deferral powers.

Presidents often use their proposed budget as a method of suggesting termination. By simply leaving a policy out of their proposed budget, presidents are signaling to Congress that they believe a termination is in order. Presidents may terminate policies in this manner, but oftentimes they simply consolidate policies into new or existing programs and recommend efficiencies.

Congress

Congressional districts have different priorities. A ruralite might care less about urban housing, whereas urbanites often dislike agricultural subsidies. Everyone, it seems, has a different sacred policy area. Members of Congress are very sensitive to constituency demands. Legislators will fight "tooth and nail" to save a program because the constituency demands it to be saved, all the while decrying wasteful government spending.

Politics aside, Congress has the tools necessary to justify policy termination. The **Congressional Budget Office (CBO)** is always available to legislators and congressional committees and can be tasked to study specific policies or programs. CBO produces copious quantities of reports that provide evidence of program relevance, effectiveness, and efficiency . . . all good information for legislators to use in the decision-making process. Reports produced by the **General Accounting Office (GAO)** are available to all branches of government, often detailing program and policy results and outcomes. Legislators also have personal staff and committee staff who can be tasked to investigate policies and programs. Through legislative committees, congressional hearings are an opportunity to directly question bureaucrats, pressure groups, and constituents about policies and programs.

Congress is, however, constrained in a number of ways. First, legislators may lack the political will to pursue termination. Second, legislators operate in a complex institutional environment—in order to get their legislation passed, they need the support of other legislators. Third, legislators lack the time needed to properly conduct termination. In order to get through the interdependent network of policies and programs, legislators would use up significant amounts of time. Often, there is no political reward for policy terminations; constituents usually want new (often expensive) policies and programs.

Courts

Historically, the courts have not had a large role in policy termination, but when they do become involved, it tends to be noteworthy. In the 1930s, the Supreme Court took their first major stab at large-scale termination. Although it is often viewed differently, one could argue that the Court's decision to declare many **New Deal** programs as unconstitutional was, in effect, policy and program termination. An interinstitutional struggle ensued, with the president successfully pressuring the Court as an institution.

The Court has been much more successful in using its power to protect individual rights and liberties in shaping termination decisions. Perhaps the most significant example is desegregation. The Court's decision in ***Brown v. Board of Education*** effectively terminated segregationist policies at the state and local level. One tends not to think of this as an example of policy termination, but in fact that is exactly what it was—the Court deliberately ended "specific government functions, programs, policies [and] organizations."

Bureaucracy

Pressure groups are usually key actors in helping bureaucracies obtain resources. A bureaucracy would have little incentive to terminate anything that might negatively impact pressure group supporters. Bureaucrats, like most everyone else, want to do a good job and help their clientele as much as possible. Terminating policies or programs might reduce the ability to serve clientele.

Also, bureaucrats are self-interested. Terminating anything will likely result in personnel either being transferred to new functions or terminated. The odds are that termination will not occur, but being transferred to a new function can be very disturbing—new locations, expectations, and colleagues.

Pressure Groups and Clients

Pressure groups generally want something from government, and usually it is not *less* government. Termination of any specific policy may not affect a great number of people, but some interest groups will be directly impacted. However, because policy is so interconnected, termination may impact a wide array of interest groups. For instance, programs that involve military transportation of fresh fruits and vegetables to schools . . . if the programs were terminated, it would likely impact military, education, agriculture, and public health agencies and budgets.

Clients are also key actors in termination. As the recipients of goods and services, clients come to depend on certain resources. Termination of a policy, program, organization, or government function may result in a loss to the client or at the very least an inconvenience.

REASONS FOR TERMINATION

Brewer and de Leon (1983) and Daniels (1997) outline five reasons for termination:

1. *Financial imperatives*
   Although the national budget is quite large, it is dwarfed when compared to the functions that government is trying to perform. A lack of resources is a very important explanation for termination.
2. *Government efficiencies*
   Government is often labeled as wasteful and inefficient; but, in reality, government must regularly determine how to do "more with less"—that is, accomplish evermore-complex goals with fewer resources. At times, efficiency means that a policy, program, organization, or government function must be terminated—possibly a great idea, but just not feasible in practice.
3. *Political ideology*
   In his 1981 inaugural address, Ronald Reagan stated, "Government is not the solution to our problems, government is the problem." Reagan made clear his view that there are things that government *ought not* do. When political majorities change in Congress, when the presidency changes party control, or when judicial philosophy changes, ideology shapes termination choices.
4. *". . . a change in behavioral theory about how administrative, human, or social services should be delivered." (Daniels 1997, 6–7)*
   Often related to the three previous points, the delivery of goods and services is a key issue—it may not be a question of *ought* but more a question of *how*. Termination might mean that instead of building large public housing projects, government would partner with nonprofits to build stand-alone residential housing for low-income individuals.
5. *Learning*
   Sometimes, termination is a sign that learning is occurring. Taking a particular policy path might seem like a good idea, but later it may appear that the wrong path was taken for all the right reasons. It is painful to admit a mistake, but the upside is that it is an opportunity to learn. Sadly, when government makes a mistake, even if for all the right reasons, taxpayers are often very unforgiving: The mistake may be termed "waste" or "fraud."

ROADBLOCKS TO TERMINATION

Peter de Leon (1976) identified six major roadblocks to termination:

1. *Intellectual reluctance*
   People do not like to admit that their ideas were wrong. Policy-makers are often intellectually gifted, highly skilled, well trained, professional individuals. Admitting failure and terminating a policy choice can be extremely painful to these individuals—a blow to the ego.

2. *Institutional permanence*

When policies, programs, organizations, or direction of government are put into place, it is generally with the understanding that they will be a part of government for quite some time.

3. *Dynamic systems*

When elected leaders are considering termination, they advertently or inadvertently signal their intentions through the institutional decision-making process. Candidates often run on slogans calling for the end of policies or programs. Presidents will signal their intentions through budget recommendations. Congressional committees will pursue termination through hearings or policy evaluations. All the while, bureaucrats are keenly aware of what is going on. As dynamic systems, bureaucracy will try to proactively adjust to avoid termination.

4. *Antitermination coalitions*

Pressure groups and clientele groups are always attentive to changes. If it appears that termination of a key policy, program, organization, or government function is approaching, key pressure groups will mobilize their members, and clientele groups will likely become more politically active. Termination is much more likely to occur if antitermination forces are unable to organize against termination.

5. *Legal obstacles*

Antitermination forces will often look for legal loopholes, indicating that termination will deny persons basic rights and infringe on civil liberties. Cases may be brought to courts where judges decide whether or not a policy can be terminated. Legal challenges are long, drawn-out processes that cost a lot of money. Policy termination may be avoided because of the high short-term costs.

6. *Sunk costs*

Voters are usually upset with government waste. Terminating a policy, program, organization, or government function usually means that all of the monies spent to organize, staff, train, and supply are lost. Avoiding the thought of loss may drive many decision-makers to pursue cheaper courses of action—termination might just prove too costly.

TERMINATION: WHEN IS A GOOD TIME?

Daniels (1997, 17) identifies five key points when policy termination is more likely to occur:

1. *Presidential administration change*

When presidents first enter office, there is usually a period of optimism or hope for a better future. Usually, the president has been elected by a majority of citizens who share that person's policy preferences. In that moment of victory and for several months afterward, the president has the greatest opportunity to reorganize things and to propose significant policy changes.

2. *Ideological change*

Americans seem to thrive on change. In the late 1960s and 1970s, government's social welfare function expanded, but in the 1980s there was a movement against social welfare programming. Twenty years later, homeland security, Medicare (Part D), and S-CHIP represent a significant expansion of government.

3. *Political turbulence*

In times of political, social, and economic turbulence, citizens are apt to find any change to be a possible sign of progress toward problem solution. In 2006, for instance, many Democrats ran for congressional office on a platform of terminating military policy in Iraq. Winning the majority, the new Democratic Congress moved swiftly to end funding for the war, but encountered opposition from congressional Republicans and President George W. Bush. With the 2008 election of President Obama and larger Democratic majorities in Congress, occurring at a time of domestic economic turbulence, the movement to terminate or at least limit military policy in Iraq has gained traction.

4. *". . . ameliorating the effects of termination . . ."*

As with everything else in life, the idea of termination begs the question, "Will it hurt much?" If one can be reassured that it is pain free, pleasant, and will produce better outcomes, then there is a much greater chance that it will be more or less enthusiastically embraced.

5. *Sunsets . . . because all good things come to an end*

Avoiding termination fights might be best accomplished by agreeing on what a policy, program, organization, or government function is supposed to accomplish—in other words, purpose and goals. Another way to do this is to put a time limit on things: a **sunset clause**.

A MODEL OF POLICY TERMINATION

Susan Kirkpatrick and colleagues (1999) developed a comprehensive model explaining how termination works in practice. They identify three general categories of factors shaping termination decisions: (1) inherent characteristics, (2) political environment, and (3) constraints.

Inherent Characteristics

A great deal of the discussion of public policy in this book is about policy history. One is tempted to ask, "Why?" Well, it turns out that what happened in the past and the length of time during which something occurred explains a lot. First, it may indicate that the goal is very important and its importance is not diminishing. Second, longevity may indicate that a policy or program has a will to live. Third, if one looks at policy history and the implementing organizations, one may find that things have become interconnected over time. Agencies discover that policy areas are interrelated and form linkages between programs for reasons of efficiency and effectiveness. Finally, the nature of benefits must be considered—benefits to clients, communities, and personnel in the form of direct cash benefits or paychecks or even community development.

Studying the inherent characteristics of a policy, program, organization, or government direction may explain the feasibility of termination. Long-term programs that have grown to become a part of society are not likely to be terminated.

Political Environment

In its later stages and the post–Cold War period—periods that witnessed tremendous increases in economic growth—social programs were touted, whereas military programs were often closely scrutinized. Prevailing political ideology changed after the 1980s when many social programs faced termination. A compromise position in the form of President Clinton's **Third Way politics** may have prevented large-scale termination efforts, focusing attention on what government *does* rather than what government *ought* to do.

Constraints

One very important constraint in termination relates to the potential aftermath. Policy is often put into place because something is wrong that needs to be fixed. Discussion of eliminating social welfare and economic control policies, for instance, is often met with fear—will things fall apart? Antitermination coalitions will often use fear of uncertainty as an important part of their message.

TERMINATION: QUICK OR SLOW?

Kirkpatrick and colleagues identify methods of termination. A self-explanatory method is called **Big Bang termination**. The second approach is a bit more subtle and occurs over time. **Long Whimper termination** is the result of reorganizations, budget cuts, personnel cuts, or the redefinition of mission and purpose. (See Figure 9.1.)

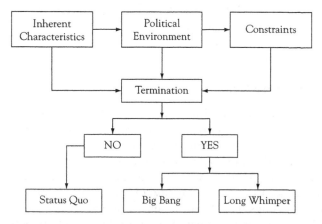

FIGURE 9.1   Process model for termination of public policy

Source: Kirkpatrick, S., J. P. Lester, and M. D. Peterson, 1999. The Termination Process: A Conceptual Framework and Application to Revenue Sharing. *Policy Studies Review,* 16(1): 219.

CASE STUDY

The Life and Death of the National Leprosarium

Quoted from: Frantz, J. E. 2002. Political Resources for Policy Terminators, *Policy Studies Journal.* 30(1): 11–28.

In 1894, the State of Louisiana established a leprosarium on an abandoned plantation on a remote peninsula of the Mississippi River just below the city of Baton Rouge. The site, near Carville, included a dilapidated plantation house and a few primitive slave houses. The first seven patients had suffered in so-called pesthouses in New Orleans before being secretly transported by raft and deposited to fend for themselves at the site. The staff was temporary and intermittent until 1896, when nuns from the Daughters of Charity of St. Vincent de Paul came to the facility. The order has provided nuns since that time (Silvers 1999, 96).

The federal government purchased the site in 1921 as a temporary place of forced exile for anyone in the United States who suffered from leprosy. Victims nationwide were transported to the primitive facility to join Louisiana's exiles. The government, unable to find a permanent location that did not inspire powerful resistance, eventually established Carville as the permanent site. A barbed-wire-topped fence around the property assured that no one was exempted from the then-prescribed treatment for the disease—exile for life. The exiles were removed from their families, denied the vote, prohibited contact with the opposite sex, ordered to assume false identities, separated from children they bore, imprisoned in the Carville bastille without trial if they escaped, and humiliated by having their outgoing mail sterilized and any money they touched chemically treated. Civil service workers at the facility were paid hazardous duty wages. According to one former patient, "This place has seen many a tear, rivers of tears. It has robbed many of us of life's joys" (Silvers 1996, 96).

There appeared to be no upside to this exile, as no effective treatment existed for the disease. Most of the patients came involuntarily, and since the disease is chronic, but rarely fatal, most lived there for decades until their natural deaths. Hidden in the language of the 1917 act (PL 64-298) that created the Center was an upside: That act required the U.S. Public Health Service (USPHS) to receive "any person afflicted with leprosy for . . . care, detention, and treatment." The language assured that victims would be detained, but it also promised lifetime care for victims of the incurable disease. The promise was amended in 1985 (PL 99-117) to assure simply that the USPHS "shall provide care and treatment (including outpatient care) without charge . . . to any person suffering from Hansen's Disease who needs and requests care and treatment for that disease." This entitlement, made the same year the Center stopped accepting new residential patients, promised free care for those who "need" it for "treatment for that disease," presumably excluding care for old age and other diseases.

Change came slowly to the leprosarium. In the 1930s and early 1940s, when the patient population reached nearly 500, a number of buildings were constructed on the property. In 1941, a doctor at the facility, Dr. Guy Faget, instituted sulfone treatments that, for the first time, gave hope to those who suffered from the disease. Faget's discovery was one of many highly significant medical discoveries made at the Center.

In 1945, the American Public Health Association (APHA) advised against isolating people with leprosy. It was by then well established that 90 percent of the population had a natural immunity to leprosy, and that it was only mildly contagious to the other 10 percent. In response, the most onerous rules at Carville were repealed. In 1946, patients were granted the franchise, and in 1948 the infamous barbed wire came down. In the 1950s, patients were allowed to marry. By 1953, patients with arrested symptoms were encouraged to leave.

The USPHS decided in the 1950s to close the Center and sent in a terminator, Dr. Eddie Gordon, as director. The resistance to closure from the patients, staff, and community must have been shocking. Gordon was forced out in less than three years. Closing the Center would be harder than expected, largely because "patients at the leprosarium possessed a considerable degree of power . . . they exercised it both within the institution and outside of it" (Gussow 1989, 177). Having cavalierly entered into a termination battle and lost, the USPHS took only tiny steps toward closure in the 1960s and 1970s. The last involuntary admission came in 1960.

In 1981, the USPHS launched another assault. Armed with an alarming budget deficit and a *political* philosophy that questioned the need for many government programs, the congressional subcommittee charged with making appropriations for the nation's health programs joined the USPHS as it targeted the nation's nine public health hospitals including the Center at Carville. Eight hospitals were closed that year. The Center stayed open (Frantz 1997).

Additional closure steps were taken in 1981 including the opening of more ambulatory care centers. The closure battle was again fully engaged. In 1982, the Office of Management and Budget (OMB) attempted to contract out jobs at the Center. Contracting out would have reduced the number of civil service employees, one of the major constituencies opposing closure. A subcommittee of the House Committee on Energy and Commerce held a hearing in Carville that led directly to a change of mind for the OMB. (U.S. Congress 1982). The OMB was especially interested in contracting out at the Center, since the supplemental hazardous pay made the payroll particularly high, but it excluded the Center when reminded that 120 of the Center's 360 patients were also on the Center payroll and unlikely to find other jobs (Peterson 1982).

The USPHS took the offensive again in 1983, when it did a formal review of the $15 million Center. By then the Center housed only 200 patients and included 98 buildings on 337 acres with "some of the amenities of a small town." The staff included 317 civil service and Public Health Service workers and 125 part-time patient–employees (USPHS 1988, 5). The USPHS recommended that the Center continue its custodial care and research programs, but asked for more outpatient clinics and a study of the elimination of residential care (1988). In 1985, the infamous hazardous-duty salary supplements were discontinued for new hires only, and the Center stopped accepting residential patients.

A 1988 USPHS report examined "whether it would be cost effective and feasible to contract out the patient care activities of the Center and transfer the research activities elsewhere" (p. 1). The report recommended: expanding the Center's mission to include other nerve-desensitizing diseases including diabetes, contracting out long-term patient care, and moving the Center's research facilities to Baton Rouge. While the Center would continue to meet "the federal government's promise of lifetime care to the current patient population," there "would be no further additions to the population, however, and over time the population would dwindle until the entire remaining facility could be closed" (p. 32). That same year, Surgeon General C. Everett Koop sent a second terminator, Dr. John Duffy, who within a year of his appointment began to loudly advocate closure. Although he favored allowing healthy residents to stay, he announced plans to move "the center's acute care, research and education functions to Baton Rouge." His recommendation was spiced with the comment that "Certainly, if given a choice between staying in this rather safe, protected world and the real world of hard knocks, most people would choose to stay, but we can't continue to create paradise forever on the backs of the American taxpayer" (Applebome 1989). His calls for change were insistent and repeated the theme " . . . a colony like this is a disgrace" (Struck 1989).

But the patients, who were organized into a Patient's Rights Federation (PRF) that dated back to the 1940s, did not want to leave and worked to keep the facility open. In 1990, the patients did agree to a plan that would gradually transform the facility into a geriatric prison. The Bureau of Prisons (BOP) rented half of the space and half of the health care services at Carville to support a small number of inmates. The prison would expand to absorb all the space and services as the Center's patient population decreased. After more than four decades, the government was finally in a position to phase out the Center as the elderly patients died. Death was imminent. The government, it seemed, had placated antitermination forces, and the Center would close (Frantz 1992).

Alas, there was considerable fight left. The geriatric prisoners arrived in 1990, and in 1992 the research branch, including 50 scientists, 150 armadillos, and 7,000 mice, was relocated to a location at Louisiana State University in Baton Rouge (Atlanta Constitution 1992). The patients, professional and nonprofessional staff, and the community fought back. In 1994, the BOP withdrew from the site claiming concern over its ability to renovate the facilities due to the designation of the site as a National Historic District (1992) and concerns about hazardous waste deposits (United States Department of Health and Human Services 1995, 34). Some of the patients took credit, claiming to have run "the Bureau of Prisons out of here" (Frink 1996). The patients called for and eventually won the resignation of Dr. John Duffy, the second terminator.

To nearly everyone's astonishment, the Center became a centenarian. A 100th birthday celebration was held in November 1994. The celebration featured a keynote speech by James Carville, a high-profile *political* supporter of then President Bill Clinton and a native of the community that housed the Center and carried his family's name (Frink 1994).

Once the celebrating was over, the USPHS and congressional budget-makers began a new assault. The staff at the Center was reduced from 344 to 216 through a 1994 government wide buy out plan (U.S. Congress, PL103-226) designed to reduce costs. Early in 1996, Congressman Richard Baker, who represented the district prior to 1992, and other government officials visited the Center to "discuss the idea of closing the center with patients and staff members" (McKinney & Frink 1996). Baker then proposed to Congress that the site be used for a job training school and that patients be given an annual living subsidy if they departed. The idea was quashed immediately when Congressman Cleo Fields, who represented the district from 1992 to 1996, objected (Carville Center Staying 1996).

Following the 1996 elections, which returned the Center to his district, Baker proposed that the site be transferred to the State of Louisiana. This time his plan was adopted. PL 105-78 provided for "relocation of the Federal facility, . . . including the relocation of the patients of the Center." There were conditions: The Carville site had to be used for health or educational purposes for thirty years, the State had to maintain the cemetery and permit burials and visitations there, and the State had to agree to permit a museum to be maintained at the site.

PL 105-78 also authorized an annual stipend of $33,000 to each patient who left the facility. The remaining patients were to be relocated within three years unless such relocation was "not feasible." The legislation offered transfer options, disability coverage, and unprecedented retirement incentives to civil service employees. It also accepted responsibility for hazardous waste problems and provided nearly $2.5 million for renovations to the property (U.S. Congress, "Report to Accompany H.R. 4272," 1999, 1). Weeks later, the U.S. Department of Labor selected the site for an $18.4 million Job Corps center for at-risk youth. In 1999, a second program operated by the Louisiana National Guard, Youth Challenge, placed its first class at the facility (Times-Picayune 1999).

The property was deeded to the State of Louisiana in August 1999. By then, some 50 patients had taken the $33,000 stipend and departed, leaving only 69. By June 2000, 37 patients remained at the site where they continued to live in their own apartments, received care from a 24-hour clinic, and shared "their own separate section in the cafeteria," which was also used by the Youth Challenge program (Frink, 2000). Roughly 24 other patients resided in a special wing at a hospital in Baton Rouge.

EXPLAINING POLICY TERMINATION

Policy termination is best explained by the following three models: game theory, group theory, and systems theory. Incrementalism could be used to explain policy termination, *especially* if one is documenting a case of Long Whimper termination—a decremental approach to ending policy, program, organization, or government policy direction.

FIGURE 9.2 Hierarchy of resistance to termination

Source: Daniels, M. R. *Terminating Public Programs: An American Political Paradox.* Armonk, NY: M.E. Sharpe, 9.

Game Theory

Policy termination is a rare event. It is rare because policy-makers have a unique interest in avoiding the conflicts associated with policy termination. Policy-makers would prefer not to spend the enormous political capital and time that it would take to eliminate a policy, program, organization, or policy direction, but it is all a matter of degree. As noted in Figure 9.2, policy or program termination is the least costly approach, whereas government function, which might incorporate a whole host of policies, programs, and organizations, is the most costly approach and perhaps the least likely to occur. Policy-makers have to be very crafty in accomplishing successful termination. Robert Behn (see Danielson 1997: 20) created a list of "One Dozen Hints" to successfully terminate:

1. Don't float trial balloons.
2. Enlarge the policy's constituency.
3. Focus on the policy's harm.
4. Take advantage of ideological shifts to demonstrate harm.
5. Inhibit compromise.
6. Recruit an outsider as administrator/terminator.
7. Avoid legislative votes.
8. Do not encroach upon legislative prerogatives.
9. Accept short-term cost increases.
10. Buy off the beneficiaries.
11. Advocate adoption.
12. Terminate only what is necessary.

Termination is about strategy and taking an indirect approach to accomplishing the goal. Avoiding compromise positions is critical because compromise only helps bureaucrats and pressure groups figure a way out of termination.

Dealing with the constituency is a critical strategic move because it effectively co-opts a key area of opposition. Enlarging the constituency is also important because it can dilute a powerful constituency and muddle the policy goals sufficiently to make it difficult to justify the purpose or need of a policy, program, organization, or government function. Goal enlargement might also have the impact of reducing resources for any specific purpose, weakening the antitermination advocates' position. Taking the opportunity to point out the harm in not terminating is also an important strategy to justify termination.

Conversely, antitermination advocates will have to counter all of the efforts of termination advocates. If terminators do not float trial balloons it will make it difficult for antitermination advocates to be proactive in their efforts. Antitermination advocates often appeal to constituents and also try to get termination decisions in front of legislators. Legislators are more likely to compromise on termination decisions, shifting policy goals to other programs—likely to do anything to avoid the conflict associated with a termination decision. Bureaucratic agencies are also key actors in antitermination movements, using their ability to deflect opponents—their "thickness" (see Daniels 1997: 24)—to avoid short-term threats to their power base.

Group Theory

As noted above, pressure groups are key actors in trying to prevent termination decisions. Pressure groups help bureaucracies by remaining vigilant to any change in political climate that might negatively impact policies, programs, organizations, or government direction related to the goals of the pressure group. Given a plethora of pressure groups, nearly every government policy area is being monitored by a pressure group. Theodore Lowi (1969) noted that liberalism is imperiled by hyperpluralism. In the case of policy termination, it is fairly evident that the ability of government to change policy direction is constrained by the presence and activity of pressure groups. Conversely, pressure groups may act as an important check on ideologues who gain policy-making power with the intent of dismantling policies that are important to citizens.

Systems Theory

Systems theory is particularly valuable in explaining why termination emerges as an issue and why it may or may not come to pass. Policy termination is not something concocted on the spur of the moment. It is usually the result of multiple iterations of policy. Policy environments change over time. As the environment changes, inputs into the policy process may also change.

Policy analysts are often keenly aware of demographic and clientele changes that might impact a policy, program, organization, or government direction. One method of avoiding termination is to co-opt new constituencies appearing on the policy horizon. In that way, programs and organizations can effectively "thicken" their walls of resistance and fend off the threat of termination.

Lessons Learned from Chapter 9

SPECIFICS

- Termination occurs for many reasons—different policy actors play different roles in termination.
- Termination can either be immediate or occur over a long period of time.
- Resistance to policy termination is dependent on the gravity of the termination decision.

THE BIG PICTURE

Termination decisions are often based on the values of policy actors. Termination decisions may be shaped by court decisions regarding the constitutionality of a policy. Segregation-related policies, for instance, were effectively terminated by landmark Supreme Court decisions. Congress often uses its budget power to terminate policies. The president uses administrative and budget power to shape termination decisions.

Key Terms

Big Bang termination	New Deal
Brown v. Board of Education	rescission
Congressional Budget Office (CBO)	sunset clause
deferral	termination
General Accounting Office (GAO)	Third way politics
Long Whimper termination	

Questions for Study

1. Why is policy termination infrequent?
2. Discuss the role of the bureaucracy in policy termination.
3. Use three models to describe and explain policy termination. Use the chapter case study as an example in applying the models.

Bibliography

Bardach, E., ed. 1976. Policy and Program Termination. *Policy sciences*. 7(2): special issue.

Behn, R. D. 1978. How to Terminate a Public Policy: A Dozen Hints for the Would-be Terminator. *Policy analysis*. 4(3): 393–413.

Brewer, G. D. 1978. Termination: Hard Choices—Harder Questions. *Public administration review*. 38(4): 338–344.

Brewer, G. D., and P. deLeon. 1983. *The foundations of policy analysis.* Pacific Grove, CA: Brooks/Cole Publishing.

Daniels, M. R. 1995. Termination, Innovation, and the American States. *American review of politics.* 15: 507–518.

_____. 1997. *Terminating public programs: An American political paradox.* Armonk, NY: M.E. Sharpe.

deLeon, P. 1982. New Perspectives on Program Termination. *Journal of policy analysis and management.* 2(1): 108–111.

Frantz, J. E. 2002. Political Resources for Policy Terminators. *Policy studies journal.* 30(1): 11–28.

Kirkpatrick, S., J. P. Lester, and M. R. Peterson. 1999. The Policy Termination Process: Framework and Application to Revenue Sharing. *Policy studies review.* 16(1): 210–236.

Court Case

Brown v. Board of Education, Topeka, Kansas 347 U.S. 493 (1954)

10

■ ■ ■

Federalism and Intergovernmental Relations (IGR)

CHAPTER OVERVIEW

Federalism shapes public dialogue regarding what government ought or ought not do. **Federalism** describes the relationship between two or more levels of government within a nation–state, wherein each level of government has leaders, who are independently chosen. Governmental units may overlap one another, and their powers, responsibilities, and interests may be interconnected. In 2007, the U.S. Census Bureau reported that there are 89,527 governments in the United States—1 national government, 50 state governments, and 89,476 local governments. Federalism is continually changing and forever impacting the nature of public policy. (See Figure 10.1.)

The specific goals for the chapter are:

- Discuss the benefits of federalism in the policy process.
- Outline the Founders' vision for federalism.
- Discuss contemporary models of federalism.
- Discuss intergovernmental relations and policy-making.

BENEFITS OF FEDERALISM

There are several advantages to federalism. First, with so many units of government, citizens have more opportunities to influence policy decisions. Second, competition between units of government in the federal system encourages government efficiency. State and local governments compete for citizen taxpayers, offering greater benefits for the tax dollar (Tiebout 1956). Third, federalism may limit the growth of government. Fourth, in the interest of maximizing its

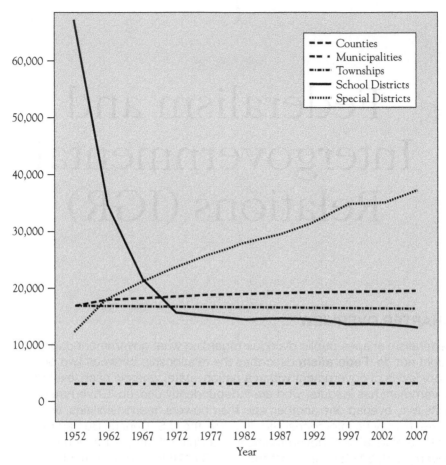

FIGURE 10.1   Units of local government 1952–2007

own benefits and minimizing its costs, governments within the federal system seek efficient and effective responses to citizen demand. Fifth, the competitive nature of federalism fosters economic growth. Sixth, federalism encourages policy innovation. Reinventing government efforts during Bill Clinton's presidency encouraged state and local governments to experiment with innovative policies. (See Box 10.1, *Origins of American Federalism.*)

BOX 10.1

Origins of American Federalism

Federalism lies somewhere between a **unitary** form of government—one that retains all power in a central government that creates local or regional government to execute policy—and **confederal government**—a government where sovereign power resides at the state, regional, or local level and central government is fairly weak.

Alexander Hamilton

The *Federalist Papers*, published under the author name "Publius," were written by Alexander Hamilton, James Madison, and John Jay. Hamilton and Madison wrote the majority of the eighty-five essays published between October 1787 and May 1788. The papers were an attempt to sway public opinion in New York in favor of the ratification of the new Constitution, but the papers hold important evidence regarding the thinking of some of the Constitution's chief architects and proponents.

In *Federalist Paper #17,* Alexander Hamilton attempted to dispel the notion that federalism will produce a strong national government and weakened state and local governments. He stated,

It will always be far more easy [*sic*] for the State governments to encroach upon the national authorities than for the national government to encroach upon the State authorities. The proof of this proposition turns upon the greater degree of influence which the State governments if they administer their affairs with uprightness and prudence, will generally possess over the people; a circumstance which at the same time teaches us that there is an inherent and intrinsic weakness in all federal constitutions; and that too much pains cannot be taken in their organization, to give them all the force which is compatible with the principles of liberty.

Hamilton went on to say that, historically, central governments have been given insufficient power to fulfill their duties and that even within unitary systems, subunits of government have often pressed central government for greater power and authority. He pointed to the origins of British government with the signing of the Magna Carta in 1215—from Hamilton's perspective, the Barons were pressing King John for greater power and authority at the expense of monarchical rule. Hamilton believed that tyranny is more likely to emerge from a weak central government—any fear associated with government power was likely related to the inequities existing between states and local governments. Hamilton supported his argument with a historical analysis of ancient Greek confederacies detailed in *Federalist Paper #18*. Hamilton argued that concerns regarding the centralizing tendency of government in a federal system are not borne out by historic evidence or logic.

In *Federalist Paper #45*, James Madison incorporated many of Hamilton's earlier arguments into a more consolidated discussion of the nature of federalism. As

James Madison

Madison envisioned it, the nature of the federal system would establish and preserve a dual governing system—a national government with clear responsibilities and powers to preserve the union of states and the basic powers of the states in relation to other states. Additionally, the national government would seek to protect the Union from external aggression and from internal discord, being mindful (as Hamilton had discussed earlier) to avoid national impositions on state lawmakers and law enforcement to protect the basic liberties of their citizens from civil discord.

The powers delegated by the proposed Constitution to the federal government are few and defined. Those which are to remain in the State

(Continued)

governments are numerous and indefinite. The former will be exercised principally on external objects, as war, peace, negotiation, and foreign commerce; with which last the power of taxation will, for the most part, be connected. The powers reserved to the several States will extend to all the objects which, in the ordinary course of affairs, concern the lives, liberties, and properties of the people, and the internal order, improvement, and prosperity of the State.

The Founders recognized that each state had different priorities and interests. The great value of federalism, therefore, would be to preserve the heterogeneity of interests without suffering those interests to be imposed by larger or politically stronger states and groups on the smaller states or the less powerful. This argument for the great strength of federal systems of government can be found in *Federalist Paper #10* in which Madison delineated the need to employ a federal government arrangement to divide the powers of governance so as to control rival factions or interests from dominating the political agenda. The division of power was further explicated in *Federalist Paper #51* in which Madison outlined the need for checks and balances in a Republican form of government—a form of government that will exist at the national and state level, thus limiting the possibility of factional control or, as discussed earlier, centralizing tendencies that would weaken state government authority. The Founders' conception of federalism, therefore, rests on the following major principles:

- The separation of powers within the national and state levels of government.
- The clear delineation of powers for the national government.
- The reduction of centralizing tendencies based upon historical evidence. A federal system of governance in the United States limits the potential trend.
- The assurance of basic rights to the citizens at the national and state level.[1]

DUAL FEDERALISM MODEL

Until Reconstruction, the federal relationship generally operated under the principles of **dual federalism**—two systems fulfilling distinct purposes without any significant overlap in function.[2] Units of government did not tightly abut one another; thus, there was little need to coordinate or cooperate. Lockean notions of liberalism were engendered through autonomous rural life.

The dual federalism model illustrates quite well a once-prevalent view of what government *ought to do*. Some Founding Fathers found dual federalism impractical, but it took more than a century to fully realize its serious limitations.[3] During the Progressive Era and the Great Depression, the Court began addressing problems with dual federalism. In theory and in practice, a few principles of dual federalism have survived. Dual federalism illustrates that different levels of government respond in unique ways to citizen needs through public policy.

COOPERATIVE FEDERALISM

The rise of the Progressive Era in the late nineteenth and early twentieth century produced a significant and lasting shift in federalism. The emergence of the so-called "marble cake" model of federalism—the notion that

PHOTO 10.1   President Franklin
D. Roosevelt (1933–1945), New Deal
legislation marked the end of a
dominant dual federalism and the
beginning of an era of cooperative
federalism.

shared policy goals existed at all levels of government—came about for a
couple of reasons:

• Awareness of change in society.
• Evolving role of government in relation to the citizenry.

   The awareness of change in society also inspired many Progressive-era reformers to limit growth in social and economic disparities. For Progressive reformers,
the America discussed by Alexis de Tocqueville and James Bryce, two sociopolitical
writers of the early and middle nineteenth century, was in peril. **Cooperative
federalism** would expedite the process of solving social and economic problems.[4]

   Cooperative federalism characterized much of the New Deal Era programming in the 1930s and 1940s. The national government helped local and state
governments produce and protect basic public goods. National hydroelectric
dams electrified cities and rural areas and provided water for domestic and agricultural uses. The New Deal programs also advanced the health and welfare
needs of citizens and promoted economic and social development. Despite the
growing presence of national government, state and local governments retained
significant responsibility in crafting public policy. Cooperative federalism promoted a shared mission but did not create uniformity. (See Photo 10.1.)

NATION-CENTERED FEDERALISM

Nation-centered federalism is consistent with the Hamiltonian view of what
government *ought* to do. Prominent during Lyndon Johnson's presidential
administration in the 1960s, nation-centered federalism employs **top-down
policymaking** strategies.

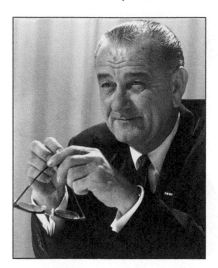

PHOTO 10.2A   President Lyndon B. Johnson (1963–1969), a proponent of nation-centered federalism.

PHOTO 10.2B   President Ronald W. Reagan (1981–1989), a proponent of state-centered federalism.

One important consideration imbued in nation-centered federalism is a belief that state and local governments either resist or downplay the need to promote political and social equality. During the 1950s and 1960s, the Supreme Court began to scrutinize government institutions, policies, and socioeconomic conditions of society to determine whether constitutional values and principles were being served; history documents the serious deficiencies.

The Court decision in *Brown v. Board of Education, Topeka, Kansas* (1954) and the passage of the Civil Rights Act of 1964 were indicative of the importance of civil rights as a policy agenda item. Policy associated with the promotion of civil rights is a primary responsibility of *all* levels of government, but best promoted and enforced through national policy attention. (See Photo 10.2.)

Nation-centered federalism was motivated by more than civil rights. Seeking to create a fair and equal existence for all Americans, President Lyndon Johnson's Great Society programs and President Richard Nixon's Equal Employment Opportunity and Affirmative Action policies focused attention on the issues of chronic poverty, educational opportunity, employment issues, and social advancement—equal treatment of adults at work and children in school.

Proponents of this view of nation-centered federalism argue that by the 1950s and 1960s, American democracy faced a serious crisis. Chronic socioeconomic and racial inequality tarnished the meaning and value of core principles. Nation-centered federalism was seen by its proponents as a practical solution to the intransigence of many state and local governments.

Critics of nation-centered federalism sharply disagree with this portrayal. In their view, nation-centered federalism violates **original intent**—that is, the Founders' intentions when framing the Constitution. The critics believe the Constitution should not be reinterpreted in ways that might affect the balance of power

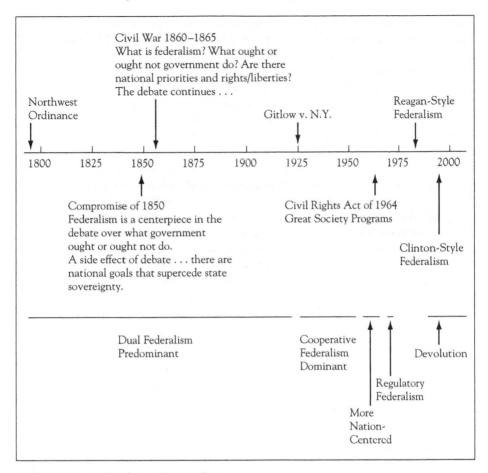

FIGURE 10.2 Federalism—the storyline

between the national and state governments. Additionally, critics of nation-centered federalism argue that the nationalization of public policy is partially a function of activism among Supreme Court justices, advancing a new vision of government and society. Furthermore, the critics state that nation-centered federalism is not the "collective will" of the people, but really a function of elite will. Finally, the critics argue that due to nationalization and growth, public policy became so complicated that elected officials divested many policy responsibilities to unelected public administrators. The critics would prefer a return to the dual federalism model, with greater focus on a state-centered federalism and local level policy-making, and a more limited role for national government in public policy. (See Figure 10.2.)

CLINTONIAN FEDERALISM AND BEYOND

The Clinton administration—along with a Republican-controlled Congress during much of the Clinton presidency—offered a new vision of cooperative federalism. Clinton's experience with public policy and government was at the state level in

Arkansas—a smaller Southern state facing many serious problems. Experience led him toward a pragmatic solutions orientation to public policy. Clinton focused greater attention on what government does or does not do, less attention on what government *ought* or *ought not* do.

As government at all levels became more results oriented in the 1990s, federalism adapted to changing needs. Increasingly, policy *goals* drove the federalism *process* rather than the other way around. Policy-makers studied the different instruments of federalism that had been developed over the decades—the various forms of grants, revenue sharing, use of funded and unfunded mandates—and tried to match policy goals with policy process. If block grants worked to best solve local attempts at growth management in burgeoning cities, then that would be the strategy adopted. If improving the impact of welfare policy was best accomplished by turning it over to state government to meet the unique needs of its citizens—**devolution**—then so be it. National government became more accepting of the idea that policy often germinates and is first tested at the state and local levels of government—the **laboratories of democracy**. In essence, there developed a certain policy-oriented pragmatism focusing on empirically demonstrated realities rather than normative issues. (See Photo 10.3.)

Although normative debate continues over the proper role and scope of government, a new policy pragmatism took American public policy beyond the scope of a simple debate about federalism. For example, public–private partnerships involving multiple levels of government became more common. Federalism has drifted away from the study of almost purely public institutional arrangements and toward a new public–private hybrid, as witnessed in the 2008-2009 federal economic bailout strategies.

PHOTO 10.3A President William J. Clinton (1993–2001), a more pragmatic approach to federalism and public policy.

PHOTO 10.3B President Barack H. Obama (2009–present), sometimes guided by pragmatism—sometimes by idealism.

INTERGOVERNMENTAL RELATIONS

The study of **intergovernmental relations (IGR)** focuses attention on the challenges of policy-making and implementation in a federal system: Different levels of government interact, frequently working together, cooperatively identifying and meeting policy goals. One of the strengths of intergovernmental relations is the ability of policy-makers at different levels of government to continually adapt their relationships to changing policy needs.

According to policy theorists Carl Van Horn and Donald Van Meter, the two major components in intergovernmental policy implementation are **policy resources** and **policy standards**. *Policy resources* come in a variety of different forms. The most identifiable resource in intergovernmental policy implementation is *money*. Policy implementation is expensive. When budgetary resources are offered in conjunction with a public policy, effective policy implementation is more likely to occur. Money, however, is only one policy resource needed for successful intergovernmental policy implementation.

The **professionalism**—*knowledge, skills, and abilities*—of implementing agency personnel are important resources. Staffing an agency is very expensive. On average, approximately 70 percent of an agency's budget is spent on personnel salaries and benefits, critical incentives in attracting, motivating, and retaining highly skilled agency personnel. Many public policies are operationalized by agency staff. At the national level, agency personnel are subject to rather uniform standards. Intergovernmental policy implementation, however, also involves agencies and personnel at the state and local level who have been acquired under different personnel systems and standards. Variations in the professionalism of personnel has a direct impact on the success of public policy implementation in the federal system.

Agency culture contributes to the success or failure of intergovernmental policy implementation. Agency culture is comprised of the norms and informal rules that shape day-to-day decision-making in an agency. The informal aspects of completing tasks in an agency are frequently as important as the formal rules and regulations. Agency culture influences the policy priorities of agencies and agency personnel. For instance, a forest management agency that has a close working relationship with timber harvesting corporations may not easily adapt to a new policy goal of forest preservation. The success of the intergovernmental policy process is shaped by the successful interfacing of different agencies with unique organizational cultures. If intergovernmental relationships can develop an effective interface despite these differences, then culture may serve as an important resource; conversely, a culture clash can harm successful implementation.

Agency culture has a substantial impact on the **dispositions of implementers.** The disposition of implementers is impacted by agency culture, evidenced by personnel responses to policy standards—the positive or negative nature of their response and the intensity of response. The disposition of implementers exists on a continuum ranging from **conservers** to **advocates**. In *Inside Bureaucracy,* Anthony Downs hypothesized that conservers wish to maintain the status quo. Careerist in mentality, they wish to simply do a job, draw a salary, and eventually retire. Change might impact their ability to smoothly move toward the aforementioned goals. Conversely, advocates are often highly enthusiastic and find personal satisfaction in advancing agency goals. They tend to be interested in new approaches in public policy, particularly changes that substantially improve accomplishment. Generally, the disposition of implementers exists somewhere between these two extreme cases. The disposition of implementers is an important issue at all levels of government, an important part of building and maintaining positive communication among policy implementers.

Socioeconomic and political conditions shape intergovernmental relationships. Economic disparity at the state or local levels of government is a serious impediment to successful intergovernmental relationships. In times of economic hardship, the ability of state and local governments to gain grant awards from national government for intergovernmental policy implementation may be constrained, yet states and localities suffering the most severe hardship, those with the greatest need of national government assistance, may be the least capable of capturing needed grant awards.

Variance in *regional norms* shapes intergovernmentalism. In his prescient studies of federalism, Daniel Elazar found that social norms impacted the effectiveness and priorities of government and the level and types of participation by citizens in shaping government policies. He referred to these norms as **political culture**. Through a sociohistorical analysis of all counties and states, Elazar identified three general types of political culture: *individualistic, moralistic, and traditionalistic.* These cultural types, which were discussed previously, shape both individual values as well as the capacity for strong intergovernmental relationships.

Individualistic political cultures, for instance, are often less receptive to national government policy influence. Governments operating in individualistic political cultures generally welcome revenues, but resist national government rules and regulations they believe will hamper their own policy-making power. Citizens living in individualistic political cultures tend to take a more classic liberal stance toward the scope and power of government. Government policy may not always be seen as an optimum solution to problems.

Traditionalistic political cultures tend to resist intergovernmental relationships. In traditionalistic political cultures, political and social elites play the primary role in the policy-making process, whereas individual citizens tend to eschew participation in the policy-making process. Traditionalistic cultures are **vertical societies** in organization; a division exists between the more powerful and the less powerful (i.e., those "above" and those "below"). Political and social elites shape the intergovernmental relationship in a way that advances their interests in maintaining the status quo.

Moralistic political cultures are often the most fruitful setting for strong intergovernmental relationships. Politics and society in the moralistic political culture tend to be **horizontal societies**; unlike a traditionalistic culture, politics and society are not stratified by separating those who have power from those who do not. Moralistic cultures foster strong social ties, encouraging citizens to collectively participate in improving community life.

Although resources are critical to policy implementation, policy standards guide policymakers toward goal accomplishment. Standards must be *clear, consistent,* and *accurate* so that all participants in the intergovernmental relationship can effectively coordinate their activities and accomplish policy goals. Standards help match expected costs with benefits, improving policy *efficiency.* Standards also define expected policy impacts, emphasizing the need to focus attention on policy *effectiveness.*

In many instances, attempts to establish clear standards are derailed by forces beyond our control. First, a new public policy is often established in response to a pressing need. Timeliness in formulation and implementation may leave little time to establish a strong theoretical foundation, clear policy standards, and an accurate identification of the target group(s). Second, the establishment of policy standards is often derailed by intergovernmental politics. Different levels of government have different policy priorities. For instance, "serious crime" may mean different things to policy-makers working in different units of government. In a small rural community, shoplifting might be seen as a serious crime, whereas in a highly urbanized area it might not be viewed the same way. State and local policy-makers may be unwilling to implement particular policies, simply because the policy is not popular with local citizens.

Enforcement of policy standards is a critical part of intergovernmental policy formation and implementation. In the implementation process, state and local governments may try to bend policy toward state or local priorities and goals. These efforts might be done for entirely harmless reasons, usually with the intent of meeting "unique" state and local needs or circumstances. In many cases, however, a policy that has been carefully considered at the national level already takes into account many of the unique conditions present in states and localities. Indiscriminate tinkering with policy during the implementation phase makes it difficult to evaluate outcomes in a uniform manner and nearly impossible to determine what works and what does not work. In order to ensure that policy is implemented according to standards, the national government must enforce policy standards.

Three general tools are available to national government policy-makers in the enforcement process and they come in two general varieties: *carrots* and *sticks.* The "carrots" are really nothing more than efforts to coax state and local governments into compliance. One form of "carrot," **norms**, are general guidelines in a public policy that help agencies make decisions consistent with the spirit of the policy, even if there are no clear guidelines for specific circumstances. Public policy-makers cannot think of every possible circumstance or condition that could confront a state or local government during the implementation process; norms are the informal guidelines that help keep the implementation process running smoothly. Another "carrot" is known as an *incentive.* The best example of an incentive is revenue to finance policy implementation. State and local governments often face financial hardships, and revenue to finance policy implementation may make these governments more attentive to national policy goals.

Although a "carrot" most of the time, incentives can also act as "sticks." If a state or local government does not respond favorably to policy standards, they may lose the incentive and the benefits of a much-needed public policy.

State and local governments are often frustrated by the alternate use of incentives as "carrots" and "sticks," particularly when there is a requirement to meet ancillary national legal requirements. National policy-makers argue that if a state or local government accepts national government assistance, then it tacitly agrees to follow national guidelines.

   Sanctions are an important "stick" in the enforcement of policy standards. The withdrawal of incentives can be considered a form of sanction by the state or local government that loses resources, but unless it involves the complete withdrawal from the implementation process on the part of the national government, it is a relatively minor form of sanction. The most serious form of sanction occurs when the national government terminates an intergovernmental relationship due to noncompliance at the state or local level. (See Figure 10.3.)

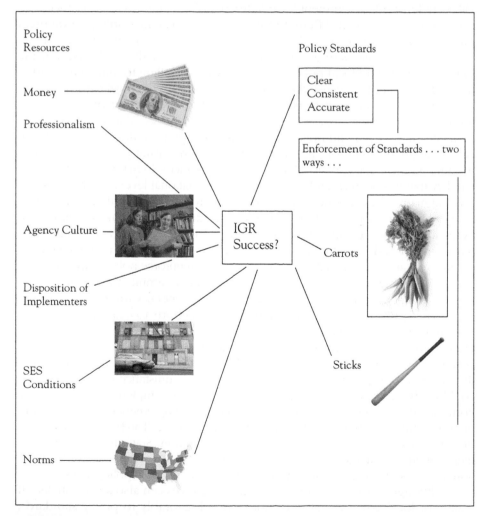

FIGURE 10.3 Factors related to successful IGR

Termination of a particular intergovernmental policy implementation relationship is usually preceded by serious attempts at negotiation between national, state, and local officials in an effort to reach policy compliance standards. The possibility of termination may be present, but it is best to eschew direct threats. In the interest of maintaining a strong intergovernmental relationship, it is better if agreement could be reached and for policy implementation to proceed.

INTERGOVERNMENTAL COLLABORATIVE POLICY-MAKING

Collaborative policy-making is a valuable method of overcoming differences and effectively responding to the needs of interest groups and citizen stakeholders. It helps to produce public policy that meets the needs of state and local citizens without compromising the core goals and values of public policy. The collaborative policy process is multidimensional and dynamic with all stakeholders actively educating each other about their understanding of a public policy, expectations, limitations, and needs. Instead of focusing on singular leadership in policy-making, it invites all stakeholders to participate in collective leadership. Support for policy-making outcomes is enhanced because it is the product of mutual agreement.

Critics of collaborative policy-making find it to be too process-oriented, focusing limited attention on the original intent of federalism. Critics argue that collaborative policy-making devalues differences between decision-making institutions and the role of elected representatives. Instead, greater emphasis is placed on the direct interaction between citizens, elected officials, and public administrators in formulating policy. Some critics see collaborative policy-making as contributing to a left-of-center communitarian approach to governance, more consistent with Rousseau's "General Will" than the Framers' Lockean notions of government and of individual rights and liberties.

FISCAL FEDERALISM

Fiscal federalism illustrates the differences between how classical liberals (many modern-day Republicans) and modern liberals (many modern-day Democrats) view the role of government. **Fiscal federalism** is the use of grants and revenue sharing by national government to shape the policy choices of state and local government. Fiscal federalism featured prominently during the era of so-called nation-centered federalism.

Categorical and formula grants have very specific policy guidelines that must be met by state and local government recipients to maintain policy compliance. **Categorical grants** are designed to meet specific policy goals using predetermined methods (e.g., rules and regulations for policy implementation). The grant amounts for categorical grants are usually firmly established. **Formula grant** amounts vary depending on the number of individuals being served by a policy or other demographic indicators.

Categorical and formula grants are built on the assumption that policy theory and methods are both valid and reliable. The assumption appears faulty when one considers the process of policymaking. For example, elected leaders, policy formulators, may lack a clear notion of the theoretical foundations of policy; worse still, competing theories may lead to an "either-or" choice or a form of compromise, diluting the impact of policy. When policy formulators have no clear notion or interest in policy theory, public administrators must operationalize policy goals as best they can with the resources and time available. Further, a lack of clear theory means that the true costs of meeting policy goals is not understood.

In the case of categorical and formula grants, many of the aforementioned dilemmas are passed along to state and local governments. If agencies simply follow policy guidelines that have not been adequately tested before implementation, then public policy may exacerbate the very problems to be solved or create new problems. Without clear causality connecting problem resolution with public policy interventions, any failure in meeting policy goals may produce conflict: Was the policy flawed or were state and local administrators incapable of following policy guidelines? Insufficient resources may also lead to crises in the implementation process. A policy may be grounded in solid theory, but without adequate funding, policy goals may not be fully realized.

Policy adoption may be a matter of choice for state and local governments. The national government will offer a limited amount of money to state and local governments that choose to develop specific public policies. State and local governments that find the policy desirable and wish to obtain resources to fund it are likely to apply; those who are not interested will not be burdened with additional policy development and implementation issues. The resources that are available in this type of grant arrangement are known as **project grants**. Project grants involve a competitive application process. State and local governments interested in applying for a project grant must develop proposals (i.e., detailing project goals, process, and costs) that meet grant requirements; the proposals are evaluated by national policy-makers and administrators, and grants are awarded on the basis of proposal merit.

In many cases, however, national policies are not a matter of choice; rather, they are **mandated**—policy goals that must be met by states and local governments. States and local governments prefer fully funded mandates, but often find that **matching funds** are better than receiving nothing at all. When a mandated policy comes with money for implementation, it is called a **funded mandate**; when it does not, it is called an **unfunded mandate**. When national budgets are constrained—particularly the case during periods of economic decline—unfunded mandates are more common.

During the presidency of Ronald Reagan, **block grants** became more common. Block grants do not specify policy goals and processes, leaving it up to state and local policy-makers to identify specific goals and policy methods. Block grants deemphasize accountability to national policy-makers, which may invite the potential for fiscal mismanagement or waste. In addition to limited fiscal accountability, block grants may not require policy evaluation demonstrating outcomes or impact, limiting the ability of policy-makers to determine the success and failure of policy initiatives.

Lessons Learned from Chapter 10

SPECIFICS

- Federalism establishes unity and coordination in the policy process without creating uniformity.
- The Founders' vision of federalism was built around classical liberal principles, the need to protect state and local government, and the goal of avoiding factional control of government and the policy process.
- Until the rise of the Progressive Era in the late nineteenth century, the dual federalism model was the dominant approach to defining the federalism relationship. As the need for well-coordinated and sophisticated public policy became more visible, the cooperative federalism model was more applicable.
- Issues of political and social equality led to alternative federalism relationships in the mid- to late twentieth century.
- Clintonian federalism emphasized the need for pragmatic policy relationships between levels of government.
- Strong intergovernmental relations are an important part of policy success in a federal system.

THE BIG PICTURE

Federalism is a work in progress—the dynamic relationship between various levels and units of government. The federal system adds tremendous strength to a nation with differing local, state, and national policy priorities and needs. The system cultivates a dialogue between units of government and individuals who live and work within these jurisdictions, allowing for policy to be formed appropriately. Federalism is as much a philosophy of government—as the *Federalist Papers* illustrate—as it is a reality that shapes public policy and, consequently, our individual lives. While commencing his presidency with a strong philosophical vision for federalism at the dawn of the twenty-first century, the vision of President Clinton led us toward a more pragmatic vision of federalism, illustrated in various policy areas. Economic crisis has led President Obama to adopt a similar pragmatic view of federalism, although the message in the early months of his presidency—and perhaps still a part of his vision for America—illustrates that the philosophy of government debates related in the *Federalist Papers* remain an active part of the U.S. public policy.

Key Terms

advocates

agency culture

block grants

categorical grants

collaborative policy-making

conservers

cooperative federalism

devolution

disposition of implementers

dual federalism

federalism
fiscal federalism
formula grants
funded mandates
horizontal societies
intergovernmental relations (IGR)
laboratories of democracy
mandate
matching funds
nation-centered federalism
norms

original intent
policy resources
policy standards
political culture
professionalism
project grants
sanctions
socioeconomic
top-down policy making
unfunded mandate
vertical societies

Questions for Study

1. What is dual federalism? Compare dual federalism to cooperative federalism and provide examples of public policy that illustrate these two models.
2. As a former state governor, President Bill Clinton had a unique vision for American federalism. What was President Clinton's vision for federal-state-local government policy interrelationships?
3. What is fiscal federalism? Identify and discuss three approaches to fiscal federalism, as discussed in this chapter.

Bibliography

Derthick, M. 1974. *Between state and nation: Regional organizations of the United States.* Washington, DC: Brookings Institution.
———— ed. 1999. *Dilemmas of scale in America's federal democracy.* New York: Cambridge University Press.
Downs, A. 1967. *Inside bureaucracy.* Boston: Little, Brown.
Dye, T. 1990. *American federalism: Competition among governments.* Lexington, MA: Lexington Books.
Elazar, D. 1966. *American federalism: A view from the states.* New York: Crowell.
————. 1987. *Exploring federalism.* University, AL: University of Alabama Press.
Graves, W. B. 1964. *American intergovernmental relations: Their origins, historical development, and current status.* New York: Scribner.
Grodzins, M. 1966. *The American system: A new view of government in the United States.* Edited by Daniel Elazar. Chicago: Rand McNally.
Hamilton, A., J. Madison, and J. Jay. 1981. *The federalist papers: A collection of essays written in support of the constitution of the United States.* Edited by R. P. Fairfield. Baltimore: Johns Hopkins University Press.
Holdstedt, M., ed. 2006. *Federalism: History and current issues.* New York: Novinka Books.
Jones, C. O., and R. D. Thomas, eds. 1976. *Public policy-making in a federal system.* Beverly Hills, CA: Sage Publications.

Karmis, D., and W. Norman, eds. 2005. *Theories of federalism: A reader.* New York: Palgrave Macmillan.

Nice, D. C. 1987. *Federalism: The politics of intergovernmental relations.* New York: St. Martin's Press.

———. 1994. *Policy innovation in state government.* Ames: Iowa State University Press.

Osborne, D. 1990. *Laboratories of democracy: A new breed of governor creates models for national growth.* Cambridge, MA: Harvard Business School Press.

Patterson, J. 1969. *The new deal and the states: Federalism in transition.* Princeton, NJ: Princeton University Press.

Peterson, P. 1995. *The price of federalism.* Washington, DC: Brookings Institution.

Peterson, P., B. G. Rabe, and K. K. Wong. 1986. *When federalism works.* Washington, DC: Brookings Institution.

Sundquist, J. 1969. *Making federalism work: A study of program coordination at the community level.* Washington, DC: Brookings Institution.

Thomas, C. S. 1991. *American union in federalist political thought.* New York: Garland.

Tiebout, C. 1956. A pure theory of local expenditures. *Journal of Political Economy.* 64:416–424.

Van Meter, D., and C. Van Horn. 1975. The policy implementation process: A conceptual framework. *Administration & Society.* 6(4): 445–88.

Wildavsky, A., ed. 1967. *American federalism in perspective.* Boston, MA: Little, Brown.

Court Case

Brown v. Board of Education, Topeka, Kansas 347 U.S. 493 (1954)

Endnotes

1. National government protections of basic rights of citizens within the states remained out of its purview for a substantial period and remains an issue of debate even today.
2. The national government tended to focus primary concern in exercising its powers enumerated in the Constitution. One important exception was the passage of the Northwest Ordinance of 1787, which provided for the development of grammar schools for the provision of basic education. The Northwest Ordinance established an important precedence for national government; early on, the national government delineated its concern with the identification and protection of public goods that states could not fully consider. In essence, the national government saw for itself a role first alluded to by Hamilton in *Federalist Paper #36*—namely, the need to ensure some basic equity between citizens (in the case of Hamilton's essay, the discussion revolved around taxation issues).

3. In many ways, the history of dominant dual federalism reflects Hamilton's conjecture in *Federalist Paper #36* that in a federal system with weak central government powers, powerful state governments may work to advance their own agenda to the detriment of weaker or smaller states and, ultimately, lead to the collapse of the federal system as originally instituted.

4. The cooperative federalism model was helped along by major reforms at all three levels of government and within the branches of government, particularly at the national level. Campaigns led to the expression of reformers' opinions to a wide audience and elections produced progressively minded political leaders. The news media and public interest groups advanced a Progressive policy agenda, detailing the social and economic issues to be addressed at all levels of government. The judiciary focused greater attention on the basic rights and liberties guaranteed in the U.S. Constitution, and began the evolutionary process of applying, through legal precedent, nationally guaranteed rights to public policy-making occurring at the state and local level.

11

■ ■ ■

Defense Policy

CHAPTER OVERVIEW

The classic question in defense policy formation is: "How much defense is enough?" U.S. commitment to defense can be very roughly measured through defense budget figures. The Department of Defense is requesting $663.8 billion for fiscal year 2010, "including $533.8 billion in base funds and $130.0 billion in Overseas Contingency Operations (OCO) funds."[1] However, budget figures alone do not answer the question of how much defense is enough. How much we *ought* to spend is a function of policy debate— namely, what *does* and what *doesn't* the Defense Department do with the fiscal resources, and what *ought* or *ought not* be done in terms of *defense*?

The specific goals for the chapter are:

- Discuss the defense policy structure.
- Outline the major participants in defense policy.
- Outline Cold War defense policy as the beginning of modern U.S. defense policy.
- Discuss the nuclear arms race and major weapons treaties.
- Discuss *post–Cold War* and *post–post Cold War* defense policy.
- Discuss ballistic missile defense.
- Discuss homeland security.

THE DEFENSE POLICY STRUCTURE

The organization of defense policy in the United States continues to evolve. Elected and appointed officials play a role in shaping defense policy, but many aspects of defense policy are delegated to U.S. armed personnel leaders. The U.S. military has three major branches: the Departments of the Army (established 1775), Navy (1775), and Air Force (1947). The U.S. Marine Corps (1775) exists within the Department of the Navy. In peacetime, the U.S. Coast Guard is attached to the U.S. Department of Homeland Security; during wartime it has historically been part of the Navy.[2]

The Cold War between the United States and Soviet Union (U.S.S.R.) fostered the need to coordinate defense policy (military) with diplomatic foreign

BOX 11.1

National Security Council: Regular Attendees

President (Chair)

Vice President	Secretary of State
Secretary of Defense	Secretary of Treasury
Director of National Intelligence	Chairman, Joint Chiefs of Staff
National Security Advisor	

Other attendees include Chief of Staff to the President, Counsel to the President, and Assistant to the President for Economic Policy. "The heads of other executive departments and agencies, as well as other senior officials, are invited to attend meetings of the NSC when appropriate" (www.whitehouse.gov/administration/eop/nsc/, accessed May 18, 2009).

policy (U.S. State Department). In 1947, the U.S. Congress responded, passing the **National Security Act (NSA)**. Revised over the last six decades, NSA created a more unified vision of defense policy.

The creation of a unified defense policy, and the linking of that policy to the diplomatic foreign affairs mission, is controversial. Proponents view it as coordinating related policy areas, currently evident in the war against terrorism. Critics charge that linking defense policy with diplomacy creates a threatening posture.

NSA created four major units:

- **National Security Council (NSC)**
  Since 1949, the NSC has resided in the Executive Office of the President. (See Box 11.1, *National Security Council.*)
- **U.S. Department of Defense (DOD)**
  The secretary of defense manages *all* military force policy. A civilian appointed by the president, the secretary of defense, and his assistants work closely with the military commanders for each branch in developing a unified defense policy.
- **Joint Chiefs of Staff system (JCS)**
  The secretary of defense coordinates activities with the JCS, comprised of a rotating chairpersonship, the force commanders for each branch of the U.S. military (to include the U.S. Marine Corps), and a director of management. The JCS are assisted by a joint staff for general areas of military function, and combatant commanders from the major military force commands, ranging from Space Command to Special Operations Command to European Command.[3] According to the *Goldwater–Nichols DOD Reorganization Act of 1986*, the JCS primarily serves as a coordinating body to assist the president.
- **U.S. Air Force (USAF)**
  USAF mission includes manned aerial missions in combat, nuclear warfare via missile systems, and global satellite surveillance.

MAJOR PARTICIPANTS IN DEFENSE POLICY

President

Article II of the U.S. Constitution gives the president the power of commander-in-chief of the armed forces. The president has the ability to shape defense policy through his vision of international policy and related defense needs. For instance, President Reagan focused his attention on the bipolarity of the United States and the Soviet Union during the Cold War. President Clinton emphasized a multilateral approach to promoting political stability internationally and shaped defense policy accordingly. President George W. Bush focused on the War on Terrorism. President Barack Obama focuses on several issues. Among the many issues he seeks to address are: reducing United States military presence in Iraq, bolstering military strength in Afghanistan, responding to pirate activity off the coast of Somalia, responding to North Korean missile tests, and reinvigorating the peace process between Israel and her regional neighbors.

Congress

Congress plays a central role in funding and formulating defense policy. Legislators are aware of the power of the defense apparatus to shape their decision-making. Defense contractors have factories or projects in many congressional districts, and legislators are aware of the potential for local economic impact resulting from congressional decisions. Military facilities are scattered throughout congressional districts and states, which is another benefit to local economies. As voters, servicemen and women influence elections, focusing legislator attention.

Interest Groups

Defense contractors—economic interests—are aware that decisions made by the elected officials and administrators impact current and future profits. Literally, billions of dollars are at stake in defense contracting. Industry lobbyists are in close contact with defense policy administrators and elected officials, discussing weapons systems development and equipment needs. Service-oriented interest groups, such as the Association of the United States Army, lobby for improved compensation. Groups such as Defense Watch scrutinize budget choices, military strategies, and implementation orientations. Human rights groups investigate the impact of defense policies on human rights.

Military Commanders and Personnel at the "Street Level"

Senior commanders develop strategic plans, but junior-level officers and enlisted personnel are most directly involved in implementing defense policy. Their leadership decisions have a tremendous impact on the success or failure of policy plans. Winning the war or winning the peace is a function of the professionalism of the *individual* in uniform. (See Photo 11.1.)

PHOTO 11.1 The commander and "street level" personnel: President Bush and a saluting United States Marine

DEFENSE POLICY DURING THE COLD WAR

Section 1084 of the 1998 National Defense Authorization Act states that the Cold War period began on September 2, 1945,[4] and ended in 1991 when the Soviet Union officially dissolved as a government.[5] From the U.S. perspective, the world was divided into three groups: Western capitalist democracies (First World), Communist regimes (Second World), and unallied developing nations (Third World).

An early policy solution was a defense and foreign diplomatic policy strategy developed in 1947 and known as the **Truman Doctrine**. Through a **containment policy**, the United States sought to stop the spread of communism, Soviet-style and otherwise. In April 1949, the United States, Canada, and ten Western European nations signed the Washington Treaty, creating the **North Atlantic Treaty Organization (NATO)**, pledging mutual defense.[6] Further containment efforts were formalized in 1954 when the United States,

Multiple nuclear warheads . . .   . . . Atop a "peacekeeper ICBM" missile

Australia, France, Great Britain, New Zealand, Pakistan, the Philippines, and Thailand formed the **Southeast Asia Treaty Organization (SEATO)**, a mutual defense pact intended to limit communist influence in Southeast Asia. U.S. defense policy followed up on these diplomatic efforts in two major ways:

- Established posts and bases in allied nations, stationed U.S. military personnel at these locations, and drew up strategic defense plans.
- The NSC and JCS developed operational plans to draw Third World nations into alliance with First World nations.

NUCLEAR ARMS RACE

The world's first major **nuclear arms race** was a Cold War phenomenon involving the United States and the Soviet Union. U.S. nuclear weapon basing used a **triad** system. Weapons were based in three general locations: on strategic bomber aircraft (for aerial bombardment), on submarines (for sea-based launches), and on land in missile silos located in the United States and allied nations.

The total number of U.S. atomic and nuclear warheads increased dramatically following World War II, from a handful of in-production weapons in 1945 to 31,700 nuclear warheads in 1966. Between 1966 and 1991, the total number of warheads declined by 42 percent. As of 2002, the United States possessed approximately 10,455 nuclear weapons. In 2004, President George Bush implemented a plan to reduce the nuclear weapons stockpile by 50 percent by 2012,

BOX 11.2

Nuclear Arms: United States and Russia 1947–2009

During the Cold War, the number of Soviet strategic warheads lagged behind the United States' strategic warhead stockpile. The number of nonstrategic warheads in the Soviet nuclear arsenal, however, actually surpassed the United States in the late 1960s and outnumbered the U.S. nonstrategic warhead stockpile for the remainder of the Cold War. The missile count became a primary measuring stick in determining "security." How much "defense" was enough? Many defense policy strategists considered either missile parity or superiority as the determining factor in answering that question.

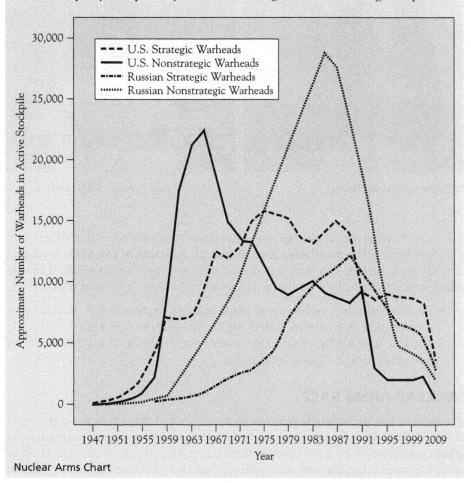

Nuclear Arms Chart

with implementation of this goal finalized five years ahead of schedule. President Barack Obama called for further reductions in the nuclear arsenal. By 2012, the United States' nuclear weapons stockpile is estimated to include approximately 4,600 warheads.[7] (See Box 11.2, *Nuclear Arms: United States and Russia 1947–2009.*)

NUCLEAR WEAPONS TREATIES

During the arms race, numerous efforts were made to prevent the proliferation of nuclear weapons. Some treaties were bilateral (United States and Soviet Union), whereas others were multilateral. Listed below are a number of **nuclear weapons treaties** by date. Although the Cold War may have ended, nuclear weapons remain a serious threat to world peace.

- 1963: *Partial Test Ban Treaty* (PTBT) [United States and Soviet Union] "This treaty prohibited nuclear testing in the atmosphere, the oceans and outer space. In essence, it was an environmental treaty that disarmed and outraged public opinion, but allowed nuclear testing to continue underground. The Treaty contained a preambular promise to continue negotiations for an end to all nuclear test explosions, which would limit the ability of the nuclear weapons states to make qualitative improvements in their nuclear arsenals" (Krieger 2005).
- 1968: *Non-Proliferation of Nuclear Weapons* (NPT) [United States, United Kingdom, and Soviet Union]. "The treaty was built on the promise that non nuclear weapons states would not acquire nuclear weapons. For their part of the bargain, the nuclear weapons states promised in Article VI 'to pursue negotiations in good faith on effective measures relating to cessation of the nuclear arms race at an early date and to nuclear disarmament . . .' The Treaty described 'research, production and use of nuclear energy for peaceful purposes' as an 'inalienable right,' and promised assistance with nuclear energy to the less developed nations. The Treaty by its terms called for an amendment conference 25 years after its entry into force 'to decide whether the Treaty shall continue in force indefinitely, or shall be extended for an additional fixed period or periods'" (Krieger 2005).
- 1972: *Anti-Ballistic Missile Treaty* (ABM) [United States and Soviet Union] "The 1972 ABM Treaty limited the anti-missile defenses that could be deployed by the United States and the Soviet Union. Each country was allowed to emplace anti-ballistic missile defenses at only two sites, its capital and one other site (later reduced to only one site). This Treaty, signed by President Richard Nixon for the United States, and General Secretary Leonid Brezhnev for the Soviet Union, was considered important because it was designed to prevent a defensive arms race that would spur a further offensive nuclear arms race. It was considered essential in order to allow the United States and Soviet Union to move ahead on limiting the quantity of their nuclear warheads and delivery systems. Following the end of the Cold War, the United States has sought to change the terms of the ABM Treaty to allow for the deployment of a National Missile Defense system, to counter perceived threats from countries such as North Korea" (Krieger 2005).
- 1972: *Strategic Arms Limitation Treaty I* (Official Title: "Interim Agreement Between the United States of America and the Union of Soviet Socialist Republics on Certain Measures with Respect to the Limitation of Strategic Offensive Arms") The United States and Soviet Union agreed not to develop any more fixed land-based long-range nuclear missile launchers nor to

retrofit old launchers for heavier missiles. Additionally, both nations agreed to "limit" the number of sea-based submarine missile launching systems and to develop a verification system to ensure treaty compliance.

- 1979: *Strategic Arms Limitation Treaty II* (Official Title: "Treaty Between the United States of America and the Union of Soviet Socialist Republics on the Limitation of Strategic Offensive Arms Together with Agreed Statements on Common Understandings Regarding the Treaty") Nuclear weaponry advancement during the 1970s led to the development of so-called MIRVs—multiple independently targetable reentry vehicles. In essence, each missile system was capable of holding several nuclear warheads that would be guided to different targets. Each missile was now the equivalent of multiple missiles. The bulk of the treaty is an attempt to limit MIRVs and thus reduce nuclear warheads rather than simply focusing on launching systems as an equivalent measure of warheads—no longer a valid central concern due to the development of MIRV technology.
- 1988: *Intermediate Nuclear Forces* (INF) [United States and Soviet Union] ". . . eliminated a whole class of nuclear weapons (those with a range between 500 and 5,000 km)" (Krieger 2005).
- 1991: *Strategic Arms Reduction Treaty I* (START I) ". . . called for reductions to some 6,500 to 7,000 nuclear weapons on each side" (Krieger 2005).
- 1993: *Strategic Arms Reduction Treaty II* (START II) Reduced the START I "number down to 3,000 to 3,500 strategic nuclear weapons on each side. . . ." (Krieger 2005). START II was ratified by the Russian Duma in 2000, but the SORT treaty has superseded START II. (See Photo 11.2.)
- 1999: *Comprehensive Test Ban Treaty* Once in effect, the treaty would ban nuclear explosions. "As of 1999, it has been signed by over 150 countries. To enter into force it must be ratified by all 44 states with a nuclear capacity. By late 1999, it had been ratified by more than half of the 44 countries. Among the nuclear weapons states, only the U.K. and France had ratified

PHOTO 11.2 President George H. W. Bush and Boris Yeltsin signing START II Treaty

the Treaty. Nuclear weapons states that [have] yet to ratify the Treaty [are] the United States . . . China, India, Pakistan and Israel" (Krieger 2005).

- 2002: *Strategic Offensive Reductions Treaty* (SORT) [United States and Russian Federation] ". . . the aggregate number of such warheads does not exceed 1,700–2,200 for each Party. Each Party shall determine for itself the composition and structure of its strategic offensive arms, based on the established aggregate limit for the number of such warheads." [8]

POST–COLD WAR ERA

In the aftermath of the Soviet Union's collapse, the United States emerged as the world's last remaining superpower. Defense policy refocused on **new interventionism**—a policy of sending military forces to various locations to quell political or social turmoil, thus avoiding broader conflict. The presidency of George H. W. Bush (Bush I) witnessed the early stages of the transition to post–Cold War defense policy and new interventionism. Two examples of new interventionism during Bush I were (1) Panama invasion (small-scale interventionism) and (2) Operation Desert Storm (large-scale interventionism).

The stated purpose of the Panama invasion was to remove Panamanian dictator Manuel Noriega from power. The United States alleged that Noriega and his regime were trafficking illegal drugs from South American nations to the United States. The dictator might have used Panama's impending control over the Canal Zone shipping lanes as a strategic weapon against the United States and other national interests. Panama was invaded, and Noriega was captured and arrested.

Operation Desert Storm was fought in the spirit of a major land war. A joint service operation, the military campaign called for massive aerial bombardment. A large ground force advanced into the enemy's territory. U.S. and allied forces rapidly extricated the Iraqi military from Kuwait.

Beginning in the 1980s, military interventionism became increasingly linked with domestic policy objectives. The war on drugs was a prominent domestic policy item for Ronald Reagan, and grew in importance during the Bush I and Clinton years. The military was tasked to search for and destroy drug production facilities in various Latin American nations, primarily Columbia and Bolivia. DOD, FBI, and CIA agents collaborated in the search for drug production and transportation facilities located in other nations.

In the 1990s, new interventionism turned toward peace keeping operations. World events led President Clinton to shift focus from domestic to foreign affairs and defense policy. Interventions in Somalia and Bosnia are two examples of efforts made during the Clinton presidency. In both cases, interventionism dealt with the impact of interethnic conflict in developing nations.

POST–POST COLD WAR ERA AND THE WAR ON TERRORISM

The post–post Cold War era began on September 11, 2001, when terrorists hijacked three U.S. commercial airliners and deliberately crashed the jets into the World Trade Center towers in New York City and the Pentagon in

PHOTO 11.3   Twin towers of the WTC burning: A new era in defense policy begins

Washington, D.C.[9] (See Photo 11.3.) The United States now finds its interests directly confronted by state (i.e., international political regimes) and nonstate (i.e., terrorists) actors. In the post–post Cold War period, the United States used focusing events to pursue shifting alliances (the "coalition of the willing," for example, comprised of many Eastern European nations and others), probing the strengths/weaknesses of post–World War II alliance structures, and establishing new basing agreements with nations in Central Asia (Peimani 2003) and talk of possible reductions in U.S. force presence in Western Europe.

QUADRENNIAL DEFENSE REVIEW (QDR) 2006

The **Quadrennial Defense Reviews (QDR)** are comprehensive defense analyses of current capacity, current and future need, recommendations to meet future need, and current progress toward current and future goals. QDR 2006 benefitted from a serious reflection on nearly five years of post–9/11 conflict. The report identifies four major current and future goals (see Figure 11.1):

1. Defeat terrorist networks
2. Prevent acquisition or use of [weapons of mass destruction]
3. Defend homeland in depth
4. Shape choices of countries at strategic crossroads.[10]

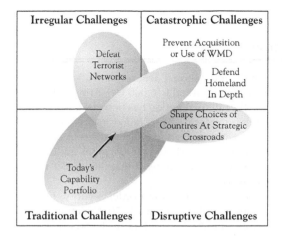

Irregular Challenges	Catastrophic Challenges
Defeat Terrorist Networks	Prevent Acquisition or Use of WMD Defend Homeland In Depth
Today's Capability Portfolio	Shape Choices of Countires At Strategic Crossroads
Traditional Challenges	Disruptive Challenges

FIGURE 11.1 Four goals of QDR 2006.
Source: Rumsfeld, D. 2006. *Quadrennial defense review report.* Washington, DC: Department of Defense.

Following is a summary of several key QDR 2006 recommendations:

- Large-scale reorganization of force structure into modules—an entirely new approach that steps away from traditional unit structure. Also, greater emphasis on permanent integrated force activities and integrated communications.
- Expansion in the number of special forces units in *all* branches of the military.
- Increased civilian–military interactions in key nations and regions. Greater emphasis on language and culture training.
- Operations tailored to mission rather than reliance on generic solutions.
- Larger and stronger U.S. Navy. Missile submarines should move toward increased use of conventional weapons, but maintain their role in the nuclear triad.
- Next generation missile technology integrated into defense system.
- Intelligence gathering updated: greater capacity and improved analysis.
- Greater integration of State Department functions with Department of Defense. Increased development of both the domestic *and* international mission of Department of Defense (e.g., see Box 11.3, *Immigration and National Defense*).
- Greater emphasis on space-based approaches to defense.

QDR 2006 illustrates the significant movement in defense policy in the last sixty years. What is not prominently featured in QDR 2006? The study does not fully consider the possibility of a large-scale military competition from major industrialized nations.

BALLISTIC MISSILE DEFENSE

In 1984, under the direction of Ronald Reagan, the **Strategic Defense Initiative Organization (SDIO)** was tasked with exploring the potential for space-based antimissile weapons as a method of overcoming the **mutually assured destruction (MAD)** policy of the nuclear arms race. In 1993, SDIO became the

BOX 11.3

Immigration and National Defense

Recent news articles tend to link immigration and national defense in relation to border control issues. In 2006, President Bush ordered roughly 6,000 U.S. Army National Guard troops to the U.S.–Mexico border.[14] Illegal immigration has become a hot topic policy issue in the United States. Immigration reform efforts failed in Congress, although there was strong pressure from special interests and conservatives to tighten border security and to build a fence along the border. Along with concerns about undocumented workers entering the United States, there are fears that the border with Mexico would serve as an entryway for terrorists.

Although many individuals might be concerned about border security, immigration plays a role in national defense. Currently, there are nearly 70,000 immigrants in the U.S. armed forces. Following September 11, 2001, President Bush and Congress eased the process by which immigrants could join the military and become naturalized citizens.[15] Since the Iraq war began, the United States has naturalized more than 32,000 immigrant soldiers who proudly serve in the U.S. armed forces.[16]

The current immigration debate focuses on illegal immigration. Although individuals who joined the military were officially recognized by the U.S. government, the fact remains that many individuals flocking to the United States are doing so because they see great value in U.S. democracy. In many cases, these individuals are willing to fight and die for U.S. interests simply to have an opportunity to realize the American dream. Public policy focusing on immigration turns out to be more complicated than erecting a fence or patrolling the U.S.–Mexico border.

Ballistic Missile Defense Organization (BMDO). BMDO sought to develop **Theater Missile Defense (TMD)** systems. Missile defense did not challenge the ABM Treaty, focusing instead on a more limited reaction to "rogue states."

In 2000, George W. Bush proposed **National Missile Defense (NMD)**, a more ambitious antiballistic missile system or "shield."[11] Despite criticism, Bush pulled the United States out of the ABM Treaty agreement in order to pursue NMD, arguing that the Cold War was over; the Soviet Union, the other party to the agreement, no longer existed; and that the treaty limited U.S. defense capabilities.[12]

A "crisis" often provides policy windows for policy agenda setters. In three instances—Cold War, post–Cold War, and post–post Cold War—political elites framed the issue in terms of a perceived crisis. Reagan's SDI policy challenged the Soviet Union. In the post–Cold War, Clinton sought to use BMDO to develop capabilities that would limit rogue states. George W. Bush, however, took things a step further toward NMD, a continuation and enlargement of a policy mission to defend against rogue states *and* terrorists.

HOMELAND SECURITY

On October 8, 2001, President Bush signed Presidential Executive Order 13228, entitled "Establishing the Office of Homeland Security and the Homeland Security Council." In 2002, Congress created the Department of Homeland Security (DHS)—a Cabinet-level department as of January 2003. The DHS has evolved over its short life into a much larger and complex organization. The major operational and support directorates and offices in DHS listed in relation to proportion of the 2010 budget request are as follows:

- U.S. Customs & Border Protection (CBP)   20%
- Federal Emergency Management Agency (FEMA)   19%
- U.S. Coast Guard (USCG)   18%
- Transportation Security Administration (TSA)   14%
- U.S. Immigration & Customs Enforcement (ICE)   10%
- U.S. Citizenship & Immigration Services (CIS)   5%
- National Protection Programs (NPP)   4%
- U.S. Secret Service (USSS)   3%
- Science & Technology (S&T)   2%
- Federal Law Enforcement Training Center (FLETC)   1%
- Domestic Nuclear Detection Office (DNDO)   1%

Approximately 3 percent of the budget not accounted for above supports all other DHS functions. Based on the budget focus, the DHS target populations are currently centered around protection of all aspects of border access, emergency response/disaster relief, first responder training, and nuclear event prevention. Following is a quick look at three top budgeted programs:

- ***U.S. Customs & Border Protection (CBP)***
  Border Patrol is one of the most visible activities, protecting ports of entry into the United States as well as "linewatch" activities—that is, prevention of illegal entry into the United States. Recently, cargo containers at ports of entry were discussed in the media. At the time, only a small percentage of the approximately 11 million cargo import containers were being inspected. CBP uses risk analysis to determine which containers require additional scrutiny. CBP monitors the international ports where goods are shipped to the United States. Pipelines, such as those containing natural gas and petroleum imports in the United States, are also monitored. The U.S. Coast Guard **homeland security** role is closely aligned with CBP, focusing on illegal entry and smuggling into the United States via waterways. Environmental protection is a closely aligned function; terrorism involving the destruction of natural resources is a serious concern for DHS.
- ***Federal Emergency Management Agency (FEMA)***
  FEMA deals with emergency planning for natural disaster relief as well as emergency response to terrorist-related events. FEMA also focuses on major fires, hazardous material spills, nuclear radiation releases, dam destruction, and related issues. FEMA plays a central first-responder and prevention role in emergency management.
- ***Transportation Security Administration (TSA)***
  Airport and passenger safety issues are central to the TSA mission. The air marshal program is a less visible TSA program. TSA manages air cargo safety, operates the Alien Flight Student Program, and developed the Crew Member Self-defense Training Program. TSA also monitors airport workers through its Transportation Workers Identification Card system.

The Office of Homeland Security had a budget of $19.5 billion in 2001 and $22.1 billion in 2002. The new Department of Homeland Security began its first full year of operations with total resources of $31.2 billion (2003). The department has a total budget authority of $52.5 billion for fiscal year 2009 and is requesting $55.1 billion for 2010.[13]

EXPLAINING DEFENSE POLICY

Elite Theories

The issue of what government *ought* to do in terms of defense is vague. In simple terms, government has a constitutional obligation to defend us, but providing for the common defense and making us feel secure may be two different things. Elites often set the defense policy agenda by convincing us that we lack proper defense and offering often costly solutions.

As commander-in-chief, the president is a key defense policy actor. The president's vision for foreign affairs often shapes his vision of defense policy priorities. The president's defense and homeland security budget proposals are tied to his vision of defense objectives.

Congressional elites craft defense policy, particularly members of the House and Senate Armed Services Committees, elected officials who have the most direct legislative responsibility in scrutinizing defense policy and establishing budget priorities. Congressional elites may have a vested interest in crafting defense policy beneficial to their continued power and influence.

Defense contractors are economic elites that have a tremendous impact on defense policy. The defense contractor landscape has changed dramatically over the last ten years. Fewer contractors are using a larger percentage of defense policy budget dollars to create and operate weapon systems. The power of the defense policy elite is tremendous. (See Table 11.1.)

TABLE 11.1 Top Defense Contractors by Contract Revenue, Fiscal Year 2009

Lockheed Martin Corporation	$14.98 billion
Boeing Company	$10.84 billion
Northrup Grumman Corporation	$9.95 billion
General Dynamics Corporation	$6.07 billion
Raytheon Company	$5.94 billion
KBR, Inc.	$5.47 billion
Science Applications International	$4.81 billion
L-3 Communications Holdings, Inc.	$4.24 billion
Computer Sciences Corporation	$3.44 billion
Booz Allen Hamilton	$2.78 billion

Source: www.washingtontechnology.com/toplists/top-100-lists/2009.aspx?Sort=Rank (accessed May 18, 2009).

In terms of defense policy, media elites often direct the mass public's attention to policy formulation. The media also plays a role in defense policy implementation and offers a form of public evaluation, discussing the costs and benefits of defense policy; in the case of military action, the loss of human life and monetary expense is often compared and contrasted with perceived benefits to taking military action.

Group Theory

In the 1950s, President Eisenhower openly rejected the state of defense policy as a function of elite *and* group-based politics. He called the relationship the "Military Industrial Complex." A small group of individuals and corporate decision-makers played the dominant role in the defense policy process. Since that time, of course, the defense policy budget has grown and the number of business groups in contention for those monies has become smaller due to consolidation within the industrial sector.

In addition to defense contractors, there are prominent groups who oppose defense policy. Critics of defense policy often point to tremendous waste in military expenditures. Another method of opposing defense policy is through the organization of antimilitary protest groups. During the Cold War—particularly during the 1960s, 1970s and 1980s—antinuclear weapon protests were common in both the United States and abroad. During the 1960s and early 1970s, anti-Vietnam War protests were examples of pressure groups mobilizing support among the mass public in opposition to defense policy. Similar protest groups have organized in response to U.S. defense policy in Iraq.

Lessons Learned from Chapter 11

SPECIFICS

- The National Security Act of 1947 formally linked defense policy with diplomatic policy.
- American defense policy has gone through a number of changes since World War II: the Cold War (1946–1991), post–Cold War (1991–2001), and post–post Cold War (2001–present).
- The Cold War era nuclear arms race and nuclear weapons treaties still shape nuclear defense policy.
- The War on Terror and QDR 2006 offer important insight into the future of defense policy.

THE BIG PICTURE

Defense policy is ultimately about what *government ought or ought not do, does or does not do.* A classical liberal might say that what *ought* to be done is to defend his or her right to life, liberty, and property. A modern liberal might argue that interventionism should be pursued to promote social and economic justice on a global scale through humanitarian aid and the prevention of large-scale military conflicts. History indicates that when we are clear on what we *ought* to do, and what *ought* to be the optimum level of defense commitment, the U.S. defense apparatus is—for better or worse—very capable of doing something.

Key Terms

Ballistic Missile Defense Organization (BMDO)
containment policy
defense contractors
homeland security
Joint Chiefs of Staff
mutually assured destruction (MAD)
National Missile Defense (NMD)
National Security Act (NSA) of 1947
National Security Council (NSC)
North Atlantic Treaty Organization (NATO)
new interventionism

nuclear arms race
nuclear weapons treaties
Quadrennial Defense Review (QDR) 2006
Southeast Asia Treaty Organization (SEATO)
Strategic Defense Initiative Organization (SDIO)
Theater Missile Defense (TMD)
triad
Truman Doctrine
U.S. Department of Defense (DOD)

Questions for Study

1. According to the chapter, the National Security Act of 1947 had a major impact on U.S. defense policy. What are three major policy outcomes of that Act? Using three policy models, describe and explain the NSA of 1947.
2. Compare the post–Cold War era with the post–post Cold War era. What are the major characteristics of defense policy during these two policy eras? Use three policy models to describe and explain the two policy eras.
3. Identify and discuss three major directorates within the Department of Homeland Security. How has homeland security impacted defense policy?

CASE STUDY

The two articles below appeared recently in *Stars and Stripes*, the U.S. military's newspaper. One article is about a military post leaving Germany after a decades-long posting in a small town, once along the now-defunct Cold War borders of East and West Germany. The other article is about a current military effort to push terrorists out of a town in Iraq. Either as a group or individually, consider how defense may have changed and how it has remained the same. If your response is in writing or in a group presentation, bring in additional news and information sources to support your case.

'Keep our little town . . . in your hearts'
Army wraps up final full day in Büdingen

By Kevin Dougherty, Stars and Stripes
European edition, Thursday, August 16, 2007

BÜDINGEN, Germany—Jules August Schröder stood Wednesday atop a short wall near the flagpole on Armstrong Barracks to address the small crowd.

"It was Friday, Good Friday, March 30, 1945," he began, harking back to the time he was 10. "My brother, my cousins, I and other teenagers of the neighborhood were standing on the sidewalk of a former eastbound throughway in downtown Büdingen."

The crowd listened intently, so the fact that Schröder didn't have a microphone to amplify his voice mattered not. Several U.S. soldiers in the audience wore black Stetsons. After all, this is cavalry country. Has been since Schröder was a boy.

"Curious, but frightened, we were watching the tan-colored Sherman tanks rolling noisily down the road. 'The Americans are here!' 'What will happen now?' someone asked suspiciously."

Then a peace token was thrown to one of the girls in his group.

"It was the first piece of chocolate most of us had seen and tasted in our lives," he recounted.

On Wednesday, lives lived and lost were remembered at a brief retreat ceremony to mark the final full day of the U.S. presence in Büdingen. Built for the German army in the mid-1930s, Armstrong Barracks has almost exclusively been a post for American cavalrymen, most recently the 1st Squadron, 1st U.S. Cavalry Regiment.

During the Cold War, the Soviet-led Warsaw Pact forces were never that far over the horizon, a point Büdingen's mayor, Erich Spamer, routinely makes.

Over the years, Büdingen-based cavalrymen left to serve their country—and their Western allies—near and far, from Bosnia to Vietnam. But the people of Büdingen, Schröder and others say, always stood in their corner, even if they didn't understand or agree.

The 40 soldiers left to close down the post were joined Wednesday by their former commander, Lt. Col. Matthew McKenna. Several others dropped by, too.

"This unit was awesome," Capt. Stephen Johnson said. "And the relationship we had with Büdingen, there's nothing like it in the Army, and there probably never will be again."

Toward the end of his remarks, Schröder asked the Americans for a favor: "Keep our little town and its inhabitants in your hearts." (See Photo 11.4.)

PHOTO 11.4 Keep our little town in your hearts

Source: Used with permission from the Stars and Stripes. © 2007 Stars and Stripes.

14 die in fight involving Iraqis and insurgents

By Joseph Giordono, Stars and Stripes
Mideast edition, Saturday, August 18, 2007

As many as 60 insurgents battled with a group of Iraqi police and armed residents on Wednesday in the southern Baqouba district of Buhriz, the U.S. military said Friday.

The battle, which Iraqi officials said started with a mortar attack on the neighborhood, left as many as 14 people dead and 20 wounded—all civilians, Iraqi police said.

American military officials reported that more than 21 insurgents were killed in the gunbattle and in airstrikes by American helicopters called in to help. The number of deaths in Iraq incidents frequently differs when reported by American and Iraqi officials.

The battle took place while some 16,000 American and Iraqi troops are participating in operations around Baqouba, the Diyala provincial capital. The purpose of the operation, military officials said, is to track down insurgents who fled the city and were believed to have holed up in surrounding towns and villages.

According to U.S. and Iraqi accounts of the battle, Iraqi police and an armed civilian group called the Baqouba Guardians traded gunfire with dozens of insurgents, some wearing suicide bomb vests. American troops from the 1st Squadron, 12th Cavalry Regiment assisted the police and coordinated with the "Guardians" throughout the battle, said Maj. Robbie W. Parke, a U.S. military spokesman.

"They were involved in the operation in the 'pursuit and exploitation' phase through most of the day on the 15th," Parke said.

The police "requested Coalition Force attack helicopter support after the first engagement. Attack helicopters arrived and engaged another large group of heavily armed fighters staging near the first attack site, killing or wounding an estimated 14 terrorists," a military press release read.

Iraqi police said the battle lasted some three hours.

"I wouldn't categorize forty to sixty insurgents as a large number," Parke said. "It's just a bit larger than a platoon, and it shows how much their operations have been disrupted.

"If you will recall from previous press releases in mid-June, the estimated enemy strength in western Baqubah when we started Operation Arrowhead Ripper was upwards of 500 [al-Qaida in Iraq] fighters.

"We liberated Baqubah—the so-called capital of the Islamic State of Iraq—from al-Qaida. I believe al-Qaida will continue to try to get a toe-hold back in Baqubah to regain lost ground . . . So far, they have been unsuccessful in their attempts and this is an example of their latest failure."

"Baqouba should be proud of their security forces and their citizen guardians today," U.S. Army Col. Steve Townsend, commander of the 3rd Stryker Brigade Combat Team, was quoted as saying in the release. "All fought side-by-side and soundly defeated a complex attack from a determined enemy. This thing could have been much worse had those suicide bombers reached their targets."

A U.S. military press release about the battle cast it as an "unprecedented combined action" between Iraqi police and armed citizens.

Source: Used with permission from the Stars and Stripes. © 2007 Stars and Stripes.

Bibliography

BBC News. "America withdraws from ABM Treaty." www.news.bbc.co.uk/1/hi/world/americas/1707812.stm (accessed March 19, 2003).

Carroll, J. 2006. *House of war: The Pentagon and the disastrous rise of American power*. Boston, MA: Houghton Mifflin.

Cimbala, S., ed. 1996. *Clinton and post–Cold War defense*. Westport, CT: Praeger.

CQ Press. 1983. *U.S. defense policy*. 3rd ed. Washington, DC: Congressional Quarterly, Inc.

Department of Defense. 2005. "Fact sheet: History of the Ballistic Missile Defense Organization." www.defenselink.mil/specials/missiledefense/history.html (accessed August 17, 2007).

Glazer, C. 1990. *Analyzing strategic nuclear policy*. Princeton, NJ: Princeton University Press.

Haass, R. 1994. *Intervention: The use of American military force in the post–Cold War world*. Washington, DC: Carnegie Endowment for International Peace.

Johnson, D., and B. Schneider, eds. 1976. *Current issues in U.S. defense policy.* New York: Praeger.

Krieger, D., 2005. "Arms control and disarmament treaties." www.nuclearfiles .org/kinuclearweapons/acindex.html (accessed January 30, 2005).

Krunzel, J., ed. 1990/1991. *American defense manual.* Lexington, MA: Lexington Books.

Lens, S. 1987. *Permanent war: The militarization of America.* New York: Schocken Books.

National Defense University. 1998. *Strategic assessment: Engaging power for peace.* Fort McNair, Washington, DC: National Defense University.

Office of Management and Budget. 2009. "Budget of the United States, Fiscal Year 2010." www.whitehouse.gov/omb/budget/fy2010/budget.html (accessed May 18, 2009).

Palmer, G. 1978. *The McNamara strategy and the Vietnam War: Program budgeting in the pentagon 1960–1968.* Westport, CT: Greenwood Press.

Peimani, H. 2003. *Falling terrorism and rising conflicts: The Afghan contribution to polarization and confrontation in West and South Asia.* Westport, CT: Praeger.

Phares, W. 2007. *The war of ideas: Jihad against democracy.* New York: Palgrave.

Roherty, J. 1970. *Decisions of Robert McNamara: A study of the role of the secretary of defense.* Coral Gables, FL: University of Miami Press.

Rumsfeld, D. 2006. Forward to *Quadrennial Defense Review Report.* Washington, DC: Department of Defense.

Stoll, R. 1990. *U.S. national security policy and the Soviet Union: Persistent regularities and extreme contingencies.* Columbia: University of South Carolina Press.

Tyner, J. 2007. *America's strategy in Southeast Asia: From the Cold War to the terror war.* Lanham, MD: Rowman & Littlefield.

Varas, A. 1989. *Hemispheric security and U.S. policy in Latin America.* Boulder, CO: Westview Press.

White House. 2009. "National Security Council." www.whitehouse.gov/nsc (accessed May 18, 2009).

Endnotes

1. Gates, R. 2009. U. S. Department of Defense: Fiscal year 2010 budget request, pp. 1–6.
2. Until 1947, the U.S. military had only two major branches: the U.S. Army and the U.S. Navy. Each branch operated independently of the other. World War II created a need for a more unified approach to defense policy, one linking the presidential role of head of state with the role as commander-in-chief.
3. www.dtic.mil/jcs/ (accessed March 22, 2009).
4. The same day, representatives of Japan's government signed the surrender documents in Tokyo Harbor on the deck of the *U.S.S. Missouri.*
5. www.dod.mil/ra/documents/pressreleases/Coldwar.htm (accessed March 4, 2003).

6. The formation of NATO was almost immediately criticized by the Soviet Union. By the mid-1950s, the Soviet Union had created its own alliance among the Eastern European nations existing within the Soviet sphere of influence—known as the Warsaw Pact (www.nato.int, accessed August 17, 2007).

7. Norris, R. S., and H. M. Kristensen. 2008. "U.S. nuclear forces, 2008," *Bulletin of the atomic scientists.* 64(1): 50–53, 58.

8. All treaty information quoted from: www.nuclearfiles.org/redocuments/treaties-all.html (accessed January 30, 2005).

9. Confirmed in the findings of the September 11 Commission, a fourth commercial jetliner was hijacked, but passengers prevented the terrorists from completing their mission to attack Washington, DC. The plane crashed in rural Pennsylvania.

10. Rumsfeld, D. 2006. Quadrennial Defense Review—2006. Washington, DC: U.S. Department of Defense, p. 19.

11. www.defenselink.mil/specials/missiledefense/history.html (accessed August 17, 2007).

12. Sanger, D. E. 2000. The 2000 Campaign; World Views—A Special report; Rivals differ on U.S. Role in the World. *The New York Times*, October 30, p. A1.

13. Napolitano, J. 2009. Budget in Brief: U.S. department of homeland security.

14. Seper, J. 2006. 55 Utah Guardsmen join Border Agents in Arizona, *The Washington Times*, June 6, p. A3.

15. McLemore, D. 2006. Immigrant Soldiers Serve the U.S. *Dallas Morning News*, November 28, www.dallasnews.com/sharedcontent/dws/news/texassouthwest/stories/112806dnteximmigmilitary.331e2bd.html (accessed August 17, 2007).

16. Montet, V. 2007. The United States has naturalized 32,000 immigrant soldiers since the Iraq war. *Yahoo News*, July 25, www.news.yahoo.com/s/afp/20070725/pl_afp/usmilitaryimmigration/070725060721 (accessed August 17, 2007).

12

■ ■ ■

Public Health Policy

CHAPTER OVERVIEW

Public health policy is often controversial. Classical liberals criticize the distributive and redistributive aspects of public health policy, believing it to be socialistic. Health issues are seen as an *individual* concern and the free market is the preferred method of delivering health care. Conversely, modern liberals find the redistributive elements of public health policy a critical part of creating a fair society and the distributive aspects a part of basic human rights. Modern liberals and many communitarians see health policy as a *societal* concern. Basic public health policy for prevention and control of epidemics is generally thought to be something government *ought to* do (see Porter 1994).

The focus of this chapter is to discuss the major public health policies administered at the national level through the **U.S. Department of Health and Human Services** (HHS).

The specific goals for the chapter are:

- Discuss major actors in public health policy.
- Discuss the seven major policy functions of HHS.
- Detail major departmental policy areas that serve the public health policy function.
- Explain Medicare, Medicaid, and the State Children's Health Insurance Program (SCHIP).

MAJOR ACTORS IN PUBLIC HEALTH POLICY

Congress

Public health policy in the late twentieth century was often shaped by congresspersons' responsiveness to citizens. Public health policy is of particular interest to the elderly, a demographic that is politically aware and active. In general, citizens support public health policies for children and the poor, which is consistent with modern liberal principles. Congress has responded to these demands through the passage of public health legislation that has expanded benefits for these groups.

President

Presidents have played leading roles in public health policy. President William Howard Taft played a prominent role in establishing the **Public Health Service**, an early Progressive health reform. President Lyndon Johnson pushed for the passage of Medicare and Medicaid. President Jimmy Carter organized HHS and Bill Clinton added a number of new agencies within HHS, expanding the public health mission. President George W. Bush urged Congress to add a prescription drug benefit to Medicare. President Barack Obama advocates broadening access to health care and seeks to reform the health insurance system.[1]

Interest Groups

Interest groups shape public health policy. The American Association for Advancement of Retired People (AARP) is one of the most powerful interest groups in the policy area, shaping the public health agenda related to the needs of the elderly. Until recently, Native American groups were underrepresented in terms of interest group influence largely because they often lacked the resources to organize effective lobbying efforts, but with gaming industry wealth at hand and control of new sophisticated organizations, their public health lobbying efforts have increased.

DEPARTMENT OF HEALTH AND HUMAN SERVICES

The U.S. Department of Health and Human Services (HHS) is responsible for a significant portion of national public health policy. HHS identifies seven broad categories of public health policy responsibilities: (1) diseases and conditions, (2) safety and wellness, (3) drug and food information, (4) disaster and emergencies, (5) families and children, (6) aging, and (7) specific populations.[2] The following HHS units are tasked with these responsibilities:

Administration for Children and Families (ACF)

Focusing on the needs of low-income individuals, the agency is primarily concerned with promoting strong and healthy families. Child nutrition programs ensure that basic food needs are available for women and their infants. Programs such as ChildCareAware and AfterSchool.gov maintain information clearinghouses on child care programs in communities nationwide, as well as child abuse, nutrition, health, and special needs programs—for example, resources for children with disabilities or nontraditional family service opportunities.

ACF monitors foster care children and adoption programs to ensure that children living in foster care are well treated. The **National Fostercare and Adoption Directory** maintains databases related to adoption agencies as well as information for prospective adoptive parents. The clearinghouse also helps adopted children learn more about their legal rights and increases their ability to gain access to vital records, like birth certificates.

Through the federal **Office of Child Support Enforcement (OCSE)**, ACF monitors child support payments. The Child Support Enforcement Program, established in 1975 under Title IV-D of the Social Security Act, requires that each state establish its own child support program to locate noncustodial parents, establish paternity, support obligations, and monitor collection of support.

The Child Support Enforcement Act of 1993 made child support delinquency a federal crime if the parent delinquent in payment resided in a different state than the child. Additionally, the **Welfare Reform Act of 1996** established **Temporary Assistance for Needy Families (TANF)** with the intention of ensuring that families not receiving child support payments were covered by state and federal support. The law established a national program to track down delinquent parents—the Federal Case Registry. The Child Support Performance and Incentive Act of 1998 encouraged states to protect the rights of children, create workable child support systems, and monitor system effectiveness.[3]

ACF also manages the Healthy Marriage Initiative, which emerged from Public Law 104-193 Personal Responsibility and Work Opportunity Reconciliation Act of 1996. Under its TANF heading, Congress made a number of findings regarding the benefits of marriage for married individuals, children, and the community. The policy currently promotes healthy marriages, premarital education, and divorce reduction programs.[4]

ACF is also tied to the Campaign to Rescue & Restore Victims of Human Trafficking, which emerged from the Trafficking Victims Protection Act of 2000. The program extends formula grants to programs offering services to the victims of trafficking and "street outreach grants" to programs that identify trafficking victims and offer help. The program also has a national resource center and hot line for individuals reporting trafficking behavior.[5]

Administration on Aging (AOA)

A growing proportion of the population is over sixty-five years old. AOA's goal is to reduce health care costs through preventative policies designed to maintain the standard of living for the elderly.

In order to help families and friends cope with aging family members, Congress passed the **Older Americans Act Amendments of 2000** (Public Law 106-501). The law created a new program managed by AOA called the National Family Caregiver Support Program (NFCSP),[6] distributing monetary resources to the states to establish partnerships within communities of caregivers. In some cases, the program offers supplemental services "to complement the care provided by caregivers."[7] National Aging Services Network (NAN) coordinates support services and centers to assist the elderly and their caregivers. NAN offers important information to help caregivers perform their tasks, and it also offers counseling support to caregivers.

AOA places special emphasis on housing and nutrition for the elderly. Despite costs and stress, many elderly wish to stay in their homes. With assistance from nonprofit organizations, AOA offers transportation to medical appointments and even helps to maintain elders' homes so quality of life is not diminished. AOA also offers information on nursing home facilities, community care retirement communities (CCRC), and special care centers for elderly disabled individuals.

Five of the top six chronic medical conditions developed by the elderly could either be prevented or better managed through proper nutrition. Responding to pressing need, Congress passed in 1972 an amended version of the Older Americans Act (1965), and government began offering home delivery of meals for malnourished elderly. On average, a year's worth of meals costs less than three-tenths of a percent of the cost of one day in the hospital.[8]

AOA promotes healthy lifestyles for the elderly. Proper exercise helps to maintain physical and mental health. Learning to manage many common ailments, such as arthritis, osteoporosis, and diabetes, may help to reduce medical problems. Health screening for conditions, such as cancer, heart disease, or stroke, helps the elderly maintain quality of life and reduces future medical costs. Aging can also bring on mental disassociation illnesses beyond Alzheimer's. Many elderly become seriously depressed, either from being abandoned by their families and friends or simply due to the mental anguish that often accompanies the aging process.

Finally, AOA tries to make the elderly aware of their legal rights. The National Elder Abuse Study conducted in 2004 found that more than a half million elderly individuals (age sixty and over) are victims of "elder and vulnerable adult abuse."[9] The National Center for Elder Abuse (NCEA)—a consortium of federal, state, and local government officials, and private organizations such as the American Bar Association—educates the public and professionals about the forms and signs of elder abuse and methods of managing these issues. (See Photo 12.1.)

Agency for Healthcare Research and Quality (AHRQ)
The agency's mission is related to findings in the *President's Advisory Commission on Consumer Protection and Quality in the Health Care Industry* (1998). President Clinton asked the commission, composed of thirty-four government and private sector health care policy leaders, to develop a health care consumer's Bill of Rights—AHRQ is tasked with establishing policy upholding those high standards:

- ". . . the right to receive accurate, easily understood information . . . in making informed health care decisions about their health plans, professionals, and facilities."
- ". . . the right to a choice of health care providers that is sufficient to ensure access to appropriate high-quality health care."
- ". . . the right to access emergency health care services when and where the need arises."
- ". . . the right and responsibility to fully participate in all decisions related to their health care . . . [and/or] the right to be represented by parents, guardians, family members, or other conservators."
- ". . . the right to considerate, respectful care from all members of the health care system at all times and under all circumstances."
- ". . . the right to communicate with health care providers in confidence and to have the confidentiality of their individually identifiable health care information protected . . . [and] the right to review and copy their own medical records and request amendments to their records."

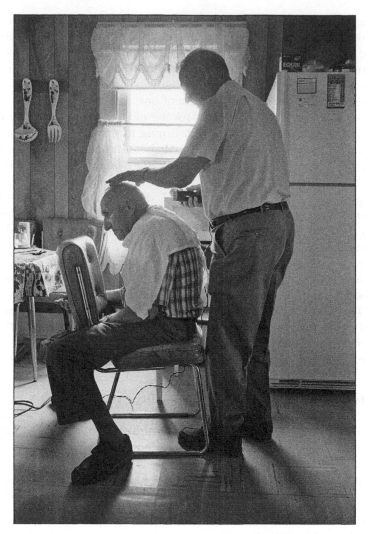

PHOTO 12.1 Helping our elderly live and die with dignity: One of our biggest health care challenges

- ". . . the right to a fair and efficient process for resolving differences with their health plans, health care providers, and the institutions that serve them, including a rigorous system of internal review and an independent system of external review."
- ". . . in a health care system that protects consumers' rights, it is reasonable to expect and encourage consumers to assume reasonable responsibilities. Greater individual involvement by consumers in their care increases the likelihood of achieving the best outcomes and helps support a quality improvement, cost-conscious environment."[10]

Agency for Toxic Substances and Disease Registry (ATSDR)[11]

The Agency for Toxic Substances and Disease Registry was created by the Comprehensive Environmental Response, Compensation, and Liability Act (CERCLA) (also known as Superfund) in 1980.[12] ATSDR was created during the Carter presidency with the mandate of improving environmental conditions and shares a mission with the Environmental Protection Agency (EPA). The public health policy aspects of ATSDR were clear in the agency's reauthorization act—**Superfund Amendments and Reauthorization Act of 1986**—placing special emphasis on developing solid scientific research on the public health impacts of toxic waste and pollution.

Centers for Disease Control and Prevention

Events such as the 1918 influenza pandemic that claimed approximately 70 million lives, and the spread of polio, tuberculosis, and typhoid fever in an increasingly urbanized world, led to the creation of the **Centers for Disease Control** (CDC) in 1946.

CDC is composed of several offices and agencies:

- National Center on Birth Defects and Development Disabilities (NCBDDD) deals with research and prevention programs for birth defects, autism, developmental disabilities, and fetal alcohol syndrome.[13]
- National Center for Chronic Disease Prevention and Health Promotion (NCCDPHP) focuses on prevention and disease management programs for diseases such as arthritis, cancer, diabetes, and heart defects.[14]
- National Center for Environmental Health (NCEH) has three major division areas. The Division of Emergency and Environmental Health Services deals with such issues as lead poisoning prevention programs, disaster-related epidemiology research, and the destruction of former U.S. military chemical weapons stockpiles. The Division of Environmental Hazards and Health Effects tracks environmental public health issues such as problems associated with air pollution and radiation exposure. NCEH also monitors human exposure to hazardous chemicals.[15] The Division of Laboratory Science is an advanced laboratory conducting research within NCEH.
- National Center for HIV, Viral Hepatitis, STD, and TB Prevention (NCHHSTP) has five major divisions: HIV/AIDS, STD Prevention, Viral Hepatitis, TB Elimination, and Global AIDS. The Division of HIV/AIDS Prevention studies infection and mortality rate trends for different races/ethnicities, genders, and age cohorts, controlling for the method of infection.

  In terms of the global AIDS mission, the president's "Emergency Plan for AIDS Relief" (PEPFAR) in 2003 pledged approximately $15 billion to HIV/AIDS programs worldwide, with special emphasis on Africa and the Caribbean (2008). *The Power of Partnerships: The President's Emergency Plan for AIDS Relief, Fourth Annual Report to Congress* (2008) reports that through global partnership efforts, PEPFAR has dramatically increased the percentage of HIV-infected individuals receiving antiretroviral medication; improved education on disease prevention, particularly mother-to-child disease spread; and promoted gender equity through the empowerment of women in issues related to reproductive health.[16]

NCHHSTP also studies STD infection rates and develops prevention programs for what it calls "hidden epidemics"[17] in the United States. NCHHSTP estimates that there are 19 million new STD cases every year. Fighting STD infection rates is the focus of the Syphilis Elimination Effort (SEE) and Gonococcal Isolate Surveillance Project (GISP), combining education with scientific monitoring of disease strains. The goal of the Infertility Prevention Project, initially a local-level demonstration project, is to reduce potential long-term impacts of STD infection.[18] The TB and Viral Hepatitis divisions have missions closely related to the HIV and STD prevention missions.

- National Center for Preparedness, Detection and Control of Infectious Diseases (NCPDCID); National Center for Immunization and Respiratory Diseases (NCIRD); National Center for Zoonotic, Vector-Borne and Enteric Diseases (NCZVED), and the National Center for Preparedness, Detection, and Control of Infectious Diseases (NCPDCID)—as well as the aforementioned NCHHSTP—share responsibilities for infectious disease response. These organizations develop global infectious disease strategies, focusing primarily on protecting the United States.
- Coordinating Center for Health Information and Service (CCHIS) is a network "hub" for the National Center for Health Marketing (NCHM), the National Center for Health Statistics (NCHS), and the National Center for Public Health Informatics (NCPHI). The centers manage health information needed by consumers and medical professionals in making informed health care choices.[19]
- Though the **Pink Book**[20], the National Immunization Program (NIP) disseminates information on disease, vaccines, even vaccinating disadvantaged individuals against preventable disease. The center also focuses on bioterrorism and the weaponization of anthrax spores and the smallpox virus.[21]
- National Institute for Occupational Safety and Health (NIOSH) monitors and reduces workplace injuries and death in the United States.[22]
- Public Health Training Network (PHTN) develops health information networks and training programs, outlining national public health standards.
- Epidemiology Program Office (EPO) collects and disseminates information regarding new and growing health risks.[23]

Centers for Medicare and Medicaid Services (CMS)

CMS was created on July 1, 2001, formerly known as the Health Care Financing Administration (HCFA). (See Box 12.1, *National Health Policy*.)

The vast majority of the HHS budget is spent by CMS in mandatory outlays for Medicare, Medicaid, and the State Children's Health Insurance Program (SCHIP). The president's estimated 2010 HHS expenditure for mandatory health programs is approximately $790 billion[24]—roughly 90 percent of HHS's anticipated total budget outlay of $879 billion.[25]

BOX 12.1

National Health Policy

President John F. Kennedy (1961–1963) proposed what is now called Medicare.

The idea of a national health system has been around for a long time. The first national health care plan was established in Prussia in 1854. In 1883, Chancellor Otto von Bismarck established a national health system in Germany. The British National Health Insurance system was established in 1911. Given our close ties to Britain, the new plan inspired a policy debate about national health insurance in the United States as early as 1912.[40] Academics at the University of Wisconsin—a leading Progressive state—studied the issue of national health insurance and sought to advance the idea on the policy agenda. Despite having a progressive Democrat in the White House (Woodrow Wilson), the policy never came to fruition, in part due to a lack of presidential leadership and the nature of the times. World War I was being fought, so attention was naturally drawn to U.S. involvement in that war. Additionally, the rise of the Soviet Union and the socialist policies it advanced led many U.S. policy-makers to eschew national health insurance. Despite the impact of the Great Depression in the late 1920s and 1930s, President Franklin Roosevelt encountered significant political and social resistance to the idea of national health insurance. Although successfully creating Social Security, national health care as a policy issue was discarded, particularly when the United States found itself engaged in World War II. The Kerr-Mills Act of 1960 expanded national government medical payments to medical care providers for the elderly who were either not covered or not sufficiently covered by their state medical programs to fully meet their medical needs.

As a U.S. Senator, John F. Kennedy revived the policy proposal for national health insurance for the elderly, which carried over as a policy priority when he became president in 1961. The proposal became known as Medicare. During his first two years as president, Kennedy tried to advance the policy proposal in Congress. Due in part to intense pressure from the American Medical Association to reject the policy proposal, the measure failed to make it through Congress. It was not until January 1965—at a time when support for Kennedy's successor Lyndon Johnson and the Democratic Party was quite strong—that Medicare became law as a part of the revised Social Security Act. Through state-level offices, the Medicare program provides health insurance to people over age 65. A 1972 amendment to the Social Security Act extended Medicare coverage to disabled persons and to individuals who had been receiving cash benefits from the Social Security program for twenty-four months. On December 8, 2003, President George W. Bush signed into law the Medicare Modernization Act, creating an outpatient prescription drug benefit for Medicare recipients. Medicaid provides access to health care for certain low-income individuals, particularly individuals who were already recipients of other forms of welfare benefits from the national and state levels of government.[41]

MEDICARE: HOW IT WORKS

Medicare is a federal program that contracts directly with health care providers.[26] It is a form of medical insurance covering the health care needs of the elderly, disabled, Social Security recipients, and certain individuals with renal failure. Medicare works from the premise that society *ought to* promote equality through medical care for individuals who may be unable to access quality health care due to infirmity or age. Medicare offers partial or complete coverage for many health services. The program has four major parts.

For the Medicare recipient, the program is not unlike any form of insurance: There are certain annual charges—or premiums—paid to maintain program eligibility. For Part A, most individuals enrolled do not pay premiums because they meet certain eligibility requirements related to work history. Part B requires a premium of approximately $60 regardless of Medicare-covered employment history.

Part A—Hospital insurance: Helps cover costs of hospitalization, nursing care facility stays, home health care, hospice care, and blood transfusions for patients staying in the hospital or during covered stays in a skilled nursing care facility. As with private insurance, Medicare does not cover all costs for every medical procedure.

Part B—Medical insurance: The Medicare program established agency rules governing the medical procedures covered by the plan and what percentage of Medicare-approved costs associated with each procedure are paid for by Medicare. Any costs over and above the Medicare contribution are the responsibility of the patient, who can opt for either voluntary enrollment for an extra premium in private insurance or government-sponsored Medigap insurance to cover remaining costs of the medical procedure. Service charges for medical procedures not covered by any insurance plan are the responsibility of the patient.

Part C—Medicare Advantage: Part C combines Plans A, B, and D into a larger, more comprehensive plan designed to increase user flexibility while reducing health care costs. Part C is noted as being beneficial to Medicare-qualified individuals who have chronic conditions requiring regular medical care. The plan relies heavily on health networks, such as HMOs, to provide care, but there is a preferred provider option. Additionally, Part C has a medical savings account plan, allowing consumers to establish medical savings accounts.[27]

Part D—Prescription drug coverage: Enrollees pay a monthly premium and a "co-pay" for the prescription depending upon the type of drugs and individual dosages.

MEDICAID

Medicaid was established under Title XIX of the Social Security Act of 1965 to serve the medical service needs of low-income individuals and families. Medicaid is a national–state cooperative health care program. The current national eligibility requirements for the "categorically needy" are:

1. Families who meet states' AFDC eligibility requirements in effect on July 16, 1996.
2. Pregnant women and children under age 6 whose family income is at or below 133% of the federal poverty level.
3. Children ages 6 to 19 with family income up to 100% of the federal poverty level.
4. Caretakers (relatives or legal guardians who take care of children under age 18 [or 19 if still in high school]).
5. Supplementary Security Income (SSI) recipients [who meet certain requirements].
6. Individuals and couples who are living in medical institutions and who have monthly income up to 300% of the SSI income standard . . .[28]

States can establish additional eligibility requirements and benefits.

Medicare and Medicaid share a unique relationship. Frequently, individuals qualifying for Medicaid will be covered under Parts A and B of Medicare. Medicaid recipients receive a prescription drug benefit and certain other benefits, such as an eyeglass benefit. For individuals who qualify under certain Supplementary Security Income (SSI) standards, the normal premiums and fee-for-service formulas are waived. (See Box 12.2, *Immigration and Health Care Costs.*)

BOX 12.2

Immigration and Health Care Costs

Immigration is often criticized in terms of the added health care costs that immigrants, particularly illegal immigrants, cost U.S. taxpayers. As a result, the federal government now requires that any individual applying for Medicaid coverage offer proof of U.S. citizenship or some form of identification that documents their residency status.[42] There are externalities that have been created by the new rule. Homeless and mentally disabled individuals will likely have a difficult time producing documents that prove their citizenship or residency status—usually indigent, these individuals are a key target population for Medicaid.

A recent study published by the *Journal of the American Medical Association* offers some evidence of the impact of immigrant (particularly illegal immigrant) demand on the Medicaid system. Although not eligible for Medicaid directly, illegal immigrants are able to access Emergency Medicaid services. Contrary to public concern, the current demand of illegal immigrant health care recipients is "a small proportion of the total Medicaid budget."[43] However, consistent with some public concern, evidence suggests that demand on Emergency Medicaid by recent and undocumented immigrants is increasing rapidly.

STATE CHILDREN'S HEALTH INSURANCE PROGRAM (SCHIP)

Established in 1997, the **State Children's Health Insurance Program** is financed by both national and state government. At the national level, it is part of CMS. The program is generally intended to insure those children who are ineligible for Medicaid benefits, yet their caregivers cannot afford private health insurance. Eligibility is generally a function of family size and family income levels. Through SCHIP benefits, children are offered immunization programs, regular health screening, and hospital and emergency room care, if possible, within their communities.[29] Enrollment in the program has increased since 2000, but costs seem to outpace enrollment. (See Photo 12.3.) (See Figure 12.1.)[30]

FOOD AND DRUG ADMINISTRATION (FDA)

The classical liberal free market approach believes there *ought to be* limited government regulation of the private marketplace, but as society has become more complex, so too have the products we consume and the services we enjoy. Regardless of whether providers are malicious, safety must be regulated to protect consumers.

In the early nineteenth century, the states took the lead in regulating food products to ensure the safety of consumers. In the 1860s, the then Department of Agriculture employed a single chemist working on issues related to food and drug safety. Rapid policy change occurred in the twentieth century.

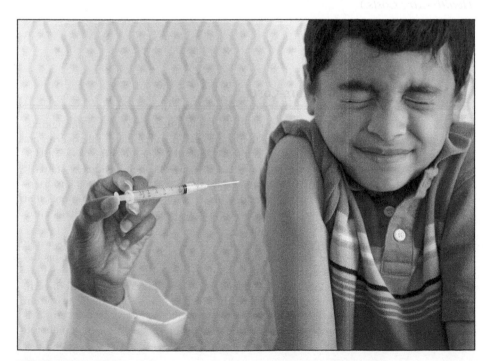

PHOTO 12.3 Children are an important part of the public health mission

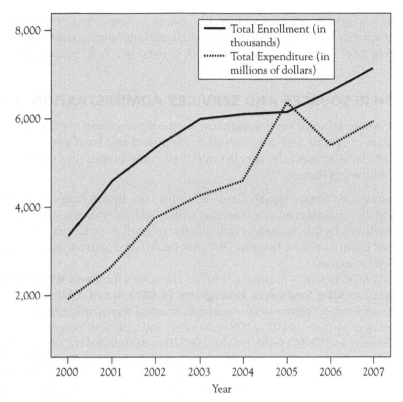

FIGURE 12.1 SCHIP enrollment and costs 2000–2007.

The **Food and Drug Administration** was established under the Pure Food and Drug Act of 1906. The FDA regulates product labeling and food safety. The FDA also conducts long and detailed scientific trials, testing the quality of new drugs and determining whether the drugs meet the medical purposes intended.

Manufacturers claim that delays in FDA approval, which may take anywhere from one to three years, lead to the unnecessary deaths of many patients who could have benefited from the drug. Additionally, manufacturers claim that the delay in FDA approval leads to higher prices for drugs. In response to these concerns, the Prescription Drug and User Fee Act of 1992 led to a decrease in the median time for most drug approval applications to approximately twelve months; priority applications now take an average of six months for approval.[31]

Under the Public Health Security and Bio-terrorism Preparedness and Response Act of 2002, the FDA (and other agencies) is tasked with the identification and control of dangerous biological agents and toxins. The FDA and partner agencies (such as Homeland Security) monitor the security of food and water supplies.[32]

Under the Federal Food, Drug, and Cosmetic Act (21 USC 301), the FDA regulates cosmetics—"(1) articles intended to be rubbed, poured, sprinkled, or sprayed on, introduced into, or otherwise applied to the human body or any part thereof for cleansing, beautifying, promoting attractiveness, or altering the appearance and (2) articles intended for use as a component of any such articles; except that such term shall not include soap." Identifying tainted toothpaste imports in 2007 is one example of the FDA watchdog role in product safety.

HEALTH RESOURCES AND SERVICES ADMINISTRATION (HRSA)

The HRSA is an information clearinghouse for the development of effective primary health care programs and offers grants to help state and local governments develop programs to meet the specific needs of communities and regions. HRSA has the following bureaus:[33]

- Bureau of Primary Health Care—Identifies the health care needs of traditionally underserved populations, which include women's health issues, children's health, homeless individuals, migrant populations, and individuals living in public housing. Primary health care also focuses on prevention programs.
- HIV/AIDS Bureau—Formed in 1997 to administer the **Ryan White Comprehensive AIDS Resources Emergency (CARE) Act of 1990**. The program grants funds to private-sector research, medical teams, and organizations for the development of HIV/AIDS prevention and treatment programs.[34]
- Maternal and Child Health Bureau (MCHB)—Authorized by Title V of the Social Security Act of 1935, MCHB distributes block grants to support strong and healthy mothers and children. The grants are awarded for special needs children, nutrition programs, and safety-related programs and related initiatives.
- Health Care Systems Bureau (HCSB)—Oversees a wide variety of responsibilities, including: bone marrow and organ transplant policies, medical facility design, next-generation pharmacy development, and administration of vaccine programs.
- Bureau of Health Professions (BHP)—Monitors the health profession workforce.
  - The report "Globalization and the Physician Workforce in the United States" (2002) concluded that in order to meet future health care needs, the United States must look beyond domestic medical schools (U.S. Medical Graduates—USMGs) and actively recruit physicians from other nations (International Medical Graduates—IMGs).
  - A shortage of skilled nurses will become dramatically worse by 2020 unless special efforts are made to encourage individuals to pursue nursing careers. BHP has developed programs to help nursing schools tap into traditionally underutilized human resource bases (Spratley et al. 2000). (See Figure 12.2.)
  - Pharmacists and dentists have increased in ratio to the population, but the number of pharmacists and dentists as compared to the population varies widely by state.
  - HRSA implements the Migrant Health Care Act of 1962.[35] Relatedly, two areas of growing interest to BHP are health care in border states, and the use of community health workers (CHW) in communities. In 2007,

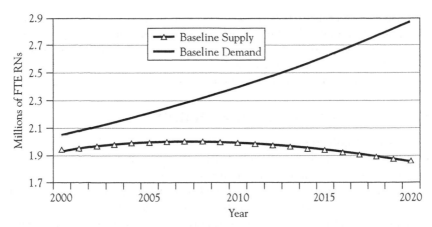

FIGURE 12.2 National supply and demand projections for FTE registered nurses: 2000–2020.
Source: Bureau of Health Profession, RN Supply and Demand Projections.

BHP found evidence of an uneven distribution of health care workers along the U.S.–Mexico border.[36] A related BHP study found that CHW numbers were increasing, but further development is needed.[37] CHW is an affordable first-line option to manage health care for underserved populations, such as migrant workers.

- Bureau of Clinician Recruitment and Service (BCRS)—Develops sustainable health care systems for communities that lack strong health care infrastructures. The bureau recruits medical personnel needed in communities.[38]

INDIAN HEALTH SERVICE (IHS)

The **Snyder Act** (25 USC 13) in 1921 established national policy authority to provide health care to recognized Native American tribes, but not until the passage of the **Indian Self-Determination Act** (Public Law 93-638) in 1975 were Native Americans given some "voice" in prioritizing their health care needs. The **Indian Health Care Improvement Act** (Public Law 94-437) of 1976 and the Public Health Service Act (see Title 28, Chapter 6 of the U.S. Code) provide the legal basis for much of the policy implemented by Indian Health Service. President Clinton's Executive Order 13084—signed in 1998—required that agencies consult with Native American tribes in crafting health care policy.

IHS coordinates many other HHS policies available to all persons, but places special emphasis on meeting the needs of Native Americans. IHS has developed an interactive database that links information on disease prevalence among various Native American tribes. HHS health care policies, such as Children's Health Insurance Program (CHIP), Medicare, and Medicaid, are coordinated for Native American clientele through IHS.

The ability to access health care is challenging for many Native Americans. Many reservations lack proper health care facilities and skilled health care professionals. IHS constructs hospitals and clinics on reservation lands and staffs the facilities with trained health care workers. Special emphasis is placed on hiring health care workers from among Native American populations. At the program level, Indian Health Service outlays account for less than one percent of the president's total recommended outlays in the 2010 HHS proposed budget.[39]

NATIONAL INSTITUTES OF HEALTH (NIH)

The **National Institutes of Health** (est. 1930) is a research-focused organization with more than twenty centers for research on various illnesses and diseases. NIH has its own laboratory facilities and continues to conduct important research on an "in-house" basis. Most NIH research is grant-funded work done in university settings. (See Box 12.3, *World War I and Anthrax.*)

Through NIH research, medical technologies and practices to treat serious illnesses have been significantly advanced. NIH research offers both current and future benefits. For example, NIH researchers have played a significant role in mapping the human genome, a probable basis for future medical science discoveries.

SUBSTANCE ABUSE AND MENTAL HEALTH SERVICES ADMINISTRATION (SAMHSA)

Substance Abuse and Mental Health Services (est. 1992) establishes databases related to mental health research findings and prescriptive practices. These databases will help policymakers craft policy solutions in a variety of policy fields. For example, it is known that crime and low socioeconomic status are often related to family mental health issues and substance abuse. SAMHSA helps develop broad-based mental health policy solutions, often linking public health to related policy fields.

EXPLAINING PUBLIC HEALTH POLICY

Systems Theory

In systems theory, institutions respond to environmental conditions. Public policy is a function of demands and constraints on policy-making institutions. Public health policy has evolved, responding to new and changing health issues. In

---

BOX 12.3
World War I and Anthrax

During World War I, the Hygienic Laboratories (the predecessor to NIH) worked to discover the cause of anthrax infections and other diseases affecting American soldiers. Of course, anthrax infections today would more likely be assumed to be acts of terrorism. The Hygienic Laboratories study, however, found a much less obvious source of anthrax infections—contaminated shaving brushes.

the late eighteenth century, public health policy focused on the threat of disease entering the United States through sailors on civilian trade vessels. In the late nineteenth century, public health focused on the threat of disease entering through immigrant populations. The twentieth and twenty-first centuries have brought a new focus on the underserved, the Rawlsian "least benefited." In addition, there is a growing focus on the possibility of bioterrorism.

Neoinstitutionalism

Institutions' outputs are a function of institutional rules as well as members' values, behaviors, and choices. The sense that public health care is an entitlement, something that government *ought* to provide, has become a prominent issue. When the Public Health Service was established in 1912, many policy-makers were White Anglo-Saxon Protestants who viewed immigrants as disease-ridden individuals. Public health policy was largely regulatory in nature. Many of the elitist early-Progressive stereotypes have disappeared from public health policy. Today, prominent modern liberal public health policy-makers focus on equity in health care provision.

Lessons Learned from Chapter 12

SPECIFICS

- Public health policy has evolved from an outwardly focused regulatory policy area toward increasingly broad distributive policy areas.
- According to HHS, there are seven major policy responsibilities of public health policy in the United States.
- A dozen major administrative offices, agencies, and centers fulfill the HHS public health policy mission.
- Medicare is a public health policy designed to serve the needs of older individuals, whereas Medicaid serves the needs of indigent or poor individuals.

THE BIG PICTURE

Public health policy is one of the oldest policy areas at the national level of government. Early public health policy was primarily regulatory, serving to prevent ship-borne diseases from entering the United States. In the late nineteenth century, public health policy focused on immigration and disease. In the late twentieth and early twenty-first centuries, public health is often promoted as a public good.

Many public health policy advocates argue that the policy is something government *ought to* do because public health is viewed as an important method of establishing a just society (in the modern liberal sense), promoting the equitable treatment of citizens and providing a public good. Conversely, classical liberals advocate individualized market-based semiprivate plans for public health rather than a unified national and state commitment through large-scale public policy.

Key Terms

Administration for Children and
Families (ACF)
Agency for Healthcare Research and
Quality (AHRQ)
Centers for Disease Control (CDC)
Food and Drug Administration (FDA)
Health Resources and Services
Administration (HRSA)
Indian Health Care Improvement
Act of 1976
Indian Self-Determination Act
of 1975
Medicaid
Medicare
National Fostercare and Adoption
Directory
National Institutes of Health (NIH)
Office of Child Support Enforcement
(OCSE)

Older Americans Act Amendments of
2000
Pink Book
Public Health Service
Ryan White Comprehensive AIDS
Resources Emergency (CARE) Act
of 1990
Snyder Act of 1921
State Children's Health Insurance
Program (SCHIP)
Substance Abuse and Mental Health
Services (SAMSHA)
Superfund Amendments and
Reauthorization Act of 1986
Temporary Assistance for Needy
Families (TANF)
U.S. Department of Health and
Human Services (HHS)
Welfare Reform Act of 1996

Questions for Study

1. Discuss two major policy actors involved in public health policy at the national level. How do their roles differ?
2. How does Medicare work? How does Medicaid work? What is the history and purpose of these policies? Using three policy models, describe and explain Medicare and Medicaid.
3. Based on the details discussed in the chapter, identify what you believe to be the three most serious public health problems facing the United States. Why did you choose these three? Support your response.

Group Project for Discussion

Statement of Senator Hillary Rodham Clinton on the President's Threat to Veto Bipartisan Agreement to Expand Children's Health Insurance, Washington, DC, July 16, 2007

"There are 8.7 million uninsured children in America—over 300,000 in New York—and our number one priority should be doing everything we can to cover them. President Bush has had six years to take action to cover these children. Not only has he done nothing, but now threatens expansion of SCHIP with a veto. It is one of our most important national priorities to cover all Americans and that should start now with all of our children.

SCHIP has been one of the most successful health care programs, with strong bipartisan support. We should build on this success by expanding the SCHIP program and working to cover every child. I have introduced legislation with Congressman John Dingell to cover all uninsured children.

Senate Finance Committee Chairman Baucus and Senator Rockefeller worked together with Senators Grassley and Hatch, who have long been strong supporters of this program, to craft this bipartisan agreement to reauthorize and expand the program. It is unconscionable that this President would veto a bill that expands and improves coverage for kids."

Courtesy of: Project Vote Smart www.votesmart.org

Discuss the statement from Senator Hillary Rodham Clinton. Is SCHIP something government ought or ought not do? Why or why not? If presenting your findings in a paper or class presentation, gather additional background information to make your case.

Bibliography

Administration on Aging. 2007. "Elder rights & resources." www.aoa.gov/eldfam/Elder_Rights/Elder_Abuse/Elder_Abuse.asp (accessed August 17, 2007).

Administration on Aging. 2009. "National family caregiver support program." www.aoa.gov/AoARoot/AoA_Programs/HCLTC/Caregiver/index.aspx (accessed May 19, 2009).

Administration on Aging. 2009. "Older Americans Act nutrition program." www.coalitionforaging.org/nutr.pdf (accessed May 19, 2009).

Administration on Health Research and Quality. 1998. "President's Advisory Commission on Consumer Protection and Quality in the Health Care Industry: Consumer Bill of Rights and Responsibilities." www.hcqualitycommission.gov/cborr/exsumm.html (accessed August 17, 2007).

Administration on Health Research and Quality. 2009. "About AHRQ." www.ahrq.gov/about/ (accessed May 19, 2009).

Agency for Toxic Substances and Disease Registry. 2009. "Webpage." www.atsdr.cdc.gov (accessed May 19, 2009).

Blumenthal, D., and R. DiClemente, eds. 2004. *Community-based health service.* New York: Springer Publishing Company.

Bureau of Health Professionals. 2006. The Registered Nurse Population: Findings from the 2004 National Sample Survey of Registered Nurses. http://bhpr.hrsa.gov/healthworkforce/rnsurvey04/ (accessed July 31, 2007).

Causey, M. 1982. "Watch Those Initials!" *The Washington Post,* July 14, C3.

Centers for Disease Control. 2009. "Tracking the hidden epidemics: Trends in STDs in the United States: 2000." www.cdc.gov/std/Trends2000/Trends2000.pdf (accessed May 19, 2009).

Centers for Disease Control. 2009. "Trends in Reportable Sexually Transmitted Diseases in the United States, 2007. National Surveillance Data for Chlamydia,

Gonorrhea, and Syphilis." www.cdc.gov/nchhstp/Newsroom/docs/STDTrends-FactSheet.pdf (accessed May 19, 2009).

Centers for Disease Control. 2009. "Chronic Disease Prevention and Health Promotion." www.cdc.gov/nccdphp/index.htm (accessed May 19, 2009).

Centers for Disease Control. 2009. "National Center for Birth Defects and Developmental Disabilities." www.cdc.gov/ncbddd/ (accessed May 19, 2009).

Centers for Disease Control. 2007. "Office of Communication: CDC timeline." www.cdc.gov/od/oc/media/timeline.htm (accessed August 17, 2007).

Centers for Disease Control and Prevention. 2007. *Epidemiology and Prevention of Vaccine-Preventable Diseases.* W. Atkinson, J. Hamborsky, L. McIntyre, and S. Wolfe, eds. 10th ed. Washington DC: Public Health Foundation.

Centers for Medicare and Medicaid Services. 2009. "CMS/HCFA history." www.cms.hhs.gov/History/ (accessed May 19, 2009).

Centers for Medicare and Medicaid Services. 2009. "Medicaid eligibility." www.cms.hhs.gov/medicaideligibility/ (accessed May 19, 2009).

Centers for Medicare and Medicaid Services. 2009. *Medicare & You.* Washington, DC: Department of Health and Human Services.

Centers for Medicare and Medicaid Services. 2009. "Overview of the Medicaid program." www.cms.hhs.gov/MedicaidGenInfo/ (accessed May 19, 2009).

Epidemiology Program Office. 2009. "About EPO." www.cdc.gov/epo/aboutepo.htm (accessed May 19, 2009).

Feit, M., and S. Battle, eds. 1995. *Health and social policy.* New York: The Haworth Press.

Health Resources and Services Administration. 2009. "HRSA Organization." www.hrsa.gov/about/orgchart/default.htm (accessed May 19, 2009).

Lawlor, E. 2003. *Redesigning the medicare contract: Politics, markets, and agency.* Chicago, IL: University of Chicago Press.

Marcus, A., and H. Cravens, eds. 1997. *Health care policy in contemporary America.* University Park: Pennsylvania State University Press.

National Center for Environmental Health. 2009. "Programs and divisions." www.cdc.gov/nceh/programs.htm (accessed May 19, 2009).

National Center for Health Workforce Analysis. 2009. "U.S. health workforce personnel factbook." http://bhpr.hrsa.gov/healthworkforce/reports/factbook.htm (accessed May 19, 2009).

National Center for Immunization and Preventable Disease. 2009. "NCIRD: Overview." www.cdc.gov/ncird/overview.html (accessed May 19, 2009).

National Center for Injury Prevention and Control. 2009. "Mission." www.cdc.gov/injury/index.html (accessed May 19, 2009).

National Institute for Occupational Safety and Health. 2009. "About NIOSH." www.cdc.gov/niosh/about.html (accessed May 19, 2009).

National Institutes of Health. 2007. "DeWitt Stetten, Jr. museum of medical research: Exhibits and galleries." www.history.nih.gov/exhibits/history/docs/page_09b.html (accessed August 17, 2007).

Office of Management and Budget. 2009. "Budget." www.whitehouse.gov/omb/budget/ (accessed May 19, 2009).

Porter, D., ed. 1994. *The history of public health and the modern state.* Atlanta: Rodopi.

Schmeckebier, L. F. 1923. *"The public health service: Its history, activities, and organization."* Baltimore: The Johns Hopkins University Press.

Social Security Administration. 2007. "The history of Social Security." www.ssa.gov/history/corningintro.html (accessed August 17, 2007).

Spratley, E., A. Johnson, J. Sochalski, M. Fritz, and W. Spencer. 2000. "Findings from the national sample survey of registered nurses." http://.bhpr.hrsa.gov/healthworkforce/reports/rnsurvey/rnss1.htm (accessed April 5, 2003).

Swann, J. P. 1998. "History of the FDA." www.fda.gov/oc/history/historyoffda/default.htm (accessed May 19, 2009).

Tester, P. B., T. A. Dugar, M. S. Medniondo, E. L. Abner, K. A. Cecil, and J. Otto. 2006. The 2004 survey of state adult protective services: Abuse of adults 60 years of age and older. Washington, DC: National Center on Elder Abuse, www.elderabusecenter.org/pdf/2-14-06%20FINAL%2060+REPORT.pdf (accessed August 17, 2007).

Tropman, J., M. Dhuly, and R. Lind, eds. 1981. *New strategic perspectives on social policy.* New York: Pergamon.

United Nations. 2004. "2004 Report on the global AIDS epidemic." www.unaids.org/bangkok2004/report.html (accessed August 17, 2007).

United Nations. 2008. AIDS epidemic update: 2007. Geneva, Switzerland, www.unaids.org/en/KnowledgeCentre/HIVData/EpiUpdate/EpiUpdArchive/2007/default.asp (accessed May 19, 2009).

U.S. Department of Health and Human Services. 2009. "Bureau of primary health care: Migrant health centers." http://bphc.hrsa.gov/about/specialpopulations.htm (accessed May 19, 2009).

U.S. Department of Health and Human Services. 2009. "HRSA HIV/AIDS bureau." http://hab.hrsa.gov/ (accessed May 19, 2009).

U.S. Department of Health and Human Services. 2009. "HSRA organization." www.hrsa.gov/about/orgchart/default.htm (accessed May 19, 2009).

U.S. Food and Drug Administration. 2002. "The Bioterrorism Act of 2002." www.fda.gov/OC/bioterrorism/bioact.html (accessed May 19, 2009).

U.S. Food and Drug Administration. 2003. "FDA's growing responsibility for the year 2001 and beyond." www.fda.gov/oc/opacom/budgetbro/budgetbro.htm (accessed August 17, 2007).

White, C. 2006. *The slowdown in medicare spending growth.* Washington, DC: CBO.

Endnotes

1. www.whitehouse.gov/agenda/health_care/ (accessed March 22, 2009).
2. www.hhs.gov/about/ (accessed March 22, 2009).
3. ACF also deals with Head Start programs.
4. www.acf.hhs.gov/healthymarriage/about/mission.html#activities (accessed March 22, 2009).
5. www.acf.hhs.gov/trafficking/about/index.html (accessed March 22, 2009).
6. Consistent with the principles of federalism, the program adopts many of the best practices used in states such as California and Pennsylvania.

7. www.caregiver.org/caregiver/jsp/content_node.jsp?nodeid=1004 (accessed March 22, 2009).

8. www.coalitionforaging.org/nutr.pdf (accessed May 19, 2009).

9. Tester, P. B., T. A. Dugar, M. S. Medniondo, E. L. Abner, K. A. Cecil, and J. Otto. 2006. "The 2004 survey of state adult protective services: Abuse of adults 60 years of age and older." Washington, DC: National Center on Elder Abuse, www.elderabusecenter.org/pdf/2-14-06%20FINAL%2060+REPORT.pdf, p. 5 (accessed August 17, 2007).

10. www.hcqualitycommission.gov/cborr/exsumm.html (accessed March 22, 2009).

11. ATSDR is attached to the Centers for Disease Control, but warrants special discussion.

12. In the 1970s the media and environmental interest groups made citizens and government officials aware of the growing problems with toxic waste in the United States. Media reports showed toxic waste containers that had been left in shopping center parking lots by private corporations that did not want to face the costs of properly disposing of these waste products. In the late 1960s and 1970s, a series of books and articles documented the environmental damage caused by private corporations and by government agencies. In her famous book, *Silent Spring,* Rachel Carson presents a fairly stark outline of the impact of environmental pollution on native plant and animal species as well as on human beings.

13. www.cdc.gov/ncbddd/index.html (accessed May 19, 2009).

14. www.cdc.gov/nccdphp/ (accessed May 19, 2009).

15. www.cdc.gov/nceh/ (accessed May 19, 2009).

16. www.pepfar.gov/documents/organization/101150.pdf (accessed May 19, 2009).

17. www.cdc.gov/nchstp/dstd/Stats_Trends/Trends2000.pdf (accessed August 17, 2007).

18. www.cdc.gov/std/ (accessed May 19, 2009).

19. www.cdc.gov/cchis/ (accessed May 19, 2009).

20. Published by National Immunization Program, reorganized under National Center for Immunization and Respiratory Diseases (NCIRD), www.cdc.gov/vaccines/pubs/pinkbook/default.htm (accessed May 19, 2009).

21. www.cdc.gov/vaccines/pubs/pinkbook/default.htm (accessed May 19, 2009).

22. www.cdc.gov/niosh/ (accessed May 19, 2009).

23. www.cdc.gov/epo/ (accessed May 19, 2009).

24. www.hhs.gov/asrt/ob/docbudget/2010budgetinbrief.pdf (accessed May 22, 2009).

25. Federal outlays by agency, *Statistical abstract of the United States,* 2009.

26. www.ssa.gov/history/corningintro.html (accessed August 17, 2007).

27. www.medicare.gov/MPPF/Static/TabHelp.asp?version=default&activeTab=3&planType=MA (accessed May 19, 2009).

28. www.cms.hhs.gov/MedicaidEligibility/downloads/MedGlance05.pdf, p. 1 (accessed August 17, 2007).

29. www.cms.hhs.gov/LowCostHealthInsFamChild/02_InsureKidsNow.asp#Top OfPage (accessed August 19, 2007).
30. Data source: Statistical abstract of the United States, 2009.
31. www.fda.gov/cder/reports/reviewtimes/default.htm (accessed May 19, 2009).
32. www.fda.gov/OC/bioterrorism/bioact.html (accessed May 19, 2009).
33. www.hrsa.gov/about/orgchart.htm (accessed August 17, 2007).
34. www.hab.hrsa.gov/heathconcerns.htm (accessed August 17, 2007).
35. Now under the Health Centers Consolidated Care Act of 1996, section 330(g) of the Public Health Service Act, http://bphc.hrsa.gov/migrant/default.htm (accessed January 31, 2005).
36. HRSA 2007. Border county health workforce profiles. www.bhpr.hrsa.gov/healthworkforce/border/ (accessed July 31, 2007).
37. HRSA 2007. Community health workers national workforce study. www.bhpr.hrsa.gov/healthworkforce/chw/ (accessed July 31, 2007).
38. www.hrsa.gov/bcrs/ (accessed May 19, 2009).
39. www.hhs.gov/asrt/ob/docbudget/index.html#Brief, (accessed May 19, 2009).
40. Doctors, health maintenance organizations, or hospitals.
41. www.cms.hhs.gov/about/history/default.asp (accessed August 17, 2007).
42. Helman, S. 2006. U.S. rule demands proof of citizenship for healthcare, *The Boston Globe*. April 11, A1.
43. DuBard, C. A., and M. W. Massing. 2007. Trends in emergency Medicaid expenditures for recent and undocumented immigrants, *Journal of the American Medical Association*. 297(10): 1091.

13

■■■

General Social Policy

CHAPTER OVERVIEW

Social policy "[has] to do with human beings living together as a group in a situation requiring that they have dealings with each other" (Tropman et al. 1981, p. xvi). Social policy has become a more prominent function of government as society has become larger and more complex.

Social policy is highly controversial in American politics. Modern liberals believe that the continued development of social policy is something that *ought* to occur. In their view, modern society necessitates government social support. Conversely, classical liberals think that extensive social policy is something government *ought not* pursue. In their view, complexity in society does not mean that individuals are incapable of meeting their own needs. Social policy is grounded in matters of *ought* and *ought not* influencing what government *does* or *does not* do.

The specific goals for the chapter are:

- Discuss major actors in social policy.
- Outline four policies related to at-risk target populations described primarily in terms of age and economic condition—the elderly, children, and the indigent.
- Explain social policy using policy theories.

MAJOR POLICY ACTORS

President

The presidency has played a tremendous role in shaping general social policies. President Franklin D. Roosevelt's New Deal era legislation led to the establishment of Social Security. Lyndon Johnson's **War on Poverty** led to the development of economic assistance, housing, and nutrition programs. President George W. Bush proposed major reform to the Social Security system, which was not enacted.

Courts

Many aspects of President Franklin D. Roosevelt's New Deal era legislation were threatened by Supreme Court judicial review. The courts saw national social and economic policy reforms as a threat to federalism. As discussed previously, the courts have broadened their interpretation of the Constitution, legitimizing the social welfare function of the national government.

SOCIAL SECURITY ADMINISTRATION

The **Social Security Administration (SSA)** deals with many areas of social policy, but the primary goal is to make direct cash payments to individuals who are eligible due to age, disability status, low income, or dependency upon an individual who is unable to provide basic social and economic needs.

The Social Security Administration can trace its legislative roots to the **Social Security Act of 1935**, but the concept of social security has a long history with many policy proposals and innovations going back to ancient Greece and early-modern Europe. England's Poor Law of 1601 and nineteenth-century German Chancellor Bismarck's pension system are two notable policy precedents.

The United States resisted most social policy until the Great Depression. In a very pointed letter to Congress in 1933, President Herbert Hoover (Roosevelt's predecessor) clearly espoused the classical liberal view of the Depression, seeing it primarily as a problem created by the private economic realm and one that would have to be remedied by the private sector. From a modern liberal perspective, FDR saw the Depression as clear evidence supporting the need for social policy for the sake of social justice. The Depression provided a "policy window" for many social policies, such as the Social Security pension system.

Social Security Reforms

Social Security policy reforms have changed the basic substance of the legislation in several ways:

COLAs

In the 1940s, Social Security was paying out very small payments and was not effectively providing assistance to the elderly. In fact, more elderly were receiving welfare benefits than were receiving Social Security benefits. In 1950, the benefits of Social Security were expanded and the payment amount per month was increased by 77 percent. The 1950 increase was designed to match economic inflation so that the spending power of Social Security payments remained steady—this is known as a **cost-of-living adjustment** or **COLA**. Since 1972, COLAs have been automatic, indexed to inflation rates.

Recipients

In 1956, President Eisenhower signed legislation that expanded Social Security benefits to disabled workers aged fifty to sixty-four and their dependents, and to disabled adult children. Disabled workers were individuals who were unable to perform their duties because of injuries related to an illness or to an accident.

The age requirement for a retired nondisabled worker had been lowered for women (1956) and men (1961). Under the revised legislation, workers who had reached the age of sixty-two could apply for and begin receiving Social Security benefits, but the payments were of a reduced amount and there was an earned-income stipulation.

Supplemental Security Income (SSI)

The original 1935 Act and the 1950s reforms led to benefit provisions for qualified disabled individuals. President Nixon signed legislation in 1972 consolidating the disability benefits programs into Supplemental Security Income (SSI), under the authority of the Social Security Administration (SSA).

Program Solvency Reforms

Following the 1972 amendments creating SSI and establishing it within SSA, the program began to face serious financial problems. Money was being distributed at a rate that would lead to program deficits. In 1977, legislation increased the Social Security payroll tax from 6.45 percent to 7.65 percent. In 1980, the disability program came under scrutiny and amendments to the Social Security Act required the periodic review of disability claimants to ensure eligibility. In 1983, the Greenspan Commission recommended that the age requirement be raised in the twenty-first century and that Social Security benefits be taxed as income. Greenspan's recommendations were signed into law by President Reagan.

In 1996, President Clinton signed the Contract with America Advancement Act, which made individuals who were disabled due to drug addiction or alcoholism no longer eligible for the SSI or Social Security disability benefits. Clinton also signed The Personal Responsibility and Work Opportunity Reconciliation Act, ending AFDC entitlements; generally made noncitizens ineligible to receive SSI benefits (the noncitizen ineligibility was rolled back in 1997 legislation); and time-limited SSI benefit recipients (i.e., "Welfare to Work"). In 2000, Clinton signed the Senior Citizens' Freedom to Work Act, eliminating the "retirement earnings test."

The twenty-first century already promises to be interesting when it comes to Social Security reforms. In 2001, the President's Commission to Strengthen Social Security—co-chaired by the late U.S. Senator Daniel Patrick Moynihan and Richard Parsons—published the following suggestions:

EXECUTIVE SUMMARY

Social Security will be strengthened if modernized to include a system of voluntary personal accounts. Personal accounts improve retirement security by facilitating wealth creation and providing participants with assets that they own and that can be inherited, rather than providing only claims to benefits that remain subject to political negotiation. By allowing investment choice, individuals would be free to pursue higher expected rates of return on their Social Security contributions. Furthermore, strengthening Social Security through personal accounts can add valuable protections for widows, divorced persons, low-income households and other Americans at risk of poverty in old age. Partial advance funding of Social Security should be a goal of any effort to strengthen the system. Advance funding within Social Security can best be accomplished through personal accounts rather than direct government investment. Personal accounts offer numerous economic benefits, including a likely increase in national saving, as well as an improvement in incentives for labor force participation. Personal accounts can be administered in an efficient and cost effective manner. This report outlines specific measures that would effectively balance desires for low administrative costs along with consumer choice and efficient financial markets. Accounts should be structured so as to allow inheritability and to strengthen the protection of spouses. Personal accounts can also contribute towards the fiscal sustainability of the Social Security system. While there are multiple paths to fiscal sustainability that are consistent with the President's principles for Social Security reform, we have chosen to include three reform models in the report that improve the fiscal sustainability of the current system, are costed honestly, and are preferable to the current Social Security system. . . .[1]

In 2005, President George W. Bush followed up on the commission's recommendations. Bush's proposal ultimately failed to be enacted by Congress, yet major reform will be needed. Despite skyrocketing assets, the Social Security Administration estimates that under current rules and based on projected Social Security tax revenues and distributions, the program will completely run out of money in 2041.[2] The influx of eligible Baby Boomer recipients, combined with smaller working age cohorts paying Social Security taxes, will have a tremendous impact on the system. (See Figure 13.1.)

U.S. DEPARTMENT OF AGRICULTURE (USDA): FOOD AND NUTRITION

The USDA plays a huge role in social policy, dating back to the Pure Food and Drug Act of 1906 and to New Deal social policy legislation during the 1930s and 1940s.[3] The USDA manages food and nutrition assistance programs. The programs account for approximately $61.8 billion of the $95 billion requested in the 2009 USDA budget.[4] The USDA's Food and Nutrition Service (FNS) operates four major programs: Food Stamp Program, Food Distribution Programs, Child Nutrition Program, and Women, Infants, and Children (WIC) Program.

Food Stamp Program
The **Food Stamp Program** began in 1939 as the Food Stamp Plan and was designed as a Depression-era program to feed needy families, and played a central role in the 1960's War on Poverty. As of 2008, the program is known as Supplemental Nutrition Assistance Program (SNAP). More than 17.2 million individuals in 7.3 million households receive benefits from the program. Food Stamps provide the less fortunate with access to a healthy diet.

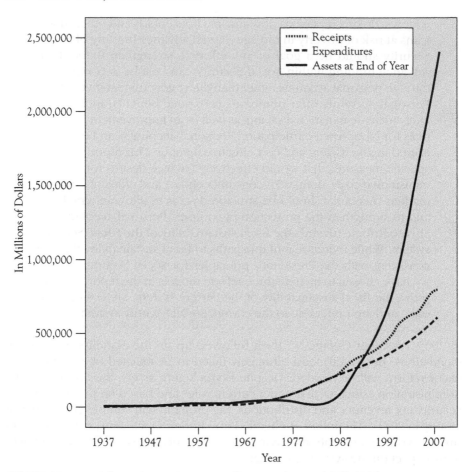

FIGURE 13.1   Social security receipts, expenditures and assets (1973–2008)

Food Stamp cards limit the use to program-designated food. In 2008, the average allotment for an individual was $101 per month—$227 for a household of three.[5] (See Box 13.1, *Food Stamps.*)

Participation standards are as follows:

- Households may have no more than $2,000 in countable resources, such as a bank account ($3,000 if at least one person in the household is age 60 or older, or is disabled). Certain resources are not counted, such as a home and lot. Special rules are used to determine the resource value of vehicles owned by household members.
- The gross monthly income of most households must be 130 percent or less of the Federal poverty guidelines ($1,907 per month for a family of three in most places, effective Oct. 1, 2008 through Sept. 30, 2009). Gross income includes all cash payments to the household, with a few exceptions specified in the law or the program regulations.

BOX 13.1

Food Stamps

"Households **can** use food stamp benefits to buy:

Foods for the household to eat, such as: breads and cereals; fruits and vegetables; meats, fish and poultry; dairy products; seeds and plants which produce food for the household to eat.

Households **cannot** use food stamp benefits to buy:

Beer, wine, liquor, cigarettes or tobacco; any nonfood items, such as: pet foods; soaps, paper products; and household supplies; vitamins and medicines; food that will be eaten in the store; hot foods."

Source: www.fns.usda.gov/fsp/faqs.htm#1 (accessed August 17, 2007).

- Net monthly income must be 100 percent or less of Federal poverty guidelines ($1,467 per month for a household of three in most places, effective Oct. 1, 2008 through Sept. 30, 2009). Net income is figured by adding all of a household's gross income, and then taking a number of approved deductions for child care, some shelter costs and other expenses. Households with an elderly or disabled member are subject only to the net income test.
- Most able-bodied adult applicants must meet certain work requirements.
- All household members must provide a Social Security number or apply for one.[6]

Food Distribution Programs

Several major food distribution programs are administered through the **Food and Nutrition Service (FNS)**. The Commodity Supplemental Program "works to improve the health of low-income pregnant and breastfeeding women, other new mothers up to one year postpartum, infants, children up to age 6, and elderly people at least 60 years of age by supplementing their diets with nutritious USDA commodity foods. It provides food and administrative funds to States to supplement the diets of these groups."[7] The Food Distribution Disaster Assistance Program "has the primary responsibility of supplying food to disaster relief organizations such as the Red Cross and the Salvation Army for mass feeding or household distribution. Disaster organizations request food and nutrition assistance through state agencies that run USDA's nutrition assistance programs. State agencies notify USDA of the types and quantities of food that relief organizations need for emergency feeding operations."[8] Authorized under the Food Stamp Act of 1977, the Food Distribution Program on Indian Reservations "is a federal program that provides commodity foods to low-income households, including the elderly, living on Indian reservations, and to Native American families residing in designated areas near reservations."[9] Although administered by HHS, the Nutrition Services Incentive Program, created under the Older Americans Act of 1965,[10] receives food and financial support from USDA.[11] The USDA's Schools and Child Nutrition Commodity Programs supports the following programs: National School Lunch Program, Child and Adult Care Food Program, and Summer Food Service Program. About 30.5 million children receive their lunch each day through the National School Lunch Program.[12] The Child and Adult Care Food Program provides, on a daily basis, meals and snacks to 2.9 million children and 86,000 adults.[13] The Summer Food Service Program provides daily meals to eligible low-income children during the summer months. According to 2004 FNS reports, 1.9 million children receive daily meals through the Summer Food Service Program.[14] In 1995, USDA partnered with the military to operate the Department of Defense Fresh Fruit and Vegetable Program, using military vehicles to deliver produce to schools, a method reducing transportation costs and increasing vehicle use efficiency.[15] The Emergency Food Assistance Program distributes food to the elderly and other needy individuals and households at no charge.[16] Finally, the State Processing Program was based on policy established in 1958, as a method of coordinating the collection and distribution of food to state and local agencies, including schools.[17] (See Figure 13.2.)[18]

Child Nutrition Program
Up for legislative reauthorization in 2009, the **Child Nutrition Program** is related to the Food Distribution Program, operating in conjunction with the School Lunch Program, School Breakfast Program, Special Milk Program, Summer Food Service Program, Child and Adult Care Food Program, and

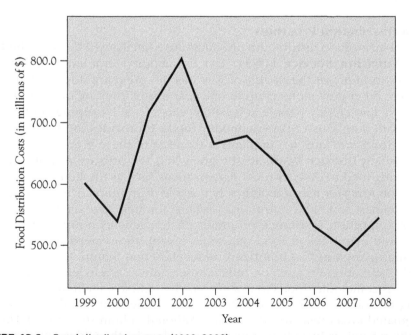

FIGURE 13.2   Food distribution costs (1999–2008)

Team Nutrition Initiative, and works for a similar target population as the State Children's Health Insurance Program. Child nutrition programs are individually and community-based programs that encourage healthy habits for individuals, households, and communities living in poverty.

Women, Infants, and Children (WIC) Program

The **Women, Infants, and Children Program** became a permanent authorization in 1975. WIC provides health care and nutrition programs to low-income pregnant women and their children up to the age of five years. Program vouchers are used by eligible women and their children for nutrition and pregnancy-related products provided by participating merchants. In 1990, a study showed that WIC participation reduces Medicaid costs for low-income women and their children. WIC participation was also linked to healthier babies and lower infant mortality rates.[19] Program participation is rising rapidly. (See Figure 13.3.) [20]

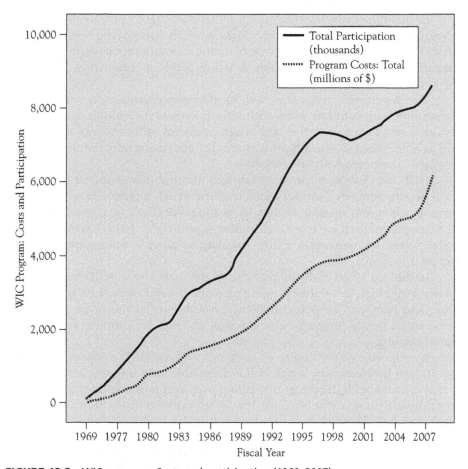

FIGURE 13.3 WIC program: Costs and participation (1969–2007)

U.S. DEPARTMENT OF HOUSING
AND URBAN DEVELOPMENT (HUD)

The **National Housing Act of 1934** represents a major national policy commitment to house those individuals displaced by economic circumstance; however, it was not until the Civil Rights Act of 1964 that principles of fair housing and the socioeconomic disparities suffered by persons of color were more effectively addressed.

As part of Lyndon Johnson's Great Society programs and War on Poverty, the **Department of Housing and Urban Development (HUD)** was tasked with the goal of renewing America's cities, providing safe housing for all individuals and families, and enforcing equity in housing availability. HUD enforcement of the **Fair Housing Act of 1968** (Title VIII of the Civil Rights Act of 1968), "prohibit[ed] discrimination in the sale, rental, and financing of dwellings, and in other housing-related transactions, based on race, color, religion, sex, or national origin . . . disability or familial status (presence of child under the age of 18, and pregnant women). . . ."[21]

In addition to promoting equity in housing, HUD promotes affordable housing development. Many individuals work in low-paying service-related jobs; the department advances urban planning statutory requirements that mandate the construction of affordable housing within a reasonable distance of workers' employment.[22]

The department cooperates with local housing planners, developers, and community leaders in providing shelter for homeless individuals. Homeless individuals often confront crime and health problems. Although not a final solution to homelessness, shelters are a method of alleviating many of the costs and problems associated with homelessness.

HUD also works to promote fair and affordable housing in rural areas. Rural poverty remains a serious problem as traditional industries in rural areas—farming, ranching, mining, timber harvesting—decline. In conjunction with HUD programs, rural areas are also finding support from HHS, USDA, and other social policy programs interested in building sustainable communities in rural and urban settings.

In the late 1960s and continuing until the early 1990s, HUD was often associated with high-rise public housing projects in major cities like Chicago, New York, and Boston. The public housing projects turned out to be one of the worst social policy programs ever devised and did not produce racially integrated housing.

In response to the failure of housing projects, HUD supports programs like Habitat for Humanity, which builds affordable homes in neighborhoods all over the nation with the intent of creating true integration and to promote dignity through home ownership for low-income individuals. Former President and Nobel Prize laureate Jimmy Carter has used his visibility to support this successful approach.

HUD played a significant role in the housing of people in the Gulf Coast region displaced by Hurricane Katrina. Temporary housing issues persist, but new construction is proceeding. A disaster sometimes creates opportunities and the HUD program is busily promoting equitable housing arrangements. In the Hurricane Katrina impact area and elsewhere, HUD is working with local contractors and national, state, and local administrators to promote green housing to reduce energy costs and environmental impact.[23]

U.S. DEPARTMENT OF LABOR—UNEMPLOYMENT COMPENSATION

Created under the Social Security Act of 1935, unemployment compensation (UC) is intended to financially provide for qualified out-of-work individuals. The **Federal Unemployment Tax Act (FUTA)** made UC almost entirely funded through employer taxes.

UC is a good example of cooperative federalism at work. The federal government has outlined many standards for unemployment compensation eligibility and for managing tax dollars collected for current and future UC purposes. The primary functions of the national government:

1. Ensure conformity and substantial compliance of state law, regulations, rules, and operations with federal law
2. Determine administrative fund requirements and provide money to states for proper and efficient administration
3. Set broad overall policy for administration of the program, monitor state performance and provide technical assistance as necessary
4. Hold and invest all money in the unemployment trust fund until drawn down by states for the payment of compensation.[24]

The state governments are responsible for the following functions:

1. Determine operation methods and directly administer the program
2. Take claims from individuals, determine eligibility, and insure timely payment of benefits to workers
3. Determine employer liability, and assess and collect contributions.[25]

Unemployment compensation is generally fixed at 26 weeks, although Massachusetts and Washington pay up to 30 weeks of compensation. Extended unemployment benefits are generally paid for an additional 13 weeks for an individual if the unemployment rate in states occurs during periods of high or rising unemployment. Optionally, a state may pay 13 weeks of extended benefits if the state-insured unemployment rate for the previous 13 weeks is at least 6 percent, regardless of the unemployment rate during the same time period in previous years (Office of Workforce Security 2008, p. 12).

Federal unemployment compensation tax money is collected from employers by state governments, which deposit the money with the federal government under the Federal Unemployment Trust Act provisions. When individuals apply for federal unemployment compensation, state government requests funds from the state account in the federal unemployment compensation fund in accordance with state unemployment compensation fund formulas—in other words,

BOX 13.2
Immigration and Employment

In recent years there has been rising concern over illegal immigrants in the labor market. "Demographers estimate that six to seven million illegal immigrants are working in the United States."[26] With U.S. unemployment rates on the rise during the recent recession, there have been heightened efforts to stop the hiring of illegal immigrants. Business interests are particularly concerned that the manual labor provided by immigrants will decline. Agriculture is particularly interested in the manual labor provided because it needs people to harvest crops.

Controlling illegal immigration in the workforce brings many different agencies together. One of the biggest concerns is that illegal immigrants can easily obtain fake Social Security numbers and other documentation. In response, the Social Security Administration and Department of Homeland Security are cooperating to create unified databases of Social Security numbers and names.[27] The Department of Labor and Internal Revenue Service are also closely tied to issues of illegal immigration and the workforce.

the states establish the parameters for the amount of money paid to an unemployed individual. When the state account is diminished, the state may apply for a loan from the Federal Unemployment Account. States must repay the loans or provide evidence of working toward repayment within an established timeframe. Outstanding unemployment compensation loan balances are subject to interest charges. States may lose the 5.4 percent tax credit to employers if these loans are not repaid. (See Box 13.2, *Immigration and Employment*.)

EXPLAINING GENERAL SOCIAL POLICY

Institutionalism

As noted earlier, the executive, legislative, and judicial branches have experienced tremendous change over the last hundred years. The executive branch—namely, the presidency—has witnessed a tremendous growth in implied powers. The president has become an important policy leader and agenda setter. As the only nationally elected leader in government, the president is often seen as the primary spokesperson for basic citizen rights, which was perhaps most evident during the presidencies of Theodore Roosevelt and his fifth cousin Franklin D. Roosevelt.

Congress has also witnessed tremendous changes in its institutional powers and organization. The Seventeenth Amendment (1913) to the U.S. Constitution provided for the direct election of U.S. senators, and the Senate became *directly* accountable to the citizenry. Given its smaller size in comparison to the House of Representatives and its visibility at the national level, the senators came to be seen as representing the national interest. Institutional changes made the passage of federal social welfare policy, with its national focus, more feasible.

Having initially rejected the social policies of the New Deal, the Supreme Court found itself under pressure from FDR. In the landmark case *West Coast Hotel Co. v. Parrish* 300 U.S. 379 (1937), Supreme Court justice Robert Owen switched from an anti-New Deal to a pro-New Deal position, creating the 5–4 majority that implicitly upheld the constitutionality of New Deal socioeconomic reforms. The decision also represented a major institutional change for the Court, which in the decades since has increasingly been a policy leader in racial and gender equality, and social policy.

Group Theory

The influence of pressure groups in social policy-making can also be used to explain the evolution and growth of social policy in the United States. Pressure groups have identified what government is not doing and argue that social policy is something government ought to do. Advocates for various social policies—groups like the National Dairy Council (advocates for the Milk Program), Association for the Advancement of Retired People (advocates for Social Security, Medicare, and Eldercare), and the Children's Defense Fund (protection of children's rights)—employ lobbyists attempting to advance the social policy priorities of their groups' membership.

Pressure groups' influence in social policy may explain why government chooses not to do certain things, and may choose to do less for one group and more for others. Pressure group formation and strength is biased. Individuals with great socioeconomic power have a greater chance of forming a successful pressure group and, ultimately, achieving their policy goals than individuals who have more limited social and economic means. Individuals who have the least power are likely to be those with the greatest need of what social policy offers.

Elite Theories

Elite theory can be used to explain social policy in a variety of different ways. One view might be that political and social elites use social policy to manipulate public opinion in their favor. A very negative view of elite power and its use, but the argument has been used by critics of social policy to explain why elites have championed social policy and successfully promoted it. In the 1930s and 1940s, classical liberal elites often complained that modern liberals promoted New Deal legislation in order to curry favor with the mass populace. (See Box 13.3, *Political Parties, Elites, a Prediction, and a Plea.*)

From another perspective, elite theory explains why social policy has been unsuccessful in meeting many of its goals. Elites have used their power to limit social policy; it may explain why government does not do certain things when it comes to social policy. For instance, we do not have a national health insurance plan because political and social elites have repeatedly blocked efforts to implement government health care—certain economic elites, for instance, might lose wealth if government regulated the price of health care.

BOX 13.3
Political Parties, Elites, a Prediction, and a Plea

One elite . . .

. . . writing to
another elite . . .

. . . about a third
elite.

"The day will come when the Democratic party [sic] will endeavor to place the responsibility for [the Great Depression] on the Republican Party. When that day comes I hope that you will invite the attention of the American people to the actual truth."

Source: Letter from President Herbert Hoover to Senator Simeon Fess (R-OH), February 1933.

New Institutionalism

New institutionalism increases our awareness of interaction between institutional rules and individual value priorities in shaping the policy agenda, and advancing that agenda to the point of policy formulation and implementation. As time progresses, policy decision-making bodies are increasingly composed of Baby Boomers and Generation Xers. The Baby Boomers had their first major significant impact on social policy during the 1970s. The general election of 1974 ushered in a huge freshman class into Congress—with a decidedly postmaterialist value orientation—eclipsing the power of an older generation of legislators, and establishing new policy priorities.

The Clinton presidency was an interesting crossroads for social policy, in part because he was a politically active Baby Boomer in the 1970s. A moderate Democrat, President Clinton campaigned as a social policy reformer, but also an advocate for national health care policy. The Republican congressional leadership—classical liberals, for the most part—used opposition to national health care policy plans as the basis of their sweep into power in the U.S. House of Representatives and U.S. Senate in the 1994 midterm election. Although they held opposing views of national health care policy, the Republican congressional leadership and the president shared a common interest in reforming social policy, particularly welfare reform, possibly due to a shared generational value set characterized by policy pragmatism. Neoinstitutionalism helps explain the convergence of institutional change and the value shifts among policymakers.

Lessons Learned from Chapter 13

SPECIFICS

- General social policy discussed in the chapter deals primarily with the needs of the elderly, children, women, and the indigent.
- General social policy is often the center of debate. Philosophically, classical liberals reject a large social policy function, whereas modern liberals embrace social policy as a method promoting social justice.

THE BIG PICTURE

Social policy is one of the largest portions of public policy at the national level. Over the last century, its growth has been meteoric and can be traced back to dramatic social and historical events, changes in our views of what government *ought to* do, and the evolution of social values. What lesson can we draw? A major lesson is that American public policy is fairly consistent in intent, but malleable enough to respond effectively to tragic errors of the past. Inequitable treatment in social policy meant that many individuals and groups, such as women and minorities, were underserved by society. Public policy—the issue of what government ought or ought not do, does or does not do—in a democratic state takes time, for better or ill, and we must remain ever vigilant of policy bias in our attempt to create what we collectively deem to be acceptable social conditions.

Key Terms

Child Nutrition Program
cost-of-living adjustment (COLA)
Fair Housing Act of 1968
Federal Unemployment Tax Act (FUTA)
Food and Nutrition Service (FNS)
Food Stamp Program
National Housing Act of 1934

Social Policy
Social Security Act of 1935
Social Security Administration (SSA)
U.S. Department of Housing and Urban Development (HUD)
War on Poverty
Women, Infants, and Children (WIC) Program

Questions for Study

1. What three major reforms have occurred in Social Security that changed the nature of that policy? Identify and discuss.
2. What are the qualifications for receiving Food Stamps? What can a recipient purchase with Food Stamps? What can they **not** purchase with Food Stamps?
3. How does unemployment compensation work? What is the role of the national government in unemployment compensation? What are the roles of state governments in unemployment compensation?

CASE STUDY

Remarks to the National Press Club
Former Senator John R. Edwards
June 26, 2006

"America has fought poverty before. Past efforts like Social Security, Medicaid, welfare reform and the Earned Income Tax Credit have made a real difference.

But poverty is still with us. Any effort to address it must face up to the reasons that past efforts have fallen short, and to the new challenges that have arisen.

First, work doesn't pay enough. A single mom with one child who works full-time for the minimum wage is about $2,700 below the poverty line. In 2005, while corporate profits were up 13 percent, real wages fell for most workers."

Second, in too many poor communities, marriage is too rare, and male responsibility is not what it should be. Welfare reform has helped reduce poverty rates among single mothers, but too many young men remain cut off from the hopes and routines of ordinary American life."

"Which is why, today, I'm proposing we set a national goal of eliminating poverty in the next 30 years."

"It's an ambitious goal, but it's one we'll meet by building the America our founders imagined—an America where if you work hard, take personal responsibility and do the right thing, you won't live in poverty, you won't just get by, you'll get ahead."

"I propose a great national goal, because Americans believe in achieving great things. Like JFK challenging America to land a man on the moon, a national goal of eradicating poverty will sharpen our focus, marshal our resources and at the end of the day, bring out our best.

Besides, we need a goal. America will never get close to eliminating poverty until we set our sights and commit to try."

"Poverty is such a low priority in Washington that politicians aren't even interested in developing an accurate statistic. The official measure is incomplete and out-of-date—overlooking as many as 1 million Americans. It's a metaphor for how poverty is ignored. Setting a bold goal is how we'll bring change."

"Tony Blair understands the power of great goals. In 1999, he announced a goal of ending child poverty by 2020. Since then, British child poverty has dropped by 17 percent. It's a remarkable accomplishment in just seven years, and there is no reason we can't see similar results here."

"But this afternoon, I want to make clear I'm not willing to settle for some Washington "pie-in-the-sky" dream that gets promised and then quickly forgotten. Poverty is an issue where we cannot fail. So to hold us accountable, I propose we also set a benchmark to measure our progress and guide our way."

"In the next 10 years, we need to cut poverty by a third, improving the lives of 12 million Americans."

"If we meet this benchmark, we'll be well on our way."

"In order to get the country on the path to eliminating poverty, we must build a "Working Society," which builds on the lessons of the past to create solutions for the future."

"At the heart of the Working Society is the value of work. Work is not only a source of a paycheck, but also a source of dignity and independence and self-respect."

"In a Working Society, we would create new opportunities to work. We would offer affordable housing near good jobs and a million last-chance jobs to people who cannot find work on their own."

"In a Working Society, we would reward work. We would raise the minimum wage and cut taxes for low-income workers. We would find ways for workers to not only have but keep their health care and other key benefits, a topic I'll return to in the future. We would help workers save for the future with Work Bonds and homeownership tax credits. And we would create a million more housing vouchers for working families."

"And in a Working Society, we would expect work. In return for greater investments, we would expect everyone who can work to work, for the sake of their country, their families, and themselves."

"Third, the debate of poverty policies is stuck in the old days. One side is driven by guilt, and the other by a deep skepticism of what government can accomplish. In reality, we need both the courage and the confidence to take a new course. And both sides should recognize that our whole economic future depends on making upward mobility universal."

Courtesy of: Project Vote Smart www.votesmart.org

The statement above by John Edwards deals with poverty in America. Using his statement as a starting point for discussion, debate your views of poverty—ought or ought not poverty-related programs exist? Why or why not? Given that they do exist, how should the programs be offered and to whom? Come to some form of compromise among group members on the need and direction of poverty-related programs, presenting a short set of recommendations to your class. If presenting your findings in a paper or class presentation, gather additional background information to make your case.

Bibliography

Food and Nutrition Service. 2009. "Nutrition services incentive program." www .fns.usda.gov/fdd/programs/nsip/ (accessed May 22, 2009).

Food and Nutrition Service. 2009. "About women, infants, and children." www .fns.usda.gov/wic/aboutwic/ (accessed May 22, 2009).

Food and Nutrition Service. 2009. "Child and adult care food program." www .fns.usda.gov/cnd/care/cacfp/cacfpfaqs.htm (accessed May 22, 2009).

Food and Nutrition Service. 2007. "Child nutrition commodities program." www.fns.usda.gov/fdd/programs/schcnp (accessed August 17, 2007).

Food and Nutrition Service. 2009. "Commodity supplemental food program." www.fns.usda.gov/fdd/programs/csfp/default.htm (accessed May 22, 2009).

Food and Nutrition Service. 2009. "Food distribution disaster assistance." www .fns.usda.gov/fdd/programs/fd-disasters/ (accessed May 22, 2009).

Food and Nutrition Service. 2009. "Food distribution program on Indian reservations." www.fns.usda.gov/fdd/programs/fdpir/ (accessed May 22, 2009).

Food and Nutrition Service. 2009. "SNAP Program: Frequently asked questions." www.fns.usda.gov/fsp/faqs.htm#1 (accessed May 22, 2009).

Moynihan, D., and R. Parsons. 2001. "Strengthening Social Security and creating personal wealth for all Americans." www.commtostrengthensocsec.gov/ reports/ (accessed August 17, 2007).

Office of Workplace Security. 2008. "Unemployment compensation: Federal–state partnership." Washington, DC: U.S. Department of Labor, www. workforcesecurity.doleta.gov/unemploy/pdf/partnership.pdf (accessed May 22, 2009).

Santow, L., and M. Santow. 2005. *Social security and the middle class squeeze: Fact and fiction about America's entitlement programs.* Westport, CT: Praeger.

Social Security Administration. 2009. "History of Medicare bill." www.ssa.gov/ history/corningintro.html (accessed May 22, 2009).

Tropman, J., M. Dhuly, and R. Lind, eds. 1981. *New strategic perspectives on social policy.* New York: Pergamon.

U.S. Department of Agriculture. 1999. "Food and agricultural import regulations and standards report." www.fas.usda.gov/itp/ofsts/us.html (accessed May 22, 2009).

U.S. Department of Housing and Urban Development. 2008. "Fair housing laws and presidential executive orders." www.hud.gov/offices/fheo/FHLaws/ index.cfm (accessed May 22, 2009).

Court Case

West Coast Hotel Co. v. Parrish, 300 U.S. 379 (1937)

Endnotes

1. www.commtostrengthensocsec.gov/reports/Final_report.pdf (accessed August 17, 2007).
2. Social Security Administration. 2007. News Release: Social Security Board of Trustees Issues Annual Report, April 23, www.ssa.gov/pressoffice/pr/ trustee07-pr.htm (accessed May 22, 2009).
3. www.fas.usda.gov/itp/ofsts/us.html (accessed May 22, 2009).
4. www.usda.gov/documents/budget2009.pdf (accessed March 23, 2009).
5. www.fns.usda.gov/fsp/faqs.htm (accessed May 22, 2009).
6. www.fns.usda.gov/fsp/faqs.htm (accessed May22, 2009).
7. www.fns.usda.gov/fdd/programs/csfp/default.htm (accessed May 22, 2009).
8. www.fns.usda.gov/fdd/programs/fd-disasters/default.htm (accessed May 22, 2009).

9. www.fns.usda.gov/fdd/programs/fdpir/default.htm (accessed May 22, 2009).

10. Older Americans Act of 1965 (amended by P.L. 108-7, Consolidated Appropriation Resolution).

11. www.fns.usda.gov/FDD/programs/nsip/nsipagreement.pdf (accessed May 22, 2009)

12. National School Lunch Program Fact Sheet, www.fns.usda.gov/cnd/Lunch/AboutLunch/NSLPFactSheet.pdf (accessed May 22, 2009).

13. www.fns.usda.gov/cnd/care/CACFP/aboutcacfp.htm (accessed May 22, 2009).

14. www.fns.usda.gov/cnd/Summer/states/ruralgrants.html; www.fns.usda.gov/pd/04sffypart.htm (accessed July 31, 2007).

15. www.fns.usda.gov/fdd/programs/dod/DoD_FreshFruitandVegetableProgram.pdf (accessed July 31, 2007); www.fns.usda.gov/FDD/programs/dod/default.htm (accessed May 22, 2009).

16. www.fns.usda.gov/cga/FactSheets/TEFAP_Quick_Facts.htm (accessed May 22, 2009).

17. State Processing Program Handbook, www.fns.usda.gov/FDD/processing/state/state-handbk.pdf (accessed May 22, 2009).

18. Data source: www.fns.usda.gov/pd/fd$sum.htm (accessed July 31, 2007).

19. www.fns.usda.gov/wic/aboutwic/ (accessed May 22, 2009).

20. Data source: www.fns.usda.gov/pd/wisummary.htm (accessed July 31, 2007).

21. www.hud.gov/offices/fheo/progdesc/title8.cfm (accessed July 31, 2007); pregnant women, disability, and family status was part of the Title VIII amendments in 1988, made effective March 12, 1989.

22. See Title 42, Chapter 130, Subchapter II of the U.S. Code.

23. Press Release: HUD Provides Technical Assistance Seminar to Assist Local Leaders and Organizations in the Rebuilding Efforts of Gulf Coast Communities, www.hud.gov/local/ms/news/pr2005-11-18.cfm (accessed July 31, 2007).

24. www.workforcesecurity.doleta.gov/unemploy/pdf/partnership.pdf (accessed May 22, 2009).

25. Ibid.

26. Porter, E. 2006. The Search for Illegal Immigrants Stops at the Workplace, *The New York Times*, March 5, Section 3, p. 3.

27. Ibid.

14

■ ■ ■

Education Policy

CHAPTER OVERVIEW

Education policy is a central part of the policy agenda. Modern liberals generally agree that the direct government provision of basic education is important in a strong democracy; through equal access to education, they believe that social, political, and economic equality is advanced. Conversely, classical liberals contend that basic education should be provided by private schools—individuals ought to be allowed to choose the schools that best fit their personal needs. Education policy is part of a larger normative debate about what government *ought* or *ought not* do, *does* or *does not* do.

The specific goals for the chapter are:

- Identify major participants in education policy.
- Discuss major education reforms.
- Discuss major policies related to education equity.
- Use policy models to explain education policy.

MAJOR PARTICIPANTS IN EDUCATION POLICY

President

President George W. Bush entered office in 2001 on a campaign platform advocating the privatization of elementary and secondary education and the use of vouchers to create a form of equality within a school choice framework. The privatization plan failed to come to fruition due to political opposition from congressional leaders and interest groups.

President Bush then changed policy tactics—instead, advocating greater public school accountability and using a modified school choice mechanism for students in "failing" schools. President Bush's 2001 education initiative, "Let No Child Be Left Behind" (NCLB) is one of the most sweeping reforms of the Elementary and Secondary Education Act since its inception in 1965. Supported by an overwhelming number of congressional legislators at its creation, NCLB is an example of presidential power in the agenda setting and policy formulation process.

President Barack Obama entered office with a similarly ambitious plan to reform education in the United States. Broadly, his plan seeks to promote early childhood education, bolster Head Start programming, reform No Child Left Behind, promote science and math education, reduce dropout rates, and promote college education. The years ahead will offer greater insight into his administration's success in promoting the aforementioned education policy goals.

Congress

Congress plays a significant role in education policy, particularly through its lawmaking and budget functions. Congress has the power to establish laws shaping how education policy is implemented at lower levels of government. Although President Bush proposed NCLB, Congress held hearings on its feasibility and amended the legislation. Legislators have different normative backgrounds and constituencies, which impacts policy-making.

Congress also plays an important policy oversight role. Congressional oversight helps illuminate policy outcomes, offering explanations for why certain outcomes may occur, offering normative interpretations of empirical results—essentially, reinforcing long-held values regarding what we collectively and individually believe *ought* or *ought not* occur.

Courts

One of the best examples of court-based policy-making is **Brown v. Board of Education, Topeka, Kansas (1954)**. In this landmark court case, the Supreme Court acted as a policy leader in the politics of racial equality. The Court noted that racially segregated school facilities deny children equal protection under the law, guaranteed by the Fourteenth Amendment to the U.S. Constitution. The Court effectively struck down the "separate but equal" doctrine.

Education policy has been impacted by the courts in a variety of other cases, often related to students' First Amendment rights. In *Morse et al. v. Frederick* 551 U.S. 393 (2007), the Court explored the balance between freedom of speech and expression with the need to control student behavior in schools. A conservative Supreme Court majority found in favor of narrower student speech rights.

The courts have slowed progress toward the privatization of public elementary and secondary education. In 1998, the Wisconsin Supreme Court found that the use of publicly provided school vouchers in religious schools was not a violation of the establishment clause. The U.S. Supreme Court refused to hear the case, a signal that the U.S. Supreme Court felt the issue was best dealt with at the state level. The following year, the U.S. Supreme Court clarified its position by finding that Vermont's and Maine's statutory limitations on the use of school voucher money in religious schools did not violate the free exercise clause of the Constitution.

In a 1999 Ohio case, the state courts argued that voucher programs are not constitutional if they are limited to a small group of schools rather than being more expansive and able to offer school choice to a wider group of individuals within the state. The U.S. Court of Appeals found that because choice was limited to a small number of schools, primarily religious-based, the voucher program in Ohio was in violation of the First Amendment's establishment clause. The U.S. Supreme Court took a more profound stab at the question when the case was appealed. In *Zelman, Superintendent of Public Instruction of Ohio, et al. v. Simmons-Harris, et al.* 536 U.S. 639 (2002), the Supreme Court found that the voucher plan was constitutional. The plan was religiously neutral—the fact that religious schools were the predominant choices available to individuals using the vouchers was irrelevant. The Court has been fairly clear in developing its privatization policy decisions: The states can delineate the extent of education reform, to include *legislatively* restricting the use of vouchers in private schools, but there is no constitutional basis for the elimination of vouchers to fund education choice. The Court's role in education policy is fairly extensive.

Bureaucracy

Bureaucrats in the U.S. Department of Education (USDOE) spend considerable time and resources testing education theory and policies to promote effective and efficient student learning. USDOE promulgates rules and regulations that directly impact education policy at the state and local levels. Through USDOE, the national government provided approximately $29 billion in aid to public schools in 2008 and is slated to disperse more than triple the 2008 amount through the American Recovery and Reinvestment Act.[1] The resources are often tied to specific policy goals, such as aid for disadvantaged or "at risk" students, disabled students, and specific learning programs in reading and mathematics.

Title I of the **Elementary and Secondary Education Act** (reauthorized under **No Child Left Behind [NCLB]**) requires that state education departments and local schools be held accountable through student testing programs to measure outcomes. NCLB requires that schools be accountable to parents and schoolchildren by developing plans to monitor and improve educational outcomes. If student test scores do not improve, then parents and school children "must be given options for seeking better and expanded learning opportunities for their children."[2]

To meet NCLB requirements, state and national education bureaucrats design examinations that measure student learning and teacher competency. The test results are calculated and monitored by bureaucrats whose reports play a significant role in determining the effectiveness of public schools.

Interest Groups

Two of the most prominent national teaching associations are the **American Federation of Teachers (AFT)** and the **National Education Association (NEA)**. Teaching associations provide membership and policy information to elected officials. The AFT and NEA often use lobbying and mobilization to pressure government. At the local level, teachers' unions negotiate collective bargaining agreements with school districts, significantly impacting school administrative policies and education policy implementation.[3]

Policy think tanks shape policy choices through research monographs, articles, and the speeches of their research fellows. Think tank *research fellows* often represent a particular view of what government *ought to do* or *ought not do*. Their research tends to link normative views with empirical evaluations of what government *does* or *does not* do. Think tanks recommend alterations in the fabric of public policy such that their normative perspective is imprinted on public.

Citizens

Citizens shape education policy. Parent–teacher associations (PTAs) and locally elected school boards are key stakeholders in education policy. Parental demands influence education policy priorities. Policy evaluations are offered legitimacy by the clientele—school-aged children and parents. Parents and other concerned citizens have often demonstrated that they can be powerful policy actors in shaping education policy.

EDUCATION POLICY REFORM PROPOSALS

Education is in the midst of a new reform effort, one that focuses on public school accountability as well as efforts to privatize public elementary and secondary education. Public school accountability can be seen in efforts to:

- Increase the professionalism of teachers through testing.
- Reduce class sizes in order to improve the effectiveness of education.
- Increase student testing to measure intellectual growth.
- Promote competition through school choice. NCLB introduces a form of school choice for students when their schools fail to meet achievement standards.

Student Testing

Since 1969, the **National Assessment of Educational Progress (NAEP)** has conducted national assessments of student learning in "reading, mathematics, science, writing, U.S. history, civics, geography, and the arts."[4] NAEP is conducted by the National Center for Education Statistics (NCES), a research unit within the U.S. Department of Education.[5]

The NAEP examination is a longitudinal analysis: The exams use standard questions so comparability is possible over time. NAEP exams are given to students in the fourth, eighth, and twelfth grades. The national NAEP exam is given to all students in the aforementioned grade levels, whereas state NAEP exams are specific to state- and local-level education assessment needs.

Analysis indicates that student learning has neither improved nor worsened significantly over the last thirty years. Looking more carefully at the aggregate test results for thirteen-year-olds from 1990 to 2007, girls have closed the gender gap on the mathematics portion of the NAEP exam. Boys continue to lag behind girls on verbal ability but the gap has closed slightly only because girls'

PHOTO 14.1   Student testing

average reading score has declined marginally—boys' reading ability has remained flat for nearly a decade. Mathematics scores have been increasing for whites, blacks, and Hispanics, although there are group differences. Average reading ability scores for thirteen-year-old black students has increased appreciably. (See Photo 14.1, Figure 14.1 and Figure 14.2.)

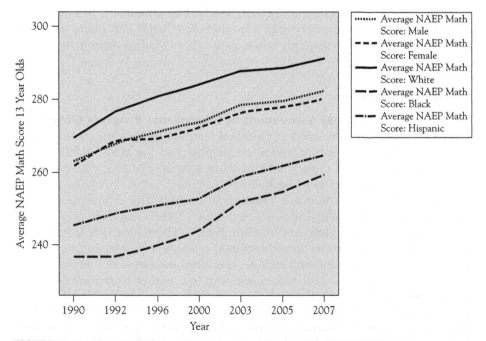

FIGURE 14.1   Average NAEP mathematics score 13-year-olds (1990–2007).

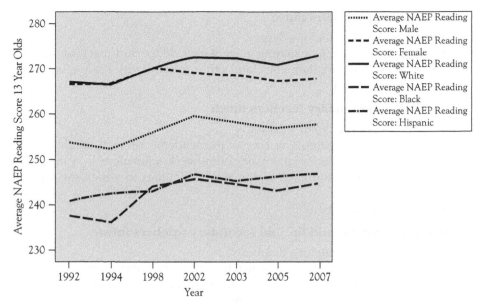

FIGURE 14.2 Average NAEP reading score 13-year-olds (1992–2007).

Teacher Quality

NCLB created new provisions for **teacher quality**. Teacher quality is an important issue relating to the equality of educational opportunity.[6] Although state governments have increasingly required that teacher quality be monitored and teacher knowledge, skills, and abilities meet state-mandated standards, the No Child Left Behind legislation is a national government attempt to create uniformity in those standards. Teacher quality is tied to national government funding for public schools. If the state governments do not institute national government standards and meet certain quality assurance deadlines, then certain national government revenue sources will no longer be made available to state and local school districts.

The standards that must be met are summarized below.[7]

States must:

- Apply evaluation standards uniformly to all teachers in the same subject and grade level throughout the state.
- Publish an annual report disclosing the professional qualifications of teachers, the percent working with emergency or provisional credentials, and the percent of classes in the state not taught by "highly qualified" teachers.

All teachers must:

- Be fully licensed or certified by the state.
- Have had no certification or licensure requirements waived on an emergency, temporary, or provisional basis.

New elementary teachers must:

- Have at least a bachelor's degree.
- Pass a state test demonstrating subject knowledge and teaching skills in reading, writing, mathematics, and other areas of any basic elementary school curriculum.

New middle or secondary teachers must:

- Have at least a bachelor's degree.
- Demonstrate competency in *each* of the academic subjects taught, *or*
- Complete an academic major *or* coursework equivalent to a major, *or* a graduate degree in each of the academic areas in which the teacher instructs, *or*
- Advanced certification.

Existing elementary, middle, and secondary teachers must:

- Have at least a bachelor's degree.
- Meet the requirements for new teachers described above, *or*
- Demonstrate competency in all subjects taught (a uniform state evaluation standard is to be used to judge competency).
- Be evaluated under a standard that must provide objective information about the teacher's knowledge in the subject taught and can consider, but not use as a primary criterion, time spent teaching the subject.

Paraprofessionals (teachers' aides) must:

- Have completed at least two years of postsecondary education.
- Be a high school graduate who can demonstrate on a formal state or local assessment the skills necessary to assist in classroom instruction of reading, writing, and mathematics.

Key deadlines for Elementary and Secondary Education Act (ESEA) teacher quality

End of the 2002–03 school year:

- Any new teachers hired and working in a program supported by Title I funds must meet the requirements of a "highly qualified" teacher.
- States and districts must begin reporting their progress toward ensuring that all teachers are "highly qualified."

End of the 2005–06 school year:

- All teachers in core academic subjects must be "highly qualified." (Core academic subjects include all subjects except physical education, computer science, and vocational education.)

Under Title II of the reauthorized ESEA, the national government provided approximately $2.7 billion to fund teacher quality policy initiatives (Solomon and Firetag 2002). The Title II funding requires that state and local governments match national government funding for teacher quality initiatives, an example of cooperative federalism.

Class Size

Class size issues became a prominent agenda item in the 1990s. News reports showed images of classes held in converted janitorial closets and classrooms with students sitting on the floor because of limited seating space. These media images, along with interest group pressure, led national- and state-level policy responses.

Many states have passed class size reduction legislation. Title IV of the reauthorized ESEA provides fiscal resources to help this process along. At least three major issues underlie class size reduction policy initiatives:

• Hiring additional high-quality teachers and administrators.
• Building new school facilities.
• Improving student learning.

The first issue is paramount in class size reduction policy initiatives, but is an exceptionally difficult task due to a shortage of qualified subject-area teachers nationwide.[8] Wealthier school districts can more easily meet these new standards because they can offer well-financed school facilities that might be attractive to new teachers. Poorer school districts now have the ability to use national government funding to improve their chances of recruiting new teachers to their classrooms. More teachers require more classrooms and, often, new school buildings. Wealthier districts are able to finance the building of new schools, whereas poorer school districts often face serious financial limitations.

The purpose behind smaller classes is to improve student learning. Yet, the evidence tends to indicate that in order to have a significant impact, classroom size would need to be reduced to below 15 students in a class—possibly even as small as a tutoring arrangement of two students for every teacher.[9] The costs of providing tutoring arrangements would be prohibitive. Rather than a "one size fits all" approach, research suggests that targeted class size reductions—based on need or class subject area—would be a more affordable solution with the potential for greater impact.

In a broader sense, class size reduction is not a universal solution to achievement—in studies of math achievement comparing the United States with eight other developed nations, class size was not related to achievement *except* in the United States. Students abroad seem to achieve (or not) regardless of class size whereas U.S. students seemingly require extra attention from instructors.[10]

Privatization Alternatives

The educational voucher system is possibly the most revolutionary market-based privatization innovation. Parents would be able to use a state-provided education **voucher** to send their children to any public or private school of their choice. **Charter schools** operate under more restricted conditions, with stipulations in their state charter regarding expected educational outcomes. Finally, **magnet schools** are public schools that operate on a semicompetitive basis with other public schools; they are given greater flexibility in their curricula, operations, and teaching methods than conventional schools.[11]

PUBLIC POLICY AND EDUCATIONAL EQUALITY

Individuals with Disabilities Education Act of 1997 Public Law 105-71 (IDEA)

The Education for All Handicapped Students Act of 1975 (P.L. 94-142) is the precursor to **Individuals with Disabilities Education Act of 1997 (IDEA)**, which guaranteed equal educational opportunity for all disabled children. Although the 1975 law was renamed IDEA in 1990 legislation, it was not until 1997 amendments that IDEA became a more fully operational policy offering high-quality education to disabled students in a manner that integrated students into the "traditional" classroom (Abend 2001). IDEA builds off the Americans with Disabilities Act of 1990, which encouraged a reconsideration of what it meant to be disabled.

Bilingual Education

In 1968, Congress passed the Bilingual Education Act (BEA)—four years after the Civil Rights Act of 1964. Reauthorized in 1999, BEA created the Office of Bilingual Education and Minority Language Affairs, which sought to promote bilingual education by offering teacher training in bilingual pedagogy and curriculum, and by providing resources to states and local school districts with the goal of promoting education equity.

The policy environment surrounding bilingual education has changed tremendously in recent years. Most prominently, California voters rejected bilingual education by passing a voter initiative supporting English-only education. A similar ballot initiative was supported by Arizona voters.[12]

The No Child Left Behind (NCLB) legislation changed the nature of bilingual education—effectively removing it from the reauthorized Elementary and Secondary Education Act. In its place, NCLB has created the Office of English Language Acquisition, Language Enforcement and Academic Achievement for Limited English Proficient Students. The policy change illustrates how target groups are identified: Previously known as "bilingual students," the NCLB now refers to "English language learners." (See Box 14.1, *Immigration and Education*.)

Head Start

A Great Society-era policy created in 1965, **Head Start** primarily serves the needs of low-income and minority students deemed educationally *at risk* due to their socioeconomic status. The program focuses on child learners under the age of six, providing them with the learning tools necessary to succeed in K–12 education. The program has a number of proponents as well as critics; both groups often cite evidence to alternately demonstrate the program's effectiveness or ineffectiveness in improving student learning and retention rates in K–12 education.

BOX 14.1

Immigration and Education

Immigration has a tremendous impact on education in the United States. More importantly, however, education has a tremendous impact on the ability of individuals to understand and participate in a democracy. Bilingual education began as a concerted effort to promote equal opportunity to all individuals, regardless of their language abilities. It has long been said that the United States is a nation of immigrants. States, such as California, long ago began their efforts to promote bilingual education; in 1967, then Governor Ronald Reagan signed legislation that allowed multilingual instruction in public schools. At the national level, the Bilingual Education Act was passed in 1968 with the goal of promoting educational opportunity for all individuals. Despite statutory advances, many individuals were still denied access to education because they were unable to understand English and no accommodation was made for them. The Supreme Court finally weighed in on bilingual education in the case *Lau v. Nichols* 414 U.S. 56 (1974) which stated that "there is no equality of treatment merely by providing students with the same facilities, textbooks, teachers, and curriculum; for students who do not understand English are effectively foreclosed from any meaningful education."

Despite the *Lau* case and more than two decades of bilingual education, a public movement against bilingualism became evident with the passage of Proposition 227 in 1998 in California, which required that all instruction in public schools be conducted in English. The California initiative also established intensive English programs for non-English speakers, thus avoiding Court scrutiny related to *Lau*. National policy has subsequently followed a similar path, with the passage of No Child Left Behind legislation, which did not reauthorize the Bilingual Education Act and instead promoted English language education. A new policy direction in education policy emerged.

EXPLAINING EDUCATION POLICY

Institutionalism

With the passage of the earliest national education initiative, the Northwest Ordinance of 1787, President Washington foresaw the relationship between education policy, national growth, and socioeconomic success. Washington realized that national expansion involved much more than the occupation of a new territory. It was critical to instill in children core social and political values—regime values.

Progressive-era presidents, such as Theodore Roosevelt and Woodrow Wilson, were also very outspoken about education policy. Largely a state and local government function, elementary and secondary education were important methods of "Americanizing" the children of immigrant families, instilling core values. Presidents Johnson and Nixon crafted national policy promoting a modern liberal vision for education, promoting equality of educational opportunity and outcomes.

Beginning with Ronald Reagan and continuing to the present day, presidents have sought sweeping reforms of education that would make schools safer, more effective, and more accountable. In the latter instance, testing and privatization are two president-led policy alternatives to make public schools more responsive to students and parents, policies that tend toward a more classical liberal viewpoint.

Congress is composed of elected representatives from local districts and states. Although representatives and senators are concerned with national issues, they also pay close attention to the priorities of their constituents. Education is a high priority for citizens at the local and state level. Although the president often proposes national education priorities, Congress frequently tailors national priorities to state and local needs. Through the congressional hearings process, legislators receive the input of policy analysts at the national, state, and local levels as well as interest group representatives and citizen stakeholders. As an institution, Congress is able to spend time pondering the issues surrounding the impact of national policy on elementary and secondary education policy at the state and local levels.

The courts are powerful policy actors in the education arena. Largely autonomous policy-makers, judges and justices at the national level do not have to concern themselves with winning reelection or meeting the expectations of a national, state, or local constituency. In the case of education policy, the courts often concentrate their attention on whether policy retains constitutional integrity. *Brown v. Board of Education* was the first major step in the movement toward greater equality in educational opportunity—a continual and important discussion in American education policy. Over time, the Court has focused greater attention on classical liberal concerns, such as the constitutionality of privatization.

Group Theory

Teachers' unions are powerful actors in education; they are well organized and members have the professional training and knowledge that make them very persuasive policy actors. Teachers' union dues are used to lobby elected officials for pro-union education policy. The unions often make sizeable campaign donations to pro-public school candidates. The teachers' unions often try to influence court decisions, either as parties to a case or through *amicus curiae* briefs.

In recent years, groups in favor of the privatization of elementary and secondary education have become visible and outspoken. Today, a growing number of businesses are operating private schools. These educational business groups pressure government to create policy favorable to the free-market approach.

Public Choice Theory

For well over a century, the local public schools were primarily financed using local taxes, collected at a tax rate determined by local citizens. In other words, citizens would determine the collective benefit of public schools and finance the schools at a level they deemed reasonable. In the last thirty years, the state and national governments have assumed the primary role in financing local schools. Public choice theorists argue that the ability of citizens to shape education policy through their individual cost and benefit calculus is lost when policy choices at the local level are diminished. Additionally, the growth of state and national government in education policy has not led to improved student performance because individualism has given way to uniformity—public choice advocates feel that education must fit the needs of the student rather than the student fitting the needs of government efforts to change society.

The movement toward private school alternatives is seen as evidence of public choice in practice. Citizens want to make choices that will best improve their lot in life. In education policy, what better way to make choices than through a policy scheme that allows citizens to pursue the educational opportunities that best fit their needs? School vouchers are seen as efforts on the part of government to promote citizens' collective and individual interest in maintaining a civil society.

Public choice bridges the gap between the issues of what government *ought or ought not do* and what government *does or does not do*. In the first instance, public choice theory argues that government *ought not* diminish the choices of individual citizens to pursue their individual interests. Public choice views the large role of state and national government in education policy as evidence of the erosion of individual choice. Public choice uses its normative argument as the basis of an empirical description of what government *does or does not do;* the theory concludes that government does not effectively educate students when there is no effective ability for students and their parents to choose their individual educational benefits in relation to the costs of education. So long as one accepts the normative argument, the public choice empirical argument becomes plausible. However, modern liberalism rejects much of public choice theory's normative argument and the empirical arguments tend to fall by the wayside, too. The power of public choice theory in describing education policy is largely a function of your normative stance—what you believe government *ought* or *ought not* do.

Lessons Learned from Chapter 14

SPECIFICS

- Education policy has certain core values that have not changed over time; however, there is considerable political and social disagreement over how to achieve educational outcomes.
- Recent public school education reforms focus on student and teacher testing to monitor and, if necessary, reshape educational processes and outcomes.
- Since the 1950s education policy has demonstrated an ever-increasing commitment to equity, which is demonstrated in policies like Head Start and the Individuals with Disabilities Education Act. No Child Left Behind legislation, however, has limited certain policies, which may be indicative of a more limited or changing approach to educational equity.

• Despite continued calls for privatization of education and challenging problems such as school violence, public education policy-makers have established an optimistic agenda for twenty-first century education.

THE BIG PICTURE

Educating future generations is critical for a number of reasons. First, education transmits social and political values to succeeding generations. Second, education policy is designed to provide young people with the basic skills and knowledge necessary for individual economic and social achievement. Finally, education is a critical part of maintaining a fair and equal society. Although some individuals will become rich and others will be middle class, education and the opportunities that formal learning experiences afford us is a critical method of preventing a class-based society that systematically restricts individuals' ability to achieve their goals.

Many goals and education policies have changed over time. The last five decades have witnessed tremendous efforts to promote equality of opportunity in education. The No Child Left Behind Act avows to continue the pursuit of equality of opportunity, but through slightly different methods and greater accountability. Private school options will likely play a larger role in K–12 education in America, impacting the children currently enrolled in school as well as a generation yet unborn.

Key Terms

American Federation of Teachers (AFT)
Brown v. Board of Education, Topeka, Kansas (1954)
charter schools
class size
Elementary and Secondary Education Act
Head Start

Individuals with Disabilities Education Act of 1997 (IDEA)
magnet schools
National Assessment of Educational Progress (NAEP)
National Education Association (NEA)
No Child Left Behind (NCLB)
teacher quality
vouchers

Questions for Study

1. Using three policy models, explain and describe education policy. Which policy model do you think best describes education policy? Why?
2. What three major policy changes have resulted from the No Child Left Behind legislation? Discuss these changes.
3. After reading this chapter, in your view, what is the most serious challenge facing education policy today? Using material in this chapter, support your response.

CASE STUDY

Excerpt from the State of the State Address, Massachusetts Governor Mitt Romney, January 15, 2004.

"If you are at home right now, watching this with your family, take a look at the faces of your children. You are looking into the faces of our future.

What legacy will we leave our children? I am convinced that our legacy should be a legacy of learning.

Massachusetts has some of the best schools and teachers in the nation. Education reform, adopted a decade ago, raised standards and closed funding gaps. But it was the first step, not the last. Let us now take every step, to prepare every child, for an ever more competitive future.

Today, I am announcing a Legacy of Learning initiative. I believe that a true legacy of learning can only come from a comprehensive effort, committed to the child every step of the way.

Let's start with our school buildings. I am asking the Legislature to work with me to launch an ambitious school building program.

We're horribly backlogged in renovating and rebuilding old and dilapidated schools.

I will propose a series of construction reforms and a refinancing program that will jump start over 100 new and remodeled school projects.

Let's start building and renovating these new classrooms now.

Great new school buildings aren't enough. We need to face up to the reality that some of our schools are just not educating our children.

Some schools are seeing as many as one-third of their students drop out of high school before the end of their senior year. Some have disappointingly low MCAS scores. An achievement gap persists. For these kids, doors to the future are slammed shut. That is simply unacceptable.

Our Legacy of Learning initiative provides emergency support for the bottom tenth of our school districts, where almost one-third of our kids go to school.

First, the state will fund full-day kindergarten in every one of these districts that doesn't have it.

Second, we will provide $20 million in additional funding for after school and summer school special help sessions.

Third, parents of children in our troubled schools need to get more involved. I propose to establish a mandatory parent preparation course to teach parents how they can support their child in school and how they can foster the discipline and hard work that are the cornerstone of education.

Fourth, Legacy of Learning will provide $5 million in grants for discipline programs. With programs tailored for chronically disruptive youth, we will take discipline problems out of the classroom so they are no longer in the way of those kids who really want to learn.

Fifth, Legacy of Learning devotes $3 million to train, recruit, and reward teachers who specialize in math and science.

Finally, my initiative will insist that principals be given the authority to remove any teacher that cannot succeed with our kids. That won't happen very often because the great majority of our teachers are terrific. But giving the principal the authority to hire and fire will put the principal, and the parents, back in charge of their school.

My Legacy of Learning initiative doesn't stop with high school. We're fortunate to have excellent public colleges and universities. But many families are having a very difficult time paying for them. And I can't stand seeing so many of our best students going off to attend college in other states.

I want our best and brightest to stay right here in Massachusetts—students like Linette Heredia.

Linette is an honors student at Lawrence High School. She earned a perfect score on the English portion of the MCAS, which is all the more impressive since her family's native language is Spanish. She's number two in her class. She's here with us tonight.

Linette, would you please stand?

Linette, we want you to stay in Massachusetts.

More than 200 years ago, John Adams wrote in the Massachusetts Constitution that our rights and liberties depend on the wisdom and knowledge of our people.

So for Linette and thousands like her, our Legacy of Learning initiative will provide funding for the John and Abigail Adams Scholarship Program.

Students who score among the top one-quarter of those who take the MCAS will be given four years at the University of Massachusetts or any state or community college, tuition free.

There's more. Any student who scores in the top 10 percent will be given four years of free tuition and a $2,000 annual payment to help pay for fees. This Adams Scholarship Program will cost about $50 million a year by year four.

And it's worth every dime.

My total budget for K–12 education will grow by over $100 million and higher education will grow by over $70 million.

Legacy of Learning puts people first, kids first. We'll be putting our money where our future is.

I know when our minds turn to education we also think of local aid. In my budget, I am proposing a modest increase in local aid. Cities and towns have worked hard to pare back their expenditures to match falling revenues. We owe our mayors and municipal officials a sincere thank you."

Courtesy of: Project Vote Smart www.votesmart.org

The article above reflects the education policy agenda of former Governor Mitt Romney, who ran for the Republican Party presidential nomination in 2007–2008. Compare his State of State comments with his campaign statements on education. As a group, discuss your level of agreement or disagreement with his public statement. Would your priorities be different or similar? If different, how so (provide specifics)? If presenting your findings in a paper or class presentation, gather additional background information to make your case.

Bibliography

Abend, A. 2001. "Planning and designing for students with disabilities." www
.edfacilities.org/pubs/disibilities3.html (accessed August 17, 2007).

Abernathy, S. 2007. *No child left behind and the public schools.* Ann Arbor, MI:
University of Michigan.

Baumgartner, F. R., and B. D. Jones. 1993. *Agendas and instability in American
politics.* Chicago: University of Chicago Press.

Clinchy, E. 2007. *Rescuing the public schools: What will it take to leave no child
behind.* New York: Teachers College Press.

Cubberley, E. 1919. *Public education in the United States: A study and interpretation of American educational history.* Boston: Houghton Mifflin.

Dewey, J. 1944. *Democracy and education.* 2nd ed. New York: Free Press.

Dougherty, K., and L. Sostre. 1992. Minerva and the market: The sources of the
movement for school choice. In *The choice controversy.* Edited by P. Cook-
son. Newbury Park, CA: Corwin Press, 24–45.

Ed.gov. 2002. *Press Releases.* Washington, DC: U.S. Department of Education
(accessed May 7, 2003).

Elazar, D. 1994. *The American mosaic: The impact of space, time, and culture
on American politics.* Boulder, CO: Westview Press.

Friedman, M. 1955. *Capitalism and freedom.* Chicago: University of Chicago
Press.

Hanuschek, E. 1998. "The evidence on class size." www.wallis.rochester.edu/
WallisPapers/wallis_10.pdf (accessed August 17, 2007).

Honig, B. 1994. *Last chance for our children.* New York: St. Martin's Press.

Kincheloe, J., and S. Steinberg. 2007. *Cutting class: Socioeconomic status and
education.* Lanham, MD: Rowman Littlefield.

Krashen, S. 1996. Surveys of opinions on bilingual education: Some current issues. *The Bilingual Research Journal.* 20(3 & 4): 411–31.

Linowes, D. 1988. *Privatization: Toward more effective government.* Washington, DC: President's Commission on Privatization.

Manley, J. 1990. American liberalism and the democratic dream: Transcending
the American dream. *Policy Studies Review.* 10(1): 89–102.

Meade, E. 1972. *A foundation goes to school: The Ford Foundation comprehensive school improvement program 1960–1970.* New York: Ford Foundation.

———. 2004. "Overview: The nation's report card." www.nces.ed.gov/
nationsreportcard/about/ (accessed January 31, 2005).

Moe, T. 2009. Collective bargaining and the performance of the public schools.
American Journal of Political Science. 53(1): 158–174.

National Commission on Excellence in Education. 1983. *A nation at risk.* Washington, DC: U.S. Government Printing Office.

National Education Association. 2007. "Teacher and paraprofessional quality:
What the law says, what NEA is doing, what you can do." www.nea.org/
esea/eseateach.html#02 (accessed August 17, 2007).

Odden, A. 1990. Class size and student achievement: Research-based policy alternatives, *Educational Evaluation and Policy Analysis.* 12(2): 213–227.

Pulliam, R. 1984. *History of education in America.* 3rd ed. Columbus, OH: Charles Merrill.

Simon, C. 2001. *To run a school: Administrative organization and learning.* Westport, CT: Praeger.

Sochen, J. 1974. *Her story.* New York: Alfred Press.

Solomon, L., and K. Firetag. 2002. The road to teacher quality. www.edweek.org/ew/newstory.cfm?slug= 27solmon.h21 (accessed May 12, 2003).

Spring, J. 1976. *The sorting machine: National education policy since 1945.* New York: David McKay Company.

———. 1986. *The American school: 1642–1985.* New York: Longman.

Taylor, F. 1912. *Principles of scientific management.* New York: Harper.

Wynn, R., and J. Wynn. 1991. *American education.* 9th ed. New York: Harper & Row.

Court Cases

Brown v. Board of Education, Topeka, Kansas 347 U.S. 483 (1954)

Lau v. Nichols 414 U.S. 56 (1974)

Morse et al. v. Frederick 551 U.S. 393 (2007)

Zelman, Superintendent of Public Instruction of Ohio, et al. v. Simmons-Harris, et al. 536 U.S. 639 (2002)

Endnotes

1. www.ed.gov/about/overview/budget/statetables/recovery.html (accessed March 23, 2009).
2. www.ed.gov/news/pressreleases/2002/11/11262002.html (accessed January 31, 2005).
3. In a recently published peer-reviewed academic journal article, political scientist and education policy expert Terry Moe found that the relative restrictiveness of collective bargaining agreements appears to be negatively related to student performance. Critics of teachers' unions and supporters of privatization alternatives may find satisfaction in the findings, particularly if the results are replicated in other state settings. Conversely, proponents of public schools and teachers' unions will likely reject Moe's findings, possibly offering a different explanation of the findings reported or perhaps publish another set of findings that challenge his results. The article is addressed here because it could serve as the beginning of a new direction in the K–12 education policy debate between privatization proponents and public school and teachers' union advocates. Moe, T. 2009. Collective bargaining and the performance of the public schools. *American Journal of Political Science.* 53(1): 158–174.
4. www.nces.ed.gov/nationsreportcard/about/ (accessed January 31, 2005).

5. The director of NCES consults with, and is advised by, the National Assessment Government Board, a bipartisan board composed of elected and appointed officials from the national, state, and local levels of government.

6. Jacobson, L. 2006. NCLB Commission Starts Gathering Testimony, *Education Week.* 25(32): 28.

7. www.nea.org/esea/eseateach.html#02 (accessed January 31, 2005).

8. Miller, M. A. 2007. *Teacher Shortage Areas Nationwide Listing: 1990–91 thru 2006–07.* Washington, DC: US Department of Education, Office of Postsecondary Education.

9. See Odden (1990). The article is a meta-analysis of previous work in class size reduction.

10. Pong, S., and A. Pallas. 2001. Class Size and Eighth-Grade Math Achievement in the United States and Abroad, *Educational Evaluation and Policy Analysis.* 23(3): 251–273.

11. Common schools, post–World War II, and Privatization sections from Simon, C. A. 2001. *To run a school: Administrative organization and learning.* Westport, CT: Praeger.

12. Ballot initiative processes are often driven by policy elites, individuals, and groups intent on using grassroots democracy to advance their policy agenda. Whether or not policy elites are in this instance responsible for these initiatives, it is instructive to note that when asked, many individuals polled lack a clear understanding of bilingual education and, depending upon question structure, opinions of bilingual education vary widely (see Krashen 1996).

15

■ ■ ■

Criminal Justice Policy

CHAPTER OVERVIEW

Criminal justice is one of the most visible confirmations of our liberal social contract—a commitment to the rule of law and due process. In recent years, the policy area has witnessed tremendous change. Many of the changes occurred prior to the terrorist acts of September 11, 2001, but a steady growth in national government influence in criminal justice has occurred over several decades. The events of September 11, however, accelerated change within criminal justice policy.

The specific goals for the chapter are:

- Discuss the major participants in criminal justice policy.
- Identify types of crime.
- Discuss causes of crime.
- Outline criminal procedure.
- Discuss perspectives on punishment.
- Discuss contemporary crime issues: hate crimes, child abduction, and racially biased policing.
- Discuss contemporary policing techniques and criminal justice issues.
- Discuss the U.S.A. Patriot Act.

MAJOR PARTICIPANTS

Courts

The lead officer in a criminal court is the judge. The judge plays the most significant role in making decisions that will protect an individual's right to a fair and speedy trial. The judge upholds policy (existing statutory and common law) and may create policy through common law decisions. Judges preside over the selection of fair and impartial juries, the actual trial process, and, if appropriate, determine punishment.

In terms of national criminal justice policy, district courts are the courts of original jurisdiction in criminal cases that involve federal law. Each state has at least one district court, but the exact number varies based on population factors. National courts become involved in criminal justice when: (1) an individual convicted of a state-level crime appeals his or her case to the national court system or (2) an individual is indicted by a federal grand jury on charges related to federal criminal law. (See Box 15.1, *Landmark Cases Related to Criminal Procedure.*)

BOX 15.1
Landmark Cases Related to Criminal Procedure

A discussion of courts as actors in criminal justice policy must not overlook the Supreme Court's role in formulating *criminal justice procedure*—the "methods that the government uses to detect, investigate, apprehend, prosecute, convict, and punish criminals."[10] Criminal procedure is outlined in the *Federal Rules of Criminal Procedure,* which serves as the basis for state and local government rules governing the methods by which suspected offenders and convicted criminals are treated.

The Supreme Court has used a series of landmark court cases to delineate specific standards for criminal procedure:

SEARCH & SEIZURE I *WOLF V. COLORADO* 338 U.S. 25 (1949)
". . . in a prosecution in a state court for a state crime, the Fourteenth Amendment does not forbid the admission of evidence obtained by an unreasonable search and seizure. The question whether Congress could validly enact legislation permitting the introduction in Federal courts of evidence seized in violation of the Fourth Amendment was left open."

EXCLUSIONARY RULE *MAPP V. OHIO* 367 U.S. 643 (1961)
Overturned *Wolf v. Colorado* (1961). ". . . it was held that, as a matter of due process, evidence obtained by a search and seizure in violation of the Fourth Amendment is inadmissible in a state court as it is in a federal court."

SEARCH & SEIZURE II *TERRY V. OHIO* 392 U.S. 1 (1967)
The Court offers a clearer definition of reasonable search. In the case of imminent danger (suspect is "armed and dangerous"), the police can, in the course of an arrest, take the seized weapon as evidence that can be used as evidence in a trial. ". . . it was held that the search was a reasonable search under the Fourth Amendment, and that the revolver seized from the defendant was properly introduced in evidence, where the police officer reasonably concluded in the light of his experience that criminal activity might be afoot and that the persons with whom he was dealing might be armed and presently dangerous." Emergent from the *Terry* case was the "*Terry* stop" and "*Terry* search." The Court found that in cases in which the police confront an armed and dangerous individual, they can enter and search private property for the promotion of community safety.

(Continued)

SELF-INCRIMINATION *MALLOY V. HOGAN* 378 U.S. 1 (1964)

". . . it was held that (1) the Fourteenth Amendment makes the Fifth Amendment privilege against self-incrimination applicable to the states; (2) the privilege, if properly invoked in a state proceeding, is governed by federal standards; and (3) judged by those standards, the petitioner's claim of privilege should have been upheld."

ASSISTANCE OF COUNSEL *GIDEON V. WAINWRIGHT* 372 U.S. 335 (1963)

". . . it was held that the Sixth Amendment's provision that in all criminal prosecutions the accused shall enjoy the right to have the assistance of counsel for his defense was made obligatory upon the states by the Fourteenth Amendment."

CONFRONTATION OF WITNESS *POINTER V. TEXAS* 380 U.S. 400 (1965)

The defendant did not have counsel, yet was denied the right to cross-examine witnesses at his trial. ". . . it was held that (1) the Sixth Amendment's guaranty protecting an accused's right to confront the witnesses against him was made obligatory on the states by the Fourteenth Amendment."

COMPULSION OF WITNESS *WASHINGTON V. TEXAS* 388 U.S. 14 (1967)

The defendant claimed to have been denied the right to have a convicted individual who was party to the crime testify on his behalf. ". . . it was held that an accused's Sixth Amendment right to have compulsory process for obtaining witnesses in his favor was so fundamental that it could be considered incorporated in the due process clause of the Fourteenth Amendment, and that the defendant was denied such right in the instant case."

SPEEDY TRIAL *KLOPFER V. N. CAROLINA* 386 U.S. 213 (1967)

Juries failed to convict an individual on the same charges on two occasions. The prosecutor had been granted the opportunity to try the individual on the same charges at an unspecified future date when the prosecuting attorney had collected further evidence. ". . . it was held that (1) the Sixth Amendment's guaranty of an accused right to a speedy trial was rendered applicable to the states through the due process clause of the Fourteenth Amendment, and (2) this right was denied accused by the procedure applied in the instant case."

CRUEL AND UNUSUAL PUNISHMENT *ROBINSON V. CALIFORNIA* 370 U.S. 660 (1962)

A drug addict was incarcerated under a California state law that makes drug addiction illegal. The Court overturned the conviction concluding that addiction is not a criminal offense; rather, addiction is an illness that requires medical treatment rather than punishment. ". . .it was held that the [California] statute inflict[ed] a cruel and unusual punishment in violation of the Eighth and Fourteenth Amendments."

Through their decisions in these landmark cases, the Court has defined and applied elements of the U.S. Constitution's Bill of Rights to national, state, and local criminal procedure. The Court's influence does not end here; the Court continues to define the constitutionality of criminal procedure through cases that come before the justices.

Attorneys

There are two major types of attorneys: **prosecuting attorneys** and **defense attorneys**. At the local level, prosecuting attorneys work within the district attorney's office. In national (or federal) criminal justice trials, the prosecuting attorneys are known as **assistant attorneys general** and work for the U.S. Department of Justice. Defense attorneys work either in private sector practice or are government-funded **public defenders**, representing defendants who are unable to afford representation.

Elected Officials

In the post-September 11 policy atmosphere, the presidency plays a much larger role in criminal justice policy. Although the president proposes policies, Congress crafts and introduces legislative bills. Legislation generally focuses on definitions of crime, criminal procedure, and programs designed to combat crime at the national, state, and local level. Criminal justice policy debates seek a balance between individual rights and freedoms, and the public good.

Bureaucracy

Criminal justice bureaucrats hold various titles. At the national level, criminal justice bureaucrats may be called federal agents or special agents. Federal or special agents work in agencies such as the Federal Bureau of Investigation (FBI) or Secret Service. At the state and local level, criminal justice bureaucrats include state troopers, sheriff's deputies, or police officers. Bureaucrats enforce criminal laws, criminal justice policies, and criminal procedures in a manner consistent with constitutional law and jurisdiction statutes.

Interest Groups

Interest groups abound in criminal justice policy. Although some groups support strong criminal justice policies and enforcement, other groups focus on the rights of the individual in relation to the power of the state to create and enforce laws. The latter groups tend to be vigilant and critical of expanded powers of the government and limitations on individual freedom.

Police unions represent the interests of law enforcement personnel. Unions seek to protect their members from liability as they do their jobs. Unions want processes to be clear cut so that officers, their members, can do their jobs with confidence. Unions support salary and benefit packages that are worthy of the law enforcement function.

The mission of the American Civil Liberties Union (ACLU) is to "Keep America safe and free."[1] More specifically, the ACLU seeks to restrain the application of the Fourth and Sixth Amendments—that is, the ACLU does not support expanded searches and seizure powers and wishes to restrain harsh sentences such as "three strikes and you're out" or capital punishment. Also, the ACLU sees the War on Terrorism as destructive to basic rights and liberties.

TYPES OF CRIME

There are two major types of crime: person-related crime and property-related crime. **Person-related crimes** involve the physical assault or threat of assault on another person's physical being or psyche or a crime against oneself with the intent to cause harm. Person-related crimes include: murder, assault, drug use or dealing, and domestic violence. Property crimes involve the taking, damaging, or destroying of property belonging to another individual or individuals. Property-related crimes include: burglary, forgery, vandalism, and arson.

Homicide and Other Violent Crimes

The homicide rate in the United States is higher than in other industrialized nations. In 1991, the homicide rate was 9.8 (crime rates are the number of crime events per 100,000 population), but that rate has been largely declining for more than a decade. In 2008, the homicide rate was 5.4—approximately 16,500 murders. (See Figure 15.1.)

Forcible rape rates steadily increased from 9.6 in 1960 to 42.8 in 1992. Since 1993, forcible rape rates have declined to 29.0 in 2008—more than 88,000 forcible rapes. Robbery rates have declined since 1991, the 2008 rate being 144.0—roughly, 440,000 robberies. Aggravated assault rates have declined to 272 in 2005 from a high of 441.8 in 1992. The 2008 aggravated assault rates are at their lowest level in 30+ years. (See Figures 15.2–15.4)

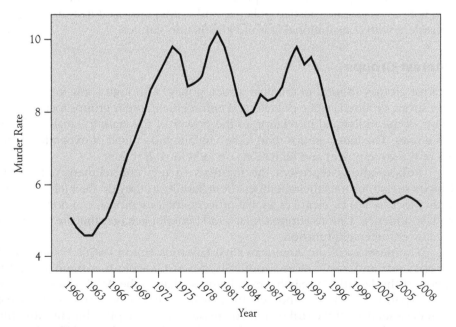

FIGURE 15.1 Murder rate (1960–2008).

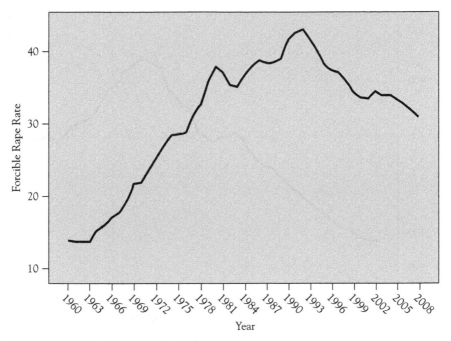

FIGURE 15.2 Forcible rape rate (1960–2008).

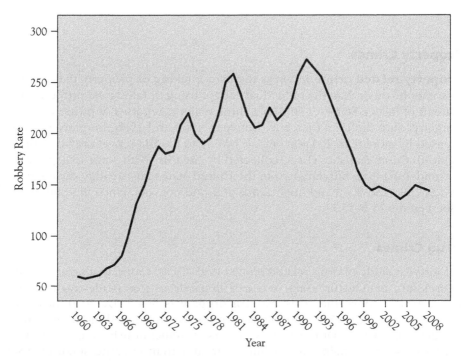

FIGURE 15.3 Robbery rate (1960–2008).

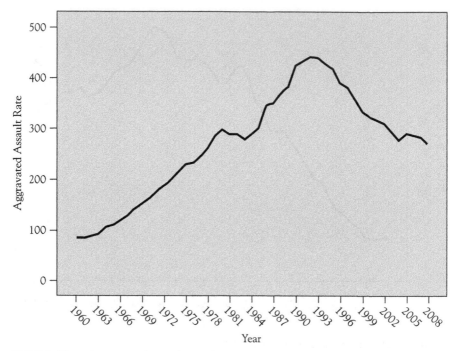

FIGURE 15.4   Aggravated assault rate (1960–2008).

Property Crimes

Property-related crime involves the use or taking of property that belongs
to someone other than the individual caught using or taking the property. The
Bureau of Justice Statistics (BJS) has three major categories of property crime:
burglary, auto theft, and larceny. Between 1960 and 1980, burglary rates increased by more than 200 percent, according to the BJS report drawn from the
Uniform Crime Statistics (UCS) collected by the FBI. With some exceptions in
the mid-1980s, the burglary rate in the United States has steadily declined between 1980 and 2008 and now stands at a rate not seen since the mid-1960s.
(See Figures 15.5–15.7)

Drug Crimes

A four-year study of drug-related crime (1995–1998) found that arrests for the
possession, manufacture, sale, or use of illegal drugs rose modestly during the
late 1990s. In 1995, the arrest rate for drugs was 564.7. By 2000, however,
the rate had risen to 587.1. Drug arrest rates have retreated moderately from
the 2000 arrest rate. Drug seizures increased tremendously since 1990, with
cannabis seizures rising at rate much greater than cocaine seizures. (See
Figure 15.8.)

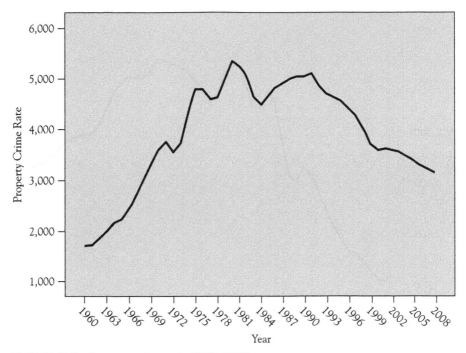

FIGURE 15.5 Property crime rate (1960–2008).

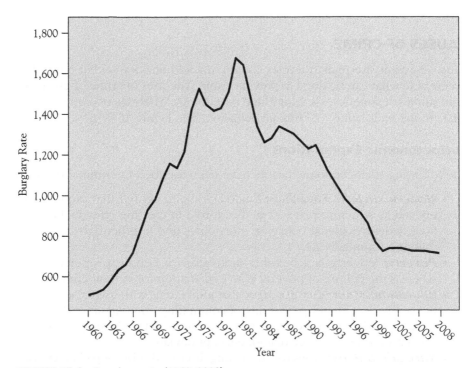

FIGURE 15.6 Burglary rate (1960–2008).

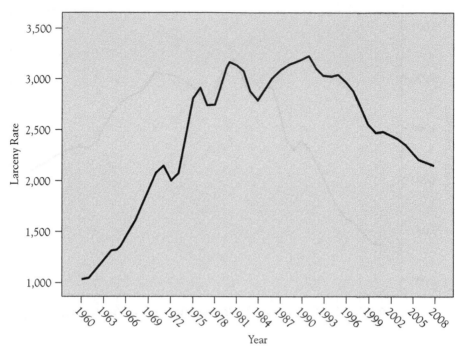

FIGURE 15.7   Larceny rate (1960–2008).

CAUSES OF CRIME

Causes of crime are really theories about criminal behavior—what it is, why it occurs, and what can be done to prevent crime. Theories of crime often emerge from studies of genetics, sociology, and psychology. Theories of crime may also relate to the "rationality" of criminal behavior. (See Figure 15.9.)

Socioeconomic Explanations

The following socioeconomic factors have been ascribed to criminal behavior:

- *Modern society:* Sociologist Emile Durkheim argued that modern society and its structure plays a significant role in creating criminal behavior. Society defines illegal behavior; individuals find it difficult to avoid committing a "criminal" act.
- *Poverty:* Poverty is a possible motivator for certain property crimes, whereas the culture of poverty is an explanation for violent crimes.
- *Education:* Crime theories argue that individuals with lower levels of education have a higher probability of committing criminal acts. The choice to reject formal education may be a "first step" in the development of antisocial attitudes, juvenile delinquency, or deviancy.
- *Race or ethnicity:* Theorists have long discussed subgroup characteristics in relation to general socioeconomic conditions and, more controversially, a

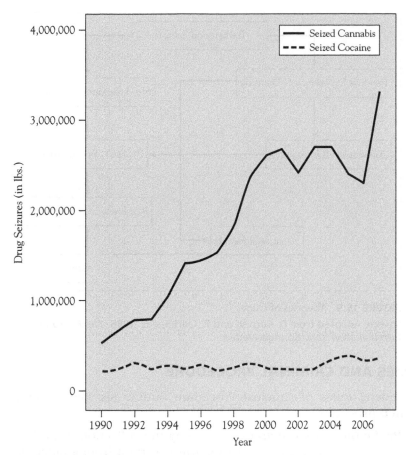

FIGURE 15.8 Drug seizures (lbs.) (1990–2007).

subculture's tendency to use violence as an acceptable method of solving disputes or pursuing personal goals.

Biological Theories of Crime

Possibly the oldest theory of crime, it was once thought that criminals were physically and emotionally weakened individuals easily possessed and influenced by evil spirits. Many biological theories have fallen into disrepute. Contemporary biological theories consider two factors:

- *Genetic composition:* Often focuses on relationships between parental characteristics and predilection to engage in criminal behavior, relating the findings to offsprings' (and siblings') criminality.
- *Intelligence:* IQ tests and psychological profiles have been used to explain and predict the probability of criminal behavior. With some exceptions, criminals tend to have lower levels of intellectual and emotional intelligence.

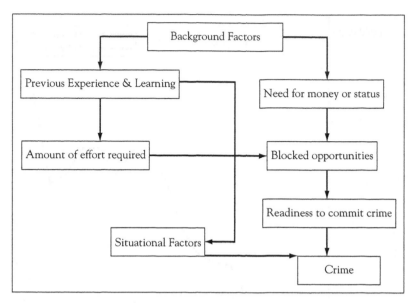

FIGURE 15.9   Theories of crime.

Source: Adapted from D. Cornish and R. Clarke, eds. 1986. *The Reasoning Criminal.* New York: Springer-Verlag.

CRIMES AND CRIMINAL PROCEDURE

The Federal Rules of Criminal Procedure outline six major elements of **criminal procedure**:

- *Preliminary proceedings:* Following the collection of evidence, the prosecuting attorney requests an arrest warrant from a judge. Law enforcement executes the arrest warrant, making an arrest. An exception to this rule is if law enforcement personnel witness a crime—criminal suspects can be arrested for community protection. Still, an arrest warrant is issued for the particular charge.

  The charges against a person (the defendant) are presented to a judge or magistrate during an initial appearance by the defendant. If the judge does not find probable cause for proceeding, the charges against the person are dropped. If the judge finds probable cause, the charges are presented to a grand jury.

- *Indictment:* Only the prosecuting attorney, judge, and grand jury are present. If the grand jury finds that the evidence is sufficient for a trial, there is an arraignment.[2]

- *Arraignment:* In an open courtroom, the charges against a defendant are made public and the defendant is asked to enter a plea of guilt or innocence. If the defendant pleads innocent, then a venue for trial must be determined. A defendant likely has chosen defense counsel at this point—private attorney or public defender.

- *Venue:* A trial date and location is chosen. The trial may occur in another jurisdiction to ensure fairness to the defendant.

- ***Trial:*** At trial, a defendant will be asked whether or not he or she wishes to be tried by jury. If a jury trial is chosen, then unbiased adult citizens (normally twelve individuals) must be chosen prior to the commencement of the trial. If the defendant is found guilty of the charges presented against him or her, then the judge establishes a date for sentencing.
- ***Postconviction procedures:*** Prior to sentencing, the victim or the victim's family are given an opportunity to speak in court to discuss the economic and emotional impact of the crime. The convicted person is also given an opportunity to speak prior to sentencing.

PERSPECTIVES ON PUNISHMENT

Rehabilitation Versus Retribution

Proponents of rehabilitation believe that socioeconomic deprivation often contributes to criminal behavior, a condition that must be rectified by society. Proponents of rehabilitation tend to hold modern liberal perspectives of crime policy—the criminal is less advantaged in relation to other members of society. The impact of rehabilitation programs is unclear, possibly due to underfunding.

Proponents of retribution see crime as a rational choice—the prospective criminal considers the costs and benefits of crime. Punishment is one way of increasing potential costs, thereby discouraging crime. Proponents of retribution tend toward a classical liberal view of crime and punishment. The impact of retributive crime policy is publicly debated.

Three Strikes and You're Out

In the 1990s, ballot initiatives were passed in many states requiring life sentences for third-time felons—twenty-six states have provisions that qualify as "three strikes" policies. Proponents argue that by the third "strike," rehabilitation efforts have obviously not succeeded and society should exact retributive justice.

Community Corrections

Community corrections facilities are for low-security-risk prisoners who have committed lesser offenses. Inmates are taught decision-making skills, helping them return to "real life" in a free society. Community corrections intends for inmates to discover the benefits of crime-free life, reducing **recidivism**.

House Arrest and Electronic Surveillance

With more than 1.5 million individuals in federal and state prisons, policy experts seek alternative methods of punishment. Technology has made it possible to restrict individuals' movements and behavior in their own homes through electronic monitoring, often used for lesser offenses. Electronic bands are attached to the prisoner; if he or she wanders from proscribed boundaries or violates curfew restrictions, law enforcement locates and apprehends the individual. Proponents argue that the method is cheaper and effective, having the effect of reintegrating prisoners into free society. Opponents argue that it does not effectively punish criminals.

Death Penalty

Critics argue that the death penalty does not deter crime and is based in a false sense of moral justice. Life in prison without the possibility of parole is seen as having the equivalent effect on a convicted criminal. Death penalty critics also argue that the punishment is applied unfairly. The proportion of blacks receiving the death penalty, although lower than that of whites, is several times greater than the proportion of blacks living in the United States. Given the disadvantaged socioeconomic backgrounds of many black criminals, critics charge that it is a socially unjust punishment. Critics of the death penalty tend to be modern liberals.

Proponents see a moral element to the death penalty and support **retributive justice**—punishment should be a form of revenge for a criminal act against other parties to the social contract. Proponents claim that higher execution rates are related to decreases in violent crime. Proponents are not overly concerned with the racial composition of the condemned—punishment focuses solely on crime itself. Proponents are inclined to support the tenets of classical liberalism. (See Figure 15.10.)

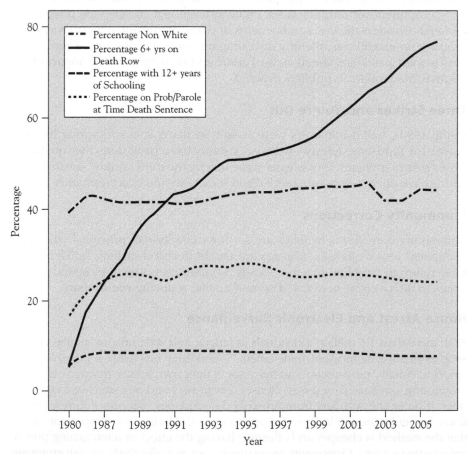

FIGURE 15.10 Characteristics of death row prisoners (1980–2006).

INCARCERATION POLICY AND MANAGEMENT

Punishment for criminal acts usually involves the loss of liberty through incarceration. When an individual is convicted of a crime and sentenced to prison or jail, the government assumes responsibility for protecting prisoners' rights and for providing for basic needs (e.g., food, shelter, and clothing). Government is also responsible for determining what it seeks to achieve for the prisoner, within the scope of the individual's rights—societal retribution or rehabilitation or a combination of both.

Control Model of Incarceration

The control model views incarceration as being both punishment leading to contrition and sense of social renewal. According to DiIulio (1987), the control model advocates that each prisoner should "do his [or her] own time," reflecting on past criminal choices. The validity of this approach is not supported by data—recidivism rates remain high.

Responsibility Model of Incarceration

The responsibility model downplays the symbols of authority that govern prisons. The model focuses attention on the variations in prisoner type, matching the prisoner to incarceration strategies. The responsibility model often rewards good behavior and self-discipline. Prisoners are offered some ability to learn new behaviors that will serve them well should they regain their freedom.

Consensual Model of Incarceration

Prison guards are expected to act professionally. But, unlike the control model, this approach can be viewed as a weak form of the responsibility model. Except for violent prisoners, the consensual model incorporates inmates into prison governance. The model often maintains prison security through nonviolent methods.

HOT TOPIC CRIMES IN THE TWENTY-FIRST CENTURY

Certain types of crime are of particular interest in the United States today. Three types of crime that are often discussed in media reports are **hate crimes**, **child abuse**, and **public corruption**.

Hate Crimes

In the early 1990s, the state of Wisconsin passed legislation implementing stronger penalties for violent crimes in which the victim had been selected on the basis of his or her race, gender, ethnicity, religion, or sexual preference. The law reflected model legislation developed by a public interest group known as the Anti-Defamation League (ADL). The legislation was supported by interest groups (e.g., National Organization for Women, gay rights advocacy groups, and groups representing various ethnic minority causes) as well as members of the broader community. The statute was challenged in *Wisconsin v. Mitchell* 508 U.S. 476 (1993), but the Supreme Court did not find the law unconstitutional. Although U.S. hate crimes law

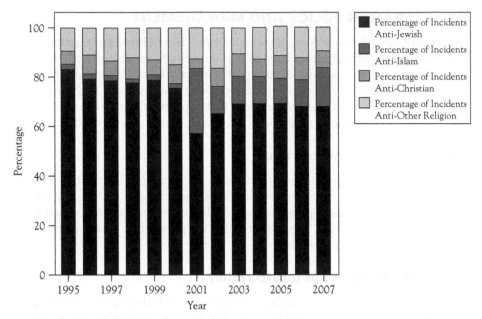

FIGURE 15.11   Hate crimes involving religion (1995–2007).

had already initiated a nationwide monitoring program (see Figures 15.11–15.15), the Court decision was key to effectively legitimizing legislation, to include:

- ***The Hate Crime Statistics Act of 1990 (28 U.S.C. 534)***
  The law required that from 1990 to 1994, the U.S. Department of Justice would collect annual data on violent or property-related crimes that

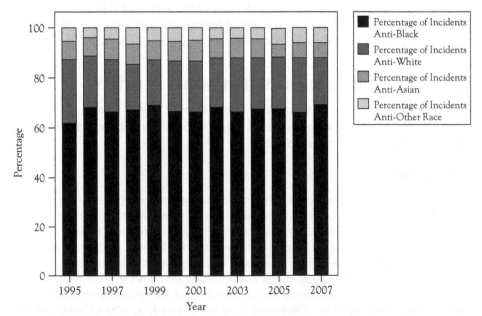

FIGURE 15.12   Hate crimes involving race (1995–2007).

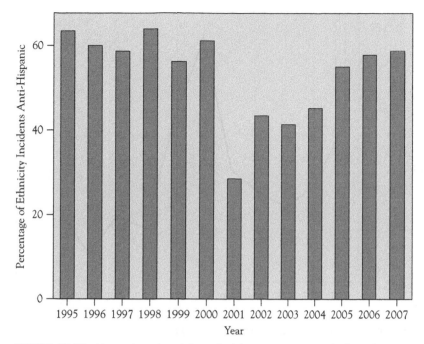

FIGURE 15.13 Hate crimes involving ethnicity: percentage anti-Hispanic (1995–2007).

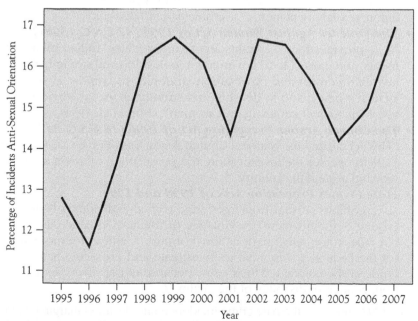

FIGURE 15.14 Hate crimes involving antisexual orientation (1995–2007).

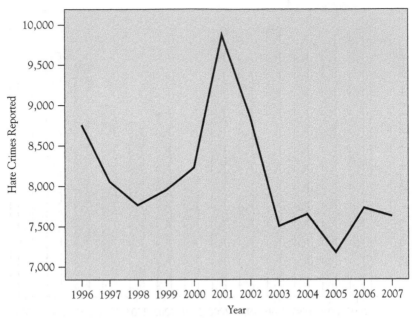

FIGURE 15.15 Hate crimes reported (1995–2007).

showed evidence of prejudice in relation to the victim's race, ethnicity, religion, or sexual orientation.

- ***The Hate Crimes Sentencing Enhancement Act of 1994 (28 U.S.C. 534)***
  "This act requires the Department of Justice to collect data on hate crimes. Hate crimes are defined as 'manifest prejudice based on race, religion, sexual orientation, . . . ethnicity, [and disability]'."[3]
- ***The Violence Against Women Act of 1994 (42 U.S.C. 13981)***
  ". . . provides for . . . grants are 'to assist States, Indian tribal governments, and units of local government to develop and strengthen effective law enforcement and prosecution strategies to combat violent crimes against women, and to develop and strengthen victim services in cases involving violent crimes against women'" (Burt et al. 1996).
- ***The Church Arsons Prevention Act of 1996 (18 U.S.C. 247)***
  "This act created the National Church Arson Task Force (NCATF) in June 1996 to oversee the investigation and prosecution of arson at houses of worship around the country."[4]
- ***Hate Crimes Prevention Acts of 1998 and 1999***
  ". . . prohibits persons from interfering with an individual's Federal rights (voting or employment) by violence or threat of violence due to his or her race, color, religion, or national origin . . . allows for more authority for the Federal government to investigate and prosecute hate crime offenders who committed their crime because of perceived sexual orientation, gender, or disability of the victim."[5]

In 1997 and 1998, the hate crime incidence rate declined marginally, but increased sharply from 1999 through 2001. The percentage of hate crimes that led to indictments is particularly high for cases involving race, ethnicity, gender or sexual preference, religion, and physical disability. Most religion-based hate crimes are directed against adherents of Judaism. Prior to September 11, anti-Islamic hate crimes reported were never greater than 3 percent of all religion-based hate crimes reported nationwide. Since September 11, anti-Islam hate crimes have increased.

Child Abuse

In the 1990s, child abductions, sexual assault, abuse, and murder became a highly visible part of criminal justice policy. The 1996 abduction and murder of Amber Hagerman in Texas led to the **Amber Alert** system, part of a nationwide effort to keep the public informed about abductions in local communities. The interstate or international transportation (e.g., Internet) of children or images for sexual exploitation is a violation of federal law.[6] The FBI and other law enforcement agencies enforce antiexploitation laws to protect children's rights.

The Violent Crime Control and Law Enforcement Act of 1996 (42 U.S.C. 14071) requires the registration of individuals convicted of crimes against children. Known as **Megan's Law**, the statute "arms the public with certain information on the whereabouts of dangerous sex offenders. . . . The law also authorizes local law enforcement to notify the public about high-risk and serious sex offenders who reside in, are employed in, or frequent the community. . . . The law is not intended to punish the offender and specifically prohibits using the information to harass or commit any crime against the offender."[7]

According to the Children's Bureau, Department of Health and Human Services, child maltreatment investigation rates have increased dramatically. Reported in the *Statistical Abstract of the United States*, there were approximately 900,000 child abuse cases in the United States in 2005. According to the Children's Bureau report cited here, the single most common perpetrator of child maltreatment is the child's mother acting alone. (See Figure 15.16 and Table 15.1.)

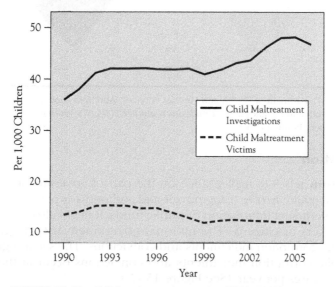

FIGURE 15.16   Child maltreatment rates (1990–2006).

TABLE 15.1 Child Maltreatment by Perpetrator Status 2006	
Perpetrator Status	**Percent of Victims**
Mother Only	40.4%
Father Only	18.3%
Mother and Father	17.3%
Mother and Other	6.2%
Father and Other	1.1%
Non-parental Perpetrator(s)	10.7%
Unknown or Missing	6.0%

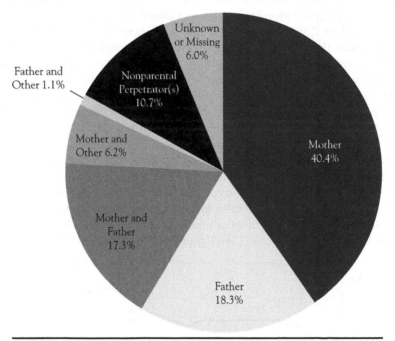

Source: U.S. Department of Health and Human Services, Administration on Children, Youth and Families 2007. *Child Maltreatment 2005.* Washington, DC: US Government Printing Office.

Public Corruption

Public corruption refers to malfeasance on the part of government officials. Public corruption could involve using power and authority for personal gain or the misuse of government information or public funds. It might also involve the abuse of coworkers or citizens. The national government has the greatest number of public corruption indictments and convictions. The second greatest number of public corruption indictments and convictions occur at the local level—nearly 300 cases per year. (See Figure 15.17.)

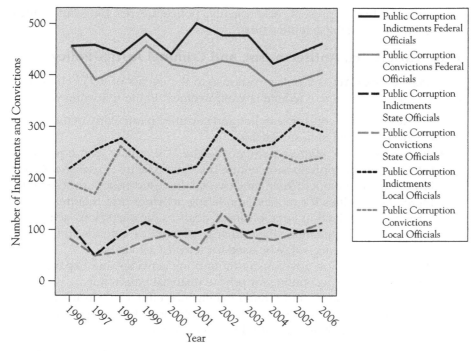

FIGURE 15.17 Public corruption: indictments and convictions (1996–2006).

CONTEMPORARY POLICING TECHNIQUES AND ISSUES

Community-Oriented Policing

Community-oriented policing (COP) represents a return to many of the historical principles of policing. The U.S. Department of Justice, which helps state and local law enforcement agencies build and continue to develop the COP programs, defines this contemporary policing paradigm as "a policing philosophy that promotes and supports organizational strategies to address the causes and reduce the fear of crime and social disorder through problem-solving tactics and police–community partnerships."[8]

Racially Biased Policing

Racially biased policing refers to ". . . law enforcement activities (detentions, arrests, searches) that are initiated . . . on the basis of race."[9] According to a 2001 study conducted by the Police Executive Research Forum (PERF), a majority of minorities and white individuals surveyed believe that police frequently conduct traffic stops and initiate searches because the individual driving the car being searched is a racial or ethnic minority. Whether police bias is widespread or a misconstrued perception, it proves to be a limitation on successful community–police relations and weakens law enforcement capacity. Many police agencies conduct analyses of traffic stop and citizen–police interactions to determine whether racial bias is present. Additionally, police are reaching out to local communities to reestablish mutual trust.

U.S.A. Patriot Act, Antiterrorism, and Criminal Justice Policy

The **U.S.A. Patriot Act** is a policy response to the events of 9/11. The Patriot Act broadens the powers of federal law enforcement in the following ways:

- Relaxes requirements for searches and seizures, particularly in the area of electronic transmission surveillance.
- Relaxes *posse commitatus* restrictions—the U.S. military can now play a role in criminal apprehension within the United States. *Posse commitatus* laws were an attempt to keep military and domestic policy areas separate.
- Increases penalties for money laundering activities and requires private businesses involved in large business deals to file suspicious activity reports (SARs), documenting the exchange of money for goods and/or services that could conceivably be used for terrorist activities.
- Reduces controls on government monitoring activities and expands government's role in accounting for private financial transactions.
- Coordinates domestic and foreign intelligence efforts to construct a more complete view of terrorism worldwide in relation to U.S. security and criminal justice policy areas. (See Box 15.2, *Immigration and Identity Theft*.)

BOX 15.2
Immigration and Identity Theft

One of the more serious issues to emerge from illegal immigration is identity theft.[11] In order to gain employment, illegal immigrants often produce some form of fake identification indicating their legal status in the United States. In the past, employers often did not have the time nor the incentive to check the accuracy of those documents. In recent years, Homeland Security has begun to crack down on employers and illegal immigrant workers who use fake documents or steal the identity of other individuals, such as citizens' Social Security numbers.

Although one approach to the problem of identity theft by illegal immigrants is through law enforcement activities—that is, regulatory policy—President George W. Bush proposed an alternative solution—a distributive policy. Namely, Bush proposed registering illegal immigrants. His plan was that after illegal immigrants have identified themselves as illegal, they are to return to their native countries for a period of time before applying for documented status. After applying for documented status, immigrant workers would be given a criminal background check and, assuming the result was acceptable, they would be given work permits to work in the United States for a period of time. Opponents of Bush's plan have called it "amnesty."

Public opinion of immigrants, however, has become more positive. Recently, the Pew Research Center[12] found that about one-third of opinion poll respondents felt that immigrants increased the crime rate. Increasingly, the public sees immigrants as hard-working individuals from close-knit families. Although opponents of Bush's plan have won the battle, an increasingly positive image of immigrants might lead to some form of official recognition of their status in the United States,[13] which in turn might contribute to a reduction in identity theft concerns.

EXPLAINING CRIMINAL JUSTICE POLICY

Elite Theory

Criminal justice policy defines crime. At the national level, the presidency and Congress are composed of elected policy elites who make major decisions about criminal justice policy. President George W. Bush's antiterrorism initiative was the newest and largest addition to criminal justice policy, although Bush's approach is currently being reevaluated by the Obama administration.

Appointed elites—federal judges, Supreme Court justices, presidential appointees—and senior civil servants have visible roles in criminal justice policy. Judges and Supreme Court justices shape criminal justice policy through court judicial interpretations. Attorneys general, the secretary of Homeland Security, and the FBI director are examples of policy elites shaping policy formulation and implementation. Senior civil servants are administrative elites who shape policy decisions.

Elites are temporary actors in the policy process—elected officials win and lose elections. Judges and justices retire from office eventually. Civil servants finish their careers and leave their posts. Policy elites, therefore, are constantly changing. These changes eventually lead to changing policy priorities. Elites represent different notions of what government *ought* or *ought not* do, and their views directly impact policy priorities.

Group Theory

Pressure groups play a substantial role in shaping criminal justice policy in the United States. The criminalization of drugs is vigorously opposed by drug-legalization advocacy groups. Other groups actively support and lobby for even more stringent penalties for drug dealing, possession, and use. The three strikes laws came into being due to pressure group advocacy leading to citizens' ballot initiative campaigns to create the policies. Death penalty advocates and opponents often work feverishly to ensure that an execution occurs, or to file legal papers to delay or stop an execution. Crime policy provokes sharp divisions about what government *ought* or *ought not* do.

Institutionalism

The institutions of government that create and implement criminal justice policy play a substantial role in what these policies represent. Community-oriented policing and racial profiling illustrate the challenges institutions face when confronted with the need for change. Community-oriented policing challenges law enforcement officers to reconsider decades of development within policing practices. Racial profiling policy requires a reconsideration of the goal and method of achieving public safety. Law enforcement at the national, state, and local levels must establish new priorities and methods of fighting crime while preserving civil rights and liberties.

Lessons Learned from Chapter 15

SPECIFICS

- There are two major types of crime: property-related and person-related.
- There are three major theories of crime: biological theory, social inequity theory, and rational choice theory.
- Basic criminal procedure is uniform to ensure that the accused are afforded legal due process.
- Two major theories of punishment are rehabilitation and retribution.
- Contemporary criminal justice issues include: hate crimes, child abduction, and racially biased policing.
- Community-oriented policing is an innovative model for reinvigorating policy practices.
- The U.S.A. Patriot Act brought law enforcement and defense policy functions into closer proximity.

THE BIG PICTURE

Criminal justice is one of the central purposes of government. It is a highly complex function that exists at the national, state, and local levels. Criminal justice policy incorporates everything from identifying suspects to incarcerating convicted criminals to fighting the illegal trafficking in drugs to fighting the war against international terrorism. For the most part, we agree that crime is bad; however, our differing views of what crime entails, why it occurs, and what should be done about it often leads us to different views about what government *ought* or *ought not do*.

Key Terms

Amber Alert
assistant attorneys general
child abuse
community-oriented policing (COP)
criminal procedure
defense attorneys
hate crimes
Megan's Law
person-related crimes

property-related crime
prosecuting attorneys
public corruption
public defenders
racially biased policing
recidivism
retributive justice
U.S.A. Patriot Act

Questions for Study

1. What is criminal procedure? Outline the process. Discuss three major landmark court cases that have impacted our understanding of criminal procedure.
2. Identify and discuss two major theories of criminal behavior and two major theories of punishment.

3. In what ways does the U.S.A. Patriot Act impact criminal justice policy? Using three policy models, explain and describe the U.S.A. Patriot Act.

CASE STUDY

Senator Samuel D. Brownback Opening Comments During Death Penalty Hearing Senate Subcommittee on the Constitution, Washington, DC, December 1, 2006 "The Fifth and Fourteenth Amendments to the U.S. Constitution provide that no person may be deprived of life without due process of law. Yet the Eighth Amendment prohibits in undefined terms the use of cruel and unusual punishment. In subsequent decisions, the Supreme Court found what it deemed to be a popular consensus against use of the death penalty in cases involving mentally disabled or minor defendants. Reading these provisions together, it seems our founding document neither demands nor prohibits capital punishment. Instead, the Constitution generally permits the people to decide whether and when capital punishment is appropriate.

"So each generation may—and good citizens should—consider anew the law and facts involving this solemn judgment. I believe America must establish a culture of life. If use of the death penalty is contrary to promoting a culture of life, we need to have a national dialogue and hear both sides of the issue. All life is sacred, and our use of the death penalty in the American justice system must recognize this truth.

"I called this hearing in order to conduct a full and fair examination of the death penalty in the United States. I believe it is important for lawmakers and the public to be informed about a punishment which, because it is final and irreversible, stirs much debate. It is my intention to explore in this hearing the various aspects of capital punishment, from the statistics on deterrence to the views of crime victims. It is my hope that by carefully reflecting on America's experience with the death penalty, the people can make informed judgments worthy of the Constitution's faith in future generations."

Courtesy of Project Vote Smart www.votesmart.org

Thinking about what Senator Brownback said about the death penalty, is it something that we *ought* or *ought not* do? Why or why not? Based on the group viewpoints presented, develop a short recommendation for keeping or ending death penalty policies. If presenting your findings in a paper or class presentation, gather additional background information to make your case—for example, exploring the policy history of the death penalty, the events that led to its creation. Use three policy models to explain the death penalty as a policy.

Bibliography

American Civil Liberties Union. 2007. "Safe and Free: Restore our Constitutional Rights," www.aclu.org/safefree/resources/17343res20031114.html (accessed August 17, 2007).

Burt, M., L. Newmark, M. Norris, D. Dyer, and A. Harrell. 1996. "The violence against women act of 1994: Evaluation of the STOP block grants to combat violence against women." www.urban.org/publications/306621.html (accessed August 17, 2007).

Cassel, E. 2007. *Criminal behavior.* Mahwah, NJ: L. Erlbaum Associates.

Cornish, D., and R. Clarke, eds. 1986. *The reasoning criminal.* New York: Springer-Verlag.

DiIulio, J. 1987. *Governing prisons.* New York: Free Press.

Durkheim, E. 1982. Règles de la Méthode Sociologique. New York: Free Press.

Fridell, L., R. Lunney, D. Diamond, and B. Kabu. 2001. *Racially-biased policing: A principled approach.* Washington, DC: Police Executive Research Forum.

Hall, N. 2005. *Hate crime.* Collumpton, Devon, UK: Willan.

Levin, J., and J. McDevitt. 1993. *Hate crimes: The rising tide of bigotry and bloodshed.* New York: Plenum Press.

Lippke, R. 2007. *Rethinking imprisonment.* New York: Oxford University Press.

Lowi, T. 1969. *The end of liberalism.* New York: Norton.

National Criminal Justice Reference Service. 2005. "Hate Crime Resources—Legislation." www.ncjrs.org/hate_crimes/legislation.html (accessed January 31, 2005).

Office of the Attorney General. 2001. *Registered sex offenders (Megan's law).* Sacramento, CA: Department of Justice, www.caag.state.ca.us/megan (accessed January 31, 2005).

Samaha, J. 1999. *Criminal procedure,* 4th ed. Belmont, CA: West/Wadsworth.

Santos, M. 2006. *Inside: life behind bars in America.* New York: St. Martin's Press.

U.S. Department of Health and Human Services, Administration on Children, Youth and Families 2007. *Child Maltreatment 2005.* Washington, DC: U.S. Government Printing Office.

University of Texas. 2007. "Community Oriented Policing." www.utexas.edu/police/cops/ (accessed August 17, 2007).

Wilson, J. 1975. *Thinking about crime.* New York: Basic Books.

Wilson, J., and J. Petersilia. 2001. *Crime: Public policies for crime control.* Oakland: ICS Press.

Zimring, F., and G. Hawkins. 1989. *Capital punishment and the American agenda.* New York: Cambridge University Press.

Court Cases

Gideon v. Wainwright 372 U.S. 335 (1963)
Klopfer v. N. Carolina 386 U.S. 213 (1967)
Malloy v. Hogan 378 U.S. 1 (1964)
Mapp v. Ohio 367 U.S. 643 (1961)
Pointer v. Texas 380 U.S. 400 (1965)
Robinson v. California 370 U.S. 660 (1962)
Terry v. Ohio 392 U.S. 1 (1967)

Washington v. Texas 388 U.S. 14 (1967)
Wisconsin v. Mitchell 508 U.S. 476 (1993)
Wolf v. Colorado 338 U.S. 25 (1949)

Endnotes

1. www.aclu.org/CriminalJustice/CriminalJusticeMain.cfm (accessed May 27, 2003).
2. A grand jury decision in favor of a trial does not mean that the defendant is guilty of the crime.
3. www.ncjrs.gov/spotlight/Hate_Crimes/Summary.html (accessed May 26, 2009).
4. www.ncjrs.gov/spotlight/Hate_Crimes/Summary.html (accessed May 26, 2009).
5. www.ncjrs.gov/spotlight/Hate_Crimes/Summary.html (accessed May 26, 2009).
6. 18 U.S.C. 110, Section 2251.
7. www.caag.state.ca.us/megan (accessed June 5, 2003); more current link to Megan's Law information: www.meganslaw.ca.gov/ (accessed May 26, 2009).
8. www.cops.usdoj.gov/Default.asp?Item=36 (accessed January 31, 2005).
9. Fridell et al. 2001, 1.
10. Samaha. 1999, 48.
11. Stana, R. 2002. "Identity Fraud: Prevalence and Links to Alien Illegal Activities." Testimony before the Subcommittee on Crime, Terrorism, and Homeland Security, and the Subcommittee on Immigration, Border Security, and Claims, Committee on the Judiciary, House of Representatives, June 25. Washington, DC: GAO. GAO-02-830T.
12. Pew Research Center. 2006. "America's Immigration Quandary: Section IV—Views and Perceptions of Immigrants," www.people-press.org/reports/display.php3?PageID=1049 (accessed May 26, 2009).
13. According to the Pew study, 76 percent of Americans favor a government identification card for immigrants.

16

■ ■ ■

Green Policy

CHAPTER OVERVIEW

Green policy is primarily concerned with our relationship with the environment, the natural world in which all species live. The environment is a **commons**, composed of goods that we cannot divide and sell but that we can consume. Powerful individuals are capable of capturing a greater quantity of these goods and holding them as property, thus limiting the ability of other individuals to obtain basic needs. The commons and **public goods** are regulated by government but ownership and use is not completely restricted.

The common resource base is also managed for the benefit of nonhuman species. Interspecial equity is viewed by green politics and policy as something that is inherently good simply because we share the Earth with other living creatures and nonliving things, and we should be responsible in pursuing our individual and collective interests.

Human populations are growing and the demands of humans are constraining the natural environment. The twentieth century witnessed one of the greatest periods of population growth known to humankind,[1] but numbers alone do not tell the complete story. Although abject poverty continues to exist around the globe, the standard of living for the vast majority of humans has increased tremendously; oftentimes, other species have suffered serious loss due to resource depletion, habitat destruction, and climate change.

The specific goals for the chapter are:

- Discuss the role of the *commons* in relation to the green policy area.
- Discuss the major actors in the green policy area.
- Detail the major national environmental laws related to green policies.
- Discuss the natural resources available in the United States.
- Use policy theories to explain green policies.

THE COMMONS

Green policy is concerned with managing the commons. There are three major principles of the commons:

- *First principle of the commons*
  Commons are those things that are consumed and *cannot be divided and sold.* Because the commons are publicly held, the political process determines "who gets what, when, and how."[2] Through political action, we collectively decide the use of common goods. Because these goods are basic necessities, they must not be denied to individuals or groups.
- *Second principle of the commons*
  The commons is *a necessary prerequisite to the maintenance of our life, liberty, and property.* Human greed may result in the misallocation of resources, diminishing the benefits of others, to include other species.
- *Third principle of the commons*
  In order to prevent misallocation and injustice, the *government must step in to manage the distribution of certain goods through regulation or direct allocation.*

Dialogue regarding the commons is related to the issue of rights. Classical liberals tend to define the commons very narrowly. For instance, classical liberals view water as a commodity rather than a common resource. The forces of supply and demand would, in their view, shape demand patterns.

One might ask, "Well, what about clean air? Isn't that something that cannot be divided? Something we all need?" From the classical liberal view, if one does not like the air quality where one lives, the individuals should move to another community. The undesirable community will, in theory, clean up its act in order to retain or attract new residents and businesses.

Modern liberals tend to view common resources in terms of Rawlsian notions of social or environmental justice. Environmental justice requires that communities identify and provide assistance to the least benefited members of *any* and *all species.* Modern liberals often view the commons in a broad sense. Basic food supplies in the ocean or in streams are seen as common goods that *ought to* be a protected and sustainable resource for all. Communitarians' view of the commons is similar to the modern liberal perspective. Right-of-center and left-of-center communitarians tend to view the commons as essential to the maintenance of a sustainable community.

KEY ACTORS IN GREEN POLICY

President

Presidential use of military and diplomatic powers led to the acquisition of land: the annexation of the Great Lakes region, the purchases of the Louisiana Territory from France and Alaska from Russia, a diplomatic relationship with Great Britain and a claim in the case of the Oregon Territory, and through the Mexican

War (1846–1848), the acquisition of Alta California and Nuevo Mexico—a large part of the American West.

A substantial portion of the land was distributed through the Homestead Act (1862). Large tracts of the acquired land remained under the control of the national government, historically used for resource extraction. A major first step toward green policy can be traced to President Theodore Roosevelt, who created national forests and parks using portions of the public lands for purposes of managed use or simply to be preserved.

Congress

In the nineteenth century land acquisitions, Congress's primary role was to: (1) passively or actively support the presidents' expansionary agenda and (2) finance the expansionary efforts. Congress often used the newly acquired lands as a basis for constituency service and reelection. Rather than simply preserving the natural environment, the parochial interests of legislators were served through programs such as water reclamation projects that dammed rivers and streams for recreational, flood control, and water resource projects designed to serve local agricultural and urban needs. In the late twentieth century, Congress's role in environmental and natural resource policy began to shift toward a green position, with greater emphasis on environmental protection.

Courts

Use of the newly acquired territorial lands posed several dilemmas regarding the nature of property rights: the role of human society in relation to the environment, the taking of lands from indigenous peoples, and the management of these lands in a federal policy-making environment. Green-related policies have and continue to be shaped by court decisions. In the now-famous case of *Northern Spotted Owl v. Hodel* 716 F. Supp. 479 W. D. Wash. (1988), the courts grappled with the balance between the need to protect the natural environment as a commons and the desire on the part of private enterprise to harvest timber on public lands as a privately held commodity. The Supreme Court's recent decision in *Massachusetts v. Environmental Protection Agency* 549 U.S. 497 (2007) found that the **Environmental Protection Agency (EPA)** has a role in regulating greenhouse gas emissions from motor vehicles. The *Northern Spotted Owl* and *Massachusetts* decisions illustrate the Court's support for green policy.

Interest Groups

After acquiring the vast lands of the Western United States, the national government was faced with a major dilemma: namely, what to do with all of it. In 1862, Congress created the **Homestead Act**. This act allowed families to acquire 160 acres of land primarily dedicated to agriculture. With the passage of the **Mining Act of 1872**, surface and subsurface mineral rights were claimed by individuals for mining purposes.

Agriculture, timber harvesting, and mining were the primary economic activities in the Western United States during the late nineteenth and much of the twentieth centuries. As these industrial sectors became more powerful, ranchers, farmers, miners, and timber harvesters coalesced into groups representing their particular economic interests. These economic groups have and continue to play a large role in environmental and natural resource policy, primarily focusing on resource extraction.

Although environmental interest groups had existed prior to the Baby Boom generation, the 1960s saw the rise of large-scale environmental interest groups. The groups have become highly influential in advancing green policies related to environmental protection, preservation, and rehabilitation. The Sierra Club and Nature's Conservancy are two highly visible groups advancing green policies.

At times, the "green" movement has brought environmental and economic interests together in rejecting **globalism**—political and economic partnerships promoting large-scale international capitalist ventures, possibly to the detriment of developing nations and the global environment. Some green antiglobalism efforts have led to memorable protests and riots. The November 1999 "Battle for Seattle" involved widespread street protests and property destruction outside of the World Trade Organization Ministerial Conference in downtown Seattle. Some scholars studying the Battle for Seattle argue that it was a form of ecoterrorism.[3]

ENVIRONMENTAL PROTECTION AGENCY (EPA)

Republican President Richard Nixon and a Democratically controlled Congress demonstrated bipartisanship in the creation of the EPA, the first nationally organized effort to regulate human-caused impacts on the natural environment. The EPA is a regulatory agency that enforces national environmental regulations.

FEDERAL ENVIRONMENTAL REGULATIONS

Prior to the 1960s, environmental policy focused attention on policies guiding methods of distributing nature's bounty found on publicly owned lands. Since the 1960s, less attention has focused on the distributive aspects of environmental policy and greater emphasis can be found in the regulation of the environment. More than a dozen major laws govern EPA regulation of the environment. A few of the landmark legislative acts are discussed here.

National Environmental Policy Act of 1969 (NEPA)
42 U.S.C. 4321–4347

NEPA created national standards governing human impacts on the environment. The law required that a Council on Environmental Quality monitor the condition of the environment, analyzing the uses and adequacy of natural resources, and the environmental impacts of state and local government policy, nongovernmental organizations, and individuals. The law requires the president to submit an annual environmental status report detailing: "(1) the status and condition of the major natural, manmade, or altered environmental classes of the Nation, including, but not limited to, the air, the aquatic, including marine, estuarine, and fresh water, and the terrestrial environment, including, but not limited to, the forest, dryland, wetland, range, urban, suburban and rural environment;

(2) current and foreseeable trends in the quality, management and utilization of such environments and the effects of those trends on the social, economic, and other requirements of the Nation; (3) the adequacy of available natural resources for fulfilling human and economic requirements of the Nation in the light of expected population pressures; (4) a review of the programs and activities (including regulatory activities) of the Federal Government, the State and local governments, and nongovernmental entities or individuals with particular reference to their effect on the environment and on the conservation, development and utilization of natural resources; and (5) a program for remedying the deficiencies of existing programs and activities, together with recommendations for legislation."

Clean Air Act of 1970 (CAA) 42 U.S.C. ss/1251 et seq.

The CAA established air quality standards regarding air emissions, intended to be met by 1975. Air emissions include particulate matter from combustion engines, nitrogen oxide, sulfur dioxide, carbon monoxide, carbon dioxide, ozone, and chlorofluorocarbons. In 1990, CAA amendments directed the EPA to promulgate regulatory policy mandating the reduction of "global warming" gas emissions.

Clean Water Act of 1977 (CWA) 33 U.S.C. ss/1251 et seq.

CWA regulates water pollution, requiring that pollutants not be discharged into navigable rivers and streams without EPA approval, and established water quality standards for surface and groundwater sources. Related, the Safe Drinking Water Act (SDWA) 42 U.S.C. ss/300f et seq. (1974) regulates the quality of potable water (water meant for human consumption).

Endangered Species Act of 1973 (ESA) 7 U.S.C. 136 and 16 U.S.C. 460

Whereas ESA is more closely associated with the U.S. Fish and Wildlife Service (USFWS) of the U.S. Department of Interior (USDOI), the EPA is involved with ESA enforcement. According to USFWS, there are over 600 endangered plant and animal species; many are threatened by pollutants, such as pesticides, impacting native species in traditional habitats. EPA enforcement includes regulations of pesticide control chemicals.

Occupational Safety and Health Act of 1970 (OSHA) 29 U.S.C. 651

OSHA protects the individual from harm in the workplace by promoting workplace safety. EPA regulation primarily relates to emissions that could negatively impact workers. Noise pollution is a particular problem in industrial employment, also monitored by EPA regulations.

Comprehensive Environmental Response, Compensation, and Liability Act of 1980 (CERCLA or Superfund) 42 U.S.C. ss/9601

The industrial age that followed the Civil War and sped along during most of the twentieth century left in its wake a series of toxic waste sites scattered around the nation. Potentially harmful production waste was buried near streams, in wooded areas, in highly populated areas, and near important watersheds. Plant and animal species were threatened by these poor waste disposal choices.

Superfund used fuel taxes to finance EPA (and related agency) efforts to clean up toxic waste sites and for proper waste disposal. Superfund was amended in 1986, and is now the Superfund Amendments and Reauthorization Act (SARA). The clean-up work continues into the foreseeable future.

Pollution Prevention Act of 1990 (PPA) 42 U.S.C. 32101

PPA is primarily concerned with the reduction of industrial and government waste. The Act promotes recycling and the efficient use of materials. PPA is a proactive effort to reduce waste at the source of pollution, focusing on changed decision-making needed to meet environmental quality standards. (See Figures 16.1–16.4.)

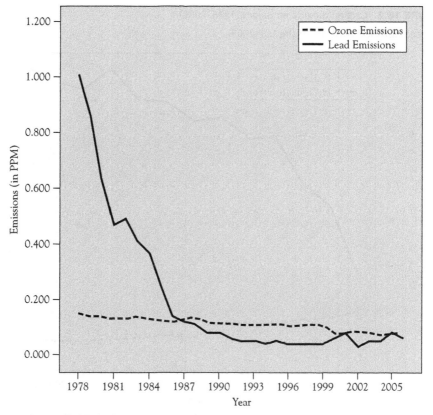

FIGURE 16.1   Ozone and lead emissions (1978–2006).

Source: Statistical Abstract of the U.S. 2009.

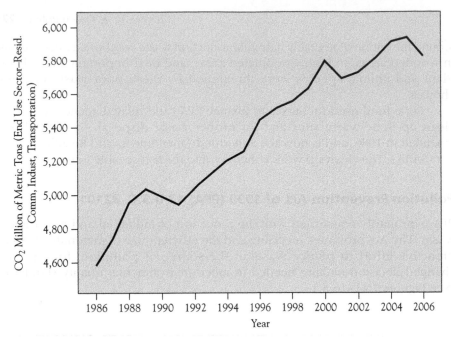

FIGURE 16.2   Carbon dioxide emissions (1986–2006).

Source: Statistical Abstract of the U.S. 2009.

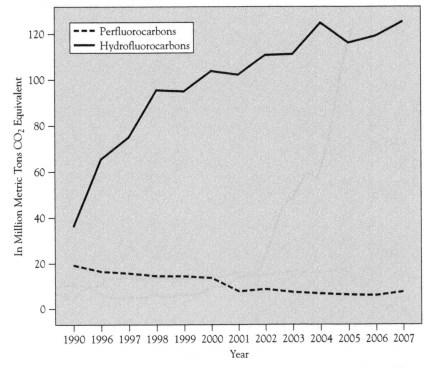

FIGURE 16.3   Hydroflurocarbon and perflurocarbon emissions (1990–2007) in millions of metric tons, CO_2 equivalency.

Source: Statistical Abstract of the U.S. 2009.

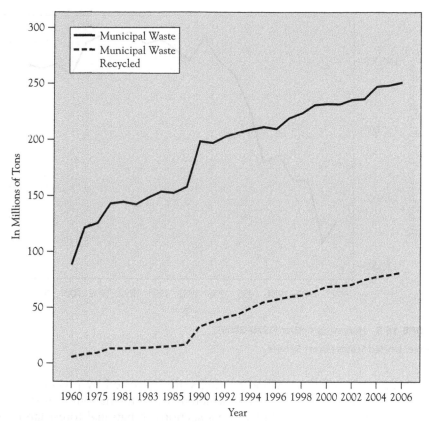

FIGURE 16.4 Municipal waste and recycling (1960–2006).

Source: Statistical Abstract of the U.S. 2009.

RESOURCE CONSUMPTION

Everything that we have created in our human world came from one of two sources: (1) plant or animal material or (2) substances that were mined from the surface of the Earth or beneath it. The most common plant material harvested from public lands is timber. Among the most common substances that is, in a sense, "mined" from the soil are fossil fuels—coal, natural gas, and petroleum.

Although many public policies seem to move policy in a green direction, resource extraction on public and private lands often poses a serious challenge to the green policy agenda. In order to understand the magnitude of nongreen practices the exploration of resource extraction is required.

Timber Resources

Roughly half of all timberland in the United States is owned privately, but the national forests (forests on national public lands) have historically provided a

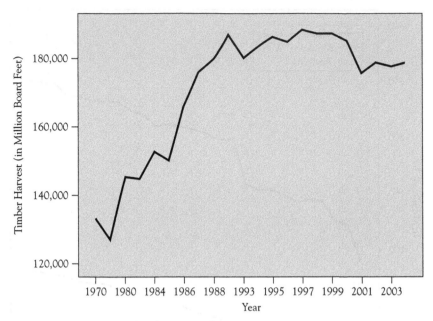

FIGURE 16.5   Harvested timber (1970–2006).

Source: United States Forest Service.

wealth of wood products. Wood products are harvested by private corporations. The U.S. Forest Service (USFS), which manages the national forest system,
is authorized to turn out to bid various sections of national forest land. (See
Figure 16.5.)

Mining in the United States

The list of minerals that are extracted from the soil is extensive. Everything from
fuels like petroleum to industrial minerals (asbestos and asphalt) to metals like
gold, lead, and zinc, are extracted from soils in the United States every year.
This section concentrates on three commonly recognized mineral fuels: coal,
natural gas, and petroleum.

Coal

In 1980, U.S. coal-mining corporations extracted 824 million tons of coal. In
2002, coal production had increased to 1.09 billion tons. Following a decline
in 2003, coal continued its upward production trend. The use of coal worries
environmental interest groups who argue that coal-burning for energy generation releases harmful greenhouse gases that could damage the planet's
atmosphere.

Coal is also used in the production of steel. The steel industry became an
especially important part of the American economy in the 1880s. Although a more
limited part of the American economy today, steel remains an important material,
used to create buildings, bridges, and other modern structures. (See Figure 16.6.)

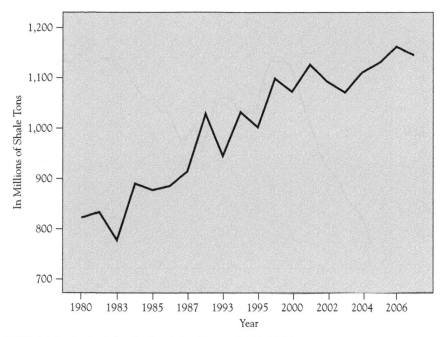

FIGURE 16.6 Coal mining in the United States (1980–2007).

Source: Energy Information Agency.

Natural Gas

In the 1980s, natural gas was hailed as a "cleaner" (fewer emissions that would damage the environment) fuel alternative to coal and oil for heating and electricity generation. Natural gas is found in cavernous pockets within the Earth and is tapped by drilling. Natural gas exploration has grown quite a bit since 1983 when gross production was at a near 20-year low of 18.7 trillion cubic feet. In 2008, gross natural gas production was 26.04 trillion cubic feet.

In 2003, U.S. Secretary of Energy Spencer Abraham announced that due to climactic and resource depletion issues, natural gas production would require further study to determine its long-term viability as a reliable natural resource for energy purposes. Natural gas reserves still exist in the United States and many gas fields are currently producing fuel. Some of the largest U.S. natural gas reserves exist under the Arctic National Wildlife Refuge—a region currently not available for the commercial mining of natural gas due to its designation as a nature preserve. (See Figure 16.7.)

Petroleum

The United States retains significant petroleum reserves beneath the land and coastal waters. Much of the easily accessible U.S. petroleum supply has been extracted, contributing to a long-term decline in production. Untapped reserves exist, but are often either very expensive to access or inaccessibly located beneath public lands. (See Figure 16.8.)

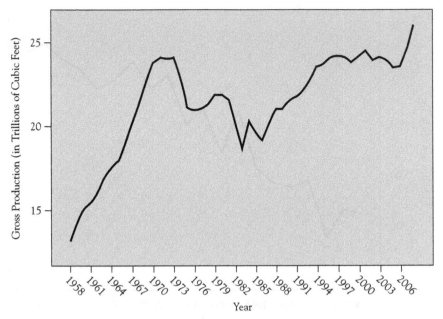

FIGURE 16.7 Natural gas production—gaseous (1958–2008).

Source: Energy Information Agency.

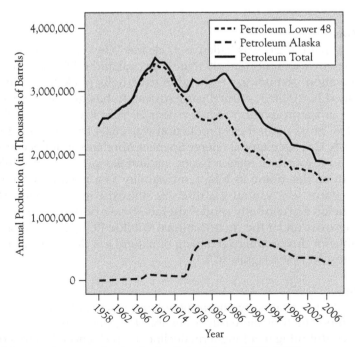

FIGURE 16.8 Petroleum production in the United States (1958–2007).

Source: Energy Information Agency.

Other Materials Mined in the United States

Besides fossil energy, corporations are actively involved in extracting other materials through mining. Uranium production remains important for defense purposes as well as meeting the material needs of the nation's 100+ commercial nuclear power plants. Precious metals such as gold, silver, platinum, and palladium are regularly extracted. Lesser known, but equally important, materials such as copper, nickel, silicon, and aluminum are basic materials used in electronics and construction. Metals—a sizeable portion of materials that are mined in the United States—are important nonrenewable natural resources that support our modern society. Many of these materials are mined on private lands, but a substantial portion is found below public lands. Mining operations are required to meet certain standards of operation that minimize environmental damage. Mining policy and politics is a classic example of balancing the public interest with private interests, a dilemma over what government *ought* or *ought not* do, *does* or *does not* do.

WATER POLITICS AND POLICY

Water is a key resource for life—a commonly used resource by all species. Yet, water is frequently treated as a commodity. In the earliest forms of government, water policy was critical to power and influence in relationships with competing societies. Public policy and the private marketplace often determine who controls water resources and how resources are used. Individuals often extracted water from streams and rivers adjacent to their property for agriculture and personal use. **Riparian rights** dictated that rivers were a *commons* that should be readily available for adjacent property owners' use, not overused by any single or group of individuals. Because water was generally plentiful, a **tragedy of the commons** did not usually occur—that is, the overuse or hoarding of a scarce common resource.

In the arid West, water supply was often quite scarce. A resource management system known as **prior appropriation** dictated water consumption. An individual who laid claim to water resources first had a right to consume the full amount of water claimed prior to the use by individuals who made later claims. Because of limited water resources, prior appropriation can lead to disparities in water consumption, impacting all forms of life. Through public policy, government reduces inequities in water management.

RENEWABLE ENERGY: PROTECTING THE ENVIRONMENT AND REDUCING HARMFUL EXTRACTIONS

What you might have noticed thus far is that there is a constant policy struggle over how to best use our resources. There is significant interest in reducing consumption of many resources for the protection of humans and other species, and to reduce environmental degradation. Fossil energy resource extraction and use is a central focus of the green policy agenda. **Renewable energy** is a green policy solution actively being pursued.

Renewable energy sources come in a variety of forms:

- *Solar energy*
  In the 1970s, solar energy policy was supported by President Carter, but was largely dismissed in the 1980s by President Reagan who favored the further development of nuclear energy. Despite a lack of clear leadership from policy-makers, there is growing demand for solar energy.
- *Wind energy*
  Wind energy has been harnessed for centuries. In properly selected sites, wind energy can produce competitively priced electricity. Some concerns exist about the turbine effect on birds, but technological developments have reduced these impacts.
- *Geothermal energy*
  Power generation involves the use of super-heated gases and water resources found deep below the Earth's surface. Geothermal resources are so extensive that resource depletion is unlikely.
- *Hydrogen*
  Hydrogen fuel cells store electrical energy for use, but produce zero greenhouse emissions. The U.S. Department of Energy's Hydrogen Initiative intends to stimulate the development of a hydrogen-energy economy.

EXPLAINING GREEN POLICY

Elite Theory

Political and social elites have played a prominent role in environmental policy. President Theodore Roosevelt is one of the most famous political elites in twentieth century environmental policy. Although by no means a "green" in today's meaning of the word, Theodore Roosevelt's policy leadership led to the establishment of the national park system and influenced Americans' understanding of nature and the role of nature in citizens' lives.

Social elites have also played a role in shaping the development of the green policy area. Prominent writers, such as Ralph Waldo Emerson, Henry David Thoreau, and poet Walt Whitman, influenced the core values of green policy. Simply stated, these authors felt that green policy is something that government *ought to* do.

In her 1962 book, *Silent Spring,* Rachel Carson documented the polluted American landscape and how that pollution was impacting citizens. Carson's work helped to advance the environmental policy agenda. Within a decade of the publication of *Silent Spring,* many of the landmark environmental laws establishing NEPA, CAA, and CWA had been passed by Congress, and now form the basis of contemporary environmental protection and regulation.

Group Theory

Interest groups have played a major role in advancing green policies. As the United States expanded westward, farmers and ranchers began to lay claim to government-granted lands. **Commodity associations** formed groups composed of individuals who raise similar food crops and share a common interest in protecting their ability to market these goods profitably. Mining and timber-harvesting industries have interest groups that work to maintain the extraction capacity of mining firms and loggers operating on public lands.

The late 1960s and early 1970s saw a tremendous change in interest group influence in the environment and natural resource policy areas—promoting a green agenda. The culture shift led to a large cohort of postmaterialists composed of environmentally aware individuals interested in promoting environmental justice and developing a balanced relationship between human society and the natural world. Groups such as the Sierra Club and Nature's Conservancy play a significant role in shaping green policy.

Institutionalism

Institutions have changed in many dramatic ways over recent decades and new institutions have been formed that have tremendous influence over environmental and natural resource policies. Created in 1905, the U.S. Forest Service (USFS) was the first major institution to manage publicly owned natural resources. Although its roots can be traced back to the Northwest Ordinance and the U.S. Land Office, the Bureau of Land Management (BLM) was officially created in 1946. The USFS and BLM play a significant role in policy formation and implementation for environmental and natural resource policy. USFS and BLM have changed tremendously since the 1960s; the institutions have changed their methods of decision-making, becoming more open to a wider spectrum of values. The creation of the Environmental Protection Agency (EPA) in 1970 also shaped environmental and natural resource policy and began to expand the goals of a safe and clean environment into the private property realm.

Congress has witnessed changes in its institutional processes that offer some explanation of green policies. As the population has shifted from rural to urban states and localities, the House of Representatives gained a higher percentage of urban representatives. Urbanites' distance from agriculture and mining means that they are less likely to view natural resources as commodities.

Since the Founding, the courts have expanded their role in shaping public policy. Court activism in environmental policy has become particularly strident since the 1960s. The courts have shaped a vision of the rights of nature. Although nature is not offered the same constitutional protections ascribed to human beings, there is a sense in court decisions that nature has rights not unlike general human rights often discussed in contemporary society.

Additionally, the courts have used their power to redefine or affirm ownership of certain natural resources. Native American tribes, for instance, have had many promises made to them in U.S. government treaties with tribes; institutional changes in the courts have led to the enforcement of treaty obligations, compelling government to reconsider its management practices—in some cases, government has been forced to relinquish ownership of certain natural resources.

Lessons Learned from Chapter 16

SPECIFICS

- Defining the *commons* is central in justifying the use of government power to regulate the environment and natural resource usage.
- Green policies require an understanding of the values, policy actors, and nature of the environment and natural resources—a unique blend of normative and empirical issues.
- The creation of major environmental laws in the 1960s and 1970s is the foundation of green policy.

THE BIG PICTURE

Environmental and natural resource policies combine to form the basis of the emergent green policy agenda. Survey research indicates that interest in these policy areas reached its peak during the mid-1980s. The higher levels of interest during the 1980s represented a unique struggle between resource extraction and environmental preservation viewpoints, culminating in the advancement of green policy. Interest in green policy has accelerated in the twenty-first century.

Key Terms

commodity associations
commons
Environmental Protection
   Agency (EPA)
federal environmental regulation
globalism
Homestead Act of 1862

Mining Act of 1872
National Environmental Policy Act
prior appropriation
public goods
renewable energy
riparian rights
tragedy of the commons

Questions for Study

1. How have statutory developments impacted green policies? Identify and discuss three major laws that have impacted environmental policy in the last forty years.
2. How would a classical liberal view green policy developments?
3. Identify and discuss three major actors in environmental and natural resource policy.

CASE STUDY

The following article reflects on Native American rights to use the natural resources of their tribal lands—a policy that would be a financial windfall for Native Americans, but create externalities for reservation residents and the surrounding communities. Explore methods of overcoming the energy independence dilemma for the Navajo. If presenting your findings in a paper or class presentation, gather additional background information to make your case. Use three policy models to explain what options are or are not available to tribal leaders as they pursue energy independence.

TRIBAL OIL REFINERY A NO-GO DESPITE HIGH PRICES, DEMAND

By *Bill Donovan*
Special to the *Navajo Times*, June 21, 2007

The Navajo Nation has given up on the idea of having its own oil refinery.

Navajo tribal officials were talking about building a refinery as far back as 1975, when the Navajo Nation was a founding member of the Council of Energy Resource Tribes.

The idea behind CERT was to create a Native version of OPEC, an entity capable of creating energy self-sufficiency for Indian Country and at the same time wielding clout in the energy policies of the United States.

The Navajo Reservation has some of the largest reserves of oil and natural gas among all of the Indian nations, so when the Navajo Oil and Gas Company was formed in the 1990s, one of its missions was to build the first tribally owned oil refinery.

But Debbie Kline, the oil and gas company's director, said recently that the idea has been abandoned, mainly because a new refinery proposal would encounter the same problems on Navajo land as it would anywhere else.

"There are just too many environmental problems connected with building a refinery today," she explained.

Refineries emit a range of toxic substances into the air, land and water. Communities near refineries along the Gulf Coast and lower Mississippi River have increased rates of cancer and various other diseases, as documented by the U.S. Centers for Disease Control.

While many scientists—not all of them on the payroll of oil companies— say the health problems are more likely the result of too much fried food and tobacco, the fact remains that almost no industry has a worse reputation for causing environmental harm or threats to health and safety.

That's the main reason why there has not been a refinery built in the United States since 1976 and no company has plans to build one, even though everyone in the industry says more refineries are desperately needed.

At one time, small refineries dotted the landscape of America, with almost every city or small town where oil drilling occurred having its own refinery where gasoline was produced for the local market.

But, according to information provided by OPEC (the Organization of the Petroleum Exporting Countries), almost all of these smaller refineries closed down in the 1970s as anti pollution standards were strengthened.

By the time Navajo leaders began to seriously consider building a refinery—where crude oil gains greatly in value as it is separated into gasoline and other fuels, asphalt, and the chemical components for a hundred other products including plastic—the door was already closing.

Even if Navajo residents had supported it, the likelihood that the tribe's non-Indian neighbors would have tolerated a refinery was, well, about the same as for a new coal-fired power plant.

As a result, although oil companies turn over a portion of the oil they extract as part of their royalty payments to the tribe, the tribe must send the oil to off-reservation refineries for processing.

The shortage of refinery capacity is often cited as the reason why oil prices have risen so much over the years.

Figures from OPEC showed that refineries in the 1980s were operating at about 77 percent of their capacity. By the mid-1990s, that had risen to 93 percent and today, it's estimated that the refineries are operating at 95 percent capacity.

Within the next 10 years, petroleum experts estimate that the refineries will be operating at full capacity and still not be able to meet the demand, which means that prices will continue to rise.

Prices are affected if anything happens to knock even one U.S. refinery out of production.

In August 2005, for instance, when Hurricane Katrina hit Louisiana, gas prices on the Navajo Reservation jumped around 15 cents a gallon almost before the hurricane had left the state. This is because Katrina forced the temporary closure of refineries that process 12 percent of the gasoline consumed in the United States.

Fortunately, damage to the refineries was much less than expected, but it still was several weeks before they were all back on line and gas prices nationwide began to drop.

Subsequently, oil companies such as Exxon reported the biggest profits in their history, demonstrating how lucrative it can be on the ownership end of an oil refinery.

Bibliography

Arquilla, J., and D. Ronfeldt. 2001. *Networks and netwars: The future of terrorism, crime, and militancy.* Santa Monica, CA: RAND Corporation.

Carson, R. 1962. *Silent Spring.* Boston: Houghton Mifflin.

Douglas, M., and A. Wildavsky. 1983. *Risk and culture: An essay on the selection of technological and environmental dangers.* Berkeley: University of California Press.

Energy Information Administration. 2003. *Emissions of greenhouse gases in the United States,* DOE/EIA-0573 (2002). Washington, DC: U.S. Department of Energy, Energy Information Administration.

Fuchs, D. 2003. *An institutional basis for environmental stewardship: The structure and quality of property rights.* Boston: Kluwer.

Jones, C. 1975. *Clean air: The policies and politics of pollution control.* Pittsburgh: Pittsburgh University Press.

Kemmis, D. 2001. *This sovereign land: A new vision for governing the West.* Washington, DC: Island Press.

Kraft, M. 2001. *Environmental policy and politics.* New York: Longman.

Larmer, P. ed. 2004. *Give and take: How the Clinton administration's public land offensive transformed the American West.* Paonia, CO: High Country News Books.

Lasswell, H. 1950. *Politics: Who gets what, when, and how.* New York: Peter Smith Publishers.

Lester, J., ed. 1989. *Environmental politics and policy: Theories and evidence.* Durham, NC: Duke University Press.

Madger, R. 1990. *America in the 21st century: Environmental concerns.* Washington, DC: Population Reference Bureau.

McCool, D. 1994. *Command of the waters: Iron triangles, federal water development, and Indian water.* Tucson: University of Arizona Press.

Simon, C. 2007. *Alternative energy: Political, economic, and social feasibility.* Lanham, MD: Rowman & Littlefield.

Steel, B. ed. 1997. *Public lands management in the West: Citizens, interest groups, and values.* Westport, CT: Praeger.

Sussman, G., B. Daynes, and J. West. 2002. *American politics and the environment.* New York: Longman.

Thoreau, H. D. 1970. *Walden, or life in the woods.* New York: C. N. Potter.

United Nations. 1998. *World population prospects, the 1998 revision.* New York: United Nations.

U.S. Census Bureau. 2007. *Statistical abstract of the United States.* Washington, DC: U.S. Census Bureau.

Vig, N., and M. Kraft, eds. 2003. *Environmental policy: New directions for the 21st century.* Washington, DC: CQ Press.

Court Cases

Massachusetts v. Environmental Protection Agency 549 U.S. 497 (2007)
Northern Spotted Owl v. Hodel 716 F. Supp. 479 W. D. Wash. (1988)

Endnotes

1. United Nations. 1998.
2. Lasswell. 1950.
3. Arquilla and Ronfeldt. 2001.

17

■ ■ ■

Cost of Policy

CHAPTER OVERVIEW

The process of prioritizing financial commitments in the policy process is known simply as **public budgeting**. The politics of public budgeting is one of the most critical aspects of policy formulation and implementation. Although budgeting is often thought of as a rather tedious subject involving ledgers and calculators, the process is anything but dull.

Budgeting is about priorities and sometimes that means making very painful decisions. For example, we might balk at being asked to put a finite dollar figure on the value of health care for the elderly. The imagination would immediately wander to the condition of sick relatives or friends— could we say that a person's health care is worth only a certain amount of money and nothing more? Yet, the budget process demands that we state in monetary terms exactly how much a public policy, and people's welfare, is worth to us.

The specific goals for the chapter are:

- Define *budgeting*.
- Explain the size of the national budget.
- Discuss the budget cycle.
- Identify major participants and influences on the budget.
- Discuss budget theory.
- Discuss the politics of entitlement.
- Discuss the budget and implications for policy.
- Use policy theory to explain budgeting.

A DEFINITION OF BUDGETING

Budgeting theorist and author of *Budgeting in America*, Thomas Lynch provides a very comprehensive definition of the term budget.

"Budget" is a *plan* for the accomplishment of *programs* related to *objectives* and *goals* within a definite *time* period, including an estimate of *resources required*, together with an estimate of the *resources available*, usually compared with one or more *past periods* and showing *future requirements* (Lynch 1985, 6).

Why Is Budgeting Necessary?

One of the most obvious reasons for budgeting is that we have *limited re-sources*. A second reason for budgeting is to establish *priorities*. With limited resources, some policies take precedence over others. Budgeting is also a method of *planning for the future*. Budgeting is a way of holding policy-implementing agencies *accountable*. Agencies are called upon to demonstrate their wise use of public monies.

EXPLAINING THE SIZE OF THE NATIONAL BUDGET

The national budget seems to be getting larger every year. Figure 17.1 illustrates the size of the budget from 1940 to 2010 (estimated). The budget increases to pay for World War II and **New Deal** programs are much smaller than our total annual national government expenditures in the early twenty-first century. In 2008 dollars, the estimated 2010 U.S. government expenditure will exceed $2.9 trillion.

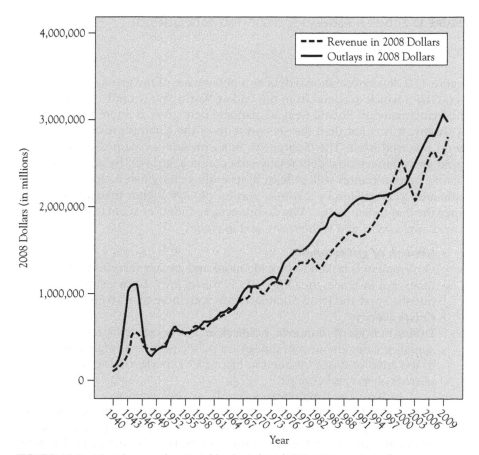

FIGURE 17.1 Historic annual national budget data (1940–2010, projected).

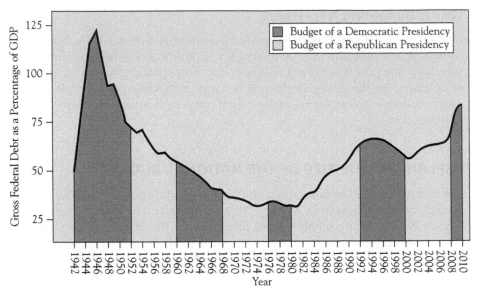

FIGURE 17.2 Debt as a percentage of GDP (1942–2010, projected).

Figure 17.2 illustrates national debt as a percentage of the gross domestic product (GDP), which declined from the end of World War II until 1981. Following the inauguration of Ronald Reagan, national debt grew at a rate faster than the economy. It was not until the second term of the Clinton presidency that the trend reversed itself. The George W. Bush presidency witnessed a return to rapid growth in national debt relative to economic growth. By all accounts, the Obama administration will, at least in its early years, push national debt to an estimated $11.8 trillion by 2010—a portion of GDP higher than anything seen since the mid-to-late 1940s. Why do budget expenditures seem to be growing at such a rapid pace, and is there any end in sight?

- *Growth of government*
  Government is tasked to provide more and greater services than in earlier times. For instance, the Office of Chemistry grew from a single employee into the Food and Drug Administration with more than 10,000 employees.[1]
- *Crisis theory*
  During periods of economic, political, and/or social crisis, the government spends greater amounts of money on public policies designed to respond to the crisis or crises. As seen in Figure 17.1, budgets tend to increase in periods of war and conflict.

  In 2009, the United States faced a serious economic downturn and Presidents Bush and Obama, majorities in Congress, and key state and local-level politicians and business leaders were proponents of government bailout for the domestic automobile, banking, and housing industries, to name but a few major industrial-sector beneficiaries. The crisis and response has contributed greatly to a rise in budget deficits and the national debt. The government response to the current crises may also lead to budget increases in a variety of ancillary policies, such as education and transportation.

- *Wagner's Law*
  Government growth tends to parallel the growth of the private sector. Government grows to meet needs created by businesses; for example, the automobile led to the need for modern roads and highways.
- *Federalism*
  The rise of cooperative federalism led to the expansion of the national government budget into policy areas previously considered to be the sole responsibility of states and local governments.
- *Public choice explanation*
  The national government has increased its level of spending because institutional changes (e.g., the Sixteenth Amendment to the U.S. Constitution) and technology changes have led to greater ease in the collection of large sums from consistent revenue streams. A current example of the role of technology in taxation, on-board global positioning systems (GPS) installed in new automobiles and trucks would make it possible for government to implement a vehicle miles taxation (VMT) policy, possibly tracking motorists' routes, miles driven, and time of travel.
- *Institutionalism*
  Increased budget expenditure for policy benefiting a voting constituency is likely to benefit institutional actors' ability to retain power through re-election.
- *Incrementalism*
  Previous expenditure levels are generally the reference point for new budget decisions—most budgets have a tendency to grow over time.

BUDGET CYCLE

Budget Preparation

At the national level, the Executive Branch is required to collect agency budget requests and to submit a unified budget document to Congress for consideration. The **Office of Management and Budget (OMB)** is the Executive Branch agency that works closely with the president and White House staff to coordinate budgeting, collecting agency budget requests and adding presidential priorities to the budget. The first step in budget preparation requires the OMB to estimate revenue availability for the upcoming **fiscal year**—the one-year period of time beginning October 1 and ending the following September 30. The OMB projects revenues by using statistical models to examine economic trends and tax revenue trends. Based on projected revenues and budget priorities, the OMB estimates agencies' expected budget size. Agency budget officers use OMB estimates to recalculate agencies' projected budget.

Budget Formulation

After agencies submit their budget requests to the OMB and adjustments are made, the agency budgets are combined into a unified budget document. The executive or president's budget is usually submitted to Congress in January, approximately ten months prior to the end of the previous fiscal year. The president's budget document is introduced to Congress and promptly rejected. Congress then divides up sections of the president's budget proposal among its **authorization committees**.

The authorization committees vote to recognize the continued legal existence of agencies and the power of agencies to make implementation and spending decisions. The committees also hold budget hearings, inviting agency executives to testify with regard to their budget requests. Also, pressure group representatives may be invited to testify to the importance of budget and policy items; the groups also directly lobby legislators.

Around the same time, **budget committees** in each legislative chamber conduct their own revenue analysis in conjunction with **ways and means** (House) and **finance** (Senate) **committees**, determining the level of funding feasible for each agency budget request, and send strict guidelines to committees reviewing agency requests. The budget committees were added to the budget process in an attempt to better coordinate budgeting activities.

After agency budgets are reviewed by appropriate committees—usually, committees whose general policy area is related to agency goals—agency budgets are amended and sent to the budget committees for review to determine whether the request will match expected revenues. Once reviewed by appropriations committees, agency requests are closely evaluated by the budget committees-since the adoption of Gramm-Rudman-Hollings in 1987, a landmark legislative act that sought to limit deficit spending.

The **appropriations committees** in both legislative chambers retain a significant role, determining whether agency requests have been reviewed and revised by appropriate legislative committees, and decide whether the requests can be adequately financed. The appropriations committees, therefore, have a great deal of power in the level of financing for authorized agencies.

Appropriations committees organize the budget into thirteen appropriations bills. If successfully reported out of the appropriations committees, the bills are debated and a floor vote occurs. Appropriations bills are generally accompanied to the chamber floor by revenue bills, outlining the taxes, fees, and duties to generate revenue needed to meet budgeted outlays. Frequently, revenue does meet outlays, the budget is not balanced, and there is a budget deficit. Government generally borrows money to make up the shortfall.

After the thirteen appropriation bills are passed in both legislative chambers, the budget goes to a conference committee composed of members of the Senate and House where differences in bills are ironed out. Once the budget resolutions are approved in conference committee, the bills are returned to each chamber for another floor vote. If the budget passes in identical form in both legislative chambers, it is sent to the president who either signs or vetoes the bills.

The U.S. Treasury generally does not give an agency its entire appropriation in one lump sum. There are at least two reasons for this:

1. *Fiscal integrity and accountability*
   The Treasury gives out smaller amounts on a regular basis to prevent the possibility of large-scale financial mismanagement leading to overspending.
2. *Cash flow*
   The U.S. Treasury does not have the entire appropriated amount because revenues are collected over the course of the fiscal year.

The U.S. Treasury uses economic projections and tax revenue projections. When "inflow of revenues" (Lee et al. 2007, 357) cannot be projected with a high degree of certainty, implementing agencies could grind to a halt. Fortunately for the national government, revenue shortfalls can be overcome through short-term borrowing. At other times, revenues exceed expenditures, and government must securely invest the money for future use.

The final stage of the budgetary process is the drafting of the next fiscal year's budget. The next two or three years' draft budget documents are likely being considered during the current fiscal year. In some instances, five-year budget projections are included in the budget request document for the next fiscal year. Projections help policy-implementing agencies use the budget as a planning document.

A BIT ABOUT NATIONAL GOVERNMENT PUBLIC FINANCE

When money is paid out by the U.S. Treasury to agencies, it is transferred into specific agency *funds* for policy-related activities. Funds are generally organized by *purpose* of funding, to ensure that money will be spent to implement public policy in a specific manner and along a specific timeline. A **preaudit** is conducted to determine whether an agency's funds and planned spending patterns are consistent with the goals of the public policies it is authorized to implement.

Agency balance sheets generally follow the basic accounting formula: Assets = Liabilities + Equity. Assets are typically the cash and other forms of revenue coming into an agency. For example, the Park Service has an **operating budget**, money allocated to it for day-to-day operations along with earmarks and **trust funds**. Trust funds are designated for a specific purpose, whereas **earmarks** are "pork barrel" monies designated for a specific project in a legislator's district or state. In this example, the Park Service assets also include monies raised from taxes, fees, and rents collected from the use of parks by individual citizens and businesses. Funds that are not spent in a relatively short period of time must be managed just as one might manage one's own money—in some form of account or investment. Secure accounts are very important for government resources, and investment is typically in U.S. Treasury bonds.

Revenue is allocated to departments and agencies over the course of the fiscal year. The bureaucracy maintains accountability, linking expenditures to specific policy goals and outcomes. Two general categories of expenditure are outlined in most budget summaries: mandatory and discretionary. Mandatory expenditures usually relate to entitlements or clearly specified requirements that must be met by the agency, whereas discretionary expenditures have greater flexibility. Expenditure is broken down further in terms of program. Within a program, expenditure is broken down along the component parts of the expenditure's program goals.

Agency accounting generally follows **Generally Accepted Accounting Principles** (GAAP), which are important in managing resources and ensuring accountability. At the end of the fiscal year, GAAP becomes particularly important to individuals conducting **postaudits** to determine whether authorizations were spent appropriately. A postaudit may also reveal the need for budgetary reformulation in the next fiscal year, reformulation that would improve policy implementation.

Government finance requires that program expenditures be tied to program outcomes, an approach known as **performance budgeting**. Usually, performance budgeting is found in program, agency, or department annual reports. Unlike the accountant's balance sheets, the performance budget reports aggregate expenditure by program and includes a narrative discussion of what was accomplished by the program during the fiscal year.

REVENUE STREAMS

Revenue comes from many sources: income taxes (personal and corporate), Social Security and retirement account taxes, unemployment taxes, excise taxes (duties on imported goods), and monies often collected in the form of permits and user fees paid into trust funds for policy areas such as transportation and the environment. Personal income taxes are by far the largest revenue stream. Corporate taxes are a much smaller amount of tax revenue generated. Social Security taxes, paid by workers and employers, are theoretically dedicated to Social Security—in reality, the money is either paid out to beneficiaries or used for other programs for current year expenditures. (See Figure 17.3.)

A **graduated income tax rate** is used to determine the amount of taxes an individual pays. This means that the more income made, the higher the tax rate. Tax rates are adjusted by Congress in the tax code and applied by the Internal Revenue Service (IRS). Personal income tax rates range from 10 to 35 percent, depending upon income level.[2] Corporate tax rates range from 15 to 38 percent.[3] Tax rates, however, explain only part of taxation. The tax code offers incentives for certain behaviors, such as buying a home (interest deduction). Capital improvements made by corporations can be deducted based on formula calculations. (See Figure 17.3.)

In presidential elections, candidates often challenge income tax systems. Democrats often claim that the tax codes are unfair to the "working and middle classes," whereas Republicans often claim that the wealthy are unfairly paying the bulk of income taxes. The issue is important because it goes back to our understanding of classical and modern liberalism. A classical liberal might favor a flat tax rate, whereas a modern liberal would want to see the least benefited paying the smallest amount. The percentile ranking of income compared to the proportion of personal income tax paid offers some insight. A significant portion of income tax paid is collected from the wealthiest members of U.S. society. (See Figure 17.4[4].)

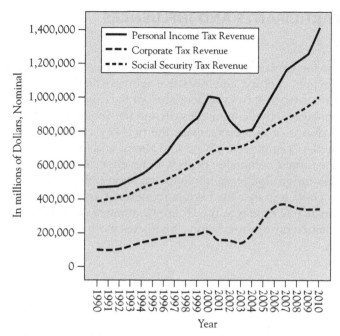

FIGURE 17.3 Three biggest national revenue streams (1990–2010, projected).

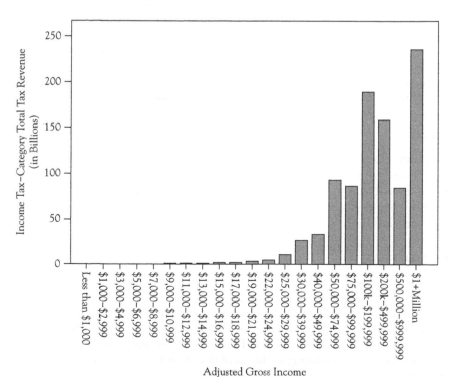

FIGURE 17.4 Individual income tax paid by income level (2005).

MAJOR PARTICIPANTS AND INFLUENCES

Congress

Congress has the power to raise revenue and to pay government debts. Until the early twentieth century, administrative agencies made their budget requests directly to Congress. Within Congress, most of the budget process was handled by four committees—two committees each in the Senate and House.

In the House of Representatives, the two key committees for budgeting decisions are the Committee on Ways and Means and the Committee on Appropriations. The former committee deals with revenue collection, of particular interest to pressure groups trying to shape taxation policy. Appropriations is in charge of stitching together the budget requests of agencies. The Senate Committee on Finance is similar to the House Committee on Ways and Means. The Senate Committee on Appropriations completes work similar to its counterpart in the House.

President

In the early twentieth century, two major changes impacted the president's role in the budget process. First, the ratification of the Sixteenth Amendment to the U.S. Constitution in 1913 authorized Congress to levy an income tax on all individual incomes in the nation, making the budget more directly relevant to all citizens.

Second, the Budget Act of 1921 created the Bureau of the Budget (BOB). The Budget Act authorized the president to submit a national budget to Congress on an annual basis. The BOB collected and analyzed agency budget requests and included these requests in the president's budget document, thus ending the practice of direct budget requests by agencies to Congress. Budgeting became more nationally focused and the president—the only nationally elected figure—was now at the center of the budget process.

Courts

The courts do not have a direct role in the budget process. Through legal decisions, however, the court can directly order agencies and elected officials to increase expenditures. For example, prison overcrowding may violate prisoners' constitutional rights, leading the federal courts to mandate improvements in living conditions; improvements cost money.

Bureaucracy

Bureaucrats play a significant and growing role in shaping budget decisions. The Office of Management and Budget (OMB, formerly known as BOB) assists the president in analyzing agencies' policy outcomes in relation to budget allocations and requests. The Congressional Budget Office (CBO) is Congress's version of the OMB. At times, the OMB and CBO use different assumptions and analytic techniques, resulting in different conclusions about revenue projections and expenditures.

Agencies submitting budget requests play a significant role in shaping the budget process, choices, and outcomes. Given their proximity to public policy and implementation, agency personnel tend to be supportive of the policies for which they are accountable—they believe that their policy function is something that government *ought* to do. Bureaucrats are, therefore, inclined to enlarge the scope of their agencies' efforts by requesting increases in budget resources. Bureaucrats provide information to elected officials about what government is or is not doing, which can shape policymakers' views of what government *ought* or *ought not* do.

Pressure Groups

Pressure groups play a significant role in the public policy process and budgeting choices are certainly no exception. Whereas pressure groups are primarily interested in shaping policy choices, policy formation and implementation require sufficient funding. Pressure groups, therefore, must remain continually vigilant of the budget process in order to accomplish their policy goals.

Media

News stories shape public awareness of extant or nascent policy issues. The U.S. Department of Education budget has grown, in part due to media stories regarding problems facing public elementary and secondary education. News reports about the plight of children, the poor, and battered women have shaped public awareness and opinion, ultimately reflected in budget priorities.

Campaigns and Elections

The budget is an inherently political document. In aggregate, the allocation of resources is a reflection of what our elected officials and administrators believe that government *ought* or *ought not* do. During campaigns and elections, candidates for office often discuss the budget, either directly or indirectly.

Direct references to the budget during campaigns and elections also reflect differences in views about the proper scope of government. Individuals who are politically left of center tend to support a larger role for government in managing the economy and shaping political and social equality. Individuals who are right of center politically generally support smaller government.

When policy priorities are discussed, the budget is being indirectly discussed because policy prioritization is often reflected in budgetary choices. When voters elect officials to public office, the official's references to the budget will likely impact budget outcomes. Vote choice represents a choice about the cost of government and a basket of goods purchased—in other words, public policy.

Domestic Socioeconomic Conditions

The chronic issues of poverty, health care, housing, employment, food and water supplies, and urban decay have become major functions of government and are reflected in budget priorities. Government tries to stimulate a weak economy through social welfare policy, public works policy, and economic stimulus policies.

Philosophy of governance, however, shapes the method by which government seeks to stimulate economic growth. In early 2008, through the Economic Stimulus Act, former President George W. Bush sought to use tax rebates as a method of stimulating *private* economic activity. In early 2009, through the $787 billion American Recovery and Reinvestment Act, President Barack Obama sought to use *public* expenditure to stimulate the economy. Alternative to these reactive solutions, government may proactively try to prevent certain forms of socioeconomic crisis from occurring rather than reacting to evolving crises.

BUDGET THEORY

Role Theory

Our eighteenth-century classically liberal Constitution provides the national government with a blueprint for revenue collection and appropriations. Congress is responsible for the budget and for revenue collection and appropriations for various Article I Section 8 duties. At an earlier time, the duties of the national government were fairly limited. The Tariff on imported goods was a fairly consistent revenue source. When budget deficits occurred, the government sold bonds for revenue. The U.S. government has never defaulted on its debts.

In the late nineteenth century, Congress experienced greater internal turbulence in the budget process. Budget items grew in number and size as the nation became more industrialized and urbanized. A growing immigrant population created new challenges for government in terms of public services. The politics of public budgeting became more complex.

In the House of Representatives, the Committee on Ways and Means, the Committee on Appropriations, and the various standing committees that dealt with authorization became embroiled in minor but noteworthy political turmoil. The decision over what government *ought* or *ought not* do was fought in relation to the budget process. Ways and Means wanted to use its power over revenue to shape decisions related to budget priorities; Appropriations felt these decisions were more in keeping with its stated purpose of determining allocations.

In the twentieth century, institutional actors sought methods of reducing conflict. An informal relationship between the House, Senate, and presidency developed with the intent of making an eighteenth-century system more effective in the modern world. The basis of the relationship is known as **role theory**.

Under role theory, the presidency is a *policy and budget advocate*. As the only nationally elected leader, it is assumed that the president's vision for the nation is the closest representation to the desires of the People. It was believed that the chief executive's annual budget submission would approximate national budget priorities.

In role theory, the House of Representatives acts as a *guardian* in the budget process. Constitutionally, money bills originate in the House, revenue policy being a critical aspect of budgeting. The House has traditionally played a supreme legislative role in appropriations decisions. As guardian, the House of Representatives was seen as a check on the president's budget priorities, limiting the size and scope of the budget and maintaining balance. The guardian role worked quite well when the nation was agrarian. Until 1920, more than 50 percent of the population lived in rural areas. Rural-dwelling individuals tend to have greater independence from society, in most instances, raising their own food. Congresspeople of the time represented largely rural individuals whose top priorities tended to be water management—dams for flood control and irrigation, or inland waterways for transportation. The House, therefore, was quite naturally a legislative body that desired to keep expenditures low and did not place in high priority national expenditures for urban problems—health, education, and social policy.

Under role theory, the Senate dealt with *appeals*. If the president and the House were in opposition in terms of revenue and expenditure priorities, the Senate would act as an institutional tie-breaker. The model worked well in the early twentieth century because the Senate was not yet a directly elected legislative body. Prior to the Seventeenth Amendment to the U.S. Constitution, senators were elected in each state by respective state legislatures. The Senate tended to be an insular body. State legislatures were dominated by social and economic elites (particularly, state-level Senates), and U.S. senators tended to be conservative.

Role theory worked well for most of the twentieth century and served as an effective remedy for modern budgeting under an eighteenth-century Constitution. As Congress evolved, the membership of the House became more urbanized. Additionally, members of Congress served multiple terms, effectively professionalizing the House. In order to retain constituency support, Congress focuses on policies that are important to constituents, such as casework—the legislative representative acting as an ombudsman or advocate for constituents in their relations with government agencies. Legislative norms (informal rules and traditions that govern the interaction between legislators) and political party control over members declined. The combined effect was that the guardian role of the House was diminished and it assumed an *advocate* role. Now directly elected by citizens of a state, the Senate has paralleled the House in professionalization and in adopting an *advocate* role.

The decline of role theory means that budgetary growth is not effectively limited by institutional constraints. The ability to prioritize budget expenditures, and to therefore establish some general sense of what government *ought* or *ought not* do, has become supremely challenging. As role theory has declined, budget reform models designed to rationalize the budgetary process and choices have become more visible in an attempt to develop new methods of reducing budgetary complexity and the potential for conflict.

Consensus Model

The consensus model of budgeting describes the budget process from the late eighteenth century until the early 1970s. The **consensus model** is an approach to public budgeting that was based largely on the idea that the budgeting process should discourage complexity and conflict in the decision-making process. In the eighteenth and nineteenth centuries, budgeting was not very complex. The policy goals of government were limited; the policy solutions were fairly simple. The United States was a growing nation with many imported goods taxed by the Tariff—a primary source of national revenue. Conflict over budget priorities was limited because revenue was consistent and policy minimal.

Twentieth-century Progressive politics led to the proliferation of public policy. The products and working conditions of the Industrial Age necessitated government regulation. The Navy commissioned a fleet of steam-powered warships. Victory in the Spanish-American War produced an American "empire" extending from the Caribbean Sea to Central America to the Philippine Islands in the western Pacific Ocean. A decade or so later, the United States entered World War I, necessitating the funding of a large army.

Combined, these massive changes stressed the budget system. The ability to achieve budgetary consensus was diminished as the process was increasingly driven by policy complexity and of the challenges of budget prioritization. In an effort to meet the goals of the consensus model, Congress divested itself of much of its budgetary authority, ceding it to the president—the foundation of role theory in which the president was designated as the budget advocate.

In *The New Politics of the Budgetary Process*, Aaron Wildavsky and Naomi Caiden argue that the budget is central to policy-making in a democratic society. Budgetary consensus reflects our representative democracy's ability to reach agreement on policy priorities and the capacity of government to be held accountable for the decisions made on behalf of citizens. The consensus model of budgeting demonstrates the strength of modern representative democracy to meet the needs of citizens through stable, adequately funded policy priorities. The authors also document the more recent failures of the consensus model, failures that have paralleled rapid growth in the national budget and—for a substantial period of time—unprecedented growth in budget deficits and national debt.

Dissensus Model

The **dissensus model** of budgeting is characterized by growing complexity and goal conflict in the budgetary process, and growing animosity between the presidency and Congress as well as within Congress. The dissensus model of budgeting is characterized by the following circumstances:

1. Efforts at budget reform that seek to limit conflict by limiting active decision-making. Balanced budget initiatives, for example, seek to limit conflict through automatic across-the-board budget cuts when revenues fall short of planned expenditure.
2. The growth of entitlement programs (e.g., unemployment, Social Security, Medicare) and the shrinking of discretionary spending. Entitlement expenditure is nondiscretionary and reactive to the needs of citizens and/or clientele. Conversely, discretionary budget expenditures involve proactive budgeting—the conscious decision to spend an amount of money on a policy or program. Reducing discretionary spending as a proportion of the

budget, however, may actually lead to greater conflict over how to spend the small portion remaining.

POLITICS OF ENTITLEMENT

Entitlement programs are linked to government's responsibility to "promote the General Welfare."[5] Entitlements are rights-based and serve the needs of the individual if the individual condition or circumstance exists within certain prescribed social, economic, racial, or ethnic parameters.

Responding to the social and economic maladies of the Great Depression, New Deal programs created a variety of entitlement programs. In the 1960s, Great Society programs were a massive expansion of entitlement programs and spending. Well over half of the national budget expenditures are designated for entitlement programs. Currently, the "big three" entitlement programs are focused on the elderly and the indigent, which is consistent with the principles of modern liberalism.

The "big three" mandatory social programs (2008 estimate, percent of total mandatory budget expenditure)

Social Security	$761.8 billion
Medicare	$508.8 billion
Medicaid	$273.3 billion
Total:	$1,543.9 billion (76.7 percent of mandatory expenditure)

Source: www.whitehouse.gov/omb/budget/fy2008/fct.html (accessed August 17, 2007).

THE BUDGET AND IMPLICATIONS FOR POLICY

Whether consensual or dissensual, the outcome of the budgetary process reveals a great deal about the preferences of elected representatives and of the People. First, the budget process demonstrates an ability or inability to establish policy priorities within the confines imposed by limited resources. In that sense, the national government has not exhibited the ability to work within budget resource constraints, thus leading to budget deficits and growth of national debt.

Second, the priorities that are established through the budget reveal the continual evolution of what we collectively think government *ought* or *ought not* do. Entitlements reflect a belief in an immutable set of core values, a belief that an identified set of least-benefited members of society has a fundamental right to social and economic justice via public policy. The entitlement programs reflect the very significant role of modern liberalism in the public policy process. With regard to their role in the dissensual model of budgeting, entitlements also reflect a conflict-burdened area of public policy, a serious debate between classical and modern liberalism. By establishing entitlements, this debate is largely ignored, possibly at our own peril as national debt continues to rise.

Third, the outcome of the budget process is an important part of legitimizing our representative democracy. Successful completion of a budget is indicative of the successful operation of the deliberative process necessary for democratic policy-making. Inability to produce a budget may reveal weaknesses in representative democracy.

Fourth, the budget reflects our demands on public policy, but it also reflects our desire to see those demands met. Budgeting allows us to measure our expenditures and to determine whether those expenditures on public policy have produced desired outcomes. It is a method of holding representative democratic government accountable to sovereigns: the citizenry.

EXPLAINING PUBLIC BUDGETING

All the models of public policy listed in Chapter 2 could conceivably be used to explain budgeting. However, only three will be applied here: incrementalism, new institutionalism, and group theory.

Incrementalism

Incrementalism accepts the impossibility of a fully rational and comprehensive decision-making process. Incrementalism is consistent with the consensual model of public budgeting. In a Congress composed of a growing number of long-serving members, one method of maintaining institutional tranquility is to eschew ongoing debate over the same set of issues—instead, institutions seek lasting compromise.

Incrementalism also helps one understand the weaknesses in the public budgeting process. First, incrementalism invites myopic decision-making. In other words, budget-makers are focused on accomplishing short-term goals, reducing process-related conflict and complexity. Significant problems on the policy horizon are often ignored. For instance, the potential for a budgetary "train wreck" for Social Security and Medicare is often discussed, but little is actually done to solve the problems. Second, incrementalism is highly pragmatic. Whatever government *does do* is seen as a given—that is, existing public policy is generally composed of accepted and largely unquestioned goals and processes. Whatever government *does not* do, however, is the source of most agenda setting. In other words, incrementalism avoids hard questions about shrinking government, but remains open to the idea of further growth. Third, incrementalism does not legitimize the representative democratic process. Public budgeting may be less responsive to current policy demands and more responsive to past choices. Paraphrasing early-twentieth-century social and political observer G. K. Chesterton, incrementalism is the democracy of the dead: an effectively conservative approach whereby past decision-makers have a hand in current budget choices.

New Institutionalism

New institutionalism theorizes that outcomes are a function of institutional rules, processes, structure, and norms, as well as the values, opinions, beliefs, and self-interest of the individuals operating within those institutions. As noted previously, when it comes to determining the cost of public policy, the roles and relative power of the constitutionally established institutions of government have changed substantially. The president has a larger role as a policy agenda setter, and this role carries over to the issue of establishing budget priorities, but the role of the president in managing government efficiency—one of the primary goals of the Budget Act of 1921—has largely been lost. With a maximum two terms in office, the president often pushes a policy agenda rather than deal with the hard issue of controlling spending.

Congress has lapsed in its role in controlling spending. Instead, it too has become an advocate for spending, but in a manner that fulfills the parochial interests of its membership and their local and state constituencies. The congressional norms and strong party controls often give way to the individual interests of the elected representatives. The members often view Congress as a career, and avoid decisions threatening chances of reelection. The personal values of Congress people often override the constraints imposed by institutional norms. The U.S. Senate is often viewed as a nationally representative body and as a "jumping off" point for a presidential bid. Senators are also interested in pursuing policy spending in areas that reflect their national policy priorities.

The bureaucracy can also be described using new institutional theory. The implementation process should be conducted in a politically neutral fashion, but evidence indicates that bureaucrats are often policy advocates. As advocates, they envision their policy area as supremely important and seek resources to implement in a manner reflective of their personal and organizational values.

Group Theory

Interest groups have also proliferated in the last thirty years. These groups pursue narrow policy agendas and attempt to achieve a "win" by influencing policy adoption and pursuing the budget resources necessary to implement those policies. Interest groups are adversarial and primarily interested in achieving their narrow goals at all costs. Interest groups influence elected officials through campaign donations, gaining access to elected officials and advancing their policy messages. The groups also influence public bureaucrats by striking informal deals to offer mutual support in the pursuit of common budget goals. Pressure groups directly and indirectly influence budget decisions through their actions and have contributed to growth in the national budget.

Lessons Learned from Chapter 17

SPECIFICS

- Budgeting involves establishing financial priorities in public policy.
- Budget growth is a function of our demands as well as the complexity of the policy issues that modern society must address.
- The budget cycle is a nearly continuous process of preparation, formulation, execution, and auditing.

- Role theory, consensus theory, and dissensus theory are three prominent approaches used to explain the politics of public budgeting.
- The "big three" entitlement programs represent approximately 76 percent of mandatory spending at the national level.

THE BIG PICTURE

Public budgeting is probably the most important part of the policy process. With few exceptions, public policy requires resources to meet goals. Without sufficient resources, it is unlikely that policy formulation, implementation, and evaluation will lead to desired outcomes. Due to institutional dynamics and the size of the national government budget, it is increasingly difficult to conduct a thorough analysis of policy priorities. Incrementalism makes budget processes less responsive to changing priorities. If the budget is any indication, it would seem that a grim pragmatism has settled upon the budget process and the debate between what government *ought* or *ought not* do has been left by the wayside, whereas what government *does* do continues to expand. The current economic crisis facing the United States in 2009 and beyond poses a unique opportunity to engage in a serious debate about the role of government. Reflecting back on the public opinion poll data reported in an earlier chapter, it would seem that younger generations lean toward public solutions to societal problems rather than the free market. With public opinion in mind, it is likely that public budgeting challenges will continue well into the future.

Key Terms

appropriations committees	graduated income tax rate
authorization committees	New Deal
budget committees	Office of Management
budget cycle	and Budget (OMB)
cash flow	operating budget
consensus model	performance budgeting
dissensus model	postaudits
earmarks	preaudit
finance committee	public budgeting
fiscal year	role theory
Generally Accepted Accounting	trust funds
Principles (GAAP)	Ways and Means

Questions for Study

1. What are the major steps in the budgetary process? Identify and discuss.
2. What are three major explanations for budgetary growth? Identify and discuss. What is an entitlement? How do entitlements impact budgetary growth?
3. Compare and contrast the consensual model of budgeting with the dissensual model of budgeting.

Group Project for Discussion

Study the president's current budget proposals (see current budget proposal spreadsheet tables at www.whitehouse.gov/omb) and determine where spending cuts *ought* to occur, if at all. Identify all major program areas where government is performing a function that you believe it ought not do and cut them from the budget—compare your decisions with the decisions of others in your group. Form some type of compromise that group members can support.

Bibliography

Chesterton, G. K. 1909. *Orthodoxy.* New York: John Lane Company.

Cox, J., G. Hager, and D. Lowery. 1993. Regime change in presidential and congressional budgeting: Role discontinuity or role evolution? *American Journal of Political Science.* 37(1): 88–118.

Kettl, D. 2003. *Deficit politics: The search for balance in American politics.* New York: Longman.

Key, V. 1940. A lack of budgetary theory. *American Political Science Review.* 34: 1137–1140.

Lee, R., R. Johnson, and P. Joyce. 2007. *Public budgeting systems,* 8th ed. Boston: Jones and Bartlett.

Lewis, V. 1952. Toward a theory of public budgeting. *Public Administration Review.* 12(1): 43–54.

Lynch, T. 1985. *Public budgeting in America,* 2nd ed. Englewood Cliffs, NJ: Prentice Hall.

Meyers, R., ed. 1999. *Handbook of government budgeting.* San Francisco: Jossey-Bass.

Nice, D. 2002. *Public budgeting.* Belmont, CA: Wadsworth.

Rubin, I. 1992. *The politics of public budgeting,* 2nd ed. Chatham, NJ: Chatham House.

Schick, A. 1990. *The capacity to budget.* Washington, DC: Urban Institute Press.

Wildavsky, A., and N. Caiden. 1997. *New politics of the budgetary process,* 4th ed. New York: Addison-Wesley/Longman.

Endnotes

1. Schmit, J. 2008. FDA receives modest boost in budget plan. *USA Today,* February 17. www.usatoday.com/money/industries/food/2008-02-04-fda-budget-food-safety_N.htm (accessed May 31, 2009).
2. Internal Revenue Service, www.irs.gov/pub/irs-pdf/f1040es.pdf (accessed August 19, 2007).
3. IRS Form 1120, U.S. Corporation Income Tax Return.
4. Data: Statistical Abstract of the United States, 2009.
5. Preamble of the U.S. Constitution.

Conclusion

■ ■ ■

Future of Public Policy

CHAPTER OVERVIEW

Sometimes, the best way to comprehend the future is to consider the past and the trends that have developed over the years. In the United States, there are at least two major visions of what government *ought* or *ought not do*. Policy history shows us how, over time, each approach rises and falls in popularity. Both approaches claim to embody the true meaning of liberal democracy and each claims relevance in addressing current issues. Sometimes, their goals and values converge, but there are several instances where they abruptly diverge.

VISIONS OF LIBERALISM

The earliest vision of liberalism is Lockean classical liberalism. It outlines a very narrow role for government. The Founders were, for the most part, Lockean classical liberals. Many of the modern-day proponents of this vision argue that the national government should do very little in the way of public policy. As "strict constructionists"—individuals who take a narrow and literal interpretation of our Constitution, the social contract—these individuals see limited powers for the national government. At the national level, government should do little more than provide for the common defense. Given that Article III powers (the national judiciary) have a limited discussion of the federal court system, the strict constructionists largely reject the powers that the national courts have, in their view, assumed for themselves through expansive interpretations of the Constitution. Lockean classical liberals often feel the same way about Congress and the presidency in terms of power expansion.

State governments are often viewed by classical liberals as the appropriate level of government for much of the public policy that exists today. Through competition between state governments, citizens are more likely to obtain the policies they want at the tax rate they desire. If citizens are not able to obtain what they want at the desired tax rate, they are free to either vote in new elected officials or move to another state and take their money with them. They vote via either the ballot box or with their feet (and pocketbooks). Classical liberals feel that this dual method of influence produces a more responsive and effective government.

Classical liberals often extend this metaphor to the marketplace, arguing that state governments will likely be unable to provide many of the public policies that citizens may desire at a given price. Additionally, without the role of the federal courts in expanding interpretations of a "public good," government will be less likely to be obliged to protect certain resources and the distribution of these resources will, therefore, be a function of private sector forces rather than legal mandate. The private sector force will be the marketplace, where citizens are free to buy and sell commodities at prices that reflect supply and demand forces. Classical liberals argue that if what is today considered a public good were of limited quantity, prices would rise and the demand on that good would decline due to the fact that costs would be beyond the financial capacity of many consumers. The laws of economics would therefore indicate that supply would dictate consumerism rather than simple demand on a good.

In the United States, a second major perspective on what government *ought* or *ought not do* is modern liberalism. Modern liberals generally find that the arguments made by classical liberals are quaint in their simplicity, but clearly outdated and unworkable in the contemporary world. The modern liberal argues that justice is not simply a function of the *process* of establishing political justice, which can be thought of as the right to vote and the right to a fair trial. Justice cannot be thought of simply as the protection of one's property. Rather, justice must be thought of in terms of social, political, and economic *outcomes*. If the outcomes are not based in some notion of fairness, then process alone will not promote two other important democratic values: namely, freedom and equality. Freedom from interference, as classical liberal notions of the term are often considered, ignores the notion that, as citizens of a democracy, our positive freedom—our freedom to do things—should also be protected and advanced. Additionally, the process-driven classical liberals focus on equality before the law, but ignore equality of outcome. One can operate within the parameters of a law but can produce outcomes that are undemocratic, unfair, and unequal.

Therefore, modern liberals tend to envision a government that must continually search for ways to produce "just" outcomes, outcomes that promote equality and freedom as well as establish a sense of order in our society. The Constitution is seen by the modern liberal as a beginning, but not an end to our discussion of the social contract. The national government is a protector of social contract. Modern liberals look at American history and see confirmation of their premise: Namely, our nation has spent decade upon decade determining methods by which we could preserve our basic principles of government and enhance the lives of our citizens in a manner that promotes their rights and liberties detailed within the social contract. The Constitution is not a perfect document, but modern liberals believe that through a continued dialogue about the meaning of the Constitution and necessary expansion of government policy, and through the power of reason and reasonable consideration of policy choices, we can in some significant ways make the principles of the Founders relevant to today's citizens and prepare for a better tomorrow.

The classical liberal and modern liberal normative perspectives are an important part of determining the direction of public policy. As you will likely note from your knowledge of American political history, the classical liberal tradition is largely ensconced in the policy positions of Republicans, whereas the Democratic Party tends to advance the principles of modern liberalism. It would be inaccurate to say that there is not a great deal of overlap; in fact, many Republicans see some value in the principles of modern liberalism and many Democrats see merit in the principles of classical liberalism. So, it is not an even split between the political parties when it comes to their philosophy of government.

The Democratic control of Congress and the presidency during the New Deal and Great Society eras had a tremendous influence on advancing the principles of modern liberalism. The policy agenda, particularly in the areas of education and social policy, expanded to introduce many new policies that promoted equality and freedom. It also challenged the society to consider further the condition of social, political, and economic justice and what could or should be done to improve conditions for all citizens.

Although the Democratic Party played an active role in shaping the policy agenda during the New Deal and Great Society eras, a resurgence of the Republican Party in the 1980s established a changed policy agenda in the United States, one that has led the nation to reacquaint itself with its classical liberal roots. The Reagan presidency was the beginning of this movement, but the Republican takeover of the U.S. Congress during the 1990s more firmly established its role in shaping the national policy agenda. Although the Democratic Party did not divest itself of all principles of modern liberalism, its leaders in the 1990s advanced a more classically liberal policy agenda, an agenda that has led to a more critical analysis of modern liberal policy goals and their feasibility. In the current political and economic environment—namely, a Democratically controlled Congress and presidency leading during a period of significant economic turmoil—it is likely that modern liberalism will reach greater prominence and achieve significant public support.

COMMODIFICATION/DECOMMODIFICATION

The classical liberal position encourages government to keep public policy to a minimum and to allow the free market to operate such that individual citizens can pursue their self-interest through economic choices. If a particular good or service is desired by a citizen, they can seek to fulfill their desire through economic choices. The modern liberal position, however, indicates that the marketplace often does not produce a desirable outcome. Many goods or services desired by individuals are in fact pursued during times of extreme need and with limited resources. For instance, how could an individual who is of low socioeconomic status pursue her needs when she is in poverty? Naturally, it would be impossible for her needs to be met and the marketplace as a solution would likely leave her without any proper assistance. The classical liberals offer a solution to this through the thoughts on social welfare expressed by John Stuart Mill (see Chapter 1), but this solution is largely private, the public policy aspects being very limited. Modern liberals point to Mill's words as evidence that classical liberalism, in a strict sense, is untenable and that it does not properly focus on the conditions of equality and freedom requisite in a liberal democracy.

Economists discuss this conflict of ideas between classical and modern liberals in a different manner, one that may shed further light on why we cannot arrive at a clear and lasting notion of what government *ought* or *ought not* do. In essence, the marketplace and the unevenness of economic conditions make free market capitalism both alluring and repugnant, constructive and destructive in the modern nation state. In times of prosperity, free market capitalism is often viewed as highly desirable by the majority of citizens because it creates wealth. In classical idiom, a rising tide lifts all boats—a successful free market environment leads to greater material wealth and many economic choices. But economic boom periods are often followed by "busts"—periods during which economic conditions deteriorate or stagnate. During these periods there is often a dearth of affordable resources and humanity turns away from the free market and toward government to provide basic goods and services via public policy, termed decommodification.

Economists who construct this view of economics and government—often termed "welfare economics"—argue that basic shifts in resource supply, marketplace conditions, and wealth distribution shape our views of what government *ought* or *ought not* do. In essence, classical and modern liberal thinkers both have something to offer us by way of explanation when it comes to our normative views of government and public policy. In one sense, our classical liberal roots tend to pull us away from collective policy choices and toward private sector free market choices. But modern liberalism is a recognition that conditions of individuals in society change with the changing tides of economics and that unequal conditions in society can be exacerbated by the very nature of the social, political, and economic system in which we live. Modern liberalism recognizes that we have a limited desire for risk and see some value in maintaining stability in our social, political, and economic position in society. Just as classical liberalism recognizes that we pledge ourselves to mutual defense of property and social order, so modern liberalism is a pledge to mutually assure a level of political, social, and economic justice in a modern free market liberal democratic state.

It is not just individuals who benefit from this balance between the free market approach and the government-based approaches to fulfilling needs. Corporations benefit from the welfare state, too. Government involvement in economic policy and in social welfare policy helps to improve economic conditions. Economic policy may lead to the lowering of interest rates for borrowing, which allows corporate enterprises to lower their economic costs and reduce their risks. Welfare policy helps to retool workers for new industries and helps to sustain workers during periods of unemployment or underemployment. In other words, the modern free market liberal democratic state necessitates that government and the private sector work together, balancing each other out and both working to solve mutual goals.

TECHNOLOGY AND THE FUTURE OF PUBLIC POLICY

Technology plays a significant role in shaping public policy formulation, implementation, and outcomes. It is the central element in the second part of policy definition: Technology shapes what government *can* and *cannot* do. Technology helps us in our development of theories and the testing of those theories. Greater specificity about the nature of policy problems and target populations is garnered through high-tech analyses. Policy formulation, therefore, is a function of the technological analyses that guide the formulation process. Implementation is also impacted by technology. Technology has helped us to more accurately pinpoint target populations and to gain a sense of the unique qualities of each member of that population, thus helping us to tailor policy implementation to best fit the needs of clientele and to improve the chances of policy success.

Technology, however, can have negative impacts on the policy process. In the effort to better understand citizens and their needs, government has collected a great deal of information about individuals. Our private economic, social, and political choices are known to various government agencies. The collection of this information often has zero impact on our individual lives. However, it can be argued, and is argued by some individuals, that such data collection and the processing of this data using high-tech statistical programs is a violation of our individual privacy.

Technology has helped government to remain relevant in the public policy realm and has made it so that government can still do the things that we desire; however, its impact on our individual lives may or may not lead to an ever-shrinking private-realm existence, a place where we remain unobserved. The debate over technology and its role in public policy returns us to the other element of our definition, namely, what government *ought* or *ought not* do.

VALUES AND THE FUTURE OF POLICY

Generation Y will soon begin to assume the reins of political power in the United States. In many ways, the basic values of this generation of citizens are not vastly different from their Baby Boomer and Generation X parents. This would imply a future stability in public policy priorities. In other ways, however, Generation Y represents a possible sea-change in public policy. Generation Y seems to respect strong beliefs that are based to a greater sense in idealism rather than pragmatism. Additionally, Generation Y tends toward support for groups that are often considered among the least benefited in our society, individuals and groups who have been historically disenfranchised or marginalized by society. Public policy will be heavily impacted by the values and the evolution of values in Generation Y. It is important for students of public policy to remain cognizant of Generation Y as it reaches maturity and produces political leaders who will shape public policy well into the twenty-first century.

CONCLUSION

This textbook was written with three primary goals. The first goal was to provide the reader with a basic understanding of the foundations of our normative debate over public policy and a sense that this debate is dynamic and continuous. The second goal was to provide the reader with a framework for the policy process that would serve as a template for a discussion of several well-known policy areas. The third goal was to provide the reader with a sense of the future or at least a framework by which to think about the future of public policy, realizing of course that the future cannot be known; rather, our glimpse into the future is based on a simple extrapolation from current knowledge and trends.

Generation Y and the idealism that it represents is an encouraging sign as American public policy advances into a new century, a new millennium. Idealism lies at the foundation of American democracy and offers public policy the lifeblood necessary to evolve in changing times. If public policy is what government *ought* or *ought not* do, then the policy debates that lie ahead will be as much shaped by our philosophic ideals as by the sheer pragmatism that emerges from a desire to pledge ourselves to the shared goal of preserving of our rights and opportunities for prosperity in an egalitarian nation state.

Bibliography

Offe, C. 1993. *Contradictions of the welfare state.* Cambridge, MA: MIT Press.

GLOSSARY

A

active managers. Individuals in management positions who delegate decision-making authority, while simultaneously attempting to maintain accountability.

Administration on Children and Families (ACF). A unit within Health and Human Services (HHS) that is primarily concerned with promoting strong and healthy families.

administrative law. The body of law developed by public agencies to better implement statutory law.

advocacy coalition. Policy networks incorporating interested citizens, pressure groups, and administrator voices, which develop policy processes, and shape policy formulation and implementation.

advocates. In Anthony Downs' *Inside Bureaucracy*, bureaucrats who are highly enthusiastic about a policy and often willing to try innovative approaches to problem solving and goal accomplishment.

agency culture. The norms and informal rules that govern the day-to-day behavior of personnel in an agency.

Agency for Healthcare Research and Quality (AHRQ). An agency within HHS, primarily concerned with analyzing the current quality of health care and conducting research to determine more effective and efficient methods of improving the quality and quantity of medical services.

aggregate level data. In policy analysis, usually data that describes a group of people.

alternative dispute resolution (ADR). An attempt to solve conflicts prior to a full legal hearing before a judge.

Amber Alert. Part of a nationwide effort to keep the public informed about child abductions in local communities.

ambiguity–conflict model. A model of policy implementation developed by Richard Matland involving two dimensions: policy ambiguity and policy conflict.

American Federation of Teachers. A nationally organized teachers' union.

analysis. A step in the scientific method, the process of analyzing empirical data collected.

Appropriations committees. The committees in Congress that determine budget expenditures.

assistant attorneys general. Prosecuting attorneys at the national government level.

authorization committees. Congressional committees that make decisions on the continued legal existence of agencies, and the power of agencies to make policy implementation and spending decisions.

B

Ballistic Missile Defense Organization (BMDO). Established by President Clinton in 1993, the organization was tasked with developing Theater Missile Defense (TMD) systems.

barrier. In policy implementation, anything besides the statute that impedes compliance.

behavioral science. A social–psychological approach that views individual behavior as partially a function of various stimuli as well as the unique qualities or condition of the individual.

benefit/cost analysis. Primarily concerned with comparing the amount of expected or known benefits produced from a particular policy choice with the expected or known costs associated with that choice.

Big Bang termination. A form of policy termination that occurs when policy is terminated quickly and completely.

block grants. A type of grant that generally does not specify policy goals and processes, leaving it up to state and local policy-makers to identify specific goals and policy methods. Block grants deemphasize accountability to national policy-makers, which may invite the potential for fiscal mismanagement or waste.

bottom-up policy-making. Policy formulation at the grassroots level.

***Brown v. Board of Education, Topeka, Kansas* (1954).** Court decision that resulted in the desegregation of education and other public services.

Brownlow Commission on Economy and Efficiency. In the mid-1930s, the Commission was tasked with determining the administrative support needs of a modern presidency, recommending the establishment of major bureaucratic support structures.

budget committees. Committees established as a method of reforming the budget process. The committees (one in each chamber of Congress) independently oversee the budget process, conducting budget analysis and making recommendations to appropriations committees on spending guidelines.

budget cycle. The process by which budgets are created, and revenues raised and expended.

bureaucratic model. A theoretical model of the "ideal" formal organization, described by Max Weber as having the following general characteristics: division of labor, clear leadership, system of files, formal communication, career employment, modern organizational structure, and merit-based hiring and promotion.

C

capture. In policy implementation, a condition where the process is significantly shaped by individual and group interests at the local level.

cash flow. In budgeting, the analysis of revenue and expenditure ensuring that adequate resources are available.

categorical grant. A grant designed to meet specific policy goals using predetermined methods (e.g., rules and regulations for policy implementation). The grant amounts for categorical grants are usually firmly established.

Centers for Disease Control (CDC). An agency within HHS that deals with, among other things: infectious disease, birth de-

fect documentation, environmental health, and occupational health and safety.

charter schools. A semiprivate school alternative in which charters (contract-based agreements) are granted to private education providers with stipulations regarding expected educational outcomes.

child abuse. Any violent actions or maltreatment committed against a child that are deemed to be physically or psychologically damaging to the victim.

Child Nutrition Program. A program within the U.S. Department of Agriculture (USDA) that nationally administers school meal programs, and adult and child nutrition programs.

class size. A policy theory arguing that smaller classes lead to improved educational outcomes.

classical liberalism. An early form of liberalism articulated in the seventeenth century by John Locke. Government is minimal, primarily designed to protect the life, liberty, and personal property of citizens.

cohort effects. A reference used by Ronald Inglehart and others to describe the impact of the general nature of the times on a group of citizens from the same generation. Impacts may be in the form of socialization experiences, values, opinions, and beliefs, as well as level and type of political participation. "Baby Boomer" is an example of an age cohort.

collaborative policy-making. A multidimensional and dynamic policy process in which all stakeholders actively educate each other about their understanding of public policy, expectations, limitations, and needs. Instead of focusing on singular leadership in policy-making, it invites all stakeholders to participate in collective leadership. Support for policy-making outcomes is enhanced because it is the product of mutual agreement.

commons. Goods that cannot be divided and sold but are consumed.

communitarianism. An approach to governance. Government is based in the emergence of social networks in society. Community, interpersonal trust, and shared interest are the basis of individual and collective action rather than a reliance on laws. In a communitarian society, "public policy" issues would often be solved through informal voluntary efforts.

community oriented policing (COP). A form of policing that focuses on community–police partnerships and neighborhood policing techniques to reduce fear of crime and increase levels of citizen trust of law enforcement agencies and personnel.

Congressional Budget Office (CBO). Created in 1974 to help Congress establish greater control over the budgeting process, the CBO studies the cost-related factors associated with policy formulation and may, if requested, discuss the financial feasibility of proposed policies reported in the bills being advanced by individual members of Congress or those being studied by various committees. The CBO also analyzes policy proposals within the president's budget as reported to Congress.

Congressional Research Service (CRS). Initially created in 1914 as the Legislative Reference Service, the Congressional Research Service conducts the bulk of policy research for members of Congress and congressional committees. The CRS deals with policy areas in both domestic and foreign policy.

conservers. In Anthony Downs' *Inside Bureaucracy,* bureaucrats who focus on agency survival rather than agency change or growth.

constitutionalism. The belief that the meaning of the Constitution is either expressly written in the document itself or can be gleaned from original writings of the Framers. Frequently used to describe the legal theories of judges or Supreme Court justices.

containment policy. A Cold War era policy advocating the control or limitation of communist influence rather than a direct assault on established communist regimes, such as the Soviet Union (U.S.S.R.) or the People's Republic of China (P.R.C.).

control group. In experimental design, under controlled conditions, the randomly selected group of individuals who do not receive the benefit of a policy.

cooperative federalism. A contemporary model of federalism, envisioning multiple systems (nation, state, and local) working together to solve problems.

corporatism. In simple terms, big government and corporations working in tandem to orchestrate public policy and the private marketplace.

cost-of-living adjustment (COLA). An adjustment made to payments usually reflecting inflation.

criminal procedure. The formal process by which an individual accused of a crime is determined to be guilty or innocent.

D

dealignment. Electoral shifts characterized by divided government and weaker presidencies and smaller and less stable congressional majorities.

decision theory. In public policy, a process by which policy analysts explore all possible contingencies extant in a particular policy; often associated with contingencies in policy formulation and implementation.

defense attorneys. Attorneys who represent the accused individual in a trial.

defense contractors. Private corporations that receive contracts from the U.S. government to supply goods and services to the U.S. Department of Defense and ancillary organizations engaged in defense-related enterprises.

deferral. In budgeting, the practice of delaying expenditures associated with policy implementation.

demography. The complex multidisciplinary process of studying populations, and their migration, present state, and changing condition over time.

devolution. In the 1980s and 1990s, the process by which many national-level policy responsibilities were returned or extended to the states and local levels to be formulated and implemented in an innovative manner and in ways consistent with state and local needs.

disposition of implementers. Usually shaped by agency culture, the often-emotive reaction of implementers to policy goals, processes, rules, and standards in the implementation process.

divided government. The condition under which one or both chambers of Congress are held by the majority of one political party, while the presidency is controlled by a person representing another political party.

dual federalism. An early form of federalism, envisioning two systems (nation and state) fulfilling distinct purposes without any significant overlap in function.

ducking responsibility. In public policy, a form of covert evaluation to avoid blame.

dystopians. Individuals who are often critical of utopianism, in part due to a perceived loss of privacy and individual choice.

E

economic theory. An approach used to explore the production, consumption, and distribution of goods and services in a community, society, or in the world. Economic theory can be divided between micro (individual choices) and macro (aggregate choices). Economic theory explores the distribution and exchange of wealth. Economics can be further divided between positivist (what "is") and normative (what "ought to be").

Elementary and Secondary Education Act. Reauthorized under No Child Left Behind (NCLB). *See* No Child Left Behind.

elite theory. A social science theory in which a small group of powerful actors (elites) control the political process and policy choices while the majority of citizens remain passive, often ill-informed, retaining minimal power. Elites are also viewed as controlling or heavily influencing social and economic conditions.

Environmental Protection Agency (EPA). An independent regulatory agency representing the first nationally organized effort to regulate human-caused impacts on the natural environment.

ethics. An individual's core beliefs regarding right and wrong, usually based in personal belief systems, professional codes, and social norms.

Executive Office of the President (EOP). The result of a Brownlow Commission recommendation, the EOP contains more than sixteen different suboffices and departments. In establishing the EOP and creating and organizing a whole host of ancillary offices within its auspices, Congress and the president recognized the chief executive's growing responsibility in policy formulation. EOP policy analysts develop public policies for the president's policy agenda, eventually proposed in draft form for congressional review, revisions, and approval or disapproval.

experiment. In public policy, under controlled conditions, the selective implementation of a policy to a randomly selected group of individuals, and comparing the change of condition for those individuals (experimental group) with at least one randomly selected group of individuals (control group) who did not receive the benefit of the policy.

experimental control. In experimental design, the intentional limiting of all influences on experimental and control groups that are not directly part of the intended treatment.

experimental group. In experimental design, under controlled conditions, the randomly selected group of individuals who receive the benefit of a policy.

expert testimony. Testimony provided by pressure groups, bureaucrats, and other interested parties to congressional committee hearings, usually with regards to public policy.

externalities. The unintended effects of a decision.

F

Fair Housing Act of 1968. Enforces elements of the Civil Rights Act of 1964, prohibiting discrimination in the sale or rental of dwellings or other dwelling-related dealings.

family social capital. The nature of family intergenerational value exchange and continuity.

federal environmental regulation. Federal laws passed to regulate environmental quality and manage common resources, such as air and water.

Federal Unemployment Tax Act (FUTA). The method by which unemployment compensation is financed.

federalism. The relationship between two or more levels of government within a nation–state; each level of government has leaders who are independently chosen and possess different types of power, responsibilities, and jurisdictions.

finance committee. A standing committee in the U.S. Senate that determines methods of obtaining revenue.

findings. In the scientific method, the comparison of data findings with theoretical expectations.

Fiscal federalism. The use of grants and revenue sharing by the national government to shape the policy choices of state and local government.

fiscal year. The one-year period of time beginning October 1 and ending the following September 30, during which public policy is financed through a budget.

focusing event. In Kingdon's model of agenda setting, the circumstances or behaviors of actors within the policy streams that cause the streams to converge.

Food and Drug Administration (FDA). Primarily responsible for the regulation of food and drug quality and safety, proper labeling of food and drug products, and to identify and control the use of biological toxins in the event of a terrorist attack.

Food and Nutrition Service (FNS). A program within the USDA that distributes food to schools, elderly, and low-income individuals.

Food Stamp Program. A program designed to ensure that indigent individuals are able to have access to a healthy diet, improving their status as healthy and productive people. As of October 2008, the Food Stamp Program is known as the Supplemental Nutrition Assistance Program (SNAP).

formal evaluation. A type of policy evaluation, usually conducted for statutory obligation.

formula grants. Grants in which resource amounts are a function of the number of individuals being served by a policy or other demographic indicators.

free good. Nonexcludable goods to which all individuals have access, at no cost to the individual.

free market economics. The basis of capitalism. Suppliers and consumers determine the price of goods on the basis of: the level of supply of a good or service and the level of demand for a good or service. Exchange between suppliers and consumers is voluntary and largely unregulated by government.

Free riders. Individuals who selfishly benefit from the efforts of others.

funded mandates. In terms of national policy, policy implemented by state and local governments with support from federal grants-in-aid.

G

game theory. In political science and policy, a theoretical approach that describes, explains, and predicts the strategic behavior of actors attempting to maximize their benefit and minimize their loss. Zero sum games result in a "win-lose" outcome, whereas Pareto-optimal games result in outcomes where some actors gain but no actors lose. Games can be competitive or cooperative.

General Accounting Office (GAO). Created in 1921, the GAO focuses a great deal of attention on policy evaluation and auditing. The GAO analyzes past policy events and makes recommendations to policy formulators.

general will. As discussed by Rousseau, a set of principles important to all citizens in a society.

Generally Accepted Accounting Principles (GAAP). A set of uniform guidelines as to how budgets should be prepared and managed.

globalism. Political and economic partnerships promoting large-scale international capitalist ventures. Globalism carries with it implications for supranational public policy formulation and implementation.

goal drift/shift. *See* goal enlargement.

goal enlargement. Occurs when goals are more broadly defined over time or when policy goals evolve as policy problems change.

grants-in-aid. In terms of national policy, money that is passed along by the national government to state and local implementing authorities.

group theory. A theoretical approach explaining how individuals with similar political, social, or economic interests coalesce into formal groups with the intent of shaping or influencing the policy process.

H

hate crimes. Crimes committed against people or their property that is racially, sexually, ethnically, or religiously motivated.

Head Start. Created in 1965, a policy primarily intended to serve the needs of low-income and minority students who are deemed *at risk* of being unable to complete their elementary and secondary educations due to the socioeconomic conditions under which they live.

Health Resources and Services Administration (HRSA). An organization within HHS that monitors the quality and availability of medical professionals in the United States.

hidden costs. Costs that cannot be prevented because they are not known.

homeland security. In 2001, an office-level organization, now a cabinet-level department, homeland security policy is designed to protect the United States against terrorist attacks and to properly respond to terrorist- and nonterrorist-related emergencies as well as to monitor border security and immigration.

Homestead Act of 1862. Allowed families to acquire 160 acres of land from the national government, primarily dedicated to agriculture.

horizontal societies. Societies that are not stratified by separating those who have power from those who do not.

hyperpluralism. As discussed by Ted Lowi in his book, *End of Liberalism,* an ever-expanding number of pressure groups lobby political and administrative decision-makers to shape policy in a manner that best suits their groups' needs.

I

incrementalism. In public policy, a model that uses successive limited comparisons over time to determine both policy goals and expected and actual outcomes.

Indian Health Care Improvement Act of 1976. In part, provides the legal basis for much of what is done by Indian Health Services (IHS).

Indian Self-Determination Act of 1975. Landmark public law giving Native Americans greater control over the prioritization of their health care needs.

individual-level data. In policy analysis, usually data that describes a person.

Individuals with Disabilities Education Act. Requires that schools respond with flexibility to student disability needs.

informal evaluation. A type of policy evaluation, usually not conducted for statutory obligation but for internal use.

information campaigns. Used by pressure groups (interest groups), an important way to maintain public awareness of a policy issue. Pressure groups use information campaigns to point out the importance of particular public policies and the need for their continued existence.

institutionalism. An approach in the study of politics and policy, the theoretical approach argues that institutional functions, rules, structures, and processes are the basis for understanding institutional choices and outcomes.

intergovernmental relations (IGR). The interrelationships of national, state, and local government in the policy process.

iron triangle. The closed, tightly coupled symbiotic relationship between pressure groups, bureaucratic agencies, and legislative committees advancing policy agendas.

J
Joint Chiefs of Staff. A non policy-making advisory and coordination body composed of representatives from all branches of the U.S. military (to include the U.S. Marine Corps).
judicial positivism. The belief that the Constitution is a generally written document because it is intended to grow and change in meaning as times change and newer problems emerge and/or older problems evolve. Judicial positivists believe that the document must be interpreted based on the nature of the times and the evolving core values of society. Frequently used to describe the legal theories of judges or Supreme Court justices.

L
laboratories of democracy. A late-1990s conceptualization of state and local government as loci for development and testing of innovative policy ideas.
legal precedence. Previous court decisions; are usually upheld.
legal standing. Refers to those individuals directly impacted by a statute who have the right to take legal action regarding the decisions of the implementing agency.
liberalism. A government of, for, and by the people, based in a social contract. People cede some freedom in order to gain the benefits of government. The basic goal of government in a liberal nation is to protect the life, liberty, and personal property of citizens. *See also* classical liberalism and modern liberalism.
lobbying. Usually, direct appeals to legislators by pressure groups (interest groups) to either adopt or reject a policy or prospective policy via statute or statutory reform. In implementation, pressure group lobbying increases politicians' awareness of the costs and benefits of fully funding the implementation of a statute. Lobbying efforts can also bring pressure groups into contact with political executives and bureaucrats.
Long Whimper termination. A form of policy termination that occurs when pol-

icy is slowly terminated over a long period of time.

M
magnet schools. Public schools that operate on a semicompetitive basis with other public schools and usually focus on specialized subject matter.
mandate. In policy, a legal requirement that must be met by units of government.
marginal benefit. The benefit associated with producing an additional unit of a good or service.
marginal cost. The cost associated with producing an additional unit of a good or service.
marketable public good. A public good that could be subject to market forces and bought or sold.
matching funds. In federalism, a situation where state or local governments pay for some portion (usually, half) the costs of policy implementation and the national government pays the remaining costs (usually, half).
materialist. An individual who views personal and political choice primarily from his or her interest in individual economic benefit.
measurement. A step in the scientific method, the process of identifying empirical measures in terms of their theoretical validity and demonstrated reliability.
Medicaid. A state-administered and nationally supervised health care program emerging from Title XIX of the Social Security Act, designed to serve low-income individuals.
Medicare. A national health care program that serves primarily elderly individuals.
Megan's Law. Informs the public of the location of dangerous sex offenders.
Mining Act of 1872. A legislative act that encouraged the development of surface and subsurface mineral rights claimed by individuals for mining purposes on public lands.
modern liberalism. An approach to liberalism promoting social and economic justice through public policy. Government is expansive and policy intends to identify

and limit any and all forms of inequity in society, promising equality of opportunity.

mutually assured destruction (MAD). A Cold War era nuclear policy reinforced by the 1972 ABM Treaty that assumed that without antimissile systems, a nation would hesitate to start a nuclear war for fear of retaliation.

N

National Assessment of Educational Progress (NAEP). The oldest continual national analysis of student learning. The NAEP began in 1969 and regularly conducts student testing in "reading, mathematics, science, writing, U.S. history, civics, geography, and the arts."

nation-centered federalism. An approach to federalism that became prominent in the 1960s whereby the national government outlined and created policy most directly implemented at lower levels of government. Nation-centered federalism was in part driven by a belief in national policy goals that must be met.

National Education Association (NEA). A nationally organized teachers' union.

National Environmental Policy Act (NEPA). Landmark environmental legislation, the NEPA created national standards governing human impacts on the environment. The law required that a Council on Environmental Quality monitor the condition of the environment, analyzing the uses and adequacy of natural resources, as well as the environmental impacts of state and local government policy, nongovernmental organizations, and individuals.

National Fostercare and Adoption Directory. Maintains databases related to adoption agencies as well as information for prospective adoptive parents. Helps adopted children learn more about their legal rights and ability to gain access to their vital records, like birth certificates.

National Housing Act of 1934. Landmark New Deal legislation, a major national policy commitment to house those who were displaced by economic circumstance.

National Institutes of Health (NIH). A research-focused organization with more than twenty centers for research on various illnesses and diseases.

National Missile Defense (NMD). First proposed by George W. Bush in 2000, an antiballistic missile system or "shield" to defend the United States and her allies against so-called rogue states that have obtained, or are in the process of obtaining, nuclear weapons for the protection of domestic and international interests. The NMD was at odds with the terms of the 1972 ABM Treaty; the United States chose to withdraw from ABM.

National Security Act of 1947 (NSA). A reorganization of national defense that created the National Security Council, Joint Chiefs of Staff, Department of Defense (DOD), and U.S. Air Force.

National Security Council (NSC). Created by the NSA, the council acts as a coordinating and advisory body to the president for national security issues, establishing a formal network between other agencies within the EOP.

negative freedom. As conceptualized in classical liberalism, freedom *from* excessive government and other interferences in the lives of individual citizens.

net profit. The profit resulting from an economic transaction after costs have been deducted.

New Deal. Social and economic programs created in the wake of the Great Depression, partially responsible for many of the social and economic programs that exist today.

new institutionalism. A variant on institutionalism, the theoretical model incorporates principles of game theory and public choice, concluding that institutional considerations *combined with* individual institutional members' opinions, beliefs, values, preferences, and related characteristics explain choices and outcomes.

new interventionism. A post–Cold War policy of sending military forces to various locations to quell political or social turmoil before it escalates into a broader conflict.

No Child Left Behind (NCLB). The George W. Bush Administration education reform.

norms. General guidelines in public policy that help agencies make decisions consistent with the spirit of the policy, even if there are no clear guidelines for specific circumstances.

North Atlantic Treaty Organization (NATO). A military alliance established in 1949 between the United States, Canada, and several Western and Southern European nations. In the post–Cold War period, NATO now includes many Eastern European nations.

nuclear arms race. A strategic move between two or more countries to out-produce rival nations in quantity, quality, and potency of nuclear weapons with the intent of gaining military and diplomatic superiority.

nuclear weapons treaties. Treaties signed between various nations to limit and regulate the proliferation, use, and type of nuclear weapons developed.

O

Office of Child Support Enforcement (OCSE). An office within the ACF that monitors child support payments.

Office of Management and Budget (OMB). Previously known as the Bureau of Budget, the OMB is responsible for coordinating all agency budget requests incorporated into the president's budget proposal.

Older Americans Act Amendments of 2000. Established the Administration on Aging and set up the National Family Caregiver Support Program (NFCSP), distributing monetary resources to the states to establish partnerships within communities of caregivers.

operationalization. A step in the scientific method, the process of developing empirical measures of theoretical concepts.

opportunity cost. The cost incurred when one chooses a particular course of action and thus loses the potential benefit of taking an alternate course of action.

organizational culture. An agency's organizational norms and informal processes; significantly impacts the ability of an agency to implement a particular policy, possibly acting as a highly potent veto point.

original intent. In terms of the Constitution, a belief that the Founders outlined inviolable rules and processes directing governance in the United States.

P

person-related crime. Involves the physical assault or threat of assault on another person's physical being or psyche, or a crime against oneself with the intent to cause harm. Person-related crimes include: murder, assault, drug use or dealing, and domestic violence.

Pink Book. Last published by the National Immunization Program, the book disseminates information globally on disease, vaccines, and even vaccinating disadvantaged individuals against preventable disease.

policy analysis. Primarily concerned with the consideration of several policy alternatives, each expected to produce different policy outcomes. Policy analysis requires careful systematic and empirical study (Lasswell 1971, 1). Policy analysis involves all aspects of the policy process, from the early stages of policy adoption and formulation to the implementation and evaluation of public policies.

Policy evaluation. The process by which policy is analyzed to determine if it is efficiently and effectively meeting goals.

policy formulation. The detailed process of using normative and empirical methods to define a policy goal, explore alternatives to achieve the goal, and then choose a preferred policy solution.

policy resources. Usually refers to money, organization, and personnel needed for successful policy processes.

policy science. The use of reliable, valid, and universally understood logico-rational (logical and rational) techniques for developing public policy.

policy standards. Usually refers to the goals, guidelines, rules, and regulations associated with a policy.

policy stream. In Kingdon's agenda-setting model, potential solutions to problems that exist in the problem stream, some of which will be adopted to solve policy problems.

policy window. In Kingdon's agenda-setting model, following a focusing event, the problem stream has become evident to the political stream actors and institutions, and particular solutions within the policy stream may become part of the policy agenda.

political culture. From Elazar, a typology of political–citizen relationships focusing on historical norms. Political culture shapes policy priorities, processes, and outcomes. The three major categories of political culture are: individualistic, moralistic, and traditionalistic.

political socialization. The experiences that shape or contribute to the development of an individual's political values, opinions, beliefs, and in turn influence his or her political behaviors.

Politics stream. In Kingdon's agenda-setting model, the stream in which solutions are debated and chosen.

positive freedom. As conceptualized in modern liberalism, freedom to exercise individual political, social, and economic rights within society's boundaries. Positive freedom assumes that rights are created and protected under the social contract.

postaudit. An audit that occurs after a budget cycle to determine whether authorizations were spent appropriately.

postmaterialist. An individual who views personal and political choice in terms of an interest in societal issues, such as the general quality of life and social and economic fairness, as well as other interests not directly related to their economic benefit.

postponement. In public policy, agency attempts to fend off external pressures, usually through delay or slow decision-making processes; often a motive for covert evaluation.

preaudit. An audit conducted to ensure that an agency's funds and planned spending patterns are consistent with the goals of the public policies that an agency is authorized to implement.

prior appropriation. Water rights, in which individuals who lay claim to water resources first have a right to consume the full amount of water as they have claimed prior to the use by individuals who have made later claims.

problem stream. In Kingdon's agenda-setting model, potential policy problems, some of which will reach the policy agenda to be addressed by public policy in some manner.

Process evaluations. Evaluations which study the systematic methods by which policy goals are accomplished.

professionalism. In public policy, the knowledge, skills, and abilities of an individual (and the organizations he or she represents) formally engaged in the policy process.

project grants. Competitive grants that are awarded on the basis of proposal merit.

property-related crime. Involves the use or taking of property that belongs to someone other than the individual caught using or taking the property.

prosecuting attorneys. Attorneys representing the government in a trial.

public budgeting. The process of prioritizing financial commitments in the policy process.

public choice. In public policy, a theoretical approach envisioning limited government, one that meets only the basic needs of citizens associated with the protection of citizens' natural rights. Citizens choose the cost of government through vote choice. Most problems are solved privately through the marketplace.

public corruption. Refers to malfeasance on the part of government officials.

public defenders. Attorneys representing defendants who are unable to afford legal advice and representation in legal proceedings.

public goods. Nonrivalrous and nonexcludable goods. Also called communal goods. Pure public goods that are not marketable because they are basic necessities for life (e.g., air).

Public Health Service. Established in 1912, focuses significant attention on internal disease control issues rather than outward-facing approaches.

public interest groups. Groups that frame issues and shape policy agendas for the benefit of all individuals.

public policy. What government *ought* or *ought not do,* and *does* or *does not* do.

Q

Quadrennial Defense Review (QDR). A policy review conducted by the Department of Defense focusing on future areas of potential threat, defense readiness, and recommendations for meeting defense policy objectives.

Qualitative studies. In policy analysis, studies that do not rely heavily on numerical analysis as the basis of policy analysis.

quantitative studies. Involves the use of numbers to describe phenomena. The analysis of numbers can simplify the study of public policy, because numbers have assigned values that may have a more universal meaning.

R

racially biased policing. A form of policing in which police action is motivated by the race of the individual viewed as a criminal suspect.

ratio-level data. In data analysis, ratio-level data is like interval-level data in all aspects except that it is possible for the data to have true zero values.

rational–comprehensive. In public policy, a theoretical approach in public policy requiring: problem identification, the development of an exhaustive list of rational solutions, and the identification and adoption of the most efficient solution. Policy is evaluated by empirically comparing policy goals with outcomes.

realignment. Electoral shifts producing overwhelming and long-lasting majorities for a particular political party and having a tremendous impact on agenda setting.

recidivism. In criminal justice, the act of re-offense.

regime values. Those values that have been encoded into and establish the basis of some form of social contract and are widely accepted within a nation.

renewable energy. Any source of energy in which the energy *source* is not consumed in the energy conversion or generation process.

rescission. In budgeting, the practice of eliminating planned expenditures associated with policy implementation.

retributive justice. A belief that punishment should be a form of revenge for a criminal act against other parties to the social contract.

riparian rights. Water rights, dictating that rivers are a *commons* that should be readily available for adjacent property owners' use; not to be overused by any single or group of individuals.

Rivalrous. A good whose ownership is a function of an individual having met a seller's price.

Ryan White Comprehensive AIDS Resources Emergency (CARE) Act of 1990. A major public law establishing comprehensive national HIV/AIDS policy in the United States.

S

sanctions. In public policy, usually a formal disincentive to an implementing agency when the agency drifts away from stated goals and processes.

scientific theory. A tentative basis for understanding phenomena. A good theory describes, explains, and predicts phenomena. In public policy, scientific theory is applied by policy science to develop policy to solve problems.

scope of government. How big or how small we want government to be, and how much we want to pay for the collective and individual benefits that government may provide.

slippage. In policy implementation, a reduced ability to produce outputs that are consistent with policy goals.

Snyder Act of 1921. A public law that established national government responsibility for Native American health care.

social capital. The combined status of civic engagement, political and social trust, intergenerational connectedness, and community networks in a society.

social contract. The written and unwritten agreement that we continually rewrite, stating what we want to do for each other collectively and what we want other members of society to do for us as individuals.

Social policy. ". . . [has] to do with human beings living together as a group in a situation requiring that they have dealings with each other" (Tropman et al. 1981, p. xvi).

Social Security Act of 1935. Established the Social Security Administration, a program offering income assistance to elderly and disabled workers and the children of disabled workers.

Social Security Administration. Agency primarily responsible for implementing key aspects of the Social Security Act.

socioeconomic. Usually refers to the general economic, education, and professional employment characteristics of individuals or communities.

Southeast Asia Treaty Organization (SEATO). A mutual defense pact intended to limit communist influence in Southeast Asia.

stakeholder. An individual who has a stake in policy formulation and outcomes (i.e., all of us, whether we take an interest or not); may or may not be a direct beneficiary of a particular policy.

State Children's Health Insurance Program (SCHIP). A program started in 1997, located at the national level within the Centers for Medicare and Medicaid Services, it is administered by the states and financed by national and state government with the goal of insuring low-income children.

steerage. How and what policy adjustments will be made to keep policy focused on intended goals.

stewardship. In presidential power theories, a theoretical approach to governance in which the president sees the use of power to extend to any behavior that is not expressly illegal and the exercise of which the president sees as being in the national interest.

Strategic Defense Initiative Organization (SDIO). Established in 1984, the organization was tasked with exploring the feasibility of SDI policy.

subgovernment model. *See* iron triangle.

Substance Abuse and Mental Health Services (SAMHSA). Established in 1992 within HHS, SAMHSA databases are related to mental health research findings and prescriptive practices that could serve as the basis of sound public policy. SAMHSA also researches the impact of mental health and substance abuse in terms of its impact on the individual and family unit.

sunset clause. A statutorily derived end date for a policy affording elected officials the opportunity to reconsider a policy's future (i.e., should it continue or has its served its purpose and be terminated?).

Superfund Amendments and Reauthorization Act of 1986. A law implemented by the Agency for Toxic Substances and Disease Registry (ATSDR), primarily intended for identification and cleanup of toxic waste sites.

systems theory. A theoretical model used in political science and public policy to study political and policy-related behavior/phenomena. Its basic elements are: political environment, input, political system, decisions or policy outputs, and feedback.

T

target population/group. Individuals and/or groups who are the intended recipients of a particular public policy. Target groups must be understood in terms of: (1) size—the number of people or organizations within the target group and (2) the amount of behavioral change the policy as implemented is intended to produce.

teacher quality. A policy concern with the level of knowledge, skills, and abilities of teachers.

technical information quandary. A term used to describe the increasingly detailed and technical language of policy-making in a highly technological policy atmosphere, and the potentially negative impact on the ability of citizens to participate in a democratic policy-making environment.

technocracy. Government by the experts. This approach challenges democratic policy-making and the active involvement of citizen "voice."

Temporary Assistance to Needy Families (TANF). A Welfare Reform Act policy that placed strict limits on assistance, with special emphasis on the program being a last resort if child support payments are not being made.

termination. In public policy, the process by which a policy or program comes to an end.

Theater Missile Defense (TMD). Consistent with post–Cold War defense policy focus on interventionism, TMD did not challenge the ABM Treaty, focusing instead on a more limited missile defense reaction to "rogue states."

think tanks. Pressure group organizations devoted almost solely to policy research to support pressure group policy agendas.

Third Way politics. A type of centrist politics that uses both government and market-based solutions to solve policy problems.

top-down policy formulation. *See* top-down policy-making.

top-down policy-making. Policy created by government (frequently national and state government) and imposed on lower levels of government and citizens.

tractability. The ability of public policy to control, influence, or reshape a particular phenomenon so as to limit what society deems to be "bad" and to promote what is "good."

Tragedy of the Commons. The overuse or hoarding of a scare common resource.

treatment. In public policy, a proposed policy or policy variation that is believed will yield more effective or efficient policy outcomes.

Truman Doctrine. A containment plan advocated by then-President Harry S Truman and followed by subsequent presidents, which effectively drew a line of demarcation beyond which Communist regimes or influence would not be tolerated by the United States.

two presidencies thesis. A theory stating that the presidency is really a foreign policy presidency and a domestic policy presidency. In the case of the former, the president will likely have greater power in setting the agenda and in formulating policy.

U

unfunded mandates. In terms of national policy, situations requiring local and state governments to implement national policies, using their own financial resources and personnel.

U.S.A. Patriot Act. A major antiterrorism and criminal justice policy that abridged civil liberties protections for citizens, while increasing the networking capacity of police and military law enforcement organizations and personnel.

U.S. Department of Defense (DOD). Created by the NSA, brings all branches of the U.S. military under the auspices of one cabinet level department.

U.S. Department of Health and Human Services (HHS). Created in 1979, consolidated health policy with other health welfare-related policies.

U.S. Department of Housing and Urban Development (HUD). Tasked with the goal of renewing America's cities, providing safe housing for all individuals and families, and enforcing equity in housing availability.

V

values. According to Schuman (1962, 175), "a normative standard of the desirable, functioning as an operational force in human behavior."

vertical societies. Societies in which a division exists between the more powerful and the less powerful (e.g., those "above" and those "below"). Political, economic, and social elites shape the intergovernmental relationship in a way that advances their interests in maintaining the status quo.

veto points. In the policy process, points where policy ideas can be eliminated or significantly altered by elected decision-makers, pressure groups, and other policy stakeholders.

vouchers. In education policy, a privatization initiative to provide state funds to parents to be used to send their children to public or private schools of their choice.

W

War on Poverty. A number of programs initiated by President Lyndon B. Johnson in the 1960s, promoting economic assistance, housing, and nutrition programs for low-income individuals.

Ways and Means. A standing committee in the House of Representatives, which determines methods of obtaining revenue.

Welfare Reform Act of 1996. A comprehensive reform of the national welfare policy, developing policy that would encourage individuals to return to an independent lifestyle and placing limits on the period of time that nondisabled individuals could receive benefits.

window dressing. A form of covert policy evaluation; a method of reducing constraints imposed by elected officials via oversight and grassroots efforts to influence agency decision-making in the implementation process.

Women, Infants, and Children (WIC) Program. Cooperative efforts at the national, state, and local level to provide health care and nutrition programs to low-income pregnant women and their children up to the age of five years.

PHOTO CREDITS

INDEX

Administrative law, 111
  and policy implementation, 111
*Agendas, Alternatives, and Public
  Policy,* 71, 81
Affirmative Action, 150
  and nation-centered federalism,
  150
Agenda setting, 71–84, 224, 300
  and biased participation, 79
  and bureaucracy, 78
  and Congress, 75–76
  and elections, 78–79
  and incrementalism, 300
  and media, 80
  politics stream, 71–72
  problem stream, 71–72
  solutions, 71–72
  and president, 75, 224
  and realigning elections, 78–79
Aid to Families with Dependent
  Children (AFDC), 193, 208
  and Medicaid, 193
  and Social Security, 208
Alternative dispute resolution
  (ADR), 114. *See also*
  intergovernmental relations
Amber Alert 78, 259
  and media, 78
American Association for
  Advancement of Retired
  People (AARP), 185
American Civil Liberties Union
  (ACLU), 245. *See also*
  regime values
*American Federalism: A View from
  the States,* 40
American Federation of Teachers
  (AFT), 226. *See also*
  education policy
American National Election Study
  (ANES), 42, 43, 47
Americans with Disabilities Act, 232
Amicus curiae briefs 84, 92, 115, 234
  and interest groups, 84, 92, 115,
  234
Analysis for Public Decisions, 61
Anti-Ballistic Missile (ABM)
  Treaty, 169
Appropriations Committee, 290,
  294, 296, 297. *See also*
  budgeting
Aristotle, 26
Austrian School of Economics, 67

Baby Boomers, 42–50, 209, 218.
  See also postmaterialism

Ballistic Missile Defense, 173–174
Battle for Seattle, 271
Benefit/Cost Analysis, 62–63
  and hidden cost, 62–63
  and marginal benefit, 63
  and marginal cost, 63
  and policy formulation, 87
Bilingual Education Act, 232–233.
  See also education policy
Bismarck, Otto von, 191, 207
Bowling Alone, 12, 38
Brewer, Robert, 60, 130, 133
Brown v Board of Education (1954),
  53, 77, 132, 150, 225, 234
  and agenda setting, 77
  and education policy, 225, 234
  and nation-centered federalism,
  150
Bryce, James, 149
Buchanan, James, 23
  and public choice theory, 23
Budgeting, 89, 91, 286–302
  budget cycle, 289–291
  committees, 290, 294, 296
  defined, 286
  entitlements, 299
  major participants, 294–295
    bureaucracy, 294–295
    Congress, 89, 91, 294
    courts, 294
    media, 295
    president, 294
    pressure groups, 295
  public finance, 291–292
  revenue streams, 292–293
  size, 287–288
  Theory, 297–299
    consensus model, 297–298
    dissensus model, 298–299
    role theory, 296–297
Bureau of the Budget, 91
  and policy formulation, 91
Bureaucracy, 30, 39, 78, 89, 91–92,
  103, 110, 111, 132, 134,
  153, 226, 245, 291, 294, 301
  and agenda setting, 78
  and budgeting, 291, 294, 301
  and criminal justice policy, 245
  and education policy, 226
  and intergovernmental
  relations, 153
  and policy formulation,
  89, 91–92
  and policy implementation, 103,
  110, 111
  and policy termination, 132, 134

Bush, George H.W., 93, 170
  and Post–Cold War, 170
Bush, George W., 72–74, 92–93,
  135, 185, 191, 206, 209,
  224, 225, 262, 288
  and agenda setting, 72–74
  and budgeting, 288
  and criminal justice policy, 262,
  and education policy, 224, 225.
    See also No Child Left Behind
  and policy formulation, 92–93
  and policy termination 135
  and public health policy, 185
  and Social Security reform,
  191, 206, 209

Caiden, Naomi, 298
Carr, Edward H., 2
Carter, Jimmy, 185, 189, 214, 280
  and public health policy, 185, 189
  and social policy, 214
  and renewable energy, 280
Centers for Disease Control and
  Prevention, 189–190. *See
  also* public health policy
Chesterton, G.K., 300
Child Nutrition Program, 212–213.
  See also U.S. Department of
  Agriculture
China, 171
Civic Engagement, 12, 38–40. *See
  also* social capital
Civil Rights Act of 1964, 150,
  214, 232
  and education policy, 232
  and nation centered federalism,
  150
  and fair housing, 214
Clean Air Act (CAA), 272. *See also*
  green policy
Clean Water Act (CWA), 272.
  See also green policy
Clinton, Bill, 76, 93, 113, 136, 140,
  146, 151–152, 171, 185, 187,
  208, 218, 288. *See also* Third
  Way politics
  and agenda setting, 76
  and federalism, 151–152
  and policy formulation, 93
  and policy implementation, 113
  and policy termination, 136, 140
  and post–Cold War, 171
  and public budgeting, 288
  and public health policy,
  185, 187
  and Social Security reforms, 208